NUCLEAR POWER

Development and Management of a Technology

Nuclear Power

DEVELOPMENT AND MANAGEMENT
OF A TECHNOLOGY

BY FRANK G. DAWSON

University of Washington Press
SEATTLE AND LONDON

Library of Congress Cataloging in Publication Data

Dawson, Frank G
  Nuclear power, development and management of
a technology.

  Bibliography: p.
  Includes index.
  1. Atomic power industry—United States—
History.   2. Industry and state—United States—
History.   I. Title.
HD9698.U52D38   1976   338.4'7'621480973   75-40880
ISBN 0-295-95445-0

Nuclear Power

DEVELOPMENT AND MANAGEMENT
OF A TECHNOLOGY

BY FRANK G. DAWSON

University of Washington Press
SEATTLE AND LONDON

Library of Congress Cataloging in Publication Data

Dawson, Frank G
  Nuclear power, development and management of
a technology.

  Bibliography: p.
  Includes index.
  1. Atomic power industry—United States—
History.   2. Industry and state—United States—
History.   I. Title.
HD9698.U52D38   1976   338.4'7'621480973   75-40880
ISBN 0-295-95445-0

Preface

SINCE the discovery of nuclear fission, the United States has provided world leadership in the development of nuclear energy for peaceful purposes. No other single technological innovation holds as much promise for alleviating energy shortages around the world; no other raises such grave questions of risk to public health and safety.

At the time of this book's preparation, the risk issues are still being debated by concerned citizens; by scientists and engineers; by local, state, and national governments; and by international organizations throughout the world. In the United States, a nuclear power moratorium is being seriously considered.

Meanwhile, the world's supplies of energy available from today's technology are being rapidly depleted. While the United States is blessed with a readily available alternative energy source, namely coal, many parts of the highly industrialized world—Western Europe and Japan, for example—are not so fortunate. Nuclear energy would appear to be their only alternative to oil and natural gas for the next twenty to thirty years.

As of 1975, the United States has 225 nuclear power plants either planned or in operation; the commitments by other "free world" nations are somewhat greater. To replace the energy to be produced from these plants over their lifetime would require the discovery of six major oil fields, each the equivalent of Alaska's North Slope. By the year 2000, the world commitment to nuclear power is projected to be four times the current plans. Except for countries with large coal resources, there are not adequate alternative energy sources. Furthermore, the national security strategies of the United States and several other world powers are dependent on large numbers of nuclear weapons and nuclear-powered naval vessels. Thus, it is unlikely that the nuclear genie will be put back in the bottle. Moreover, nothing short of a total, worldwide moratorium would eliminate the risks of nuclear power to both present and future societies.

The answer, therefore, lies not in abolishing nuclear power but in properly managing its use. As with the development of nuclear power, the United States should assume a world leadership role in dealing with its control and regulation.

Despite fission's inherent problems, however, the technological development of nuclear power should be considered a success. As a case study, it provides a model for joint government-industry intervention in the solution of a long-term societal problem. Many aspects of other current and future world problems— food shortages, the need for alternative energy sources—may be amenable to similar systematic solutions.

This book presents the history of nuclear power development in the United States—from its inception as a secret military stratagem through its metamorphosis as a peaceful commercial energy source. The primary emphasis is on the key governmental policies, decisions, and actions that influenced the development and its subsequent management and regulation. Hopefully, this perspective and the analysis of the technological delivery system can also provide a data base for those interested in the management of other technologies involving a government-industry partnership.

Acknowledgments

MOST of the material for this book is derived from my doctoral dissertation. The underlying research was done in 1971, when Battelle Memorial Institute underwrote the completion of my graduate studies in nuclear engineering at the University of Washington. In the course of these studies, I had the privilege of working with Dr. Edward Wenk, Jr., on a research program supported by the National Science Foundation on the social management of technology. One of the five technologies studied was commercial nuclear power. This work, together with my long-time professional interest in nuclear power development, provided the springboard for the dissertation.

The concept of a technological delivery system discussed in the book was first introduced to me by Professor Wenk during the NSF research. Moreover, a significant part of the beginning of Chapter VI, on the regulatory process, was taken from the NSF study. I am indebted to Professor Wenk and to Professor Ronald Geballe, who headed the NSF nuclear power study, for their permission to use this material and for their encouragement and counsel during the preparation of the dissertation, and also for their suggestion that it be expanded and modified for book publication.

I also want to express my appreciation to the other researchers involved in the NSF study; to the staff of the University of Washington nuclear engineering department and its chairman, Professor Albert Babb; and to Battelle and members of its staff, particularly Dr. Ronald S. Paul, for their contributions and assistance.

Contents

Figures

Tables

NUCLEAR POWER
Development and Management of a Technology

CHAPTER I

Introduction

THIS book presents a case study of the development and deployment of commercial nuclear power in the United States. It is an expanded and edited version of the author's doctoral dissertation, which was submitted to the University of Washington in October 1973. Since the preparation of the dissertation, the Atomic Energy Commission has been split into two parts: one responsible for research and development; the other, for regulation. While the text has not been completely modified to reflect this change, the new organizations are briefly described in the second chapter.

The introduction of commercial nuclear power parallels a growing concern in the nation and the world about the value of technological progress *per se* to society and its impact on our environment. Some of the aspects deal with complex societal judgments that may be transitory; certainly they are never constant. The book was prepared at the end of the initial reactor development period—an early stage of nuclear power's commercial introduction and evolution. It is being published at a time when strong objections are being raised not only to the construction and operation of specific, individual reactors but to the promotion and use of nuclear power in general. Since the first commercial reactor has been in operation only a few years, and since the expected life of a single plant is approximately thirty years, clearly nuclear power has not yet had enough time to demonstrate its sustained reliability and safety. There has been no final solution to the problem of radioactive waste management; moreover, because of the nature of radioactivity, evaluation of any solution implemented may not be valid for centuries. Serious questions are also being raised concerning the safeguarding of nuclear materials from clandestine diversion. Because of the uncertainties involved in all these complex issues, a nuclear power moratorium in the United States is a real possibility. From an energy supply standpoint, such a moratorium could make the energy crisis facing the nation and the world much more difficult to solve. This book is being published to give an his-

3

torical perspective to the development of nuclear power and its controversy and hopefully to present some insight into the operation of the system used to develop it.

The government's role in the development of nuclear power consisted of a major intervention in the creation and evolution of a commercial product for the generation of electrical energy—an alternative to power systems traditionally devised and manufactured by private industry. As a national policy, the government declared that the development of nuclear energy be directed so as to make the maximum contribution to the general welfare of the nation.[1] It was recognized at the beginning that atomic power had great potential benefits as an energy source for the nation, but success was uncertain and at best long-range, requiring large financial resources and greater risks than private industry alone was willing to take. Through government leadership, a partnership was established with industry to provide a framework for a technological delivery system to exploit this new energy source. The system resulted in a commercial product that is capable of meeting a major fraction of man's energy needs. Nuclear energy could become the predominant fuel for electric power generation, thus releasing oil and natural gas for other more valuable purposes.

In the future the national interest is again likely to require government initiative and government-industry cooperation to carry out the development programs for new technologies. To the degree that the development of nuclear power can be considered successful, it is possible that the policies, legislative actions, processes, system components and their relationships, and other aspects of the system that have contributed to its success may have general or specific applicability. The concept of viewing the development in terms of a technological delivery system (t.d.s.) will be presented in Chapter VII. It is conceivable, for instance, that a similar t.d.s. might be applicable for one or more other energy resources—e.g., fusion, solar, and/or geothermal energy— some of which are already in the early development stages, and some of which have recently been proposed as areas requiring extensive government assistance. An understanding of the nuclear power technological delivery system may help minimize the shortcomings of similar future systems.

Nader has stated that "scientific and technological developments can modify the political situation so rapidly that policies are needed to deal with current changes and anticipate and channel subsequent ones in order to achieve desired objectives. The design of such policies requires an environment which will encourage the initiative of special interest groups within a common frame of reference."[2] Policy decisions concerning the commercial nuclear power program typically have reflected the interaction of a number of sometimes conflicting considerations:

> *Technical*—The optimum size and type of reactor; the relative emphasis given to basic research, prototype development, and construction of demonstration plants; and the optimum uses of scientific manpower and other limited resources.

Fiscal—The overall level of federal expenditures, public priorities, allocation to power reactor development, and the degree of government assistance to cooperative projects with industry.

Political—The desirability of public versus private ownership of nuclear plants, fuels, materials, and facilities; conflicts of power structures within the government and between government institutions and interest groups; and the roles and interrelationships of the Executive and Legislative Branches, the supply industry, and the utilities.

Foreign Policy—National security, the need to protect the competitive position of American industry in foreign markets, and the importance of establishing or maintaining American primacy in nuclear technology, both as a matter of national prestige and as a means of demonstrating U.S. determination to use atomic energy for peace rather than for war.

Safety and Environmental—The acceptable degree of risk of a nuclear accident, the acceptable level of radiation exposure to nuclear workers and the public, and the degree of assurance of adequate radioactive waste management and special nuclear materials safeguards.

Energy Resource Requirements—The availability of uranium reserves, the approach to uranium utilization, and the timing of availability of nuclear energy as an alternative energy resource.

Green has stated that "the atomic energy experience is a useful example of the accommodation of Government and legal mechanisms to meet the demands of mushrooming technological development which seemingly outraces the ability of society to accommodate itself to the past and present, let alone the future." [3] The innovative nature of the first atomic energy law passed by Congress laid the basis for the practice and policy of innovation and improvisation that was to pervade the atomic energy development process. Because of the military origin of the nuclear power plant, there were considerable opportunities for institutional distortions in its introduction as a service to society. The process has been characterized as an "inverted form" in that it emerged from an effort tightly regulated by government, rather than from an effort initiated by industry. [4] Nonetheless, the policies and practices formulated and implemented by the government have been effective in deploying the development within the traditional industry framework.

There have been a number of studies on the evolution of the nuclear power reactor. For example, several studies by Green, including his book, *Government of the Atom*, [5] examine in great depth the characteristics and the role of the Joint Committee on Atomic Energy (JCAE); Orlans [6] has investigated the contracting policies employed by the Atomic Energy Commission (AEC); Zinn [7] and Glasstone [8] have described the technical programs and reactor concepts explored; and other researchers have conducted and published studies of limited scope on the various aspects of the development. This book discusses the combined system of the Atomic Energy Commission, the Congress, and industry as components of a technological delivery system. These institutions provide a well-defined and stable political subsystem [9] operating over an extended period of time. The role of the public through intervenors is also discussed. While significant uncertainties still surround the results of the t.d.s., the product is clearly defined, and many aspects of it and of the system producing it can be described and analyzed. Many of the factors affecting the highly complex development process can also be examined, based on reasonably accessible data.

The history of the establishment of an Atomic Energy Commission free from existing bureaucratic quagmire, the evolution of a viable government-industry relationship, and the formation of a major industry that has had a large impact on society present engineers, physical scientists, political scientists, and public and private administrators with a remarkable case study of government and industry in partnership. Many of the essential events are well documented. Seldom has it been possible to see so clearly what happens when a new agency is projected into the administrative organization of the government—into an essentially political environment—and develops such a close relationship with private industry. It is hoped that from the accumulated data an historical perspective can be gained of governmental policies, key decisions and actions, and accomplishments in the field of commercial nuclear power. Chapter VII presents an analysis of these policies, decisions, and accomplishments to determine what factors have had either a negative or a positive influence; and to evaluate the performance of the system by employing a set of criteria. Evaluation of possible system application to other technological developments is also given. The book will also provide a data base for other researchers.

The book focuses primarily on governmental policies that had significant impact on technological and industrial developments. The approach is historical. Some of the specific areas examined are: technical programs, legislative actions, AEC-industry relationships, JCAE-AEC relationships, the role of related military applications and research, and the deployment of nuclear power in the commercial arena.

While the written record of nuclear power development is extensive, it does not fully reflect the interplay among the components of the operating system, since parts of this interplay were never recorded. Even those aspects that have been recorded may not fully reveal the true purpose or intent of actions taken or statements made. In an attempt to remove part of this limitation, a significant number of interviews were conducted with key individuals. A list of persons interviewed is given in Appendix A. The purpose of the interviews was to gain additional insight into particular aspects of the process, to obtain specific data in some cases, and to obtain various points of view and opinions from knowledgeable participants.

The material in the book is for the most part chronological and can be viewed in four separate phases. Significant events occurring in these phases are given in Table 1. A brief synopsis of Chapters II through VI is presented below in order to give readers an overview of the subject and some indication of the issues faced in the discussion.

TABLE 1

SIGNIFICANT EVENTS IN THE HISTORY OF NUCLEAR POWER DEVELOPMENT

1938–1952 (Chapter II)	1952–1954 (Chapter III)	1955–1963 (Chapter IV)	1964–1975 (Chapters V and VI)
Fission discovered.	Experimental Breeder Reactor-I operated; first nuclear power generated in token amount.	AEC expands R&D programs.	AEC phases out support of light-water reactors except for safety R&D.
First nuclear reactor operated.		JCAE takes actions to spur progress.	
Manhattan Engineer District formed.	Dual-purpose reactors studied by industry, using classified data.	Cooperative demonstration program between government and industry initiated.	AEC changes objectives on reactor development to breeders.
Nuclear weapons developed.			Industry allows (and later requires) ownership of nuclear fuels.
Civilian control of nuclear energy established.	Five-year government experimental reactor program announced.	Government constructs and tests large number of prototype and large-scale reactors.	Toll enrichment of private uranium provided by AEC.
Atomic Energy Commission and Joint Committee on Atomic Energy established.	Atomic Energy Act of 1954 passed. Allows greater private participation in nuclear development.	Price-Anderson Act passes, indemnifying private owners and operators of nuclear reactors.	AEC buyback of plutonium from industry terminated.
Postwar priority given to weapons.			AEC phases out uranium purchase program.
Uranium ore exploration and development program initiated.		Several large demonstration reactors start operations.	Utilities purchase a large number (~ 225) of nuclear power plants.
AEC division of reactor development formed.	JCAE takes active role in power reactor development planning.	Power output of reactors greatly increased to gain advantage of economy of scale.	Significant number (~ 55) of commercial plants put in operation.
Navy reactor program initiated.			Power rating of nuclear plants more than doubled.
			Licensing and safety of plants become controversial issues.
			Government promotion and regulation of nuclear power are administratively separated.

This detailed examination and the description of the policies, legislative actions, processes, system components, and their relationships are necessary for providing the data base for the analysis and evaluation contained in Chapter VII.

Chapter II describes the first phase (1938–52) of nuclear development. This was a period when wartime and postwar priorities and government secrecy prevented any substantial progress in peacetime application of nuclear energy, but activities during this period were very important to the development of nuclear power and its ultimate introduction and use by industry. During World War II, technical feasibility was demonstrated with respect to both the nuclear chain reaction and the nuclear reactor as a large energy producer. Immediately after the war, government institutions were established for managing and regulating nuclear developments and uses; the two most important of these were the Atomic Energy Commission, in the Executive Branch, and the Joint Committee on Atomic Energy, in Congress. Nuclear energy for electrical power generation and other peaceful purposes was considered, but governmental priorities for weapons production and military reactors, governmental policies controlling nuclear technology and the use of nuclear materials, and the shortage of uranium, all acted to retard the initiation by either government or industry of a major nuclear power research and development effort. The war and postwar government efforts did, however, leave a legacy of laboratories, production facilities, and contracting policies that were significant factors in events that followed.

Some of the key issues presented in Chapter II include: government monopoly of nuclear energy, effects of monopoly on nuclear energy utilization, problems arising from governmental control and ownership of the technology, effects of military developments, and effects of technical and resource constraints and governmental priorities.

Phase two (1952–54), described in Chapter III, was a period of transition. The Joint Committee on Atomic Energy started taking a much more active interest in nuclear power development and became concerned over the slow progress being made. The AEC initiated a five-year experimental reactor development program for the purpose of evaluating various reactor concepts. At the invitation of the AEC, and using secret data, industry conducted survey studies of possible reactor concepts for power and weapons material production. Due largely to a government incentive program to encourage uranium exploration by industry, uranium became more plentiful; this increase provided a firmer basis for nuclear power as a major energy source.

During this period, members of the AEC proposed that nuclear power development become a national objective. It was generally recognized that to accomplish that objective, however, private industry and electric utilities must be allowed to become more directly involved. The AEC and the president made proposals for major changes in the atomic energy law to accomplish this. A significantly different new atomic energy law was prepared by the JCAE and was enacted by Congress in 1954. One of the most important features of the new law was that private ownership of nuclear power reactors was finally allowed. The new act was a major step in opening the door to industry and in initiating a substantial developmental program. Notable issues emerging during this period were: progress of peacetime uses of nuclear energy, private industry involvement, policies on government control, and the JCAE's role in promoting nuclear power.

Chapter IV describes the third phase (1955–63), a period of rapid expansion of government support for civilian nuclear power research and development. Most of the R&D efforts in this area and much of the technology were removed from the cloak of secrecy. Through legislative action, the government also removed the roadblock of the financial risk to industry of potential catastrophic accidents. A government partnership with industry emerged in research and development through contracting arrangements and cooperative programs. This partnership not only provided a mechanism for governmental support, but also gave industry an opportunity to gain necessary experience and knowledge of the technology and to apply measures making the cost of nuclear power competitive with that of other energy sources.

The pattern of civilian nuclear power deployment was essentially determined during this period through demonstration reactor projects. It was also a time when conflicts of power between the Congress and the Executive Branch were resolved and important relationships between government and industry were established. The JCAE became a strong supporter and prodder of the AEC and the development of nuclear power became a national goal, seldom questioned by special interest groups or the public. The major questions were: when would commercially viable nuclear power be achieved, and how cheap would nuclear power costs be? The breakthrough occurred in 1963 when the first commercial plant was sold in competition with alternative fuel sources.

Major issues during this phase were: technical constraints on reactor materials and components; evaluation of reactor prototypes; introduction and evaluation, as a cooperative effort of government and industry, of demonstration reactors with commercial potential; selection of reactors for commercial exploitation; the roles of the various components of the technological delivery system and their relationships; and the financial risks to be assumed by government and industry.

The last phase of the development, described in Chapters V and VI, started in 1964 and has been a period of rapid acceptability and purchase of the nuclear reactors by the user industry, the electric utilities. The chief components of the supply industry to the utilities have also emerged. Because of the long lead time necessary for constructing and government licensing of nuclear plants, it remains a period in which operational performance and reliability are being evaluated but have yet to be fully demonstrated. The AEC reactor development objectives have shifted to new reactor types with potential for better uranium resource utilization. The government's role in the uranium supply field has been significantly altered. Reactor safety, waste disposal, and nuclear material safeguards have become major issues and are still to be fully resolved. Other significant issues during this phase have been: the government's continued involvement in the commercial product and supporting industries; acceptability and reliability of the product; competition in the industry; and new objectives for the government.

Chapter VII presents an analysis and evaluation of the nuclear technological delivery system (t.d.s.)—that is, the system by which inputs to the development of nuclear power were integrated in order to achieve outputs. Based on the case study material presented in Chapters I through VI, an analysis is made of the institutions and policy-making processes of the nuclear t.d.s.

In the first part of the analysis, a set of process questions is discussed. The answers to these questions identify the factors determining the system's outcomes, and bring into focus the key aspects of the processes involved. In the second part of the analysis, a set of outcome variables is used to evaluate the system's performance. Finally, the strengths and weaknesses of the nuclear t.d.s. are discussed in terms of their applicability to other systems.

CHAPTER II

Early Development

and Management of the Atom

NUCLEAR ENERGY—A WARTIME LEGACY

ORIGIN OF THE FIRST NUCLEAR REACTOR

PROBABLY no scientific discovery has had greater impact on world politics or has presented man with a greater opportunity for self-destruction or for fulfillment of his insatiable appetite for energy than has nuclear fission. The discovery of fission was made in Germany late in 1938 when Otto Hahn and Fritz Strassman found a radioactive barium isotope among the products resulting from their bombardment of natural uranium with neutrons. The neutron had been discovered in 1932 by Chadwick.[1] Physicists expected and later confirmed that the splitting of the uranium atom also released neutrons. These neutrons would make possible a chain reaction producing large amounts of energy, which was determined later to be controllable because of the fact that the emission of a small fraction of the neutrons is delayed in time. Unlike a controlled nuclear reactor, a nuclear bomb does not require these delayed neutrons.

A complication became apparent when physicists found that in natural uranium only the rare isotope U-235, which constitutes 0.7 of 1 percent of naturally occurring uranium, was fissionable by slow neutrons. The principal uranium isotope, U-238, fissions only when very fast neutrons are absorbed. However, it was later discovered that U-238 could be converted, through neutron capture, to the plutonium isotope, Pu-239, which is also fissionable by slow neutrons. These fundamental facts have played a major role in nuclear reactor design and are the basis for the reasons that the world is now embarking on a multibillion-dollar program to develop the highly complex "fast breeder" reactor, which does make use of the U-238 isotope. The conversion of U-238 to Pu-239, a chemically separable element from which a nuclear explosive

11

could be made, became the impetus for developing the first nuclear reactor. This man-made material, Pu-239, has become a major source of controversy in the later stages of nuclear power utilization.

An experiment by Enrico Fermi and others in 1942 demonstrated that the nuclear characteristics of U-235 permit a chain reaction using even natural uranium. Thus, the first nuclear reactors, as well as the power reactor programs of several nations, utilized natural uranium, a choice which places major constraints on nuclear power plant designs and operation. For this and other reasons (such as economics), natural uranium was not the fuel of the first commercial nuclear power plants in the United States, although it did play a major role in building the U.S. and the world's atomic arsenal.

In 1939 Fermi, Szilard, and others considered conducting chain reaction experiments using ordinary water, heavy water, or carbon for slowing down the fast neutrons emitted from fission, but no such experiments were undertaken until sometime later. It was recognized in 1939 that the immediate potential of the fission process was as an explosive.[2] The Navy was also interested in fission as a source of power for protracted undersea operations, as the process requires no oxygen. It was at this point that the Navy made the first governmental overture to support atomic energy, offering $1,500 to Carnegie Institute. Carnegie rejected the offer for internal policy reasons.[3]

Szilard, a Hungarian physicist working with Fermi at Columbia University, became quite concerned over the possibility that the Germans might exploit fission for military purposes. He was primarily responsible for inducing Einstein to write the famous letter to President Roosevelt and for having Alexander Sachs, a Lehman Corporation economist who had access to the White House, assist in presenting it to Roosevelt.[4] Einstein stated in his letter, dated August 2, 1939: "Some recent work by Fermi and L. Szilard, which has been communicated to me in manuscript, leads me to expect that the element uranium may be turned into a new and important source of energy in the immediate future. . . . This new phenomenon would also lead to the construction of bombs. . . ."[5] Sachs convinced the president of the potential military importance of the discovery of fission, and Roosevelt took immediate action by setting up the Advisory Committee on Uranium. The committee was headed by Lyman J. Briggs, a government soil scientist who was then director of the National Bureau of Standards.[6] The formation of this committee marked the beginning of government intervention in nuclear energy. However, it was the creation of the National Defense Research Committee (NDRC) in June 1940[7] and the establishment twelve months later of the Office of Scientific Research and Development (OSRD), containing both NDRC and the Uranium Committee,[8] that provided the institutional framework for further development of the fission concept. Vannevar Bush, a scientist with considerable interest and background in military requirements, was appointed to head OSRD, and James B. Conant of Harvard became head of NDRC. These two men played a major role in pushing forward the idea of developing fission energy for weapons purposes.

Fundamental to the possibility of producing a nuclear explosive was the feasibility of a nuclear chain reaction. The proof of feasibility of a chain reaction was not only a difficult and painstaking task, but it was also competing with alternative ways of producing the necessary material for a nuclear explosive. It was not until December 2, 1942, that sufficient graphite and natural uranium of the necessary purity were obtained for assembling a "pile" large enough to yield a sustained fission reaction process. It was on this date that Fermi was able to report that "the Italian navigator has just landed in the New World," thus signaling the advent of nuclear power.[9]

THE BOMB

Four approaches were considered simultaneously for supplying the fissionable material required for the atomic bomb. Three were conceived as isotope separation systems to produce uranium highly enriched in the fissile isotope U-235. These systems were based on three isotope separation processes: gaseous diffusion through a special barrier material; electromagnetic; and centrifuge. The fourth process was a graphite-moderated reactor fueled by natural uranium, which would convert unusable U-238 to the fissile Pu-239 isotope. This was similar in concept to the first chain reactor, assembled by Fermi.

The gaseous diffusion method of separation and the reactor approach became the mainstays of the weapons program, and both have had a significant impact on the development of commercial nuclear power. The centrifuge, which was rejected after initial consideration, is now being seriously reconsidered as a means of meeting the increased demand for enriched uranium projected by the commercial reactor market. The government's gaseous diffusion plants will supply the needs of the civilian power reactor industry for enriched uranium until the early 1980's.

The first reactor that had a substantial power output—approximately one million watts of thermal energy (~ 1 Mw_{th})—was the Clinton pile at the government laboratory in Oak Ridge, Tennessee, which went into operation on November 4, 1943.[10] It used graphite as a neutron moderator and contained aluminum-clad natural uranium slugs cooled with air for the fuel. Its primary purpose was to produce plutonium in the uranium in order to study chemical processes for separating the desired plutonium.

Eleven months later, on September 27, 1944, the first large plutonium production reactor began operation at Hanford, Washington.[11] This reactor was similar to the Clinton pile, except that water was chosen as the coolant instead of air or helium, which had also been considered. Heavy water was considered as a neutron moderator instead of graphite. Heavy water was later used as the moderator in production reactors at the Savannah River plant near Aiken, South Carolina. It was subsequently learned that the Germans had also considered both materials, but because of impurities in the graphite, they had received false indications of its usefulness as a moderator, and had selected heavy water instead. The Germans did not, however, create a sustained nuclear reaction during the war. These two moderator materials—heavy water and graphite—were chosen by several nations for their power reactor programs. In most cases, both materials were eventually abandoned in favor of the U.S. light-water technology. Canada and the United Kingdom are exceptions; their power reactors employ heavy water or graphite.

Approximately ten months after the first Hanford reactor started operations, sufficient plutonium had been produced, separated from the uranium, and put in the form required for a weapon. On July 16, 1945, the first atomic bomb made from the Hanford plutonium was exploded at Alamogordo, New Mexico.[12] On August 6, 1945, a U-235 bomb was dropped on Hiroshima, Japan. On August 9, a bomb (plutonium) was dropped on Nagasaki.[13] Each of the Japanese cities had been virtually destroyed with a single bomb. Early in the morning of August 10, Japan agreed to accept the surrender terms that had been presented at Potsdam.[14] The war ended and the awesome new force of atomic energy had been introduced to the world.

WARTIME MANAGEMENT AND LEGACY

The nuclear weapons development program was carried out in complete secrecy under the auspices of the Army. During the early experimental stage, the project was under OSRD; the crash program, however, called for large construction projects. The procurement of materials and the recruiting of manpower were crucial and came at a time when industry had war contracts exceeding the total production of the national economy in any prior year.[15] Therefore, to meet these difficult management challenges and to centralize authority and responsibility for the project, the Manhattan Engineer District (MED) was established in the Army and was given complete control over all aspects of the project, including construction of facilities, operations, information, materials, developments, and security. Government control of the atom was absolute from the beginning.

Although the only objective of the MED was the rapid development of the bomb, several early decisions by the MED were to have major significance in the later development of commercial nuclear power. First was the complete secrecy of all operations and developments. Lack of information was to be for many years a deterrent to private entry into the field and continues to place restrictions on certain commercial developments as late as 1975. The areas of significance to the industry that are still restricted are uranium enrichment technology and laser-induced-fusion research. The MED's exclusive control put the government in the position of being the only sponsor of atomic energy research and development. With this pattern established and with the tight secrecy maintained long after the end of the war, the government also became the only legitimate peacetime sponsor of research and development in the field. Thus, the basis was laid for government intervention in the development of a major commercial product which it has supported directly since then in unprecedented ways.

A second factor that contributed significantly to the government's involvement in peacetime nuclear applications was the physical legacy left from the wartime effort. Major facilities had been constructed to use in the weapons program and a large number of outstanding scientists, engineers, and other personnel had been accumulated to conduct the research and development and to operate the plants. While most of the laboratories and production facilities continued to be used primarily for military purposes in the postwar period, several have been designated "national laboratories" and are used primarily for nonmilitary programs. Even laboratories directly supporting the weapons program have contributed to or have essentially been reassigned to nonmilitary developments in significant ways.

Production facilities that have had the greatest impact on power reactor development are the large uranium enrichment plants. Without these, it would not be feasible for the United States to have commercial nuclear reactors that use enriched uranium. The availability of enriched uranium from these former weapons facilities allows greater flexibility in reactor design than would be possible if restricted to natural uranium. On the other hand, the current power reactors create a demand for the utilization of the enrichment plants that cost the government several billions of dollars to build, and that are no longer needed in the weapons program.

A third factor coming from the war effort that was of significance to commercial development was the contracting practices implemented by the Manhattan Engineer District. General Leslie Groves, head of the MED project, believed that contracting with a few of the nation's largest and best qualified companies and universities was the most expeditious and effective way to develop, design, and produce atomic bombs.[16] This contracting policy was continued after the war and allowed these large companies, as government contractors, to become knowledgeable about the atom even while it was still under heavy secrecy. It also resulted in a cadre of trained manpower in industry readily accessible to the operating contractors for commercial developments. The results of this policy have made possible the effective large-scale transfer of government nuclear technology to private industry.

Although the Manhattan Engineer District considered little else but the weapons program during the war effort, many of the participating scientists became concerned about the postwar future of atomic energy. By the summer of 1944, scientists such as Bush and Conant concluded that the time had come for earnest thought about arrangements for both domestic and international controls of atomic energy technology. Arthur Compton, director of the metallurgical project in Chicago, initiated discussions with General Groves regarding the future of the government laboratories.[17] At Compton's request, a long-range planning study was undertaken by Henry D. Smyth. It proposed that new possibilities be investigated, including reactor concepts, use of thorium, and potential military, scientific, industrial, and medical applications. Compton also suggested basic research in nuclear physics, chemistry, biology, and metallurgy.[18]

He saw that vigorous exploration of these areas was necessary if the United States was to maintain its leadership after the war. Later, in the fall of 1944, two committees were established. One was the Committee on Postwar Policy, chaired by Richard C. Tolman, scientific advisor to General Groves; the other was the "Jeffries Committee," appointed by Arthur Compton and headed by Zay Jeffries, a General Electric executive and consultant to Compton.[19] The Jeffries Committee then prepared a report, "Prospectus on Nucleonics," that called for objectives similar to those in the Smyth report; namely, worldwide control and aggressive research and industrial applications by the United States. "They hoped for a future marked by happy collaboration between the universities, the government and an independent nucleonics industry." [20] These were some of the first seeds of a peaceful atom.

The first major step toward policy development on postwar control of the atom was the formation by President Truman in May 1945 of an "Interim Committee," with Henry L. Stimson as chairman.[21] The first committee concern was national and international control of the atom. The management concepts for regulation and development suggested by the committee served as the basis for legislation, proposed by Truman soon after the end of the war, that led to the Atomic Energy Act of 1946.

POSTWAR CONTROL OF THE ATOM

THE MAY-JOHNSON BILL

Immediately after the war, the public was given a brief account in a press bulletin of the amazing development of atomic energy. This was issued with a report prepared by Henry D. Smyth that summarized the technical achievements of the wartime program.* The War Department set the tone of measures to be proposed for controlling the atom by stating, "The best interests of the United States require the utmost cooperation by all concerned in keeping secret now and for all time in the future all scientific and technical information not given in this report or other official releases of information by the War Department." [22] Smyth saw things quite differently, as is indicated by the preface of his report. Hewlett and Anderson summarized Smyth's viewpoint as follows:

> The ultimate responsibility for the nation's policy on the questions raised by atomic energy rested with its citizens. Heretofore, military security had restricted their consideration to the scientists and a few high officials. Now the great political and social questions that might affect all mankind for generations were open for the people to debate and decide through their elected representatives. Men of science, Smyth hoped, would use the present semitechnical account to explain the potentialities of atomic bombs to their fellow citizens and help them reach wise decisions. The people of the country must be informed if they are to discharge their responsibilities wisely.[23]

* The classic report, *A General Account of the Development of Methods of Using Atomic Energy for Military Purposes under the Auspices of the United States Government, 1940–45* (Washington, D.C.: GPO, 1945), was published as a means to satisfy public interest but at the same time to release only that information that could be easily duplicated by others.

The fundamental difference between the War Department's desire for control and secrecy and Smyth's belief that public debate was necessary in order to discharge the government's responsibilities was to become the basic controversy in developing legislation to establish the country's policies on the use of atomic energy. If Smyth's advice had been more closely followed by the government, the nuclear issues now facing the nation would be better understood by the public and by decision makers; this understanding might have led to wiser decisions on the future of nuclear power.

On October 3, 1945, President Truman sent his atomic energy message to Congress.[24] He proposed both international control of this new force and domestic legislation based on the War Department's draft. The latter was prepared principally by two lawyers, Brigadier-General Kenneth C. Royall and William L. Marbury.[25] Truman called for the prompt creation of an atomic energy commission to regulate all research, experimentation, and operations concerning the new discovery for any purpose. The War Department draft, which had been modified to reflect Stimson's Interim Committee * recommendations, was introduced in Congress by Representative Andrew J. May (D., Colorado). The May-Johnson Bill provided for an Atomic Energy Commission of nine part-time members to be appointed by the president, with the consent of the Senate, and to serve for nine years without pay. An administrator and a deputy administrator were to be appointed by the commission and be responsible only to it. Military officers were allowed to serve on the commission or as administrators. Truman had further recommended that the commission:

1. Control all fissionable material by purchase or condemnation.

2. Control all land containing fissionable material.

3. Conduct all necessary research for military, industrial, scientific, and medical purposes.

4. Issue licenses to use fissionable materials.

5. Establish security regulations on materials and information.

Representative May, chairman of the Committee on Military Affairs, held hearings on the bill on October 9 for one day and heard from only four witnesses, all of whom had participated in the war effort. One was Secretary of War Patterson, who testified that the War Department "had taken the initiative in proposing that it be divested of the great authority that goes with the control of atomic energy, because it recognizes that the problems we now face go far beyond the purely military sphere. The War Department bill would place control of this terrible force in the hands of men who would be representative of all that is best in our national life." [26]

There was mounting pressure against the May-Johnson Bill. Particularly vocal were scientists outside of the Washington circle.[27] Nader summarized the views of the scientists who argued against the bill; according to them it failed "(1) to establish effective liaison with the executive for the integration of

* A committee with representatives from industry, government, science, and universities.

foreign policy and atomic energy policy; (2) to give the executive and Congress the proper supervisory and review controls over the Commission and the administrator and his deputy; (3) to make civilian control explicit; and (4) to provide the best conditions for conducting scientific research and exchanging information.'' [28] Members of the House Foreign Affairs Committee also could not agree on fundamental points of the bill. Representatives Chet Holifield (D., California) and Melvin Price (D., Illinois), both of whom were later to play major roles in atomic energy developments, were convinced that the commission should be composed of full-time, well-paid members; that they should be subject to the president's normal removal powers; and that the administrator should be a civilian appointed by the president.[29] They, as did the Republican members of the committee, submitted minority reports with the majority report of Representative May on November 5, 1945.

Once aware of the problems implicit in the bill, President Truman withdrew his support, but offered no substitute.[30] With this loss of presidential support and the open controversies, the May-Johnson Bill was doomed.

THE ATOMIC ENERGY ACT OF 1946 (THE MCMAHON BILL)

A substitute bill came from the Senate Special Committee on Atomic Energy, which was established October 23, 1945, by Senate resolution at the initiative of Senator Brian McMahon, who became its chairman. McMahon, a freshman Democrat from Connecticut, called on James R. Newman from Truman's staff to assist him in formulating a new bill.[31] Newman found the May-Johnson bill inadequate in at least two significant respects: it overemphasized military uses, and it failed to stress the potentially more significant civilian application. On December 20, after much in-fighting within Congress and pressures from special interest groups, McMahon introduced in the Senate his bill, S. 1717, for the domestic control of nuclear power. In a White House conference on December 4, 1945, he obtained Truman's support; the president reemphasized that ''the entire program and operation should be under civilian control and that the government should have a monopoly of materials, facilities, and processes.'' [32]

Hearings were held on the bill from January 22 until April 8, 1946. It was reported out of committee on April 19 with only one significant amendment, the Vandenberg amendment, which gave the Military Liaison Committee authority to advise and consult on all atomic energy matters that, in the committee's judgment, related to military application. On June 1, 1946, the bill passed the Senate, almost without debate. House amendments were made but did not affect the fundamental principle of civilian control. The House passed the bill in July and Truman signed the Atomic Energy Act of 1946 [33] on August 1. The Atomic Energy Commission took over from the Manhattan District on December 31, 1946.

The ''Declaration of Policy'' and purpose of the act are:

Section 1.(a) Findings and Declaration.—Research and experimentation in the field of nuclear chain reaction have attained the stage at which the release of atomic energy on a large scale is practical. The significance of the atomic bomb for military purposes is evident. The effect of the use of atomic energy for civilian purposes upon the social, economic, and political structures of today cannot now be determined. It is a field in which unknown factors are involved. Therefore, any legislation will necessarily be subject to revision from time to time. It is reasonable to anticipate, however, that tapping this new source of energy will cause profound changes in our present way of life. Accordingly, it is hereby declared to be the policy of the people of the United States that, subject at all times to the paramount objective of assuring the common defense and security, the development and utilization of atomic energy shall, so far as practicable, be directed toward improving the public welfare, increasing the standard of living, strengthening free competition in private enterprise, and promoting world peace.

(b) Purpose of Act.—It is the purpose of this Act to effectuate the policies set out in section 1 (a) by providing, among others, for the following major programs relating to atomic energy:

(1) A program of assisting and fostering private research and development to encourage maximum scientific progress;

(2) A program for the control of scientific and technical information which will permit the dissemination of such information to encourage scientific progress, and for the sharing on a reciprocal basis of information concerning the practical industrial application of atomic energy as soon as effective and enforceable safeguards against its use for destructive purposes can be devised;

(3) A program of federally conducted research and development to assure the Government of adequate scientific and technical accomplishment;

(4) A program for Government control of the production, ownership, and use of fissionable material to assure the common defense and security and to insure the broadest possible exploitation of the fields; and

(5) A program of administration which will be consistent with the foregoing policies and with international arrangements made by the United States, and which will enable the Congress to be currently informed so as to take further legislative action as may hereafter be appropriate.

In most respects the McMahon Act overcame the objections of scientists, led by the Federation of Atomic Scientists and others who had opposed the May-Johnson Bill. It provided for a five-member civilian commission whose members are appointed by the president with the advice and consent of the Senate. Congress was given a major role through the Joint Committee on Atomic Energy established by the act.

The act gave great powers to the Atomic Energy Commission regarding use and control over the development of nuclear energy. The controls were manifested in exclusive government ownership of fissionable materials and the facilities for their use or production, a power that gave the government a virtual monopoly over the development and exploitation of peaceful applications of atomic energy. The act also essentially banned the granting of normal patent rights for inventions in atomic energy. The act established a completely new system of information control which placed great constraints on flow of information from the government developments to private institutions. The control used the concept of data being "born classified"; that is, data did not require affirmative action by anyone to make judgment that they indeed were classified. As a result of the events that followed, namely the rapid nuclear developments by the Russians, these restrictions were not reduced until some eight years after passage of the act. As discussed earlier, these restrictions, along with higher military priorities, placed major roadblocks in the way of peaceful development of atomic energy. Secrecy also prevented the widespread dissemination of nuclear information, both to the public and to policy and law makers in government.

GOVERNMENT MANAGEMENT OF THE ATOM

ATOMIC ENERGY COMMISSION

Purpose, Authority, and Scope of Activities

The Atomic Energy Act of 1946 set forth the broad policy of the United States development and use of atomic energy. Programs specifically called for in the 1946 Act in support of this policy were identified in the previous section.

The Atomic Energy Commission (AEC) was established by the act to administer these programs. In addition the AEC was charged with the responsibility of protecting the health and safety of the public with regard to use of nuclear energy, and of regulating the control and use of source, byproduct, and special nuclear materials. The AEC was authorized and directed to make arrangements (including contracts, agreements, and loans) to conduct research and development activities relating to the following: [34]

- Nuclear processes.
- The theory and production of atomic energy, including processes, materials, and devices related to such production.
- Utilization of fissionable and radioactive materials for medical, biological, health, or military purposes.
- Utilization of fissionable and radioactive materials and processes entailed in the production of such materials for all other purposes, including industrial uses.
- The protection of health during research and production activities.

It was also authorized and directed to conduct such activities through its own facilities.[35] Except for a few minor operations, the AEC has not used this authority and has conducted its programs through operating contractors.

The 1946 Act also gave the commission unprecedented powers. These included:

- Ownership of all nuclear facilities capable of "producing within a reasonable period of time a sufficient quantity of fissionable material to produce an atomic bomb or any other atomic weapons." [36] This ruled out private ownership of power reactors, which was not allowed until passage of the 1954 Act.
- Ownership of all fissionable material.[37] Private ownership of special nuclear materials was not allowed until 1964.

- Authority to license persons to transfer, receive possession of and use fissionable material after its removal from its place of deposit in nature.[38]
- Establishment of regulations for the control and dissemination of scientific and technical information on atomic energy.[39]
- Authority to control all patents.[40] The 1954 Act granted nearly normal patent rights, but compulsory licensing of patents pertaining to nuclear energy utilization was required.

The types and magnitudes of special programs can be seen from AEC expenditures and budgets. For illustrative purposes, two sets of data are presented. The first, Table 2, shows expenditures for the 1947–52 period in various categories. The programs of particular interest here are reactor development, physical research, and biology and medicine, since they contributed to civilian nuclear power either directly or indirectly. It is worthwhile to note that very early in the development of atomic energy, the last category, essentially the effects of radiation on man, was receiving substantial attention.

TABLE 2

ATOMIC ENERGY COMMISSION EXPENDITURES, 1947–52
(Dollars in Millions)

	1947	1948	1949	1950	1951	1952
Procurement and production of nuclear materials	$167.4	$141.0	$110.6	$168.5	$188.3	$ 278.3
Weapons development and fabrication			92.9	112.0	163.6	229.2
Development of nuclear reactors			19.3	31.5	44.5	64.4
Research in chemistry, metallurgy, and physics	24.5	53.4	26.1	28.9	29.8	34.7
Research in cancer, biology, and medicine			15.2	17.8	21.3	24.5
Community operations—net	18.9	23.7	25.6	19.9	17.3	16.4
Administrative expenses	16.0	24.8	25.2	22.9	24.5	31.4
Other expenses and income —net	32.4	85.3	61.4	13.3	5.3	5.3
Plant construction	59.1	134.4	255.5	256.1	459.2	1,082.2
Totals	$318.3	$462.6	$631.8	$670.9	$953.8	$1,766.4

Source: Hewlett and Duncan, *The New World*, p. 677.

Table 3 shows similar data for fiscal years 1973, 1974, and 1975. It can be seen that all three categories have grown markedly along with the operating funds of the AEC. The categories have been rearranged and new ones added, however, so that direct comparisons with Table 2 unfortunately cannot be made. Reactor development expenditures in Table 2 include those of the military. Expenditures for civilian reactors in the late 1940's and early 1950's were small (see Table 6).* Two points can be made on the basis of these data:

* More information on the funding of reactor development programs is provided later in this chapter and in Chapter IV.

1. From the beginning, nuclear materials and weapons absorbed the largest part of the AEC expenditures.

2. Attention to the effects of radiation on man was an important concern of the AEC from the early days.

TABLE 3

ATOMIC ENERGY COMMISSION EXPENDITURES, FISCAL YEARS 1973–75
(Dollars in Thousands)

	1973 Actual	1974 Estimates	1975 Estimates to Congress
Nuclear materials	$ 429,460	$ 531,848	$ 654,610
Weapons	844,115 (1972)	867,729 (1973)	883,300 (1974)
Naval reactor development	149,526	154,200	161,500
Civilian reactor development	255,907	290,390	385,510
Reactor safety research	33,858	40,683	52,940
Applied energy technology	10,610	14,565	32,320
Space nuclear systems	38,590	26,100	27,000
Physical research	243,727	252,340	286,800
Controlled thermonuclear research	37,001	53,000	82,000
Biomedical and environmental research and safety	111,423	124,563	168,643
Regulation activities	45,307	54,430	67,835
Program support	141,024	154,270	170,055
Cost of work for others	26,922	11,900	9,100
Other costs and credits	346	—	—
Total program costs, funded	$2,385,970	$2,544,344	$2,973,543
Change in selected resources	6,916	219,986	167,580
Gross obligations	$2,392,886	$2,764,330	$3,141,123
Plant and capital equipment:			
Capital equipment	$ 163,439	$ 170,072	$ 200,160
Construction	262,007	435,745	496,200
Plant and capital equipment	$ 425,446	$ 605,817	$ 696,360

Source: U.S., Budget Bureau, President's Budget to Congress, Fiscal Year 1974, and *Nuclear News*, 18, 3 (March 1974), p. 35.

Organization

The 1946 Atomic Energy Act established two governmental bodies to control and develop the atom: one administrative, the AEC; and the other legislative, the Joint Committee on Atomic Energy (JCAE).*

It will be remembered that much of the debate that surrounded passage of the 1946 Act was on the question of what type of management and organization should be established for the AEC, particularly regarding military versus civilian control. The act established two important management functions: first, a

* In addition to the use of the abbreviations, AEC and JCAE, the two organizations are also frequently referred to as "the commission" and "the joint committee" or simply "the committee."

five-member commission which would be primarily a policy-formulation body; and second, a general manager who would provide the day-to-day administrative and executive function. The Senate Special Committee on Atomic Energy had this to say about the organizational form selected:

> This form of organization is based on administrative experience developed in both government and industry. Such experience points to the need for a high level policy group which can discharge its functions without the additional burden of passing on current operations. Day to day administration is best directed by a single manager. While the scope and importance of his duties are such as to require his appointment directly by the President, the manager is to work under the general supervision and direction of the Commission, to discharge such of the administrative and executive functions of the Commission as the Commission may direct.[41]

Relating to military matters, a Division of Military Application and a Military Liaison Committee were established.*

A General Advisory Committee (GAC) was established "to advise the commission on scientific and technical matters relating to materials, production, and research and development."[42] The GAC is composed of nine members appointed by the president from civilian life. They hold office for a term of six years. The GAC is instructed by law to meet at least four times per year. It is an internal advisory committee to the commission. Except for the early postwar years, there is little in the recent public record, e.g., JCAE hearings, to indicate the nature of GAC activities or influence. Opinions obtained from interviews, as well as the lack of public statements, indicate that its influence is not nearly so important today as it was during the period 1946–52. As the GAC's influence has waned, the JCAE's influence has increased.

According to the act, the commissioners were appointed by the president, by and with the consent of the Senate. The term of office was five years except when a person was appointed to fill a vacancy of an unexpired term. The president designated one member to be the chairman of the commission; he also had the power to remove a commissioner from office for "inefficiency, neglect of duty, or malfeasance in office." Although the president appointed the commissioners, the criteria for removal limited the political pressure that could be applied on them once appointed. Table 4 lists the chairmen who have held office since the inception of the commission. They have had experience in the fields of finance, administration, law, the military, and science.

The general manager was originally appointed by the president, but an amendment to the act adopted in 1950 established that he was to be appointed "by the Commission, shall serve at the pleasure of the Commission, shall be removable by the Commission. . . ."[43]

The commission/general-manager form of management had both advantages and disadvantages. Management by a commission is a more deliberate process than management by a single administrator. The general manager's being re-

---

* Since these did not affect commercial developments directly, they will not be discussed further.

TABLE 4

ATOMIC ENERGY COMMISSION CHAIRMEN, 1947–73

Year Appointed	Name	Background
1947	David Lilienthal	Administrator; chairman, Tennessee Valley Authority
1950	Sumner Pike (Acting)	Engineer and associate of Wall Street financial firm; one of the first AEC commissioners
1950	Gordon Dean	Lawyer, AEC commissioner 1949–50
1953	Lewis Strauss	Associate of Wall Street banking firm, admiral, U.S. Navy; one of first AEC commissioners
1958	John McCone	Executive
1961	Glenn Seaborg	Scientist
1971	James Schlesinger	Administrator, economist
1973	Dixie Lee Ray	Scientist

sponsible for day-to-day operations presumably freed the commissioners for activities involved in long-range planning and policy making. Nonetheless, the form of management has been criticized many times, and proposals were made even by the five-man commission itself that the commission be abolished.[44] The joint committee, however, did not push for abolishing the commission, as such action presumably could reduce the joint committee's inflence over policy matters and increase that of the president. Critics claimed that the commissioners were indecisive and slow in taking action on important issues. Others believed that the more deliberate approach inherent in decision making by a commission provided several points of view on the issues, and was thus less likely to result in serious mistakes.

The initial reasons for having both an executive commission and a joint committee in Congress no longer exist. These reasons had their basis in the newness and awesomeness of the atomic weapon and the secrecy with which all atomic activities were to be controlled. The rationale behind establishing these forms was the belief that a single administrator should not control the agency.

Orlans' stated view of this issue is that "the charges of excessive caution and indecision . . . should, however, be put in some perspective. It is strange that an agency against which such charges have so often (and, apparently, so justifiably!) been leveled should nonetheless have an outstanding record of technical achievement." [45]

In June 1972, in his message to Congress, President Nixon proposed reorganization within agencies concerned with energy and natural resources that would split the Atomic Energy organization. In this proposal, the commission would be kept for the regulatory function which is consistent with other government regulatory functions. The civilian developments would be combined in a new energy research and development agency under the direction of one administrator. In the interview with Robert Hollingsworth, general manager of the

AEC, he expressed a view that can be summarized as follows: except for the regulatory responsibilities, there is no real need for continuing the commission form of management, either for the AEC's current responsibilities or for its new role in the proposed energy research and development agency. It was also his opinion that the regulatory function could be successfully split off from the development side of the AEC. This split was accomplished in 1974 and will be discussed in the next section of this chapter.

In addition to creating a Division of Military Application, the 1946 Act also called for "such other program divisions (not to exceed ten in number) as the Commission may determine to be necessary to the discharge of its responsibilities. Each division shall be under the direction of a Director who shall be appointed by the Commission. . . ." [46] The AEC initially established four headquarters divisions: research, military applications, production, and engineering. [47] The directors of these divisions essentially had staff positions rather than "line" responsibilities. The actual line authority rested with the managers of the initial five field offices: Oak Ridge, New York, Chicago, Hanford, and Santa Fe. [48] The AEC was at that time a highly decentralized organization with contract and program authority delegated to the field offices. However, this organizational arrangement soon came under attack from several sources. [49] For example, Donald F. Carpenter (a vice-president of Remington Arms Company), whom Strauss had induced to serve on the AEC's Industrial Advisory Group and who became chairman of Military Liaison Committee, [50] recommended that the divisional directors be given line authority with responsibility to coordinate and supervise the field offices. [51] Furthermore, the General Advisory Committee, seeing little ability to influence commission programs with the existing organization, recommended reorganization along the lines of Carpenter's proposal, [52] which specifically called for directors of research, weapons, reactors, and production with line authority, plus an overall administrative officer. On August 5, 1948, the AEC announced a reorganization essentially as had been proposed. [53] Various changes or additions were made to the Washington, D.C., organization as the AEC programs evolved, but the basic philosophy of management remained similar to that established in 1948, with one exception. This exception, which occurred in the 1960's, was a change in the way some of the responsibilities were divided between the AEC headquarters and the field offices. Program planning, budgeting, and control had been primarily headquarters' responsibility, with the field offices responsible for contractor performance and supervision. In the 1960's, changes in this split of responsibility gave headquarters, particularly the Division of Reactor Development and Technology, more responsibility for the direct supervision of programs in the laboratories under the purview of the field offices. Figure 4 (Chapter VII) is a chart of the AEC organization structure in the early 1970's.

Regarding the regulation of atomic energy, a civilian applications division called for in the 1954 Atomic Energy Act was established in June 1955. [54] On December 18, 1957, the division's functions were reassigned to two new organizational units: the Division of Licensing and Regulations, and the Office of Industrial Development. The latter was responsible for developing commission policy for encouraging and assisting private activities in the civilian applications of atomic energy, exclusive of the reactor program.[55] As can be seen from the organization chart in Figure 4, the licensing and regulatory function, headed by the director of regulation, was completely separate from the operating and developmental functions, headed by the general manager. The director of regulation and the general manager both reported directly to the commissioners. Also reporting to the commissioners were the Advisory Committee on Reactor Safeguards and the Atomic Safety and Licensing Board Panel, both of which were important to reactor licensing.

AEC operations were carried out largely by industrial concerns and by private and public institutions under contracts administered by the field offices, which by 1973 numbered eleven. The largest part of their programs was conducted in AEC-owned facilities, but a not insignificant part was conducted in nongovernment facilities. Contributions to the power reactor development program came from many of the AEC facilities, including particularly the three major multiprogram "National Laboratories" (Argonne, Illinois; Brookhaven, New York; and Oak Ridge, Tennessee); the two naval reactor program laboratories (Knolls Atomic Power Laboratory, New York; and Bettis Atomic Power Laboratory, Pennsylvania); the National Reactor Testing Station in Idaho; and research and development laboratories associated with plutonium production facilities at Savannah River, South Carolina, and Hanford, Washington. Other AEC facilities have been important in developing and producing supplies of special nuclear materials. The two major laboratories associated with weapons development, E. O. Lawrence Radiation Laboratory, California, and Los Alamos Scientific Laboratory, New Mexico, have also made significant contributions to the AEC's power reactor development programs.

By 1974 the total number of employees in the AEC's program was: AEC—7,988, operating contractors—94,662; and construction contractors—10,561. This compares with about 5,000 staff and 50,000 contractor personnel transferred to the AEC from the War Department on December 31, 1946 [56] (construction personnel not given).

ERDA AND NRC

During the preparation of this book, a major reorganization of the AEC and the nation's government energy research and development occurred. Through the Energy Reorganization Act of 1974,[57] the nonregulatory part of the AEC—e.g., reactor development, physical research, military application—became part of the newly formed Energy Research and Development Administration (ERDA), and the licensing and regulatory functions were placed under a separate organization, the Nuclear Regulatory Commission.

The head of ERDA is a civilian administrator appointed by the president with the advice and consent of the Senate. Also appointed by the president with the advice and consent of the Senate are a deputy administrator and six assistant administrators. The six assistant administrators manage six areas of research within ERDA specifically called out by Congress: (1) fossil energy; (2) nuclear energy; (3) environment and safety; (4) conservation; (5) solar, geothermal, and advanced energy systems; and (6) national security. The objective of the reorganization was not only to split up the promotional and regulatory functions of the AEC, but also to place greater emphasis on nonnuclear energy developments and to bring them closer in priority ranking with nuclear energy. Along with the reorganizational emphasis, rapid budget escalations have occurred in nonnuclear research through 1975 and are continued in the president's proposed FY 1976 budget to Congress. For example, coal R&D is expected to increase by 60 percent over FY 1975, solar by 551 percent, and geothermal by 106 percent—while nuclear power development is only about 10 percent,[58] essentially keeping up with general inflation.

Other government energy research programs were also transferred to ERDA; these included solar energy programs from the National Science Foundation, and the Office of Coal Research and Bureau of Mines energy centers from the Interior Department. A major objective of these moves was to place the nation's energy research under one organization so that a more consistent set of energy research policies and priorities could be formulated. It is interesting to note, however, that ERDA's FY 1976 budget request of $311 million for fossil fuel research and development is less than half the Interior's request of $717 million for energy R&D,[59] including coal, goethermal, uranium, and thorium. In addition, the Environmental Protection Agency is continuing major energy research activities.

The Nuclear Regulatory Commission (NRC) is composed of five members, one of whom is designated chairman. Members of the commission are appointed by the president with the advice and consent of the Senate; not more than three members can be of the same political party. Except for the initial members, whose appointments are staggered by increments of one year, the term of office is five years. As with the AEC commissioners, political pressure on members is lessened by the stipulation that they can be removed by the president only for inefficiency, neglect of duty, or malfeasance in office. Members cannot, moreover, engage in any outside business, vocation, or employment during their tenure in office.

The Atomic Safety and Licensing Board and the Atomic Safety and Licensing Appeal Board were transferred to NRC and specific offices were established for each of the following three functions: nuclear reactor regulation; nuclear material safety and safeguards; and nuclear regulatory research. The directors of these offices are appointed by the commission and their proposed budgets for FY 1975 and FY 1976 are, in millions of dollars: $51.9 and $65.7, $7.5 and $11.0, and $61.4 and $97.2, respectively. Included in the FY 1976 nuclear regulatory research budget is over $17 million for nonreactor research, including safeguards, fuel cycle, and environmental research. These items, especially with regard to plutonium, are becoming major issues in the nuclear power debates.

Budgets

Some budget data were given in a previous section of this chapter (Purpose, Authority, and Scope of Activities) to illustrate types of AEC programs; those given here represent expenditures directly related to nuclear reactor developments.

The budget and accounting system of the AEC evolved and changed over its history. Therefore, the data given for the various categories may have somewhat different bases from year to year. The data given in Tables 5 and 6 are cost data, not budgets or appropriations. The cost data include a facility and equipment depreciation cost, except that in Table 6 the pre-1957 reactor development costs include actual construction and equipment costs for each reactor program. Costs for 1960 and 1965 were also reassigned between general reactor research and development and specific reactor programs. Because of the overlapping nature of the programs, it is not always obvious where certain costs should be assigned. Even though variations and inconsistencies can be demonstrated, the absolute size of the expenditures and the relative expenditures are useful for extracting certain information on the government's priorities and emphasis over the history of the AEC.

First, AEC operating costs rose rapidly until 1959, but remained within a narrow range since then. Heavy construction costs were incurred in the early 1950's for plant expansion for weapons material production.

Second, it can be seen from Table 5 that the total reactor development costs were less than five percent of the AEC's costs until 1955. They then climbed rapidly until about 1963, remaining in the range of about $500 million to $570 million through 1974; this funding represents roughly 20 percent or less of AEC operating costs.

Third, the civilian reactor development expenditures grew rapidly in the 1950's, remained relatively constant until about 1966, and increased substantially since then. Table 3 (presented earlier in this chapter), which gives projected expenditures (on a different basis from that of the data shown in Tables 5 and 6) for fiscal years 1974 and 1975, shows that the growth trend continued. It is interesting to note that the AEC's program costs for support of civilian reactors in 1974 and 1975 were approximately 10 percent or less of the total operating costs, even including all the general research and development costs. By the early 1970's, the majority of the general R&D funds had been used primarily for support of civilian reactor development. Military activities still absorbed the overwhelming majority of AEC funds.

Fourth, excluding the general R&D costs, the cumulative expenditures for civilian power reactors through 1974 were comparable in total with those for naval reactors and aircraft and space nuclear developments; each of these latter categories totaled less than $2.5 billion. In the last category, aircraft propulsion

TABLE 5

ATOMIC ENERGY COMMISSION COSTS, FISCAL YEARS 1947–74
(Dollars in Millions)

Fiscal Year	Total	Cost of Operations [a]	Construction and Equipment Costs	Reactor Development [b]
1947	—	$ 259	$ 59	?
1948	—	328	134	?
1949	—	376	255	$ 19
1950	$ 671	415	256	32
1951	954	495	459	45
1952	1766	684	1082	65
1953	2031	905	1126	105
1954	1255	1040	1215	100
1955	2133	1290	843	119
1956	1910	1608	302	170
1957	2275	1968	317	254
1958	2589	2299	290	287
1959	2796	2497	299	356
1960	2951	2619	332	399
1961	3045	2612	433	437
1962	3120	2696	424	433
1963	3124	2713	411	507
1964	3116	2739	377	561
1965	2941	2570	371	536
1966	2773	2440	333	484
1967	2737	2447	290	528
1968	2838	2507	331	549
1969	2984	2566	418	508
1970	2937	2504	433	496
1971	2933	2501	432	505
1972	2960	2575	385	510
1973	3118	2677	441	546
1974	3288	2744	544	571

Sources: U.S., AEC, Financial Reports, 1956–74; and Hewlett and Duncan, The Atomic Shield, Appendix 7.

[a] Costs include operating costs plus facility depreciation cost.

[b] Reactor development costs are included in second column, "Cost of Operations."

developments dominated the expenditures until 1961, at which time that program was terminated.[60] Other space nuclear developments since 1961—e.g., nuclear rocket engines and auxiliary power plants—substantially exceeded the expenditures for aircraft propulsion, and until 1967 were larger on a yearly basis than those for the civilian reactor program.

Most of the AEC's technology development and assessment leading to the commercial light-water reactors occurred before 1964. At about that time the civilian reactor program started phasing out the support of the light-water reactor and started emphasizing breeders and advanced converters.[61] Except for light-water reactor safety, most of the AEC's civilian reactor effort in 1975 was on one reactor type, the liquid-metal fast breeder reactor (LMFBR).

TABLE 6

NUCLEAR REACTOR DEVELOPMENT COSTS, FISCAL YEARS 1948–74 [a]

(Dollars in Millions)

Year	Naval	Space and Aircraft	Civilian	General R&D
1948–50	$ 8.8	?	$ 3.1	—
1951	29.8	$ 5.5	5.1	—
1952	38.0	17.0	6.3	—
1953	57.3	20.2	10.1	—
1954	49.0	22.0	18.9	—
1955	39.7	25.9	28.4	—
1956	50.7	52.0	51.6	—
1957	79.1	92.9	58.2	—
1958	81.9	78.5	79.0	41.1
1959	90.6	102.3	105.3	43.3
1960	88.8	112.9	117.8(100.0) [b]	60.4(81.4)
1961	93.5	115.5	102.3	86.1
1962	95.4	117.6	94.3	104.1
1963	108.9	170.2	88.1	121.1
1964	113.8	181.3	98.5	136.6
1965	102	179 (196.9)	98 (116.6)	140.4(104)
1966	89.6	159.4	120.0	112.0
1967	105	165.6	141.0	116.0
1968	123.5	141	166.5	117.4
1969	128	111	152.4	117.4
1970	139.5	107	147.7	102.0
1971	154.7	99.2	155.7	95.2
1972	157	64	185.0	104.5
1973	167.4	45.9	216.5	115.8
1974	172.1	31.6	---------- 367.6 --------------------	
Total	$2,364.1	$2,211.5	$2,490.0(est.)	$1,742.2(est.)

Source: U.S., AEC, *Financial Reports,* 1956–74.

[a] Costs to 1957 included costs of operation plus actual cost of facilities and equipment; after 1957 depreciation costs for facilities and equipment were used.

[b] Numbers in parentheses show a new distribution of costs after reassignment of certain costs from one category to another.

Of the total projected civilian reactor development program FY 1975 budget of $385.5 million, direct support of the LMFBR accounted for $207 million, and another $14 million was for the LMFBR demonstration plant. Indirect support of the LMFBR came from the nuclear safety program, $40.1 million (excluding $52.9 million for reactor safety, primarily light-water reactor safety, administratively separate from the civilian reactor safety program); and the technology and engineering program, $67.5 million. Other AEC support of civilian reactor development projected for FY 1975 included light-water reactors, primarily Rickover's breeder, $21.1 million; gas-cooled reactors, $27.8 million; molten salt breeders, $4.0 million; and engineering evaluation and support, $4.0 million.

AEC Policy toward Industry

The tone of the AEC's policy toward industry was established by the basic wartime policy of General Leslie Grove and the Manhattan project. Even though the development of atomic energy was probably the most secret large-scale project ever undertaken by government, the government took the position that "contracting with a few of the nation's largest and best qualified companies and universities was the most expeditious and effective way to develop, design, and produce atomic bombs." [62] The government has continued this policy and in 1975 still operates its extensive laboratories through contracts with private organizations. Orlans points out that:

> This has been a deliberate policy, for the AEC was not, like the National Science Foundation, proscribed by statute from operating its own laboratories; on the contrary, one avowed purpose of the Atomic Energy Act of 1946 was to provide for a program of federally conducted research and development. This self-denying policy was the more remarkable in view of the unprecedented and exclusive powers given by this act to the AEC to own all fissionable material and all facilities for its production, and to license and control its distribution and use.

Orlans gives several reasons why government operation of AEC facilities was never favored by either a majority of the five-man commission or the Congress:

1. Most of the key industrialists and scientists opposed it, believing that military or civil service management would be less effective than that of a private organization, and would handicap recruitment of the best people.
2. The 1946 Atomic Energy Act already gave the government monopolistic and in some respects draconian powers (the phrase "shall . . . be punished by death" recurs a good many times), abrogating in the nuclear field traditional rights of private ownership, private patents, and the free exchange of information.
3. From the outset, even in the days when fissionable material was most scarce, nuclear technology most secret, and civilian application most uncertain, the explicit objective of the government was, in the words of the 1946 Act, "strengthening free competition in private enterprise."
4. Finally, contracting with outside groups had the double advantage of keeping these groups informed about highly classified activities . . . and, in turn, bringing to government a continuing flow of knowledge, ideas, and advice from a larger and more distinguished number of industrialists and scientists. . . .

Newman states that "the preference shown by Congress for the maximum safe participation of private industry in atomic matters has been interpreted by the AEC as a dogma. . . . The Commission has elevated private participation above every other principle except possibly security." [63]

In addition to the policy of having its research and development performed by private contractors or public and private universities, other AEC policies had a bearing on nuclear energy development. These policies, apparent in the commission's programs of employment, research laboratory and contractor distribution, and reactor development, were: *

---

* These policies are discussed in other sections dealing with the various AEC programs.

1. To disburse contracts widely throughout the nation.

2. To assist private firms in the development of reactor programs, rather than building reactors itself.

3. To support private industry and public organizations in the research and development required for commercial reactors.

On the one hand, the AEC was assigned the mission of developing nuclear reactors for electric power. It was thus the promoter of nuclear development. On the other hand, it was to establish the safety criteria for construction, operation, and regulation of nuclear plants. Thus it may be seen that the potential for conflict of goals was built into the organization. Government policies gave the AEC primary responsibility for providing programmatic leadership and financial support to develop the base technology, conduct safety and waste management research and development, initiate advanced reactor concepts, construct advanced reactor prototypes, and financially assist industry-owned demonstration plants.

AEC policy had a mixed impact on the pace of nuclear development. On the one hand, secrecy, government monopoly, and political problems may have had an inhibiting effect on nuclear power development. On the other hand, government development assistance, in the form of both financial aid and technical information compiled during years of military and civilian research, was made available to domestic industry. This was particularly true of the Navy's propulsion reactor program. Licensed noncommercial reactor operators were provided with research and development funding, free use of nuclear fuels and other materials, fuel reprocessing, and waste storage. Other incentives for nuclear development have included low-cost fuel loans and waivers of payment, government purchase of byproduct plutonium and U-233, AEC-funded research and development, and government liability insurance. Most significant of these was AEC-funded research and development. The assistance to nuclear power development has been justified by the AEC on the basis of supporting foreign policy, accelerating development, and avoiding government ownership.

JOINT COMMITTEE ON ATOMIC ENERGY (JCAE)

The 1946 Act established the Joint Committee on Atomic Energy (JCAE) and specified that it was to be composed of nine members from the House and nine from the Senate, to be appointed by the Speaker of the House and President of the Senate, respectively.[64] It further stated that in each instance not more than five members were to be members of the same political party. The responsibilities were spelled out as follows:

> The joint committee shall make continuing studies of the activities of the Atomic Energy Commission and of problems relating to the development, use, and control of atomic energy. The Commission shall keep the joint committee fully and currently informed with respect to the Commission's activities. All bills, resolutions, and other matters in the Senate or the House of Representatives relating primarily to the Commission or to the development, use, or control of atomic energy shall be referred to

the joint committee. The members of the joint committee who are Members of the Senate shall from time to time report to the Senate, and the members of the joint committee who are Members of the House of Representatives shall from time to time report to the House, by bill or otherwise, their recommendations with respect to matters within the jurisdiction of their respective Houses which are (1) referred to the joint committee or (2) otherwise within the jurisdiction of the joint committee.[65]

These led to unique powers for the JCAE. First, it was given full jurisdiction over all legislative matters pertaining to atomic energy; second, it was accorded the right to be "fully and currently informed" and to "make continuing studies of the activities of the Atomic Energy Commission." These authorities gave the JCAE strong investigative powers. The JCAE is the only joint committee of Congress authorized to receive and recommend to the Congress proposed legislation.[66] It is one of the few committees established by statute, rather than by rule of each house.[67]

The chairmanship of the JCAE was clarified by the Atomic Energy Act of 1954, which provided that:

Vacancies in the membership of the Joint Committee shall not affect the power of the remaining members to execute the functions of the Joint Committee, and shall be filled in the same manner as in the case of the original selection. The Joint Committee shall select a Chairman and a Vice Chairman from among its members at the beginning of each Congress. The Vice Chairman shall act in the place and stead of the Chairman in the absence of the Chairman. The Chairmanship shall alternate between the Senate and the House of Representatives with each Congress, and the Chairman shall be selected by the Members from that House entitled to the Chairmanship. The Vice Chairman shall be chosen from the House other than that of the Chairman by the Members from that House.[68]

In performing its legislative function, the JCAE usually holds extensive hearings on proposed legislation and then reports out identical bills to each house. It also takes the responsibility for bills on the floor and in conferences, and conducts confirmation hearings on presidential appointees.

As a "watchdog," the JCAE maintains close surveillance of the various aspects of the atomic energy program and the work of the AEC, with a view to insuring that adequate progress is being made and that appropriated public funds are being expended wisely and efficiently. The authority to carry out this function comes from the rather innocuous-sounding phrases quoted above from Section 15 of the 1946 Act.

The JCAE also uses its policy and review functions as the basis for proposing policy changes or innovations in the atomic energy program. The JCAE points out as examples of this that it has "expedited and supported the naval nuclear propulsion program, the hydrogen bomb project, an expanded atomic power program, the preservation of food through irradiation, the utilization of atomic energy for space applications, and the liquid metal fast breeder reactor program." [69]

The JCAE has been a consistent and avid supporter of atomic energy development and a firm prodder of the AEC. Although the JCAE was responsible from the beginning for all legislation dealing with atomic energy, it did not have authorization powers until some time later. The 1954 Act provided limited legislative authorization responsibilities; that is, JCAE authorization was required for construction and real property acquisition.[70] On July 3, 1957, the JCAE gained additional control over the civilian reactor program when a bill [71] was passed giving it authorization power over essentially all nonmilitary reactor projects. Total authorization power was obtained when an amendment to Section 261 of the 1954 Atomic Energy Act was passed in 1963.[72] This amendment required prior congressional authorization of all appropriations for the AEC, including both construction and operating funds. The JCAE views this power as necessary to "further insure adequate congressional control over the atomic energy program." [73] The authorization requirement allowed the JCAE to receive detailed testimony on the needs for the appropriations requested by the AEC, thereby giving the JCAE sufficient background information on the AEC's activities and plans to enable it knowledgeably to influence program plans and priorities. Much of the power and influence of the JCAE, not only with the AEC but with Congress and particularly with the appropriation committees, probably came from the extensive knowledge that its members have of the atomic energy program. In the early years, the program's secrecy put them in an even more elite position in this regard.

The JCAE obtained other methods of influence by requiring that certain AEC planned actions or criteria for actions be placed before the committee for thirty days or more, while Congress was in session, before the AEC plans could be finalized. For example, appropriate proposals had to be submitted to the JCAE for a period of forty-five days before the commission could establish a "guaranteed purchase price" or a "guaranteed purchase price period" for licensee-produced plutonium or U-233, or before the commission could establish any criteria for the waiver of use charges on special nuclear materials.[74] Likewise, under the cooperative power reactor demonstration program, for the AEC to enter into or amend an agreement that had not been previously approved by authorizing legislation, it had to sumit that agreement to the JCAE for forty-five days before the agreement could become effective. Similar requirements applied to the AEC's adoption of criteria for enriching services.[75] In some cases the JCAE could waive these requirements, but in general they gave the JCAE an opportunity to review the submitted plan, to offer changes if it desired, or even to introduce additional legislation relating to the desired action. These requirements thus made the JCAE review powers even more extensive. The membership of the JCAE actively used its powers and became a strong partner of the AEC in formulation of policies and plans.

Organizationally, the committee is composed of the following seven subcommittees: Research, Development, and Radiation; Legislation; Agreements for Cooperation; Communities; Military Applications; Security; and Raw Materials.[76] The subcommittees are charged with the responsibility of conducting detailed studies of the problems and progress in their assigned areas of the atomic energy program and reporting their findings and recommendations to the full committee. There is some indication, however, that most substantive matters are now taken up directly in the full committee rather than through the subcommittees.

Green and Rosenthal have conducted a detailed study of the JCAE and have concluded that the JCAE is probably the most powerful congressional committee ever to exist.[77] It acquired this power in part because it had access to information, participated in policy formulation and implementation, invaded the sphere of executive privilege, maintained direct contact with all levels of the executive branch without regard to "chain of command" procedures, and performed an advocate role toward AEC programs instead of the usual braking role of congressional committees.

Green and Rosenthal provide further insight into the committee in their summary of its evolution over the years:

> In considering the role of the JCAE during its fifteen-year existence, one is impressed by the manner in which its role and activities fall neatly into separate eras. The years 1947, 1948, and 1949 may aptly be characterized as a period in which the Joint Committee played a relatively passive role, functioning primarily in a 'watchdog' or oversight capacity. Commencing late in 1949, the Committee's role appears to have changed markedly. While it continued to function as a 'watchdog' to the same extent, it also began to assume a role of vigorous leadership in the national atomic energy program. In this role, it generally encouraged and exhorted the willing but cautious AEC to expand programs which the JCAE regarded as important, and functioned as a 'big brother,' cooperating with and protecting the AEC against its critics and those who favored curtailment of its program. This period extended through the end of the Truman Administration, and through the first year of the Eisenhower Administration. Then, in 1955, largely as a result of the Dixon-Yates controversy and the atomic power policies of an economy-minded Republican Administration, a Democratic-controlled Joint Committee sought to accelerate the nation's civilian power program. The years 1955 to 1958 were marked by sharp controversy with the Executive Branch. During this period, the JCAE became a policy-forging institution, greatly expanding the exercise of its statutory authority and exerting influence the Executive deemed unwarranted. Finally, 1958 through 1960 were years of relative calm during which the JCAE, having won a position of leadership in the national atomic energy program, entrenched and consolidated its position with little opposition from the Executive.[78]

These comments were made in 1961. There is some evidence that the leadership role of the JCAE has diminished in the early 1970's. While implementation of a 1973 AEC reorganization of water reactor safety was supported by the joint committee as a whole, it was opposed by two of the committee's most influential and longest standing members.[79]

The JCAE also seems to be experiencing something of a transition period, in that membership is being assigned to more junior members of Congress and in that Senate members are taking a much less active role than the House members. The latter situation has been attributed to the higher priority the Senate members place on other committee assignments and to the fact that the number of senators in Congress is less than one fourth that of the representatives, even though they are responsible for essentially the same issues. These problems could result in a breakdown of the effectiveness of a joint committee. In addition, two of the most influential members of the JCAE, Holifield and Hosmer, have resigned from Congress.

While interview data indicated that lack of Senate-member attendance at JCAE meetings is a current problem, an analysis by Orlans of attendance for the 1964 and 1965 authorization hearings shows that the same situation existed then:

> "This is no longer a Joint Committee; it is a House Committee," one observer remarked, and an examination of attendance at hearings bears him out. On the average, only one Senator (usually Pastore, Joint Committee chairman that year) attended each day's authorization hearings in 1964, and less than two, the following year. The Senators remain, of course, alert to and active in protecting the nuclear interests of their area; but they have been content to let the House members and committee staff assume much of the burden of hearings and monitoring Commission activities.[80]

Concern with protecting nuclear interests in their area is not limited to the Senate members. Many of the influential members of the joint committee of both houses have had significant constituency interest based on major atomic energy installations in their state. These have included such members as Senator Henry Jackson (Hanford, Washington), Senator Clinton Anderson (Los Alamos and Sandia, New Mexico), Senator Albert Gore (Oak Ridge, Tennessee), Representatives Chet Holifield and Craig Hosmer (Lawrence Radiation Laboratory and Stanford, California), Representative Melvin Price (Argonne, Illinois), and Representative James Van Zandt (coal district in Pennsylvania). On the other hand, members of the joint committee have generally supported the broad scope of nuclear power development and since the early 1950's have consistently promoted "a vigorous, imaginative, and aggressive atomic-energy program, demanding boldness and risk-taking rather than caution and economy." [81] With few exceptions, their support has been bipartisan. The few exceptions have included quarrels over patent restrictions and public versus private power controversies. Neither of these issues is of any consequence today, but the public power issue could have had a major impact on the structure of the utility industry.*

EARLY POSTWAR DEVELOPMENTS (1946–52)

In its first annual report to Congress in 1947, the AEC announced that a broad program initiated by the Mnnhattan Engineering District for the production of electrical power from nuclear energy was underway with Monsanto Chemical, operator of the Clinton Laboratory (Oak Ridge National Laboratory), and the General Electric Company. It also stated that "the Commission

---

* This issue is discussed further in Chapters III and IV.

plans immediately to consult with representatives of interested American industries in such fields as utilities, electrical manufacturing, chemical and others, in order to assure broad participation by private enterprise in the research and development program, looking toward the industrial application of atomic energy.'' [82] While these statements set the tone of the approach that the AEC has used ever since, they implied a much more aggressive program than actually existed.

In January 1947, in a report to the General Advisory Committee, Walter Zinn, Director of Argonne National Laboratory, summarized the status of research reactors operating at that time. These included two small reactors at Los Alamos, the rebuilt Fermi pile and a small heavy-water-moderated reactor at Argonne, a test reactor at Hanford, and the X-10 graphite reactor at Clinton Laboratories.[83] The first five were essentially zero-power reactors, but the X-10 had a neutron flux level sufficient for radioisotope production and radiation research. None met the need for a very high neutron flux and access ports for test irradiation of reactor materials and components; however, the Clinton Laboratories had started designing a reactor which did meet this need.[84]

Several power reactor types were being considered by the AEC. Because of the existing shortage and potentially high cost of uranium, the breeder concept * was under active consideration. The Knolls Atomic Power Laboratory (KAPL), operated by General Electric, was investigating an intermediate neutron spectrum breeder reactor. Argonne was designing a "fast" breeder that would use high-energy neutrons. The breeding concepts were considered marginal, however, neutron economy being the foremost consideration. A "thermal" reactor (utilizing low-energy neutrons in the fission process), to be used primarily for power production, was being designed by Farrington Daniels and his associates at the Clinton Laboratories.[85]

Because of technical reasons, the AEC and members of the Clinton pile division had little enthusiasm for the "Daniels pile," and later in 1947, AEC general manager Wilson and research director Fisk terminated the project.** The high-flux reactor at Clinton was also uncertain. At that time, the Clinton Laboratories were undergoing contractor change and were also without a director—a situation that resulted in little programmatic direction.[87] Even the construction of the intermediate breeder reactor at KAPL was seen "far in the future," since the supporting "zero-power pile" was not to be ready for operation until 1948.

The General Advisory Committee (GAC) was deeply troubled by the commission's failure to take hold of reactor development. After extensive review,

* The term "breeder" is used to describe those reactors that produce more fissile material than they consume. The production of fissile atoms—e.g., Pu-239 or U-233—occurs as a result of the capture of an excess neutron by a "fertile" atom such as U-238 or Th-232.

** Also, the reactor development committee had stated that the commission should not waste time on projects like the Daniels reactor, which would do nothing more than demonstrate the obvious fact that electrical power could be generated from atomic energy (Hewlett and Duncan, *The Atomic Shield*, p. 118).

on November 23, 1947, the GAC issued a statement that described some of the complex economic factors involved in building a nuclear power system. Hewlett and Duncan summarized the report as follows:

> These included the need for high-temperature operation, new materials for components, long fuel cycles, high specific power, and a low net consumption of fissionable materials. Two reactors then under development, presumably the high-flux and the fast-breeder, would probably produce atomic power within two or three years; but neither could conceivably be thought of as an economical producer of power. The outlook would probably be brighter if low-grade ores proved plentiful or if breeding should be possible. Since the engineering difficulties associated with breeding were enormous, the best hope seemed to lie in increasing ore supplies through geological research and prospecting. On the assumption that breeding would not prove practical in the immediate future, atomic power would not compete with conventional fuels in the United States except in high-cost regions unless the cost of uranium concentrates could be brought appreciably below $100 per pound. In any case construction costs would always be higher for plants using nuclear fuel than for those operating on conventional fuels. In summary, the committee did "not see how it would be possible under the most favorable circumstances to have any considerable portion of the present power supply of the world, replaced by nuclear fuel before the expiration of twenty years." [88]

This statement by the GAC has proved to contain considerable insight into the problems of nuclear power development. Fisk favored extensive component development before full-scale power reactors were attempted, while Glenn Seaborg, a member of the GAC, thought the best way to identify technical problems would be to build a reactor, and suggested that Westinghouse be asked to develop a high-temperature power reactor. [89]

In an attempt to resolve the issues, the AEC established a reactor development group consisting of members having leadership roles in reactor development at Argonne, Schenectady, and Clinton. [90] After an appeal from the Navy and the Air Force, the group gave the nuclear-powered submarine highest priority. [91] The GAC saw a program built around the Air Force and Navy requirements as a worthwhile start toward giving direction to reactor development. [92] The GAC also favored developing a breeder proposed by Argonne. The question of adequate uranium ore supply continued to have a significant impact on the reactor program.* In its third semiannual report to Congress, the commission stated: "Both the military and industrial potential of atomic energy justify the effort to solve the problem of breeding." [93] The commission, like the GAC, saw that the timetable for significant amounts of useful nuclear power would extend through two decades. [94]

Another possible impediment to reactor development was a pessimistic analysis by Edward Teller of the consequences of a reactor accident, a position that the GAC believed exaggerated the danger. [95] Teller was the first to frame the reactor siting problem in mathematical terms. Simply stated, the higher the power

---

* A discussion of the AEC's program to alleviate this constraint is provided in Chapter V.

level, the greater the area over which population density control was needed.[96] This formula continues in practice today.

On October 19, 1948, Wilson proposed to the commission a plan encompassing four reactor projects: the high-flux reactor (to be called the materials testing reactor—MTR), the Argonne fast breeder (EBR-1), the General Electric intermediate breeder, and the Navy-Argonne submarine propulsion reactor. The last was a thermal, water-cooled reactor concept previously studied at Oak Ridge.[97] On November 10, 1948, the commission approved the plan. A fifth reactor, Alvin Weinberg's homogeneous reactor concept, was added to the plan.[98]

On February 1, 1949, Lawrence R. Hafstad became the first director of the AEC's reactor development division.[99] Also, early in 1949, the commission selected a remote area in Idaho as a site for testing its nuclear reactor concepts.[100] This has become the National Reactor Testing Station, and has been used extensively for Navy, aircraft, and experimental power reactor testing. Also, three materials and components testing reactors and several safety experiments have been located there.

On December 10, 1948, Westinghouse accepted the assignment to work with Argonne on the submarine thermal reactor.[101] General Electric continued working on the intermediate breeder. At this time W. Rudolph Kanne was carrying out experiments on irradiated special foils of plutonium in the Hanford reactors, and Thoma M. Snyder was working on critical assembly at KAPL. These crucial experiments, however, did not demonstrate the expected breeding.[102]

The pessimistic outlook on breeding led General Electric to study the intermediate breeder as a power source for submarines. Moreoever, new uranium discoveries in the United States and elsewhere had made ore procurement a matter of economics rather than availability, a fact that deemphasized the earlier importance of breeders. In March 1950, the commission decided that: the intermediate breeder would be postponed indefinitely; KAPL would concentrate most of its effort on Hanford production reactor problems; and the intermediate breeder reactor at KAPL would be redesigned as a prototype for submarine propulsion.[103] Admiral Hyman Rickover, head of the Navy program, favored this decision. This further biased the AEC position on power reactor development in favor of the military. The decision did, however, bring industrial experience and participation more actively into the reactor program, thus meeting a long-standing objective of the commission. This experience was to be of major importance in developing a nuclear power industry.

The emphasis on building a weapons stockpile, the shortage of uranium, the need for secrecy, and particularly the increase in Russian weapons developments,* [104] all contributed to the delay in formulating a well-defined civilian power reactor program. As of the early part of 1950, the only power-type reac-

* Russia exploded its first atomic bomb on September 23, 1949.

tor under construction was the experimental breeder reactor (EBR-1). The other approved power reactor project was the study of the homogeneous reactor. Even these two reactors were considered potentially important to the military plutonium production program.[105] Hafstad, director of the AEC reactor development program, contended that for the short run, the commission should concentrate on military propulsion reactors and plutonium producers and that, while nuclear energy for electric power production would be significant in the long run, private industry might better do that job.[106] The General Advisory Committee, meeting in December 1951, gave a pessimistic view of the future of nuclear power, but did recognize the significance of the large increase in the availability of uranium ore vis-à-vis the difficult problem of developing the breeder.[107] Some members of the GAC thought that the United States should concentrate on plutonium and propulsion and leave power reactors to the British.

Another decision made in 1950 put additional strain on the manpower and research capabilities of the AEC and on the funding of its program. It was Truman's decision on January 31, 1950, that the AEC should "continue its work on all forms of weapons, including the so-called hydrogen bomb." [108]. The hydrogen bomb required not only fissile material but also tritium. Tritium would have to be made from a target material using a neutron source, either a reactor or an accelerator. The AEC considered several reactor types and finally selected a uranium-fueled reactor, moderated and cooled by heavy water. It was to be an enlarged version of the CP-5 research reactor that Walter Zinn, director of Argonne, had planned to build.[109] DuPont, which had built and operated the Hanford plant during World War II,* was called on to design, construct, and operate the new production facilities,[110] to be located on the Savannah River, near Aiken, South Carolina.[111] In addition, construction of five large reactors at Hanford was authorized in 1951 and 1952, bringing the total number of production reactors to thirteen. Construction of the Paducah, Kentucky, gaseous diffusion plant was also started during this period.[112] All of these decisions involved major policy questions and planning efforts that occupied much of the time of the AEC, GAC, and JCAE. Power reactor development was receiving second priority.

---

* General Electric operated Hanford after World War II.

CHAPTER III

Period of Transition, 1952–54

THE 1952–54 period was a major turning point in the development of atomic energy for electric power generation. The JCAE began taking a much greater interest and a more active role in the development of not only military and production reactors but power reactors as well. The AEC established an industrial participation group in 1951, and a large number of companies and industrial teams began studies on power reactors. The AEC expanded its experimental reactors program, put forth a five-year plan, and made major policy shifts.

In 1953, Gordon Dean, retiring as chairman of the AEC, recommended to the JCAE that early development of commercial nuclear power be established as a national objective. He urged modification of the Atomic Energy Act of 1946 to allow private ownership of reactors and reactor fuels so as to encourage private enterprise to enter the nuclear field.[1] Lewis L. Strauss, who succeeded Dean as chairman, reaffirmed this position. In December 1953, Eisenhower presented his historic Atoms-for-Peace proposal and on February 17, 1954, he presented a message to Congress recommending substantial changes in the 1946 Atomic Energy Act. Among other things, these changes allowed for much wider participation of industry in nuclear power development. The 1954 Atomic Energy Act, implementing many of Eisenhower's proposals, was signed into law August 30, 1954. The other significant development of this period was the discovery of large uranium deposits, both in North America and elsewhere, making prospects for nuclear power even brighter.[2] This chapter deals with the AEC experimental programs, the expansion of industrial participation, the increasing role of the JCAE, and the 1954 Act.*

* The development of the uranium supplies is discussed as a major topic in Chapter V.

DEVELOPMENT OF EXPERIMENTAL REACTORS

In 1952, even after a decade of atomic energy development, the AEC was putting little emphasis, in terms of funds expended, on nuclear reactor development purely for electric power production. The main interest was still on expanding the production of fissionable materials and devices for weapons. While substantial efforts were being applied to reactor development, these were either for production reactors or for military purposes. The major area of development included naval vessel propulsion—primarily submarine reactors. A contract was let for studying the use of nuclear power for a large naval vessel, such as an aircraft carrier. Work was also underway for developing a nuclear power plant for aircraft propulsion. However, during the 1952–54 period, several prototype and testing reactors were put in operation and a major five-year experimental reactor program was initiated.

EARLY PROTOTYPES

In 1952, tests were being conducted on two small experimental prototype projects on reactor concepts that had potential for electric power generation.[3] Both had the potential for breeding. With earlier uncertainty in uranium ore supply, this characteristic had particular importance. One project was the Experimental Breeder Reactor (EBR-1), which started operation in 1951 and was the first reactor facility to generate electrical power. The purpose of the test being conducted on this reactor was to gather data on the possibility of breeding in large power units. The EBR-1 was developed by Argonne National Laboratory for the AEC and was operated at the National Reactor Testing Station (NRTS). Breeding feasibility was demonstrated in 1953. The second project was the Homogeneous Reactor (HRE-1), which first operated in the spring of 1952 at Oak Ridge National Laboratory (ORNL),[4] reached full power in 1953, and generated a small amount of useful electric power as a demonstration. Another reactor, the Materials Testing Reactor, was completed and put in service in May 1952.[5] As implied by its name, its purpose was to test reactor materials, including structural materials and fuels, under high-radiation fields. Priorities for its early use emphasized military developments; however, its reliance on water cooling and its later use in testing reactor fuels and materials were to be of particular value to civilian power development.

In July 1953, the first major "full-scale" nuclear power plant project was authorized by the AEC.[6] Westinghouse Electric was assigned the responsibilities for development, design, and construction of the reactor, which was to have an electrical capacity of 60 Mw$_e$. This pressurized-water reactor, known as the Shippingport reactor (located at Shippingport, Pennsylvania), was a major advance toward realization of civilian nuclear power. Duquesne Light Company was the utility operator of this AEC-owned facility and received the power output. Organizationally, the reactor development was and remains within the Westinghouse-operated naval reactor laboratory at Pittsburgh, known as the

Bettis Atomic Power Laboratory. It was recognized that the electric power from this reactor would be far from economically competitive, but it was thought that nuclear power costs would never be known until several such reactors were built and in operation.

The pressurized light-water reactor design was selected, in part because more was known about that type than any other. The technology came from a number of earlier water-cooled reactors and specifically from the work on the Navy's Submarine Thermal Reactor (STR) and on the large ship-reactor program at Bettis, which had been canceled.

The rationale for government funding of the Shippingport reactor was that at that stage of reactor development the expenditures required were larger than private industry was prepared to make. This conclusion was based on industrial testimony at the nuclear power hearings before the JCAE in July 1953.[7] The justification of government funding was based in part on the relationship of the development of nuclear power to the international scene, since many countries outside the Soviet bloc had urgent need for new sources of power.

Ground was broken on September 6, 1954, for construction of the Shippingport reactor; this was the nation's first "civilian" nuclear power plant.[8] President Eisenhower emphasized the symbolic nature of this peaceful use of the atom by initiating an electric signal at Denver, Colorado, that used a neutron source and a fission detector and that was transmitted across the country to start a remote-controlled bulldozer at the Shippingport site. Still, many of the data developed concerning the reactor were classified and were made available only to authorized personnel at a series of classified seminars at the Bettis plant.

The development effort on a sodium-graphite reactor by North American Aviation (now Atomics International of North American Rockwell) was also receiving attention in 1953.[9] It drew on the graphite technology developed largely at Hanford and the sodium technology developed for the Submarine Intermediate Reactor (SIR) by Knolls Atomic Power Laboratory—both, incidentally, operated by the General Electric Company. By 1954, development was sufficiently encouraging to justify construction of a prototype. Ground was broken for America's first sodium-cooled, graphite-moderated reactor (SRE) at Santa Susana, California.[10] North American Aviation, the prime contractor for the SRE, was to contribute 25 percent of the estimated $10 million required for the project over the 1954–58 period of the contract. The design used metallic fuel elements of either enriched uranium or a combination of thorium and uranium, and also employed graphite blocks clad in zirconium as the moderator. Because of physical instability of metal fuel exposed to intense radiation, the concept was later determined to be a major limitation of the design.

FIVE-YEAR EXPERIMENTAL REACTOR PROGRAM

At the request of the JCAE, the first comprehensive program toward industrial nuclear power development was submitted to Congress by the AEC on February 5, 1954.[11] The program called for five distinct technological approaches with experimental reactors, and was estimated to cost nearly $200 million; associated research and development were estimated to cost about $8.5 million annually over a five-year period. The program was totally funded by the government. The reactors are summarized in Table 7. These reactors were constructed and operated by AEC contractors, with no major participation by outside industry, and provided a basis for technological evaluation of the various reactor concepts. Data on the reactors built under this program are given in Table 9 (see Chapter IV). All except the HRE concept led to the building of additional reactors under the Power Demonstration Reactor Program initiated in 1955. From 1955 to 1958, Westinghouse Electric seriously considered the further development of the HRE concept under utility sponsorship; however, this plan was dropped in 1958, when the development work at ORNL encountered serious difficulties.

TABLE 7

Experimental Reactor Program, 1955–58

Project	Estimated Cost (dollars in millions)	Estimated Completion	Experimental Scale
1. Pressurized-water reactor	$85	1957	Full
2. Boiling-water reactor	17	1956	Medium
3. Sodium-graphite reactor	10	1955	Medium
4. Homogeneous reactor	47	1956–58	Medium
5. Fast breeder reactor	40	1958	Medium

Significant findings were made in the summer of 1953 on the boiling-water reactor concept.[12] Previously, it had been believed that boiling within the core of a water-cooled reactor would cause unstable operation. Tests on a small water-cooled and -moderated reactor (BORAX-1) at NRTS were set up to impose conditions that could be expected to cause a "runaway" if analyses were correct. It had been previously assumed that under these conditions the core would melt and allow fission products to escape. In experiments that allowed the power to rise to several thousand kilowatts in a fraction of a second, the steam formed was found to cut off the nuclear reactor completely before dangerous temperatures were reached. The mechanism was seen to be a potentially important safety device in an ordinary water (light water)-moderated and -cooled power reactor. It was recognized that a reactor used as a direct source of steam in a power plant would reduce capital costs by eliminating the need for an external heat exchanger (steam generator), by reducing the pressure of the primary coolant system, and by decreasing the pumping power required for the system.

The first reactor of the BORAX series was destroyed on July 22, 1954, when it was purposely put on a large power excursion in which the power rose to well over a million kilowatts in a tenth of a second.[13] The destruction of the core had been considered a distinct possibility. A second reactor built for similar purposes, but at a higher steady-power level (6,000 kw) and pressure (300 psi) than the first, began operation on October 19, 1954.

While the BORAX-1 experiments were extremely encouraging, other questions regarding the boiling-water reactor concept still had to be investigated. Plans were initiated in 1954 for the Experimental Boiling Water Reactor (EBWR).[14] An important aspect of the EBWR was to determine whether it could operate without troublesome or hazardous deposits of radioactivity in the turbine, condenser, feedwater pumps, or other equipment outside the reactor. Radioactivity in the steam could create maintenance problems as well as increase radioactive releases; these difficulties, in turn, could negate the advantages of this reactor type. In the following decade, the BWR concept was to undergo extensive investigation, leading to the first commercial reactor sale in 1963. Like the pressurized-water reactor (PWR), the BWR is moderated and cooled by ordinary water and employs slightly enriched uranium; both reactors are included in the generic name, light-water reactor (LWR).

MILITARY REACTORS

In addition to the rapidly expanding activities on commercial reactors, a number of significant events occurred in the military reactor programs during the period 1952–55. Some of these developments, particularly early research and development of naval reactors, had a major bearing on commercial power reactors.

Reactors for the first two nuclear power submarines, the *Nautilus* and the *Sea Wolf,* were under development. The *Nautilus* reactor, known as the Submarine Thermal Reactor (STR), was developed by Westinghouse and Argonne. It utilized ordinary water for the moderator-coolant and zirconium for cladding of the fuel; these materials are now used in commercial light-water reactors (PWR's and BWR's). The coolant for the Submarine Intermediate Reactor (SIR), developed by General Electric for the *Sea Wolf,* was sodium. This same coolant material was later selected by the AEC for its Liquid-Metal Fast Breeder Reactor program of the 1960's and 1970's.

The land-based prototype of the STR achieved criticality on March 31, 1953, and was generating power two months later.[15] The *Nautilus,* powered with the STR Mark II, was commissioned on September 30, 1954.[16] The SIR prototype was likewise completed in 1954.[17] In addition, development of a Submarine Advanced Reactor (SAR) was underway at Knolls Atomic Power Laboratory, and development of a new reactor for large ships was started by the AEC and the Navy at Westinghouse.[18] As previously mentioned, the Shippingport reactor project, which was the first prototype for today's commercial pressurized-water reactor, came from the naval reactor program, and in fact was conducted by the AEC's naval reactors group.

Many in the reactor industry believe that the early work in the Navy program was the most significant of any in providing a direction and technological base for the current commercial light-water reactors. Important contributions were made in developing the initial light-water reactor concepts, uranium oxide fuels, zirconium cladding for the fuel, and burnable poisons for reactor control. The Shippingport reactor has continued to operate as an experimental facility in commercial reactor developments. An attempt by the Navy reactor group to develop a light-water breeder employing the thorium fuel cycle has utilized the Shippingport facility since the late 1960's.

While the aircraft propulsion project was of less direct importance than the Navy program to the development of today's light-water commercial reactors, the civilian reactor program also derived accrued benefits from this project conducted throughout the late forties and fifties. Two of these benefits were the development of shielding technology and the development of high-temperature materials. Like the Navy and production reactor programs, the aircraft propulsion project also provided a training ground for nuclear engineers. The programs were conducted by General Electric, Oak Ridge National Laboratory (operated by Carbide and Carbon Chemicals Company), and Pratt and Whitney Division of the United Aircraft Corporation.[19] The work was highly classified.

In January 1954, the Department of Defense requested that the AEC cooperate with the Army Corps of Engineers in a program to meet military requirements for nuclear power plants. The AEC established an Army Reactors Branch in the Division of Reactor Development.[20] Studies by the Army and the AEC had previously established that the installation of nuclear power plants at remote military bases appeared to be technically feasible, and that such bases would have strong military advantages. The two organizations agreed to build a small prototype based on an ORNL pressurized-water concept. It was to be built using proven components that required minimum development and was to be contracted on a lump-sum basis with a private firm selected through competitive bids. In December 1954, after receiving eighteen proposals from various industrial firms to design, build, and test-operate the prototype Army package power reactor (APPR), the AEC let the contract to the American Locomotive Company.[21] The APPR was built and operated at the Army Corps of Engineers Training Center at Fort Belvoir, Virginia. Other Army reactors were built and operated, with emphasis on small portable power supplies. However, no technical innovation from this program has had a major impact on commercial reactor design, nor has nuclear power become a significant energy source for the Army.

In addition to funding work on specific reactor projects, the AEC conducted, primarily in its own laboratories, development work on: reactor physics, fuel elements, structural materials, coolants, instrumentation, shields, and controls; recovery of fuel from radioactive waste; storage of the waste; and possible uses of fission products. These programs were conducted in support of both military and nonmilitary uses of atomic energy.

WIDENING INDUSTRIAL PARTICIPATION

AEC PROJECTIONS FOR INDUSTRIAL DEVELOPMENT

In the early 1950's, involvement of industry in both military and civilian reactors R&D still required security clearance. Also, all power reactors and their fuels were the property of the government. It was becoming increasingly apparent to the JCAE and the AEC that in order to develop economic nuclear power and a reactor industry, major changes would have to be made in the 1946 Atomic Energy Act. On June 2, 1954, the AEC submitted a statement to the JCAE on the "Probable Course of Industrial Development of Economic Nuclear Power." In summary, although the AEC's projections were highly qualified, they were still rather optimistic regarding the timing and extent of required developmental efforts. The following is a summary of the AEC's views in 1954 with respect to key factors in achieving and applying economic nuclear power:

- *Timing.* The AEC considered the five-year program important, and constructed five different reactor prototypes with the aim of making nuclear power competitive. The commission felt that if the demonstrations were accomplished, a small number of full-scale, privately owned and operated reactors would be likely to be on the line in ten years—that is, by 1965. This projection was approximately met.
- *Energy Resources.* It was thought that the uncertainty in fossil fuel reserves, as well as the pressure toward higher cost of power due to increased fuel cost, made the development of a new source of energy an essential goal. In 1975, this reasoning is still an important justification of the need for nuclear energy.
- *Competitive Power.* Achieving competitive power costs was not a certainty but seemed to be a good probability. In order to achieve widely competitive nuclear power, the generating cost had to be in the range of 4 to 7 mills per kilowatt hour, while 8-mill power would be competitive in high-power-cost regions. Competitive costs were and continue to be achieved with nuclear power; its costs are considerably lower than those of coal- and oil-fired plants.
- *Impact on Current Industry.* The commission expected that tens of millions of kilowatts of nuclear power capacity could be absorbed into the rapidly expanding utility industry, projected to grow in ten years from 100 million kilowatts to 300 million kilowatts, without displacing any existing capacity. Consumption of coal was expected to triple in ten years and the demand on coal, oil, and gas for industrial and domestic use would far outweigh any share of the market obtained by nuclear power. It was also thought that if its costs could be brought down to 4 to 5 mills per kilowatt hour, nuclear power would enable continued growth of the aluminum industry as the availability

of additional low-cost gas and hydroelectric sources decreased. The situation as of 1975 is that nuclear-fueled generating plants have not yet displaced a large fraction of fossil-fueled plants. However, the 225 plants that are in operation or planned total approximately 50 percent of the 1975 electric generating capacity of the United States.

• *National Security and Welfare.* It was felt that nuclear power facilities would provide a supplemental source of nuclear weapons material, and that the dependence of electric power generation in vital areas on vulnerable fuel transportation facilities would be reduced. The supply of weapons material has only been associated with one power reactor project in the United States: the Hanford dual-purpose reactor.

• *Foreign Countries.* It was projected that nuclear power might appear earlier and be more pervasive in foreign countries, both developed and underdeveloped, than in the United States. So far, nuclear developments in foreign countries have paralleled those in the United States. Energy problems in these countries could eventually make nuclear energy more important there than in the United States.

• *Institutions.* It was thought that, as nuclear power became competitive, it should be integrated in established institutions of the nation and should be produced by the existing utility systems. It was believed that the inescapable restrictions and safeguards which society must impose on the utilization of atomic energy could be made consistent with allowing freedom of initiative to power producers and equipment manufacturers.[22] These policies have been practiced.

These projections clearly indicated a need for greater activity of private industry under less restrictive measures. The AEC saw that, as long as fossil fuels remained cheap and abundant, reducing costs was the key to the success of nuclear power generation. It believed that this difficult job could best be accomplished by joint efforts of industry and government working as a team, bringing in industry's management and engineering experience with cost cutting "sparked by the profit incentive." [23]

The AEC suggested that the following benefits might result from increased use of nuclear power:

1. Nuclear power may help make it possible to undertake large new industrial activities at sites that would otherwise be uneconomic in the face of punishing transportation charges or the absence of transport facilities for conventional fuels.
2. It may provide an economic solution to the problem of providing additional cheap electric energy in locations where the demand is expected to outrun the availability of hydroelectric power and fossil fuels are lacking.
3. It may permit and perhaps encourage the development of strategically decentralized areas of industrial production requiring low-cost electric energy.
4. It may provide blocks of electric energy for government and military installations where the cost of power is important, but not controlling in site selection.
5. It may help electric utility systems in metropolitan areas to adjust to such limiting

factors as rail transportation and smoke nuisance arising from a major increase in electric energy generation from coal.

6. It may contribute in some measure to the introduction of new production techniques in electroprocess industries.

7. It may become technically feasible and economic for commercial propulsion purposes, such as for powering merchant ships.

8. It will take on increasing importance as a strong force both in holding down energy costs as exhaustible resources are used up and in assuring the availability of fuel for continued economic growth.

9. It may stimulate consumption of electricity beyond present projections and accelerate the trend toward using a larger portion of our energy in the form of electricity.

10. A sound basis will be established for assisting other nations in applying nuclear power for economic development.[24]

The AEC projected that it would be after 1975, however, before nuclear power would make a significant contribution to the nation's economy.

SURVEY STUDIES BY INDUSTRIAL TEAMS

Until the early 1950's, industrial involvement in reactor development consisted primarily in contractors' operating major AEC facilities. General Electric and Westinghouse were the major naval reactor development contractors, and General Electric and DuPont were the production reactor operating contractors. The power reactor developments EBR-1 and HRE-1 took place at the AEC's ANL and ORNL laboratories and were operated by the University of Chicago and Union Carbide, respectively. The operating contractor for NRTS was Phillips Petroleum Company.[25] ANL as well as ORNL played an important part in submarine reactor developments in the early days. ORNL then became more involved with aircraft reactor developments in the late forties and throughout the fifties.

In 1952, studies conducted by four industrial teams reported separately on a survey of "dual-purpose" reactor technology, production of plutonium for weapons, and generation of electric power.[26] These studies were classified; however, according to the AEC, each team indicated that in a few years it might be possible to build large reactors capable of furnishing economical power to the utilities. The cost projections were contingent on the AEC's buying weapon-grade plutonium at the current cost of producing plutonium at the AEC's Hanford plant.

It is interesting to look back on the make-up of these "first four industrial teams." They were:

- Monsanto Chemical Company and Union Electric Company, both of St. Louis.
- The Detroit Edison Company and Dow Chemical Company of Midland, Michigan, with Babcock and Wilcox Company and Nuclear Development Associates.

- Commonwealth Edison Company and Public Service Company of Northern Illinois, both of Chicago.
- Bechtel Corporation and Pacific Gas and Electric, both of San Francisco.

Many of these companies have had an active role in the development and utilization of nuclear power.

During 1952, the studies by these four teams were extended for another year. A fifth study team, Pioneer Service and Engineering Company of Chicago and Foster Wheeler Corporation of New York, was added in September 1952. In addition, ten more utilities and an architect-engineering company, Vitro Corporation of America, were added to the Dow-Detroit Edison team. Of all the members of these five study teams, only Babcock and Wilcox and Foster Wheeler were equipment manufacturers. Both still represent a significant segment of the reactor component manufacturing industry, but only Babcock and Wilcox continues as a reactor manufacturer.

Twelve more companies were associated with the Dow-Detroit Edison group in 1953, including seven utilities, two architect-engineering firms, Allis-Chalmers Manufacturing Company, Ford Motor Company, and Bendix Aviation. In that same year, the AEC approved five new industrial teams for surveying reactor technology, allowing them access to AEC laboratories, plants, and contractor scientists and engineers.[27] The teams consisted of:

- The Duquesne Light Company of Pittsburgh and Walter Kidde Nuclear Laboratory of New York.
- A five-company group, including Commonwealth Edison Company of Chicago, Union Electric Company of St. Louis, Bechtel Corporation of San Francisco, Pacific Gas and Electric Company of San Francisco, and American Gas and Electric Service Corporation of New York.
- General Electric Company of Schenectady, New York.
- Newport News Shipbuilding and Dry Dock Company of Newport News, Virginia.
- The Tennessee Valley Authority.

The five-company group included three companies of the original four teams. The new groups' studies were not bound by the original design criteria of reactor concepts for dual-purpose operation.

In the same year that these new study groups were being formed, the original teams were reporting their results.[28] The Foster Wheeler-Pioneer Service group studies showed that promising concepts included: (1) thermal reactors using circulating fuel and breeding U-233 from thorium (HRE type), (2) fast plutonium breeders with easily processed fuel, (3) pressurized-water reactors with long-life fuel elements, and (4) sodium-graphite reactors with long-life fuel elements. The circulating fuel breeder was selected for further study of cost and development requirements.

The Dow-Detroit Edison group was concentrating on the fast breeder concept, employing an enriched, low-melting-point alloy fuel element. Operation of the reactor and its chemical fuel processing facilities were to be integrated at one location. Experimental work on fuel development and fabrication and liquid metal test loops was underway.

In June 1953, the Commonwealth Edison group submitted a technical evaluation of several reactor types, including homogeneous and sodium-graphite reactors and a power breeder design developed by KAPL. They had also studied a helium-cooled graphite reactor fueled with natural uranium, which appeared uneconomical; a pressurized heavy-water reactor fueled with natural uranium; and a light-water reactor fueled with slightly enriched uranium. The last was selected for further study operation in the ''power only'' mode.

The Monsanto-Union Electric group completed feasibility studies on a dual-purpose, graphite-moderated, sodium-cooled reactor and began preliminary design of a 150 Mw$_e$ unit that would also produce plutonium or U-233. Monsanto proposed a $5-million program, the cost to be ''divided appropriately with AEC,'' whose purpose was to determine whether to proceed with the construction of a full-scale production reactor and power plant. Monsanto concluded that sale of plutonium or U-233 under a long-term contract with the AEC was the only way a privately financed business could get underway promptly.

The Bechtel-Pacific Gas and Electric group investigated a heavy-water-moderated, light-water-cooled reactor using natural uranium to avoid enrichment expenses. However, it considered the sodium-cooled breeder to have the most promise for the long range. Both weapon-grade plutonium and electricity were to be produced.

From the initiation of the industrial participation program in 1951 to the end of 1953, industrial contractors had invested an estimated $3 million in surveying reactor technology, in making preliminary designs and economic studies, and in carrying on research and development.[29] In the first six months of 1954, consistent with its policy of encouraging industrial participation in the development of economic nuclear power, the AEC approved five new study group agreements with commercial firms; this brought the total number of participating teams to thirteen.[30] The five new industrial groups were:

- Babcock and Wilcox Company of New York, which performed an independent study concentrating on the design, development, and manufacture of equipment needed in operating nuclear power plants.
- American Machine and Foundry Company of New York, which studied machines and equipment associated with nuclear power plants, and explored the feasibility of developing low-power reactors for industrial research.
- Bendix Aviation Corporation of Detroit, which studied the future of atomic power and its byproducts, and anticipated the development of new reactor designs and discovery of new uses for radioactive fission products.
- Westinghouse Electric Corporation of Pittsburgh, which surveyed the commission's reactor development activities, determining engineering, technical, and economic aspects of practical applications of atomic power.
- Pacific Northwest Power Company of Spokane, which studied the engi-

neering, economic, and technical feasibility of constructing a nuclear reactor for the production of electrical power. The Pacific Northwest Power Company included: the Montana Power Company, Washington Water Power Company, Pacific Power and Light Company, Portland General Electric Company, and Mountain States Power Company.

In 1954, an Industrial Liaison Branch was established in the AEC's Division of Reactor Development.[31] Industry participation continued to expand through the last half of 1954, as the AEC approved six additional study groups:

- Bethlehem Steel Company, which was to conduct a study on the application of atomic power to the propulsion of commercial ships.
- Consumers Public Power District of Nebraska, which was to study the engineering, economic, and technical feasibility of constructing a nuclear power reactor for the production of electric power.
- Kaiser Engineers, which was to study the engineering, economic, and technical feasibility of constructing and operating a power-producing reactor.
- Pennsylvania Power and Light Company, which was to make a detailed study of the economic and engineering feasibility of a large-scale, nuclear-fueled power plant in its own system.
- Rocky Mountain Nuclear Power Study Group, which was to conduct a study of the commission's reactor development activities to determine the engineering, technical, and economic aspects of peacetime applications of atomic power. The group included Arizona Public Service Company, Phoenix; Ebasco Services, Inc., New York; Fluor Corporation, Ltd., Los Angeles; Idaho Power Company, Boise; Minnesota Mining and Manufacturing Company, St. Paul; Phillips Petroleum Company, Bartlesville, Oklahoma; Public Service Company of Denver, Colorado; Riley Stoker Company, Worcester, Massachusetts; and Utah Power and Light Company, Salt Lake City.
- Vitro Corporation of America, which was to make a study of chemical and metallurgical problems associated with nuclear power systems.[32]

In 1954 the AEC accepted from the Dow-Detroit Edison group, which had been participating in the program since its inception in 1951, a proposal for the group to spend $2.3 million for research and development on a special type of reactor for generation of electric power and production of fissionable material and fission products.[33] In this connection the AEC established a policy that allowed the group to conduct research in AEC facilities when it could best be done there and did not interfere with higher priority AEC work. Another policy established by the AEC was that when the investigations of the group required work that was of direct interest to the AEC and formed part of its approved program, the expense of such work would be borne by AEC. This was the beginning of direct support on specific industrial projects. The large number of companies and study groups indicates the widespread interest of industry in participating in the development of this new field of nuclear energy. At the time there was great optimism that nuclear energy would yield major benefits to mankind in the long run, in a variety of ways.

With the evidence of rapidly expanding industrial interest, the AEC recognized that full participation by industry in the development and use of reactors raised unique policy and contractual problems over such matters as ownership of nuclear plants, licensing and use of fissionable materials, secrecy, patent rights, public safety, competition, and liability in case of disaster. Under the 1946 Act, fissionable material and nuclear reactors could not be owned by anyone other than the Atomic Energy Commission. These conditions resulted in additional pressures on the AEC and Congress to change the 1946 Atomic Energy Act.

ACTIVE JCAE PARTICIPATION

THE JCAE HEARINGS ON INDUSTRIAL DEVELOPMENTS

While the JCAE had been actively interested in military and production reactor programs, it had not paid much attention to commercial development until about 1952.[34] In a letter to the AEC dated August 19, 1952, Senator Carl Durham (D., North Carolina), chairman of the JCAE, notified the commission that he planned to recommend that the JCAE hold a series of meetings on industrial participation during 1953, and requested the AEC to submit a review of its policies in that area. In identifying its interest, he quoted from the October 19, 1951, JCAE report to Congress as follows:

> The Committee is keenly interested in the current study program involving eight private industrial firms. These are exploring the possibility of offering to build reactors wholly or partly at their own expense, with the dual purpose of producing power for sale to the public and plutonium for sale to the government. It is recommended that the complex factors entering into such a possibility be brought rapidly to a point of crystallization, so that they may be properly evaluated and judged.[35]

As a preface to the 1953 hearings, the joint committee staff prepared material bearing upon the atomic power development problems. This material included: (1) discussions of problems in such areas as law, technology, secrecy, and the roles of government and industry; (2) speeches of AEC commissioners and the director of the AEC's reactor development division; and (3) a chronology of significant developments, statements, and articles.[36]

In mid-summer of 1953, the JCAE held extensive hearings on the subject of atomic power development.[37] Several executive sessions had been held earlier, in which both classified and unclassified information was discussed. The hearings themselves, however, were designed to be totally unclassified, so as to give not only Congress but the American people a "better understanding of the prospects for atomic power development, along with a fuller appreciation of the problems which must be solved." [38] When put in the context of the sensitive security era of that time, these hearings were a significant break from the past. They were the first such hearings to be held by the joint committee, and were endorsed and encouraged by the administration.[39]

In his opening remarks, Representative W. Sterling Cole (R., New York), chairman of the JCAE, presented a statement jointly prepared with Senator Bourke Hickenlooper (R., Iowa), the vice-chairman, pointing out some of the grave responsibilities that the country faced for seeing that atomic energy benefited mankind. Representative Cole saw the possibility of atomic energy's solving the problem of "increasing discrepancy between man's requirement for energy in modern civilization and his ability to provide it for the use of an expanding world population."[40] At that time, the Russians were making rapid advances in atomic weaponry. The cold war and McCarthyism were dominant, and the spread of communism was a major concern to the nation. Representative Cole saw the atomic power development race as a continuing part of the "battle for the minds of men."[41] He declared that "we must show ourselves and the world that the vigor of America continues to lead the way to a decent standard of living today, tomorrow and always for us and for our friends."[42] It was in this international political environment that these public hearings were held.

The JCAE hoped that the hearings would lay the groundwork for determining what changes, if any, should be made in the existing atomic energy law. It was recognized that there would be wide differences of opinion concerning what public policy should be followed. Some of the fundamental questions were outlined by Representative Cole:

How will the development of atomic power bear upon the military security of the United States?

How will unfolding progress in this area affect America's leadership of the free world?

Whose money should be used to develop atomic power—the taxpayers' or private investors'—and in what proportion?

What type of policy will best protect the public's multi-billion-dollar investment in the national atomic energy program?

How can the genius and skill of the American private enterprise best be enlisted in developing atomic power?

How can we reconcile wider participation of free enterprise with the requirements of atomic security?[43]

PROPOSED AEC MAJOR POLICY CHANGES

Because of the unknown factors at the time of its enactment, the 1946 Act had anticipated that the initial legislation would be subject to revision from time to time, and that the policies put forth by the commission would certainly require significant changes. Early in 1953, in response to a request by the joint committee, the AEC reexamined the government's policies toward nuclear power development, designing a policy position that recognized the development of economic nuclear power as a national objective. The policy position promoted and encouraged free competition and private investment in development, while at the same time accepting on the part of the government certain responsibilities for furthering technical progress. On May 26, 1953, the following AEC policy statement was submitted to the Congressional Joint Committee on Atomic Energy:

Statement of Policy on Nuclear Power Development
1. We believe the attainment of economically competitive nuclear power to be a goal of national importance. Reactor technology has progressed to the point where realization of this goal seems achievable in the foreseeable future if the Nation continues to support a strong development effort. It would be a major setback to the position of this country in the world to allow its present leadership in nuclear power development to pass out of its hands.
2. Accordingly, we recognize it as a responsibility of the Commission to continue research and development in this field and to promote the construction of experimental reactors which appear to contribute substantially to the power reactor art and constitute useful contributions to the design of economic units.
3. In addition, it is the conviction of the Commission that progress toward economic nuclear power can be further advanced through participation in the development program by qualified and interested groups outside the Commission.
4. We recognize the need for reasonable incentives to encourage wider participation in power reactor development and propose the following moves to attain this end:
    (a) Interim legislation to permit ownership and operation of nuclear power facilities by groups other than the Commission.
    (b) Interim legislation to permit lease or sale of fissionable material under safeguards adequate to assure national security.
    (c) Interim legislation which would permit owners of reactors to use and transfer fissionable and byproduct materials not purchased by the Commission, subject to regulation by the Commission in the interest of security and public safety.
    (d) The performance of such research and development work in Commission laboratories, relevant to specific power projects, as the Commission deems warranted in the national interest.
    (e) More liberal patent rights than are presently granted to outside groups as may seem appropriate to the Commission and consistent with existing law.
    (f) Consideration of a progressively adjusted code for safety and exclusion area requirements as may appear reasonable in the light of operational experience with reactors. Competent state authorities will be encouraged to assume increasing responsibility for safety aspects of reactor operation. Financial responsibility associated with reactor operation will be assigned to the owners, in keeping with normal industrial practice.
    (g) Giving full recognition to the importance of reactor technology to our national security, a progressively liberalized information policy in the power reactor field as increasing activity justified.
5. It is the objective of this policy to further the development of nuclear plants which are economically independent of government commitments to purchase weapons-grade plutonium.
6. We view the next few years as a period of development looking toward the realization of practical nuclear power. On this basis we conclude that the time is not yet

at hand for the report called for in Section 7 (b) of the Atomic Energy Act of 1946.[44]

This statement was submitted for the record by the first witness, Gordon Dean, chairman of the AEC.[45] Regarding the long-range potential of nuclear power as an energy source, Dean presented some tantalizing figures. He listed the following world reserves: oil and gas, 8Q; * coal, 72Q; and uranium, 1,700Q (assuming 100 percent utilization of uranium, which implied breeders).[46] In 1950, the world annual fuel consumption was 1/5Q and was projected to be 1Q by the year 2000. With further use of his crystal ball, Dean estimated that nuclear power might be furnishing 10 percent to 12 percent of U.S. energy needs in the year 2000. Based on current projections, this may well turn out to be a very accurate prediction. He also made an additional observation that is meaningful with respect to the "energy crisis" of the early and mid-1970's: that "there will always be some kind of requirement, of course, for fluid fuels; and as your petroleum runs out, . . . you have got to go to coal in order to get fluids from coal." [47] Thus, although nuclear power was shown to have great long-range potential as an energy source, it was not being sold by the commission as a panacea.

In addition to the purely technoeconomic problems, Dr. Bugher, director of the AEC's division of biology and medicine, stated that "it is obvious that the successful development of commercial power from nuclear fuels must be consistent with the standards of public health and safety." [48] He identified not only the radiation hazard problem from reactor operations, but potential hazards of the very long-lived fission products which would have to be properly dealt with. He pointed out that these problems had been of major concern since the inception of the atomic reactor program in 1942.

> Under these circumstances, referring to the circumstances of 1942, and pending the inauguration of a vigorous research program it was necessary to establish criteria of radiological safety of a very conservative character. These considerations, plus those of security and the necessity for dispersal of huge installations, required the isolation of the operations within large tracts of land. With the experience gained by actual operation, and with the accumulation of knowledge as research has progressed, it has been possible to achieve a certain degree of relaxation of some of the original criteria. The performance record of the plants is such that there have been very few radiation accidents, and the general health of the people fully engaged in the atomic-energy program is certainly as good as that in any other section of our national economy.[49]

Dr. Bugher's further testimony pointed out the excellent safety record of the AEC. He stated, "We have sufficient practical knowledge to insure safe operation of power reactors of the types now contemplated. For the longer view, we are confident that our research programs, vigorously prosecuted, will enable us to maintain sound safety criteria for future developments." [50] This statement is evidence that public safety was and continues to be a major concern of the AEC.

* One Q equals 10^{18} Btu's of energy.

A major policy question was how to proceed with private industry involvement, particularly in view of security constraints and the long-range development required before nuclear power could be competitive and economically viable. The director of the AEC's reactor development division believed that private industry could not proceed independently without certain classified data.[51] The commission's view was, therefore, that it would be necessary to carry out a largely developmental program over a period of four to five years which would include the building of several prototypes and experimental reactors by the AEC, while industry was brought in through joint studies.[52] After that time, industry would be in a better position to invest risk capital.

Senator John Pastore (D., Rhode Island) stated, "I am for private enterprise, and I think, myself, that they should be involved in a joint effort. There should be a partnership." [53] These and the policy statements of the commission represented the beginnings of the strong and effective joint government-industry partnership which has existed since that time. The JCAE was concerned about the delay in obtaining the benefits of nuclear power by taking this more deliberate approach to reactor development. Senator Pastore said that the public had been led to believe that atomic energy would be available soon; this now appeared not to be the case. Dean emphatically agreed.

In testimony from the public side of the utility industry, Mr. Samuel Morris of the American Power Association, representing 700 utilities in thirty-eight states, supported the AEC's technical approach, requested that both private and public power be allowed to participate, and warned against patent policies that would result in a monopoly of the atomic energy field.[54] The private utilities, which at that time accounted for 84 percent of the electric generating revenues in the United States, were represented by Mr. Edgar Dixon, chairman of the Edison Electric Institute's Atomic Power Committee. Mr. Dixon made the following recommendations:

1. Permit industry to own both source materials and fissionable materials, and facilities for the production and utilization of such materials;
2. Deal fairly with patent rights and incentives for new developments; and
3. Permit industry to obtain workable licenses from appropriate regulatory authorities for projects in this field.[55]

He foresaw continued government participation but wanted private industry to have the right to own and operate its own facilities, "subject to appropriate regulation in the interest of national security, health, and safety." [56] Basically this was the same position taken by General Electric Company, which had operated the Hanford plutonium production plant since 1946 and had built and operated the Knolls Atomic Power Laboratory.[57] Westinghouse, another major AEC contractor, did not take so strong a position regarding need for change in the existing law, but did recommend that "Congress move toward giving free enterprise a chance to function normally, so far as national security permits." [58]

Westinghouse saw private ownership of nuclear reactors as being primarily the concern of the users, the utilities; [59] the manufacturers' stake was in securing normal patent rights. [60]

Congressman Holifield was one of the major dissenters from the proposed policies of the commission. He was very concerned about there being, among other things, a possible "give-away" program and subsidies to private industry. His views along these lines have continued over the many years of legislative history on the atomic energy program and are discussed in more detail in Chapter IV.

It was apparent from the various views presented by the AEC and industry that if industrial development of the atom was to go forward in an expeditious manner, major changes would have to be made in the existing laws governing the atom. Based on these hearings, recommendations by the AEC, and proposals made by President Eisenhower, a major new atomic energy law was soon to be written that would replace the original 1946 Act and open the door to private industry.

OPENING THE DOOR TO INDUSTRY—THE 1954 ACT

As discussed in Chapter II, the Atomic Energy Act of 1946 had put major constraints on industry's involvement in the peaceful development of atomic energy for power generation. Government priorities, moreoever, had placed little emphasis on power reactors. In a speech before the Economics Club of Detroit on March 3, 1952, Gordon Dean listed the following as the government's objectives: first, to create a bigger stockpile of fissionable material; second, to develop better weapons; third, to develop the hydrogen bomb; and fourth, to develop power reactors, with the submarine reactor having first priority. [61]

Despite the relatively low priority of reactor development, there were those in industry and government who felt that more should be done to encourage work in this area, and they felt that action was needed to remove the existing constraints. In March 1950, David E. Lilienthal, then chairman of the AEC, called for revision of the law and stated "as fundamental policy of this country, that development of the industrial atom shall be in accord with the American system." [62]

It will be remembered that in 1953, Gordon Dean, then retiring as chairman of the AEC, went to the JCAE and recommended that early development of commercial power be established as a national objective. He urged modification of the Atomic Energy Act of 1946 to encourage private enterprise to enter the nuclear field. [63] This was a reversal of a position he had taken in mid-1952. Lewis L. Strauss, who succeeded Dean, reaffirmed this policy.

NEW LEGISLATION PROPOSED

The testimony of the 1953 hearings also indicated to the JCAE the need for major revisions of the 1946 Act. As part of their advance preparation for the

1953 hearings, the staff of the JCAE had prepared a report that discussed the issues and documented the various government and industry positions on the problem of accelerating the peacetime development of the atom.[64] In a section on "Power and the Control of Atomic Energy," the staff identified the following as being major issues: policy toward ownership of fissionable materials and reactors; proper scope and use of secrecy; the exercise of judgment in health and safety measures; patent rights; the proper roles of government and industry; and state regulation of utilities. In their review of public statements on the issues, the staff did not find a consensus. However, during the hearings on the proposed bill, Senator Carl Durham from North Carolina expressed what was probably the majority sentiment of the JCAE: "No one wants this completely socialized industry to continue forever. . . . It has been in the minds of the members of the original committee ever since the beginning . . . that when we met the military problem, it was our duty . . . to get this interest started into the private enterprise system. . . ."[65]

In response to Senator Durham's 1952 request, the AEC submitted both a policy statement (see section entitled, "Proposed AEC Major Policy Changes," this chapter) and a legislative draft to the JCAE for their hearings in May 1953. The draft had not been cleared by the Bureau of the Budget, and therefore was considered informal and was not made public by the JCAE.[66] The committee used the Durham documents as a focal point for discussion of possible new legislation.[67]

During June and July of the 1953 hearings, the JCAE held fourteen open meetings on atomic power development and private enterprise; testimony and statements were received from 112 witnesses representing 83 organizations.[68] With these testimonies, plus the survey data from its staff and specific proposals from the AEC, the JCAE was ready for detailed discussions on a new bill.

President Eisenhower gave additional impetus to the discussions for new legislation when he made his famous "Atoms for Peace" speech on December 8, 1953, before the General Assembly of the United Nations. The speech called for a beginning of peaceful atomic development through the mechanism of an international agency—an atomic pool from which all nations might profit equally and which might serve as a first constructive step toward a peaceful atomic world.[69] At this time, Russia had already developed both the atomic and hydrogen bombs. The president called for an international atomic energy agency to be established under the aegis of the United Nations; principal governments would make joint contributions to the agency from their stockpiles of normal uranium and fissionable materials. Not only would the agency stockpile and safeguard the material, but according to Eisenhower's proposal:

> The more important responsibility of this Atomic Energy Agency would be to devise methods whereby this fissionable material would be allocated to serve the peaceful pursuits of mankind. Experts would be mobilized to apply atomic energy to the needs of agriculture, medicine, and other peaceful activities. A special purpose

would be to provide abundant electrical energy to the power-starved areas of the world. Thus, the contributing powers would be dedicating some of their strength to serve the needs rather than the fears of mankind.[70]

On February 17, 1954, the president sent a special message to Congress recommending changes to the Atomic Energy Act of 1946. He recommended that the following objectives be sought through amendments of the act:

> First, widened cooperation with our allies in certain atomic energy matters;
> Second, improved procedures for the control and dissemination of atomic energy information; and
> Third, encouragement of broadened participation in the development of peaceful uses of atomic energy in the United States.[71]

The first two objectives deal predominantly with military matters and were not particularly important to nuclear power development. To prevent confusion from arising regarding the relationship of these objectives with those in the earlier "Atoms for Peace" proposal, in the February message Eisenhower clearly dissociated the area of cooperation through the United Nations from the proposed amendments by stating: "These recommendations are apart from my proposal to seek a new basis for international cooperation in the field of atomic energy as outlined in my address before the General Assembly of the United Nations last December. Consideration of additional legislation which may be needed to implement that proposal should await the development of areas of agreement as a result of our discussions with other nations." [72]

Regarding domestic development of atomic energy, President Eisenhower stated that the complementary efforts of government and industry should continue, but called for legislation that would allow industry to assume a substantially more significant role. He specifically recommended the following amendments:

1. Relax statutory restrictions against ownership or lease of fissionable material and of facilities capable of producing fissionable material.
2. Permit private manufacture, ownership, and operation of atomic reactors and related activities, subject to necessary safeguards and under licensing systems administered by the Atomic Energy Commission.
3. Authorize the Commission to establish minimum safety and security regulations to govern the use and possession of fissionable material.
4. Permit the Commission to supply licensees special materials and services needed in the initial stages of the new industry at prices estimated to compensate the Government adequately for the value of the materials and services and the expense to the Government in making them available.
5. Liberalize the patent provisions of the Atomic Energy Act, principally by expanding the area in which private patents can be obtained to include the production as well as utilization of fissionable material, while continuing for a limited period the authority to require a patent owner to license others to use an invention essential to the peacetime applications of atomic energy.[73]

The subject of patent rights became one of the more controversial areas. Eisenhower's position was further clarified by his statement:

Until industrial participation in the utilization of atomic energy acquires a broader base, considerations of fairness require some mechanism to assure that the limited number of companies, which as Government contractors now have access to the program, cannot build a patent monopoly which would exclude others desiring to enter the field. I hope that participation in the development of atomic power will have broadened sufficiently in the next 5 years to remove the need for such provisions.[74]

Although the JCAE did not see fit to use Eisenhower's exact proposal in drafting a bill, the bill finally introduced by Representative Cole and Senator Hickenlooper, chairman and vice-chairman, respectively, of the JCAE, did encompass most of the objectives of that proposal regarding civilian nuclear power. The JCAE thought the proposal gave the president too much power in both the domestic and international fields.[75] Representative Cole stated:

Thereupon the vice chairman and I and others . . . sat down and drafted our own bill. It had been my personal purpose and thought to treat these 3 phases of the amendments . . . in 3 separate bills. However, as we got into this subject, we discovered that the three problems were very interlocked and interwoven. We realized also that the act itself was in dire need of being overhauled and modernized and brought up-to-date. We therefore concluded that all 3 of our objectives, along with the overall revision, would be treated as 1 bill.[76]

The bill was introduced in the two houses of Congress on April 15 and 19, 1954.

In a joint statement for the *Congressional Record,* Cole and Hickenlooper claimed the bill gave the president what he wanted regarding transfer of restricted data to NATO allies and a basis for licensing industrial use of atomic energy, but it placed specific requirements on the president regarding cooperative arrangements with another nation, to be approved by the AEC and to be submitted to the JCAE for thirty days while Congress was in session. The bill's provisions were summarized as follows:

1. The bill would permit the Commission to determine that any material which would release substantial quantities of energy through nuclear fission or through nuclear transformation can be determined by the Commission to be "special material." This permits the Commission to determine that materials which are utilizable in a fission process should be classed as special materials along with those items already determined to be specially utilizable in fission processes. The term "special material" is then used through the act in place of the prior terms of "fissionable material."
2. Title to all special material would be retained in the United States as an exercise of the powers of the United States to arm itself, and to prepare for its defense.
3. Regulation of the industry is accomplished by exercise of the powers over the property of the United States contained in article 4, section 3, of the Constitution, as well as its powers over interstate and foreign commerce and its power to provide for the common defense.
4. Title to reactors and other facilities utilizing or producing special materials is allowed to be held by the private persons who would be licensees.
5. In order to encourage prospecting to increase our domestic supplies of uranium, the earlier provisions retaining rights to source materials in public lands have been eliminated.

6. Normal patent rights would be permitted in the peaceful applications of atomic energy.

7. Standards for licensing are established in order to provide sound statutory bases for guidance of the Atomic Energy Commission in this new field. In addition, normal administrative procedures have been established as far as possible consonant with the requirements of secrecy in the field because of common defense and security.

The criminal provisions of the present act, dealing with the unlawful disclosure of restricted data, have been reexamined and tightened. The bill proposes imposing absolute liability on those lawfully having access to restricted data who disclose the restricted data to persons not authorized to receive it.

In additon to these matters, many items of organizations and powers of the Commission, of its advisory committees, and of the joint committee have been reexamined and strengthened. Wherever changes had been thought generally desirable, they were suggested.[77]

The JCAE did not provide for private ownership of special nuclear materials as suggested by Eisenhower. This was not to come until ten years later. The new act did, however, provide a more liberal patent clause, facilitate private industry access to atomic information, and allow for private ownership of nuclear reactors.

HEARINGS

This first bill, HR 8862 (S 3323), was sponsored by the authors, Representative Cole and Senator Hickenlooper, both Republicans. The bill, as intended, was then referred back to the committee for hearings, which were held in May and June of 1954. The bill was originally submitted to Congress as a point of focus for discussion, appraisal, and likely modification. It served that purpose and was continually being modified during the hearings. This modification process created problems and criticisms, since neither the witnesses nor the JCAE members were completely certain what the status of the draft was at any given time. The following exchange exemplifies the problem. The discussion concerned the definition of "and others" in connection with one of the stated purposes of the bill: that of encouraging "widespread participation by private enterprise and others in the development and utilization. . . ."

> Representative Holifield (in response to a statement by Mr. Francis K. McCune of General Electric): Then you have no objection to us spelling the "and others" out?
> Mr. McCune: No.
> Representative Hinshaw: Say "a program to encourage the widespread participation in the development of atomic energy."
> Chairman Cole: I have been advised by one of my assistants that the revision has already been done.
> Representative Holifield: We are at a little bit of a disadvantage because we do not have a clean bill before us and we are not aware of the language changes that have been made by the staff.

Representative Holifield had two points to make: first, to have put into the record that the intent of the legislation was to include participation by government, private, and public institutions, both profit and nonprofit; and second, to inject some criticism on the way the bill was being modified. He also opposed the domestic provisions of the bill.[78] However, it was through this technique of continuous evolution of the bill's features that the committee developed the final version that was then submitted to the full Congress for consideration.

The hearings were divided into two parts: the first was held during the middle of May 1954 and included a broad spectrum of nongovernment witnesses from fifty different organizations; the second part was held in June and included witnesses from eight Federal organizations. The first group included individuals representing manufacturing, private and public utilities, labor, the press, law associations, education, insurance, industry, engineers and scientists, and other special interest groups. The government witnesses were from the following departments: Defense, Interior, Justice, and State; and from the AEC, FPC, TVA, and Congress. This wide coverage gave opportunity for broad participation in the formulation of the legislation. However, as Holifield had objected, since the bill was continuously changing during the hearings, none of the witnesses was testifying on the final bill. Holifield suggested that additional hearings might be required on the revised bill, and Hickenlooper responded that the course to be followed would be determined by the full committee.[79] A revised draft, dated May 26, was transmitted to the AEC for comment before the June hearings.

Other opponents of the bill were unhappy with the way Representative Cole conducted the hearings and with the fact that much of the testimony had not been on the final version. At the time of his May testimony, Clyde Ellis, representing the National Rural Cooperative Association, requested that he be heard again during the June hearings after the bill was finalized; he was told to submit his additional testimony in writing. He, as well as representatives from the American Public Power Association and the CIO, complained in writing to Senator Herbert Lehman (D., New York) during the time the bill was before the Senate, that he had not had the opportunity to testify on the bill before the Congress.[80]

Green's and Rosenthal's general comment on the problems and objectives of JCAE legislative hearings is particularly pertinent to this issue:

> Hearings on proposed legislation are not held to enable the public to draft legislation or to change the basic views of legislators. Instead, much like other congressional committees, the JCAE holds hearings: (1) to make a public record available to the Congress; (2) to clarify as many issues as possible; (3) to provide a basis for agreement within the Committee, and especially between the Committee and the Executive Branch, by means of bargaining and compromise; and (4) to protect, and sometimes enhance, the powers of Congress, and the JCAE in particular.[81]

Their evaluation of the JCAE's performance in these areas is as follows: (1) "The Joint Committee has often gone out of its way to make public a record of its deliberation"; (2) "During hearings Committee members try to clarify for themselves chiefly—but for other members of Congress and the public as well—the factual situation, the legislative provisions, and the policy implications associated with a particular bill''; (3) ''The Joint Committee's use of legislative hearings for bargaining and horse-trading with the Executive Branch is particularly noteworthy''; and (4) ''Congress has seldom been known to be adventurous. The JCAE has probably been more adventurous than most congressional committees, but it has insisted that atomic ventures be either of its own choosing or else subject to its persuasive influence.'' [82] Although criticism was levied against the JCAE, much credit must be given to the committee for allowing such broad-spectrum participation, particularly in light of the period, a time when the desire for atomic secrecy was paramount and long before public involvement in government policy issues was occurring on a large scale.

One of the most controversial issues during the hearings centered around private versus public development of atomic energy. The focal point was most often the patent clause, although private ownership of reactors was also challenged. In addition, a ''public power preference clause'' was inserted in the legislation. The public power advocates looked at the proposed patent clause, which would have allowed normal patent rights for nonmilitary (peaceful) applications, as a major giveaway by the federal government.

On the patent issue, the Cole-Hickenlooper proposal was considerably more favorable to private industry than that proposed by Eisenhower. Eisenhower's position was frequently referred to by the public power advocates in defense of maintaining AEC control over patents, a control authorized by the 1946 Act. Mr. Benjamin Sigal, representing the CIO, expressed the following concern over monopoly development; his statement typified the public power view:

> In our opinion, it is contrary to the public interest to make any change in the present patent provisions applicable to the atomic energy industry. The people of the United States have already invested over $12 billion in the course of acquiring the technical and scientific knowledge concerning the production of atomic energy. It is true that much of that investment has gone into the manufacture of atomic weapons. However, if the proposed amendments are adopted the know-how acquired in the course of that manufacture will be placed at the disposal of the few fortunate companies who have been or will be in a position to acquire access to all of this know-how. It requires no great insight to see that the present contractors who have been running AEC plants, or who have had contracts for experimentation and development, have a running start on the whole field. They have the experienced personnel and the technical knowledge which will enable them to obtain control and determine the future industrial development of atomic energy. [83]

After Sigal, in support of his own position, had quoted Eisenhower's suggestion for a transition period regarding patents, a little political by-play ensued:

> Mr. Holifield. I want to compliment the CIO on backing President Eisenhower. I find that the Democrats on the Hill are in that position quite frequently, that we are supporting the President. I would like to see the principles that the President enunciated written into this bill. I believe it would be good for the Nation.
> Mr. Sigal. I must hasten to add, Mr. Congressman, that our approval is qualified.

Mr. Patterson. I am glad to see that the CIO recognizes the attributes of the Republican Party.

Mr. Sigal. We are very happy to give credit where credit is due and where good work is done to applaud it, whether Republican or Democratic in origin.

Chairman Cole. In view of the enthusiasm which my friend from California, Mr. Holifield, has expressed in his support of the President's urging of the adoption of revision of the Atomic Energy Act, I fully expect his aggressive and dynamic support of the enactment of the bill. I am happy to hear him now say that he approves of the recommendation of President Eisenhower with respect to changes in the Atomic Energy Act.

Mr. Sigal. Of course Mr. Holifield will have to speak for himself as to whether he does approve the proposed bill.

Senator Pastore. Let me say this for myself: That I will find myself in almost complete support of this bill if we do write in that protection which the President spoke about. That to me represents the crux of this whole issue. If we can allow private industry to participate, and write in the law the procedures and mechanics as expressed by the President to protect all in the public interest, without trying to create a monopoly, I think myself we will have better luck.

Mr. Sigal. With all due respect of course to the President, we take issue on this point as to whether or not the 5-year limitation that he proposed is sufficient to provide the protection.

Senator Pastore. You take the position youself that 10 years is the experimental period from your point of view.

Mr. Sigal. I say the committee thinks so.

Senator Pastore. Somewhere between 5 and 10, I should think should be sufficient.[84]

This colloquy also serves to point out the feeling of others in the JCAE regarding a transition period.

Another public power advocate, National Rural Electric Cooperative Association, represented by Clyde T. Ellis, presented extremely strong-worded testimony urging defeat of the bill:

A modern industrial society is made possible by harnessing inanimate sources of energy to machines. America has led the world in industry. One absolutely basic explanation has been our vast supplies of inanimate energy, coal, oil, gas, hydro—and now atomic. We cannot for the sake of our standard of living, for our military security, permit any group or groups to cripple or hamstring us in the use of this new and probably greatest source of inanimate energy. The enemy of abundance is monopoly, and we urge that this Congress guard this new resource against monopoly, high prices, and restriction of output. The bill before you does not meet the requisites of a policy to achieve abundance, in our opinion. We urge you to defeat this bill and return to the problem after the proper investigation and reports have been made and the people given an opportunity to discuss the pros and cons.[85]

Mr. Ellis went on to make a threat to the elected representatives and particularly aroused the ire of Chairman Cole by stating:

I don't want to be misunderstood in making this concluding statement, but I feel it my duty to make it. It is not a threat, of course, but a prediction. I predict that if Congress yields to the demands of the monopolistic power companies and permits the granting of exclusive patents in the field of atomic power development and if the Atomic Energy Commission proceeds to grant such exclusive patents, the adverse reaction will be voiced at every farm breakfast table and in every rural ballot box in the United States.[86]

This provoked even Representative Holifield, a public power advocate himself, to make a statement clarifying the position of private power companies. He stated that while testimony indicated that the power companies were in favor of normal patent rights, the utilities as such were not particularly interested in patents. He pointed out that "there is no utility company that I know of that specializes in obtaining patents. But they are working hand-in-glove with the machinery people and the chemical people, who do want the patents, and they are acquiescing in going along with their demands that there be exclusive patenting." [87] This statement essentially sums up the position of private power companies.

Under the provision of the bill, the primary benefactors of a normal patent provision would be the manufacturers of equipment and the suppliers of fuel. Many potential equipment suppliers were already in a favorable position regarding access to technology know-how. The act proposed to make restricted data more generally available to qualified organizations who were interested in nuclear power studies.

While the manufacturers of equipment were certainly in favor of normal patent rights, some were conciliatory in their position. For example, Mr. McCune of General Electric suggested that if full patent rights were not to be granted, the final patent provision should be such that it would have a minimum effect on private incentives gained through patents. He suggested further that compulsory licensing of a patent to others at a reasonable royalty, with the AEC acting as arbitrator, be one approach, but that this provision be limited to five years.[88] General Electric generally supported the proposed bill.

Representative Cole strongly opposed the five-year period and believed that the principle of compulsory licensing would discourage inventive efforts. Although the AEC had proposed the compromise provision, Mr. Strauss agreed with Representative Cole.[89]

The bill reported out by the JCAE provided for the compulsory licensing of a patent obtained by a private company from efforts solely its own. The patent owner was entitled to reasonable compensation from the licensee, and if agreement could not be reached, the royalty fee was to be determined by the commission. This provision was to be effective until September 1, 1959. The commission could also be licensed to use the patent. The five-year transition period to normal patent rights had been recommended by the AEC, and although he was opposed to it in principle, Senator Hickenlooper viewed it as a way to reconcile the contribution made by the government with that of the private investor.[90]

When the bill was debated in Congress, Representative Cole proposed an amendment to grant normal patent rights for nonmilitary inventions not developed from government support. It carried, 203 to 159. The split in votes was essentially along party lines: Republicans in favor and Democrats opposed, with few switches. The Republicans controlled the House.

In the Senate, however, Senator Robert Kerr, Democrat from Oklahoma, after having had an amendment tabled that would have reverted back to the 1946 Act provision, proposed a ten-year transition period. In a conciliatory effort, Hickenlooper agreed to the provision and the amendment carried.[91] The difference in the patent clause between the House and Senate versions would have to be worked out in conference.

CONGRESSIONAL ENACTMENT

The revised bill, HR 9757 (S 3690), incorporating revisions reflecting the hearings, was introduced in Congress on June 30, 1954. According to the JCAE report accompanying the bill, it "accomplishes the purposes set forth in the President's February 17 message to Congress." [92] In summary, it provided the following:

1. Authorization for negotiating bilateral agreements for cooperation with foreign nations in peacetime uses of atomic energy, under carefully stipulated safeguards.

2. Improvement of the procedures for control and dissemination of atomic energy information, primarily as it relates to weapons.

3. AEC licensing of private industry to possess and use special nuclear materials. The government was to retain title to such materials.

4. Ownership by private persons, under license of the AEC, of reactors intended to produce and utilize special nuclear materials.

5. The requirement that holders of patents on inventions of primary importance to the peacetime uses of atomic energy license such patents to others in return for fair royalties. This compulsory patent license clause was to expire five years after enactment of the bill.

6. A directive to the AEC to declassify any information that could be published without undue risk to the common defense and security, and to make continuous reviews of restricted data and classification guides so as to determine which data could be released.

7. The requirement that the JCAE conduct hearings on the state of the atomic energy industry during the first sixty days of each congressional session.

Although the JCAE was unanimous in favorably reporting the bill out of committee, several members held disparate views on the various sections.

Representative Cole strongly disagreed with the compulsory patent provision. He was formally supported in his view by Representative James Van Zandt (R., Pennsylvania). Cole stated that "compulsory licensing is not creeping socialism; it is socialism run rampant." [93] He believed the provision to be: (1) unconstitutional; (2) unnecessary, either to the public interest, or to prevent the accrual of undue benefits or preferential position to persons and corporations currently engaged in the atomic program; and (3) wholly foreign and hostile to American tradition and practices and the system of private enterprise. He urged a return to the original provision for normal patent rights, with a protective clause that would require the patent applicant to present a sworn statement on how and when the discovery was conceived. The AEC would be allowed to interpose an objection to the commissioner of patents if the AEC found that the invention was conceived during the course of any relationship with the government by the applicant; in such a case, the patent would be the property of the government.

Representatives Holifield and Price submitted a rather lengthy minority report, which included the following objections:[94]

1. Congress should take a two-step approach to the legislative changes. It should act first on those amendments required to implement the president's international proposal. Then Congress could take "a long, hard look at the pending proposals to confer private ownership and patent rights in the atomic field." [95]

2. A finding of "practical value" should be submitted by the AEC, as required in the 1946 Act, before issuing a license for any type of utilization or production facility. The 1946 Act required the following:

> Report to Congress. Whenever in its opinion any industrial, commercial or other nonmilitary use of fissionable material or atomic energy has been sufficiently developed to be of practical value, the Commission shall prepare a report to the President stating all the facts with respect to such use, the Commission's estimate of the social, political, economic, and international effects of such use, and the Commission's recommendations for necessary or desirable supplemental legislation. The President shall then transmit this report to the Congress, together with his recommendations.[96]

The proposed bill would require a finding of "practical value" for issuance of a license for a commercial facility, but such a finding was not required for an R&D facility. The "finding of practical value" clause was to continue to be a point of controversy for many years to come. Holifield and Price at this point were using it to try to block private ownership of nuclear reactors.

3. The bill should be revised more nearly to reflect the Federal Power Act of 1920. Specifically, it should accord preferred consideration to public bodies where their applications conflict with those of privately owned systems. In safeguarding the public interest (benefit) in this national resource, Holifield and Price felt that nuclear power paralleled hydropower development. The Federal Power Commission had testified that:

> . . . it becomes pertinent to test any legislative proposals with respect to non-Federal development of atomic energy to see whether the public interest in atomic energy is protected and benefited as adequately as the Congress of an earlier generation sought to do for the Nation's interest in water power . . . the grant of the (license) privilege should depend not solely on the negative consideration that national defense will not be harmed, but on the affirmative ground of benefit to the public interest in electric power and other products of the operation of nuclear reactors as well.[97]

Holifield and Price wanted the bill modified to reflect "this advice from the Nation's outstanding independent power agency." [98] They also called for a provision that would subject an applicant's request for a construction permit to the same procedural safeguards, assuring interested parties full opportunity for notice, hearings, and appeal before the AEC issued a license. The "interested parties" that Representatives Holifield and Price had in mind were the public power groups.

4. Other organizations should have more participation in deciding how nuclear power was to be developed. Holifield and Price proposed:

> If the use of nuclear energy as a source of commercial electric power is to be accorded the consideration which its importance warrants, this should be reflected in the statutory organization of the Commission. It cannot be left wholly to the discretion of the Commission which may be at any given time, and is now, weighted in favor of playing down the Government responsibilities in this field.
>
> Specifically, we believe there should be a statutory Division of Civilian Power Application, counterbalancing the statutory Division of Military Application, with positive responsibility for the commercial development of nuclear electric power by Federal or non-Federal public and private agencies.
>
> There should also be an Electric Power Liaison Committee, corresponding with the Military Liaison Committee, with provision for full cooperation between the Atomic Energy Commission and those Federal agencies responsible for carrying out other phases of Federal power policy. This would provide a basis, now lacking in the bill, for Federal construction and operation of nuclear powerplants where required in connection with Federal regional programs.
>
> The Electric Power Liaison Committee might well be composed of one representative each of the Federal Power Commission, the Securities and Exchange Commission, the Rural Electrification Administration, The Tennessee Valley Authority, the Bureau of Reclamation, the Bonneville Power Administration, the Southwest Power Administration, the Southeast Power Administration, and the Corps of Engineers, with an independent Chairman appointed by the President, by and with the consent of the Senate serving at the pleasure of the President. [99]

Holifield and Price went on to say that:

> This Committee would advise with the Atomic Energy Commission in connection with all activities directed at the development of power from nuclear energy with a view to assuring its maximum contribution to the general welfare. Such advice would include assistance in the formulation of standards as specific problems arise. But dependence on ad hoc decisions alone for the determination of standards affecting the economics of atomic power development and use would be unsatisfactory in the extreme. It is for this reason that we favor amendments which would authorize and direct the Division of Civilian Power Application and the Federal Power Commission, in their respective spheres, to apply substantially the same public interest safeguards in connection with the licensing of atomic powerplants as are applied in licensing hydroelectric developments under the Federal Power Act. [100]

Again they attacked consideration of the bill as premature, since they felt it might result in the "transfer of atomic power development to private monopoly."

5. The compulsory license period should be left open, or at a very minimum

should extend for ten years. It was also suggested that the patent rights clause be changed back to that of the 1946 Act.

6. The provision that the government would lease fuel to private parties and that the commission would compensate the reactor owner for special nuclear materials produced at "guaranteed fair prices" was considered a subsidy to industry.

7. They also attacked the clause designating the chairman of the AEC as the "official spokesman" of the commission. The JCAE had previously changed this language from "principal officer" in the earlier version of the bill. Holifield and Price appeared to be particularly concerned that the dominant role of the current chairman, Lewis Strauss, not be strengthened. Since, moreover, Strauss was also special advisor to the president on atomic energy, they further objected to his dual status. Representatives Holifield and Price believed that because of Strauss's latter role, the other commissioners and the committee would not be kept fully informed. They acknowledged that Mr. Strauss was a "strong and vigorous Chairman," but concluded that under his direction the AEC "has fallen to a low point in harmony and effectiveness." [101]

8. They objected strenuously to the Dixon-Yates Contract, which, as they saw it, would make the AEC into a power broker, purchasing power from a private corporation to service an area (Memphis) "far removed from its [AEC] activities." [102] While this contract had all the trappings of a public versus private power struggle, it did not have any direct effect on commercial nuclear power development, since nuclear power was not involved. However, the Dixon-Yates debates during consideration of the 1954 Act probably did detract from the discussions on the important issues of the act itself, and certainly extended them greatly.[103,104]

The views of Representatives Holifield and Price defended the public power interest. They saw the AEC under Mr. Strauss as being very much in favor of turning to private industry for joint development of nuclear power, and they saw the 1954 Act as providing the legislative mechanism for doing so. Their apparent motives were that nuclear power should remain a government industry. They carried their battle to the floors of the House and Senate.

On the second reading of the bill, a myriad of amendments was introduced; Representative Holifield and his colleagues alone proposed thirty-three for the record. Below are summarized only those amendments that had a significant effect on nuclear power development.

Patents. Senator John Sparkman's (D., Alabama) amendment to extend time for compulsory patents from five to fifteen years was tabled by a vote of 43 to 24. Representative Cole's amendment to grant normal patent rights was adopted 203 to 159. Senator Kerr's amendment to retain the patent provisions of the 1946 Act was tabled on a motion from Senator William Knowland (R., California) by a vote of 41 to 37. The Kerr amendment to extend compulsory licensing from five to ten years was adopted. The conflict between the Kerr and Cole amendments was left to be resolved in conference.

Public Power. Representative Holifield proposed amendments calling for the establishment of government and nongovernment production and distribution of electrical power generated by atomic energy. These activities were to aim at achieving the maximum public benefits. The amendments were rejected. Holifield's amendment to establish an Electric Power Liaison Committee was likewise rejected, as was the same motion made by Senator James Murray (D., Montana) in the Senate, by a vote of 56 to 30. Representative Metcalf's amendment to empower the AEC to produce and dispose of electric power was amended by Representative Aime Forand (D., Rhode Island) to provide that preference be extended to any purchaser in high-cost power areas. The amended amendment was adopted. Representative Cole substituted for this clause an amendment barring the AEC from distributing or selling electrical energy except that generated as a byproduct in AEC research and development facilities. The House adopted this revision by a vote of 161 to 118. The Senate passed by a vote of 45 to 41 Senator Edwin Johnson's (D., Colorado) amendment to authorize the AEC to generate electric power and to require that preference be given to public bodies and cooperatives in disposing of excess power from AEC plants.

Uranium Mining. The Senate also passed Senator Anderson's (D., New Mexico) amendment requiring that leases for prospecting for source material in national parks be granted solely by executive order.

Civilian Application Division. The Senate adopted Senator Hubert Humphrey's (D., Minnesota) amendment providing for an AEC division responsible for civilian applications.

Recommittal. HR 9757 passed the House by a vote of 231 to 154 after a recommittal motion by Representative Holifield was defeated by a vote of 222 to 165. The Senate passed S 3690 with the Senate amendments by a vote of 57 to 28.

Conference. The three major differences in the House and Senate bills were the patent clauses, the public power preference clause, and the question as to the conditions under which the AEC could generate electric power. Representative Cole insisted that his provision providing normal patent rights be allowed to stand, while the Senate Democrats considered the ten-year period of compulsory patent licensing which their version included to be absolutely necessary. The first JCAE conference report [105] retained Cole's patent clause and watered down the public power preference clause by adding the words "insofar as practicable." The Republicans held the majority in the committee. The Johnson amendment allowing the AEC to become a power producer was also dropped in the first conference report. The conference report was accepted in the House, but was rejected by the Senate. During the discussion in the Senate, Senator Hickenlooper inserted in the record a letter from President Eisenhower favoring the bill; the letter stated ". . . the REA cooperatives should and still have protection as preference customers. The bill adequately provides for such protection. . . . Its provisions with respect to patents adequately meet my recommendations. . . .'' [106] Seeing the deadlock between the Senate and House, and fearing that no bill at all would be passed, the second JCAE conference quickly agreed on a five-year patent clause; the phrase ''insofar as practicable'' was deleted.[107] The Senate passed the compromise bill 59 to 17 [108] and the House passed it on a voice vote.[109]

Green and Rosenthal have analyzed the voting according to parties on the various amendments.[110] The analysis clearly shows that the two political parties, following their respective leadership, were solidly aligned against each other. The Democrats favored issues giving the government more control over patents and public development of nuclear power, while the Republicans pressed for a greater emphasis on private development; for example:

- In the House, 94 percent of the Republicans voted for and 84 percent of the Democrats voted against Cole's normal patent rights amendment.
- In the Senate, 100 percent of the Republicans voted for and 95 percent of the Democrats voted against Senator Knowland's motion to table an amendment by Senator Kerr that would have retained the patent clause of the 1946 Act.
- In the Senate, 73 percent of the Democrats voted for and 71 percent of the Republicans voted against an amendment by Senator Johnson that would authorize the AEC to produce electric power and would give preference to public bodies and cooperatives in disposing of excess power from the AEC plants.
- In Holifield's attempt to kill the bill (recommit), 93 percent of the Republicans voted against and 72 percent of the Democrats voted for recommittal.

The Republicans, who controlled both houses and therefore the JCAE, together with a few conservative Democrats, mostly Southerners, provided a sufficient vote margin for the Republicans to defeat nearly all of the amendments proposed by the liberal Democrats.[111]

Interwoven with the debates on the bill was the Dixon-Yates controversy [112] mentioned earlier in this section. The controversy was over a proposed contract in which the AEC would have become essentially a ''power broker'' between a private utility and the TVA, purchasing power that in essence would have been used not by the AEC but by the city of Memphis, Tennessee. The Dixon-Yates issue did parallel the public versus private power issue that permeated the debates and the positions taken by the two political parties. This issue remained alive during the remainder of the 1950's and early 1960's and was to be the partial basis for further controversy on nuclear power.*

SUMMARY

The 1954 Act paved the way for a new relationship between the AEC and industry in developing commercial nuclear power. It allowed private ownership

---

* See Chapter IV, under ''The Gore-Holifield Bill,'' for further discussion on the private versus public power issue.

of nuclear reactors under AEC licensing and provided for near-normal patent rights. The government maintained ownership of special nuclear materials but was allowed to lease these to industry. This provided an additional government incentive mechanism in that the AEC's pricing policy for these materials could affect the economics of nuclear power.

In their report to Congress, the JCAE explained the purpose and philosophy of increasing private industry's role in the development of nuclear power and stated the need for a combined government-industry effort:

> It is now evident that greater private participation in power development need not bring with it attendant hazards to the health and safety of the American people. More-over, the atomic-reactor art has already reached the point where atomic power at prices competitive with electricity derived from conventional fuels is on the horizon though not within our immediate reach. For more than 2½ years, the experimental breeder reactor has actually been producing relatively small amounts of electricity at the national reactor testing station in Idaho. The land-based prototype of the atomic engine propelling the U.S.S. Nautilus has already produced more than enough power to send an atomic submarine around the world, fully submerged and at full speed. The Westinghouse Electric Corp., and the Duquesne Power & Light Company, are now constructing the Nation's first large-scale atomic-power reactor, which will generate 60,000 kilowatts of electricity—an amount sufficient to furnish light and power for a sizable city.
>
> Many technological problems remain to be solved before widespread atomic power, at competitive prices, is a reality. It is clear to us that continued Government research and development, using Government funds, will be indispensable to a speedy and res-olute attack on these problems. It is equally clear to us, however, that the goal of atomic power at competitive prices will be reached more quickly if private enterprise, using private funds, is now encouraged to play a far larger role in the development of atomic power than is permitted under existing legislation. In particular, we do not believe that any developmental program carried out solely under governmental aus-pices, no matter how efficient it may be, can substitute for the cost-cutting and other incentives of free and competitive enterprise.[113]

Holifield and Price of the JCAE had a different view of the status and needs of nuclear power development. Their minority view saw the bill as premature, and wanted the AEC to be more involved in power generation:

> The profit-making opportunities in atomic enterprise are years distant. Unless the United States Government strikes out boldly in a comprehensive program of reactor development and undertakes to produce and distribute electrical power derived from nuclear fission, we will soon find other countries forging rapidly ahead in this field. . . . Accordingly we propose that the United States undertake a billion dollar "crash" program for peacetime atomic-energy development to let the whole world know that we are serious about putting the atom to work for peace.
>
> This billion dollar program, spread over the next 5 years, would represent about five times the expenditures now planned for atomic reactor development.[114]

These statements were more than hollow rhetoric. Later, Holifield, as chairman of the JCAE legislative subcommittee, took a leadership role in pushing for a major government construction program. Some have called these later plans a "nuclear TVA."

The planned strategy of combining legislation on the domestic and international aspects of atomic energy in the 1954 Act was successful over the objections of Holifield and Price. Based on this new legislation, the AEC was soon to launch a new era in government-industry cooperation in the development of a major commercial product. Three years after the passage of the act, the former chairman of the AEC, Gordon Dean, stated his view of the legislation:

> It is still too early to see concrete results of these modifications in the law, but there is no doubt in my mind that, as time passes, the participation of industry in our atomic energy program on a risk basis will have many desirable effects. Not the least of these will be the introduction of cost-cutting methods in manufacture and design which will serve to hasten the achievement of real economic atomic power.[115]

While the public power advocates in Congress retained some government control over patents, they lost out on the key Johnson amendment, which essentially would have allowed the AEC to become a commercial power producer. While the act allows the AEC to sell electric power generated incidental to R&D or to production facilities, it expressly forbids the commission to enter into sale or distribution of electricity for commercial use, except that generated by these sources.[116] The act allows public and cooperative utilities to own and operate reactors on the same basis as private utilities.

Although the public power advocates retained the compulsory patent after much debate and controversy, their success appears to have had little effect on the progress of development or competitiveness of the industry. This conclusion is supported by opinions obtained from interviews. The clause has never been exercised since it would require the government to rule that a private patent so affects the public interest that it should be subject to compulsory licensing. Paraphrasing Joseph Hennessey: the patent clause has not deterred the interest of manufacturers to innovate and build on government technology. He believes that it has had the effect of establishing a fairly liberal attitude by industry in licensing their patents. To what extent companies elect to keep inventions a trade secret rather than face the compulsory patent requirements is not known. The patent clause has been extended for additional five-year periods three times since 1954, and was due to expire September 1, 1974.[117]

The 1954 Act provided the AEC with workable authority to permit greater international cooperation, to increase participation by private enterprise, and to assure effective dissemination of both scientific and industrial information. It provided for bilateral agreements with friendly nations in which the United States would provide them with special nuclear materials for power and research reactors, furnish assistance in the design and construction of the reactors, and exchange certain classified information on nonmilitary utilization of atomic energy. The new law also recognized that the initiative and resources of private industry in the development and use of atomic energy for peaceful purposes should be encouraged and drawn more specifically into the national program. It specifically empowered the commission to license private and public groups to build, own, and operate research and power reactors, provided the licensees agreed to observe adequate health and security regulations. It did not, however, allow private ownership of the necessary fissionable materials—U-233, U-235, and plutonium—for such facilities, and reaffirmed that these could only be leased from the commission.

The passage of the 1954 Act truly represented the birth of a new era in atomic energy development. Its enactment brought the JCAE squarely into the middle of the AEC reactor program, where it has remained since.

CHAPTER IV

Ten Years of Rapid Development, 1955—64

THE year 1954 was a critical one in the development of U.S. commercial nuclear power. In the following decade a number of important legislative actions were taken, broad policies regarding government-industry relationships were established, and major reactor development programs were initiated and carried out. These programs and policies led to a substantial reduction of the government monopoly and allowed the growth of a more normal private enterprise that would parallel existing industry in the electric power field. At the end of the ten years of development, large nuclear power plants were being sold and were competing with other sources of energy for the electric power industry.

The key legislative action that laid the foundation for private industry participation and the "partnership" that developed between government and industry was the Atomic Energy Act of 1954. Congress may not have recognized at the time that short-term economic incentives were insufficient to induce industry to "go it alone." However, it soon became clear that the AEC would have to maintain an active role to assure that progress in this new technology would be rapidly and adequately expedited.[1] The evidence indicates that the joint committee, or at least some of its members, believed that the technology was sufficiently developed to embark on major power reactor construction programs; it felt that if industry was not willing to undertake this action, the government should. The AEC's policy position was one of a more deliberate and therefore longer-term technology assessment program.

As the involvement of industry increased and private ownership of large power reactor facilities was contemplated, it became apparent that to commit enormous financial resources in an area with the potential, however remote, for a catastrophic accident was too great a risk for private industry to take in view of the lack of short-term economic incentives. Recognizing this fact, the JCAE, supported by the AEC and by much of industry, was responsible for removing this "roadblock" through the enactment of legislation in 1957 that provided for government indemnification against liability arising from a nuclear catastrophe. This unwillingness of industry to accept full responsibility for nuclear accidents is used by nuclear opponents to indicate that the nuclear industry itself does not believe nuclear power is safe.

In the years from 1955 to 1964, the government's partnership with industry was developed and strengthened; in the same time frame, the JCAE became the supporter as well as the prodder of the AEC. Thus, the three major components of the nuclear energy field joined to form a political subsystem that was well established by the end of the decade.[2] The two government components were the AEC and the JCAE; the industry component consisted of an amalgam of industry special interest groups with representatives of private and public utilities.

The key legislative actions, government policies and programs, and industry response during the crucial decade of technical legislative and industrial development are summarized in the following sections.

GOVERNMENT DEVELOPMENT PROGRAMS

How did the AEC view the new atomic energy act? Section 1 of the act stated: "The development, use, and control of atomic energy shall be directed so as to promote world peace, improve the general welfare, increase the standard of living, and strengthen free competition in private enterprise." In its January 1955 report to Congress, the AEC stated: "The paramount objective to the AEC was not altered—to make the maximum contribution to the common defense and security. What is new is added emphasis on the development of peacetime use of atomic energy."[3] They also viewed the act as a mandate to increase private participation to the greatest extent possible. Although the AEC considered that its efforts had not neglected the development of peacetime uses, in 1954 AEC civilian power reactor support represented less than 20 percent of its reactor development costs and less than 2 percent of its total costs. The AEC's interest in having private industry as the major contributor to nuclear power and the JCAE's sense that the commission lacked an aggressive government program in its development became major points of controversy in the following few years. As the JCAE became more impatient with the progress being made by the AEC, it proposed major programs of its own design, and generally prodded the AEC into a more broadly based program. The development program took on a new dimension in both funding and scope: the funding of the civilian reactor rose from a cost of less than $20 million in 1954 to over $100 million five years later; and the scope was greatly expanded toward reactor construction and demonstration.

This expanded reactor development program can be classified into three major areas: general research and development; reactor experiments and prototypes; and demonstration reactors. From a funding standpoint, the commission's stated policy was to "continue to bear the burden of basic research and assist the development of nuclear power by the construction of experimental reactors.'' [4] However, because of AEC contracting policies, a significant amount of the AEC-funded work in all areas was conducted in AEC facilities operated by potential nuclear industry companies. Companies also conducted similar development programs that were privately funded, either internally or by utilities. In addition to these programs, research and development were conducted in both AEC and private facilities in such complementary areas as the biological effects of radiation; fundamental research in physics, chemistry, metallurgy, and mathematics; and the development of sources of special materials such as uranium, zirconium, beryllium, and heavy water.

ESTABLISHING A TECHNOLOGICAL BASE

AEC Support of Research and Development

From the beginning, the development of nuclear reactors of all types has rested on a broad program in basic technology supported by the AEC. For the reactor proper, the objective of these programs was to find fuels, moderators, coolants, and structural and operating components that would be mutually compatible for long periods at high temperatures and in intense radiation fields; would minimize neutron losses by absorption; and would permit efficient heat transfer. External to the reactor, developments were required for economical and safe methods of fabricating new fuels and reprocessing spent fuels, whereby useful fissionable and fertile materials could be reclaimed and fission products could be removed and safely stored. There was also the need for developing the numerous types of facility components required for reactor operation: pumps, heat exchangers, controls, instrumentation, etc. No attempt will be made to describe these efforts in detail, but it is essential at least to indicate the degree to which the AEC has considered it necessary to develop in-depth understanding of the components and materials basic to nuclear reactors, as well as an understanding of their behavior under both normal and abnormal conditions.

It would be a horrendous, if not impossible, task to reconstruct exactly how much money was spent for each category of research and development efforts. Table 8 presents data as published in the AEC's financial reports. These reports began to separate the categories from overall reactor development in 1958. In addition to those funds shown in Table 8, it should be recognized that each reactor project also had associated with it major efforts in physics, fuels, materials, engineering, components development, and safety.* These efforts have likewise been included in other AEC programs, such as the Plutonium Utiliza-

---

* For example, the AEC's LMFBR FY 1975 budget to Congress for R&D operating funds (excluding construction) includes requests for funding as follows (dollars in millions): fuels, $14.0; physics, $1.7; components, $68.5; systems and plants, $21.3; EBR-2 (test reactor) fuels and materials, $17.0; zero-power reactors (physics), $3.4; liquid metal center (sodium coolant development), $16.0; Fast Flux Test Facility, $64.6; and LMFBR demonstration reactor, $14.0. These funds are in addition to the general reactor technology and safety funds.

tion Program listed in Table 8. Initially, the "General R&D" category was for research and development applicable to all nuclear reactors, including military reactors. Starting in the middle 1960's, however, programs such as physics, fuels, and materials were largely redirected toward the liquid-metal fast breeder reactor (LMFBR), while the safety program is directed toward both the LMFBR and the extant commercial reactors. In other words, what was initially a general R&D program has become, in most instances, a program aimed primarily at a limited class of reactors.

In recent years, the increases in supporting development have come primarily in the area of reactor safety—to a large degree in light-water reactor safety. The total AEC proposed safety budget for FY 1975 is approximately $93 million, of which one half is in support of the current commercial LWR's. Undoubtedly, this change in priorities was brought about to a large degree by the pressures placed on the AEC by intervenors and others concerned with the safety of these reactors.

Physics Research

The physics program is a good illustration of the impact and scope of the AEC's supporting technology for reactor development. This program has been funded in the range of $7 million to $10 million per year, and included both theoretical and experimental developments. Theoretical methods were developed, adapted to computer models, and then correlated with experimental data. These analytic methods were then used to predict the behavior of nuclear reactors under steady-state or time-dependent operations. Successful methods were made available to the AEC contractors and industry, either directly from the laboratory developing the method or from the Argonne Computer Code Center.

The general experimental physics program consisted of two parts: measurements of the probability of a neutron's interacting with materials (nuclear cross-sections), and critical or near zero-power experiments designed to simulate neutron behavior in various reactor concepts. Nuclear cross-sections are essential to reactor analysis. Fundamental cross-section measurements were also performed in the AEC's Division of Research. Critical experiments provide integral data on the neutronic characteristic of a reactor configuration, including information on reactor kinetics, fuel requirements, power distribution, and neutron absorptions. These data are important to the understanding of such processes as reactor breeding or conversion,* safety, and heat generation. A large number of facilities for conducting these programs were built at AEC, university, and industry laboratories.

At this point a brief technical description of one of the physics parameters will serve to indicate its particular importance to the area of design options and constraints, that is, its importance in determining what types of reactors are technically and/or economically feasible.

* Breeding or conversion is the process of converting a nonfissile material, e.g., U-238 or Th-232, into a fissile material, e.g., Pu-239 or U-233, respectively.

TABLE 8

GENERAL RESEARCH AND DEVELOPMENT
EXPENDITURES, 1958–72 [a]
(Dollars in Millions)

Category	Fiscal Year								
	1958	1959	1960	1960 [b]	1961	1962	1963	1964	1965
Physics plus advanced reactors	$ 7.3	$ 9.4	$16.2	$29.3	$33.1	$ 8.0 +20.0	$ 7.4 +24.7	$ 8.6 +29.5	$ 9.2 +30.3
Reactor fuels and materials	6.3	10.4	17.4	17.4	19.7	28.3	30.0	29.3	29.6
Plutonium utilization [c]	—	—	—	—	—	10.3	12.2	11.8	11.1
Reactor components [d]	1.4	1.9	2.6	2.6	2.7	—	—	—	—
Engineering	—	—	—	—	—	—	—	—	—
Fuel element chemical separations	8.1	6.0	7.2	7.2	6.6	7.8	8.4	9.5	9.9
Waste storage and disposal [e]	3.2	3.6	4.7	4.7	2.5	—	—	—	—
Reactor safety	8.6	8.4	10.2	10.2	12.1	17.3	26.3	33.2	32.8
Euratom	—	—	—	—	—	2.6	3.8	4.2	4.5
Operation of service facilities and other	6.1	3.5	2.1	9.9	9.4	9.8	8.2	10.5	13.1
Total	$41.1	$43.3	$60.3	$81.3	$86.1	$104.1	$121.1	$136.6	$140.5

Category	Fiscal Year							
	1965[b]	1966	1967	1968	1969	1970	1971	1972
Physics plus advanced reactors	$ 9.2	$ 10.2	$ 10.4	$ 10.3	$ 9.9	$ 9.7	$ 9.3	$ 10.3
	+16.9	+21.5	+14.5	+ 8.9	+ 7.4	—	—	—
Reactor fuels and materials	29.6	31.2	33.2	32.5	30.4	32.1	27.1	22.8
Plutonium utilization [c]	—	—	—	—	—	—	—	—
Reactor components [d]	—	—	—	—	—	—	—	—
Engineering	5.9	4.4	4.7	5.0	5.3	5.0	5.0	4.4
Fuel element chemical separations	9.9	10.1	10.9	8.5	8.7	7.7	9.7	14.2
Waste storage and disposal [e]	—	—	—	—	—	—	—	—
Reactor safety	23.2	24.9	32.9	37.7	38.4	43.1	40.3	49.1
Euratom	4.5	3.4	2.8	2.6	2.0	—	—	—
Operation of service facilities and other	4.9	6.0	6.6	11.9	15.3	4.5	3.8	3.7
Total	$104.1	$112.0	$116.0	$117.4	$117.4	$102.0	$ 95.2	$104.5

Source: USAEC Financial Reports, 1956 through 1972.

[a] Includes depreciation; excludes construction and equipment.

[b] Reflects redistribution of costs in 1960 and 1965.

[c] Removed as an item under this general category and placed under "Water Cooled Reactors." Program continued until FY 1973.

[d] Combined with other budget categories after 1962.

[e] Waste Management is placed under "Nuclear Materials" category. Budgets for FY 1972, FY 1973 (est.), and FY 1974 (est.) are $6.2, $7.4, and $15.0 million, respectively.

The physical parameter in question is the number of neutrons emitted per neutron absorbed in the nuclear fuel. This parameter is commonly identified by the Greek letter eta. Eta differs among isotopes and varies with the energy of the neutron producing the fission. Its magnitude varies roughly between one and one half and three for fissile isotopes over the neutron energy range existing in reactors. It is greater than unity in a typical neutron energy spectrum only for the fissile * isotopes, namely U-233, U-235, Pu-239, and Pu-241, of which only U-235 occurs naturally. Eta generally has an intermediate value at low-neutron energies (thermal energies), low value at intermediate-neutron energies, and high value for high-neutron energies. Because of neutron absorption in structural materials, neutron losses through leakage, and so forth, eta must be greater than unity to permit a sustained nuclear reaction and greater than two for breeding to occur. In "converter reactors" ** the "fertile" † material, thorium or U-238, is converted to U-233 or Pu-239 through the absorption of a fraction of the extra neutrons; but this does not occur as rapidly as the fissile material is consumed. In a breeder reactor, more fertile material is converted to fissile material than fissile material is consumed.

The "effective" eta of natural uranium, which is the combined eta of the natural mixture of U-235 and U-238, is very low, but still sufficient to sustain a chain reaction in some configurations. This fact limits not only the types and quantities of structural materials that can be employed in a reactor but also the life of the fuel. The AEC's gaseous diffusion plants "enrich" the uranium in the isotope U-235 by partially separating the two isotopes. These plants were originally built to produce weapons uranium, highly enriched in U-235. With only slightly enriched uranium (a few percent U-235), reactor design flexibility is greatly increased. For example, the light-water (ordinary-water reactors— LWR's) and fast reactors are made technically feasible with enriched uranium fueling. The other fissile isotopes made from thorium or uranium can also be used for enrichment. The fast breeders having good breeding capabilities would employ either plutonium or U-233 because of their higher eta values. Breeding in thermal reactors is technically feasible with U-233 and has had much developmental attention, but it is difficult to accomplish because of the marginal eta value for thermal neutrons.

Neutrons resulting from the fission reaction emerge with high speeds and the extent to which they are slowed down is determined by the amount and distribution of moderating material placed in the reactor. Thermal reactors employ moderating materials, such as water or graphite, while fast reactors do not. Some slowing down occurs as a consequence of neutron interaction with all of the reactor materials, including the fuel itself. In fast reactors, this degradation

---

* Fissile isotopes are those fissionable by absorption of a thermal (very low-energy) neutron.

** Current commercial reactors, LWR's and the high-temperature gas-cooled reactor (HTGR), are "converters."

† Fertile isotopes are those which can be converted to fissile isotopes through capture of a neutron.

of neutron energy generally decreases the breeding capabilities because of the lower eta value in the intermediate-neutron energy range.

Basic characteristics of reactor materials are among the parameters examined by the physics research program, and have had a profound impact on related aspects of reactor design and programmatic decisions. Research in this area has helped determine the technical infeasibility of the proposed intermediate breeder; the dependence of light-water, uranium-fueled reactors upon enriched uranium available only from the huge government diffusion plants; the severe design constraints and limited fuel life of natural uranium reactors; the greatly increased number of reactor design options in countries where enriched uranium is readily available; the probable necessity of having to produce difficult-to-design breeders (thermal breeders are still possible) in order to utilize uranium resources fully; and the significant impact of fuel availability on the decisions of most foreign countries in selecting reactor types (those countries without their own sources of enriched uranium and unwilling to be dependent on a foreign source can select only the natural uranium concept).

Other Areas of Research and Development

As with any technology, nuclear energy research and development are necessary in many areas to solve the problems of reactor design and increasingly stringent performance requirements that evolve over time. In the case of fuels and materials, for example, the final selection for the light-water reactors was uranium oxide pellets encapsulated in zirconium tubes. Many alternative combinations of fuel and cladding material were considered. The development of zirconium can be credited to a crucial neutron cross-section measurement made by Herbert Pomerance at Oak Ridge in 1947,[5] and the aggressive Navy program conducted in the late 1940's and early 1950's. Zirconium was recognized as having high corrosion resistance to water, but appeared to have a great affinity for neutrons. Pomerance discovered that this affinity was not due to zirconium but instead to the hafnium that was present in commercial-grade zirconium. The Navy's work developed a process for its removal and further developed zirconium as an excellent cladding material. Similarly, high-density carbon coating of the high-temperature gas-cooled reactor (HTGR) fuels was developed by the Rocket Project at Los Alamos Scientific Laboratory (LASL), Project Rover.

Two areas that are of major importance to the health and safety of the public and that have required R&D efforts are radioactive waste management and reactor safety. These areas are discussed in Chapter VI.

TECHNOLOGY EVALUATION THROUGH EXPERIMENTATION

The problem of introducing nuclear power as a commercial energy source in the 1950's was one not of technical feasibility but of economics. It had been demonstrated that large reactors could be built—plutonium reactors were operating at Hanford. Furthermore, in 1951 EBR-1 demonstrated that electricity could be generated from nuclear energy. But these were far from economic solutions to the use of nuclear energy for electric power generation. The problem was to determine what type or types of reactors from the vast number of possible reactor concepts would prove to be the most successful. Industry studies and AEC developments, briefly reviewed in the previous chapter, indicated that there were many types with significant potential. Therefore, it was necessary that the initial AEC program be one of technology evaluation through experimentation, followed by larger scale demonstration projects of the more promising types. This was a deliberately designed approach, as will be seen from the AEC testimony presented in later chapters, and one that contributed much to the final selection of the currently successful power plants.

Five-Year Power Reactor Development Program

The first phase of the reactor development program involved construction of small reactor experiments and prototypes. While industry constructed a few prototypes, most of this phase was funded and conducted by the AEC.

The "Five-Year Power Reactor Development Program," discussed briefly in the last chapter, was proposed by the AEC on February 5, 1954. It was presented to the joint committee in response to a letter from the committee chairman, Representative Sterling Cole, at the end of the 1953 hearings. Representative Cole stated that there had been "a substantial number of references by witnesses during our hearings to the indefiniteness of commission plans for research and development in the field of atomic power components, pilot plants and prototypes." [6] He requested from the AEC a three- to five-year program of specific R&D projects.* The actual construction and operation of the reactors extended over more than ten years. In fact, one reactor, the EBR-2, is still in operation today as a test facility for the ERDA's LMFBR program. The types of reactors constructed are summarized in Table 9.

The Pressurized-Water Reactor. Although substantially larger than the other reactors, the pressurized-water reactor, listed first in the table, was not expected to be competitive with conventional power plants, but was to yield data on large plant operation in such areas as reliability, and operating and maintenance costs.[7] A conversion from a project for a reactor for a large naval ship, it contributed both to the development and testing of fuel elements for long irradiation life, and to advancing the physics of ordinary water-moderated and -cooled reactors that are fueled by slightly enriched uranium. The project was also expected to yield data on the design and construction of large pressure vessels for reactor conditions; on charging and discharging of fuel through a pressure shell; and on control of a reactor with closely spaced fuel pins. After a total of the equivalent of 27,780 full-power hours, the reactor was shut down in 1964 for refueling with a second core.[8] It had successfully demonstrated the use of zircalloy (zirconium alloy)-clad fuel in a two-zone seed blanket concept,

* See Table 7, Chapter III.

TABLE 9

FIVE-YEAR EXPERIMENTAL REACTOR PROGRAM

Reactor Concept	Name	Location	Scheduled Completion Date	Moderator	Coolant	Fuel	Heat Output (kw)	Electrical Output (kw)
Pressurized Water	Pressurized Water Reactor (PWR)	Shippingport, PA.	1957	Ordinary water	Ordinary water	Slightly enriched uranium	264,000	60,000
Boiling Water	Experimental Boiling Water Reactor (EBWR)	Argonne Nat. Laboratory near Chicago, IL.	1956	Ordinary water	Ordinary water	Natural and highly enriched uranium	20,000	4,500
Sodium Graphite	Sodium Reactor Experiment (SRE)	Laboratory near Santa Susana, CA.	1957	Graphite	Sodium	Slightly enriched uranium	20,000	6,000
Fast Breeder	Experimental Breeder Reactor-2 (EBR-2)	National Reactor Test Station, ID.	1958	None	Sodium	Uranium-plutonium alloy	62,500	16,500
Homogeneous	Homogeneous Reactor Experiment-2 (HRE-2)	Oak Ridge National Laboratory, TN.	1957	Heavy water	Heavy water	Highly enriched uranium in UO_2SO_4 solution	5,000	300
	Homogeneous Thorium Reactor (HTR)	Not selected	1959	Heavy water	Heavy water	Highly enriched uranium in UO_2SO_4 solution	65,000	16,000

which consisted of a highly enriched zone and a natural uranium zone, respectively. The reactor was restarted in 1965 with a maximum rating of 505 Mw_{th}—almost double the initial power.

On January 1, 1965, a memorandum of understanding was executed by the AEC and the Department of Water Resources, State of California, which provided for a cooperative arrangement for construction of a large (525 Mw_e) nuclear central station plant based on the Shippingport reactor developments.[9] Public Law 89-32 authorized the Large Seed-Blanket Reactor (LSBR) project and authorized $91.5 million for the AEC's portion of the cost.[10] However, in April 1965, the AEC canceled the project because of the expectation that technical difficulties would interfere with the development of the very-long-life fuel planned for the reactor core—a fuel which would permit a nine-year span between refuelings.[11] The Shippingport Laboratory was then reoriented toward developing a light-water breeder (LWBR). The successful development of this concept "could ultimately make available for power production about 50 percent of the energy potential available in this country's thorium fuel resources—a source of energy many times greater than the known coal, oil, and natural gas reserves of the United States." [12] The concept is particularly important in that it uses already developed light-water-reactor technology; if successful, it could presumably make the development of the LMFBR either unnecessary or at least not so urgent—a highly desirable goal. The breeder cores could possibly be placed in the commercial PWR's.[13] However, even though moderately funded ($25 million to $30 million per year), the concept has yet to be successfully demonstrated. Because of the difficulties of attaining good neutron economy in such a concept, the claim that it is a true breeder may not be justified. The Shippingport reactor program has been and continues to be performed at the AEC's Bettis Atomic Power Laboratory, operated by Westinghouse. It was probably directly responsible for Westinghouse's selecting the PWR concept for its current commercial reactor type. The PWR is also the choice of two other reactor vendors, Babcock and Wilcox and Combustion Engineering.

The Experimental Boiling-Water Reactor. Based on encouraging results from BORAX experiments, the EBWR was designed as a pilot plant to produce 20 Mw_{th} (5 Mw_e), the minimum power considered necessary to enable sound extrapolation to large-size central station power plants.[14] The boiling-water reactor had the advantage of producing steam directly in the reactor, rather than in an external heat exchanger as was done in the pressurized-water reactor. The facility went into operation in late 1956 and was dedicated on February 9, 1957, when it began its first full-power tests.[15] At the dedication ceremony, AEC Chairman Strauss stated, "This occasion marks a milestone in the development of the peaceful atom—another important step toward the fulfillment of President Eisenhower's promise to the world that the United States will . . . 'devote its entire heart and mind that the miraculous inventiveness of man shall not be dedicated to his death but consecrated to his life.' . . ." [16] With other reactors scheduled to start operation that year, Strauss saw the year 1957 as a possible turning point in power reactor development for peaceful purposes. He said 1957 was the year "when we begin to see something of the results of our comprehensive nuclear power program—the year when our research and development begins to pay off. . . ." [17] At that time he was under great pressure from the JCAE to expand the nuclear program.

The initial operations of the reactor indicated that the EBWR could probably operate satisfactorily at twice the design reactor power of 20 Mw_{th}.[18] After successfully completing the planned program at 20 Mw_{th}, the EBWR was shut down July 3, 1959, to be modified for a new set of experiments.[19] This modification included additional heat removal capabilities to 100 Mw_{th}—five times the original design capacity. The increased power level allowed for verification of maximum stable power-density operation, investigation of in-reactor steam separation phenomena, determination of hydrodynamic characteristics, and evaluation of carbon steel material.[20] On November 15, 1962, the reactor reached a power level of 100.4 Mw_{th}.[21] The experiments continued until the end of the year and then the facility was put into standby condition. Its next and final mission was to test plutonium-uranium oxide fuel in a boiling-water reactor environment.[22] The reactor was restarted with a partial zone of the plutonium fuel on October 11, 1966,[23] and thus became the first boiling-water reactor to use plutonium in significant quantities. A series of experiments was performed on the reactor, which was able to operate at the planned power level for a substantial time; however, the program was terminated [24] for lack of programmatic priority before the fuel had received the planned irradiation exposure. Thus, a long, successful history of use in the development of the boiling-water reactor (BWR) ended for the EBWR. The BWR was the first reactor type sold on a purely competitive basis and remains one of the three commercial types in use today.

The Sodium-Graphite Reactor. Construction of the sodium-graphite reactor was started in 1954. It was a graphite-moderated, metallic-uranium-fueled reactor, cooled with sodium. The sodium coolant gave the potential of sufficiently high temperatures for superheating steam in an external heat exchanger. Thus it was to have a higher thermal efficiency than water reactors and was comparable to modern fossil-fueled plants. The reactor, built and operated by Atomics International, first went critical on April 25, 1957. Its electrical power output of 6 Mw_e was purchased by Southern California Edison, which used its own generator equipment. Although there were some early component and fuel problems, the reactor reached its design power in 1958. However, swelling of the metallic uranium limited its life. Developmental work on alternative fuels—thorium-uranium, uranium-molybdenum, and uranium carbide—was initiated in 1958.[25] The reactor was shut down in July 1959 because of fuel failure caused by overheating. The problem resulted from a flow blockage produced by the leak of a compound into the sodium coolant. The reactor was restarted in 1960 with a core fueled by a thorium-uranium alloy.[26] The program was then directed toward developing a fuel for sodium-cooled reactors, with particular emphasis on the Hallam Nuclear Power Facility planned for Nebraska.[27] The reactor was again shut down in April 1962 in order to replace two defective moderator cans; it was restarted in August 1962, and continued to supply power to Southern California Edison.[28] In 1966, the Sodium Reactor Experiment (SRE) was considered for possible use as a test facility in the then high-priority LMFBR program, but since it would have required extensive modification, it was not used. In December 1966, the AEC announced the deactivation plans for the facility.[29] Because of sodium leaks into the graphite moderator cans in December 1965, the AEC also terminated its program in the Hallam demonstration plant, which had followed the SRE.[30] The concept was no longer a viable alternative for commercial development; on the other hand, the experience gained can be applied to improving the reliability and performance of other sodium-cooled reactors, such as LMFBR's.

The Experimental Breeder Reactor-1. During the period covered by this chapter, the EBR-1 was the only fast reactor in operation. This first prototype fast breeder reactor was authorized by Congress in 1948. As stated in the previous chapter, the purpose of the reactor was to demonstrate that breeding was technically feasible and that the operation of a fast reactor was stable. The EBR-1 became critical in August 1951. The first known generation of electricity from nuclear energy was realized from the EBR-1 on December 1, 1951, and the reactor operated for four trouble-free years. Although a pseudobreeder (i.e., a prototype which was not a breeder itself because of size), the EBR-1 achieved its objective in proving that breeding, stable operation, and power production were feasible with a liquid-metal-cooled fast reactor.

During a series of experiments in 1955, a second core was designed to study the behavior of the EBR-1 under extreme conditions with no coolant flow. As a result, a power excursion occurred and the temperature rose sufficiently high to melt the uranium fuel. After this incident, a third core, made of modified fuel pins and designed to eliminate the fuel bowing that had occurred in the first core, was operated in a stable manner. On November 27, 1962, the operation of EBR-1 with plutonium fuel was demonstrated. On December 31, 1963, after other test facilities had become available, EBR-1 was shut down at the conclusion of its experimental program. To summarize its accomplishments, the EBR-1 was the first nuclear reactor to:

- Produce usable amounts of electricity (December 20, 1951).
- Demonstrate the feasibility of breeding (1953).
- Achieve a self-sustaining nuclear reaction with a plutonium-fueled core (November 27, 1962).
- Produce usable amounts of electricity with plutonium fuel (July 1963).
- Demonstrate the feasibility of using liquid metal (sodium-potassium) at high temperatures as a reactor coolant.

The Experimental Breeder Reactor-2. The EBR-1 was replaced by the EBR-2 which had a much higher power level: 62.5 Mw_{th} (20 Mw_e) versus 1.2 Mw_{th} (0.15 Mw_e). The objective was a further development of the highly desirable breeder concept. Using sodium as a coolant, the reactor also had potential for higher thermal efficiencies than the LWR's. EBR-2 achieved "wet" (with sodium in the core) criticality in November 1963.[31] The EBR-2 facility was designed as a fully integrated facility with the capability of accomplishing the entire fuel cycle: fuel fabrication, fuel irradiation (reactor operation), and fuel reprocessing. This concept eliminated off-site shipment of highly dangerous irradiated fuels to a chemical processing plant and the return of fresh plutonium-uranium fuels to the reactor. The fuel was also rather innovative. It contained 49 percent U-235 (replaced later by 20 percent plutonium), 46 percent U-238, and 5 percent fissium (fission products alloy).[32] Thus, some of the fission products were recycled into the core. Because of problems of radiation stability, the metal fuel has since been replaced by plutonium-uranium oxide which is the prototype fuel for the LMFBR; however, most EBR-2 fuel is still metallic uranium. The concept of a closed, integrated fuel cycle which leaves radioactive material mixed with the plutonium could have significance for waste management and plutonium safeguards. This point will be discussed further in Chapter VI.

EBR-2 operation has provided valuable data in such areas as plant design, reactor components, instrumentation and control, sodium technology, physics, and safety. It reached its design power level of 62.5 Mw_{th} in 1969, but had operated at significant power levels (> 30 Mw_{th}) since initial power operation in 1964.[33] Today it is the only fast reactor test facility in operation in the United States. It is currently used for irradiation testing of fuel and materials for the Fast-Flux Test Facility and the high-priority LMFBR program.

The Homogeneous Reactor Experiment 2. The HRE-2 was developed at ORNL. This concept simplified fuel processing in that it occurred continuously as a part of the operation and had the potential of breeding. Construction began in August 1954 and nuclear operation was initiated on December 27, 1957.[34] The HRE-2's fuel was a heavy-water solution of uranyl sulfate and the reactor was operated initially with a heavy-water blanket. The blanket consisted of a thorium solution in which breeding of U-233 occurred. The plant included chemical processing equipment for purifying the irradiated uranyl sulfate solution through the removal of solid corrosion and fission products. With these characteristics, fuel fabrication and out-of-plant processing of irradiated fuel were eliminated.

Corrosion and reactor stability were of serious concern and had undergone much study. The HRE-2 reached full power of 5 Mw_{th} on April 4, 1958;[35] shortly thereafter, the core solution was discovered in the blanket region as a result of corrosion. The corrosion was caused by an instability of the fuel solution. Because of lack of resolution of the fuel solution instability problem, operation of the reactor was terminated April 28, 1961, and the program was also terminated.[36]

The Homogeneous Thorium Reactor listed in Table 9 was planned but was never conducted. Westinghouse and Pennsylvania Power and Light Company had initiated studies on the intriguing concept in 1955 and had proposed a prototype power plant under PDRP in 1957; however, they withdrew the proposal in December 1968.[37]

In summary, based on the planned five-year program proposed by the AEC in early 1954, two of the five reactor types led to commercially competitive systems within ten years; two were abandoned; and one, the fast reactor, continues as part of the current high-priority LMFBR program. These prototypes were completely funded by the AEC.

Other Experimental Reactors

Not all of the experimental investigations of reactor concepts were made under the five-year program. Many others were tested in various AEC laboratories and a few were built by private industry. Some of the experimental reactors did lead to or give support to demonstration plants. Others produced sufficient evidence to discourage further development.

Many reactor concepts were proposed. Reactors constructed by the AEC are listed here:

BORAX-1 through -5: A series of boiling-water-reactor experiments starting around 1953 for the purpose of testing various design and safety parameters, including nuclear superheating of the steam.

HWCTR: A heavy-water-components test reactor to provide basic information on heavy-water-moderated and -cooled reactors.

PRTR: A heavy-water reactor used to develop the technology of recycling plutonium in thermal reactors.

OMRE: An organic-moderated and -cooled reactor using Santowax, a mixture of diphenyl and the three terphenyls, with a boiling point of 640°F at atmospheric pressure.

EOCR: A second experimental organic-cooled reactor constructed to test various organic coolants and fuels.

EGCR: A gas-cooled reactor using a helium coolant, a graphite moderator, and stainless-steel-clad, enriched-uranium fuel elements.

UHTREX: Ultrahigh-temperature, gas-cooled reactor employing graphite as a moderator and uranium carbide as a fuel.

Clementine: The first known fast reactor employing plutonium. It went into operation in 1946 at a power level of 10 kw, which was increased to 25 kw in 1949. Mercury was the coolant.

LAPRE-1 and -2: Aqueous homogeneous reactors using an enriched uranium trioxide dissolved in phosphoric acid. The extremely corrosive nature of the fuel solution necessitated the use of gold or platinum cladding of components.

MSRE: A graphite-moderated reactor cooled with a molten salt composed of fluorides of lithium, beryllium, zirconium, uranium, and thorium.

LAMPRE: The Los Alamos Molten Plutonium Reactor Experiment—a fast reactor with a eutectic mixture of plutonium and iron contained in tantalum capsules and cooled with sodium.

Three small experimental reactors were privately financed: the Vallecitos Boiling-Water Reactor and the Vallecitos Experimental Superheat Reactor (VESR), both constructed by the General Electric Company; and the Saxton Nuclear Experimental Reactor, developed by Westinghouse. These projects were carried out in cooperation with one or more utilities and were instrumental in developing the light-water reactor concept. The VESR was used in an unsuccessful attempt to develop the technology for superheating steam in the reactor. Had it been successful, the process would have reduced the thermal pollution inherent in the light-water reactor type, a drawback of current nuclear power plants often pointed to by environmentalists. Several small materials-testing reactors were also built by industry; these supplemented the AEC's capabilities in this area.

Of those listed above under "Other Experimental Reactors," only the EGCR was full-scale. This reactor will be discussed further in a later section. It was a reactor sponsored by the JCAE, to tie in with the TVA system; it was built at Oak Ridge, but was never operated.

The MSRE led to the Molten Salt Breeder Reactor (MSBR) concept, one of the few reactor concepts still under active consideration. However, the AEC support was relatively low and erratic, resulting in significant uncertainty for its future.

All of the tests, except as noted, were totally financed by the AEC, with industry participating primarily as operating contractors for the AEC laboratories. Although it would appear that the examination of such a large variety of reactor types would have provided a sound experimental basis for technological assessment, the total number of reactors investigated was in fact too large for each to be constructed and tested on an equivalent, firm, technical basis. Some of these concepts were extremely speculative and proper evaluation of the reactors would have shown that they should not have been built. But the 1950's were the "honeymoon" decade for nuclear technology development, a time when almost any ideas proposed by scientists and engineers could find support in the Atomic Energy Commission. Moreover, in general these experiments were relatively low cost and could be put into operation in a relatively short time.

COOPERATIVE DEMONSTRATION PROGRAM WITH INDUSTRY

The five-year experimental reactors program and other experimental and prototype reactors built primarily by the AEC laid the technology foundation for large-scale demonstration of the practical value of nuclear power for commercial use, but they were not designed as a mechanism for transferring to industry the knowledge and experience needed for commercial introduction of nuclear power. More direct industry involvement was required. The Shippingport reactor project was a significant step in bringing industry into the development effort, but it was built under the terms of the 1946 Act, which did not permit private ownership of large reactors. Therefore, the AEC was the owner of this facility.

The 1954 Act gave the AEC the statutory authority to construct large-scale reactors for research and development purposes, but the AEC was not allowed to build reactors for the sole purpose of generating or selling power. Even with the authority to build and operate large-scale plants for R&D purposes, however, it resisted taking this route of development; it believed that competitive forces of industry would bring about economic nuclear power faster. There were a few exceptions, but these reactors were brought about specifically by JCAE pressures or legislative action. The AEC developed policies that were deliberately designed to encourage industry participation.

The problem facing the AEC in 1954 with respect to its attempts to bring industry into the development of this new technology was that there was no strong market "suction force" for commercial nuclear power. While many looked to nuclear power to play a major role in the energy supply of the nation and the world, this development was not expected to take place soon. Furthermore, it was certain that nuclear power plants could not be constructed and operated on an economically competitive basis with conventional fuels until significant advances were made. There were, however, pressures for rapid development of this technology. In a 1957 article, Harold P. Green stated that "there is general agreement—and little articulated disagreement—among all political and economic groups in the United States that nuclear power must be developed as rapidly as possible." [38] He cited the National Coal Association as the only group seriously challenging that position. Green saw the pressures coming not only from the potential role of nuclear energy in meeting the nation's expanding power requirements, but also from the role of the United States in world affairs:

> The rapid development of atomic power has become a primary element in the cold war, and it is regarded as of paramount importance that the United States, rather than the Soviet Union, be able to take the lead in bringing nuclear power to those areas of the world which are desperately in need of cheap power in order to industrialize and to raise their standards of living and health. It is similarly regarded as quite important that American industry be able to compete effectively with industry of other nations in the race for overseas nuclear markets. These considerations require that nuclear power be rapidly developed within the United States to the point at which it can be effectively and profitably exported to other nations. They preclude reliance upon the forces of the marketplace as determinants of the rate of nuclear power development and require an aggressive program of Government intervention to assure substantial activity in the nuclear industry even though such activity cannot be justified on conventional economic grounds. [39]

Even the coal industry did not object to the development of nuclear power *per se*. In 1955, the National Coal Association established a special committee on atomic energy. In a resolution of the NCA on atomic energy policy, they declared their overwhelming support of the government's development of atomic energy, referring to the "need for the Government to continue the power demonstration program to optimize the conditions under which atomic power is generated." They further declared that atomic energy should "be utilized principally in whatever ways or processes it will contribute efficiently to the energy requirements of the United States and the world." [40] It was generally agreed that nuclear energy would not replace coal to any degree for many decades, by which time use of coal and other fossil fuels would also have expanded.

The coal industry objections generally concerned the degree of subsidization, which in their view gave an unfair competitive advantage to nuclear power over coal. James Van Zandt, the representative from the coal-rich twentieth district of Pennsylvania and a member of the JCAE, suggested that a national policy governing commercial uses of atomic energy be developed so that hardships would not be created for the country's coal, oil, and natural gas industries. [41]

In 1955, optimism for nuclear energy was high. The nation was eager to put this new power to work for the betterment of mankind and there was essentially no opposition to the government programs for its development. Furthermore, the recently passed 1954 Act opened the door for a new phase in this development.

THE POWER DEMONSTRATION REACTOR PROGRAM—ROUND ONE

The 1954 Act introduced significant changes in the law controlling atomic energy and provided the opportunity for much greater private industry participation. The AEC interpreted the 1954 Act as a mandate to rely primarily on normal industry for the final demonstration of nuclear power. Undoubtedly, the AEC chairman at that time, Lewis L. Strauss, played a key role in formulating the AEC policies that were to follow.

The first step was Strauss's announcement on January 10, 1955, of a Power Demonstration Reactor Program (PDRP) "designed to open the way for American industry to develop, fabricate, construct, and operate experimental nuclear reactors." [42] The objective of the program was to bring private industry into the engineering of nuclear reactors and to advance the time when nuclear power would become economically competitive. The AEC requested competitive proposals for cooperative projects from applicants who were "willing to assume the risk of construction, ownership, and operation of reactors designed to demonstrate the practical value of such facilities for industrial or commercial purposes." For their part, the commission was to consider assisting these privately financed projects by waiving charges for loan of source and special nuclear material (fuels) for up to seven years; performing in its laboratories, without charge, certain mutually agreed-upon research and development; and buying from the participant, under a fixed-sum contract, technical and economic data developed from the project. The reactor owner was to pay for any special nuclear material consumed in the operation. The fixed-sum commitments put a ceiling on AEC participation and placed the economic risks of the project on

TABLE 10
POWER DEMONSTRATION REACTOR PROGRAM

Plant	Location	Reactor Type	Reactor Owner/Operator	Reactor Contractor	Start of Project	Initial Operation
Round One						
Yankee Nuclear Power Station	Rowe, MA	Pressurized water	Yankee Atomic Electric Co.	Westinghouse Electric Corp.	CP 1957	1960
Hallam Nuclear Power Facility	Hallam, NB	Sodium graphite	AEC/Consumers Public Power District of Nebraska	Atomics International	A 1960	1962
Enrico Fermi Atomic Power Plant	Lagoona Beach, MI	Sodium-cooled fast breeder	Power Reactor Development Corporation	Atomic Power Development Association	CP 1957	1963
Round Two						
Elk River Reactor	Elk River, MN	Boiling water	AEC/Elk River Rural Co-op Power Assn.	Allis-Chalmers Manufacturing Co.	A 1959	1962
Piqua Nuclear Power Facility	Piqua, OH	Organic cooled	AEC/City of Piqua, Ohio	Atomics International	A 1960	1962
La Crosse Boiling Water Reactor	La Crosse, WI	Boiling water	AEC/Dairyland Power Co-operative	Allis-Chalmers Manufacturing Co.	A 1963	1967
Boiling Nuclear Super-heat Reactor (BONUS)	Punta Higuera, PR	Boiling water, nuclear superheat	AEC/Puerto Rico Water Resources Authority	General Nuclear Engineering Corporation	A 1960	1964

Round Three

Name	Location	Reactor type	Utility	Vendor	Permit	Operation
Big Rock Nuclear Power Plant	Big Rock Point, MI	Boiling water	Consumers Power Co.	General Electric Co.	CP 1960	1962
San Onofre Nuclear Generating Station	San Clemente, CA	Pressurized water	Southern Cal. Edison and San Diego Gas and Electric Cos.	Westinghouse Electric Co.	CP 1964	1967
Malibu Nuclear Plant	Corral Canyon, CA	Pressurized water	Dept. of Water and Power of City of Los Angeles	Westinghouse Electric Corporation	(CP) 1964	canceled
Connecticut Yankee Atomic Power Station	Haddam Neck, CT	Pressurized water	Conn. Yankee Atomic Power Company	Westinghouse Electric Corp.	(CP) 1963	1967
Carolinas-Virginia Tube Reactor	Parr, SC	Heavy-water pressure tube	Carolinas-Virginia Nuclear Power Association	Westinghouse Electric Corp.	CP 1960	1963
Pathfinder Atomic Power Plant	Sioux Falls, SD	Boiling water, nuclear superheat	Northern States Power Company	Allis-Chalmers Manufacturing	CP 1960	?
Peach Bottom Atomic Power Station	Peach Bottom, PA	Gas cooled	Philadelphia Electric Co.	General Atomic	CP 1962	1966
Fort St. Vrain	Platteville, CO	Gas cooled	Public Service Co. of Colorado	General Atomic	CP 1968	?

Source: Walter Zinn, Frank K. Pittman, and John F. Hogerton, *Nuclear Power USA* (New York: McGraw-Hill, 1964).
A—Project authorization
CP—Construction permit granted
(CP)—Construction permit filed

the applicant. Thus, the arrangement provided a definite incentive to the utility
to seek minimum costs for the project; the utility, in turn, would apply pressure
on the reactor supplier and others involved to reduce the high costs existing for
nuclear power plants.

The following criteria were established by the AEC for evaluating the proposals:

1. Probable contribution of the proposed project toward achieving economically competitive power.

2. Cost to the AEC in funds and materials.

3. Risk to be assumed by the maker of the proposal.

4. Competence and responsibility of the maker of the proposal.

5. Assurances given by the maker of the proposal against abandonment of
the project.

The cutoff date for receiving proposals was April 1, 1955, but the AEC indicated that if this first round was favorable and appeared to provide an effective
mechanism for private industry participation, subsequent requests for proposals
might be made.

Four proposals were received. One of these, a proposal from Commonwealth
Edison Company, did not seek AEC financial assistance but was dependent on
leasing fuel from the AEC, the only allowed owner of special nuclear materials
under the 1954 Act. The other three proposals, shown in Table 10, resulted in
contracts for cooperative reactor projects. Two of these were from private
groups and the third was from a public utility. Breakdowns of the actual costs incurred by the respective contractors and the government are given in Table 11.

The first contract was signed on June 4, 1956, with Yankee Atomic Electric
Company, a corporation created and owned by a group of New England utilities. The AEC committed itself to fund up to $5 million in R&D in support of
the project, $1 million of which was to be performed in AEC laboratories and
$4 million to be reimbursed for R&D performed in private facilities.[43] This arrangement provided a definite mechanism for government-industry interaction
conducive to effective technology transfer. The AEC also agreed to waive its
normal charge for use of special nuclear materials to fuel the reactor, a figure
amounting to approximately $3 million for the first five years of operation of
the reactor. Yankee contracted with Westinghouse for the reactor portion of the
plant, estimated to cost $18.5 million. The reactor was a pressurized-water type
having a 134 Mw_e capacity. The total estimated cost of the plant was $34.5
million, all of which was to be borne by Yankee. The plant continues to
operate today as a private facility.

A similar arrangement was contracted with Power Reactor Development
Company (PRDC) of Detroit, a corporation owned by twenty-three utility and
industrial companies. The Fermi reactor was a fast-breeder type having a capacity of up to 300 Mw_{th}. Detroit Edison Company supplied the electrical generators. PRDC contracted with Atomic Power Development Associates
(APDA) to supply various development, design, engineering, and fabricating

TABLE 11

Costs of Cooperative Power Reactor Projects [a,b]
(Dollars in Millions)

Plant	Research/Development/Design		Plant and Training of Operators		Waiver of Use Charge	Fuel Fabrication		Total
	AEC	Participant	AEC	Participant	AEC	AEC	Participant	
Yankee Nuclear Power Station	$ 5.0	$ 0.2		$ 39.2	$ 3.8	—	$ 1.7	$ 49.9
Hallam Nuclear Power Facility	16.7	—	$33.5	20.1	—	$ 6.6	—	76.9
Enrico Fermi Atomic Power Plant	3.2	38.2	—	71.4 (71.2)	6.0	—	3.6	122.4
Elk River Reactor [c]	—	—	13.1	1.6	—	1.2	—	15.9
Piqua Nuclear Power Facility	3.6	—	10.9	4.1	—	1.2	—	19.8
LaCrosse Boiling Water Reactor [c]	—	—	15.4	8.8	—	3.9 (1.5)	—	28.1
Boiling Nuclear Superheat Reactor (BONUS) [c]	1.3	0.2	14.2	5.9	—	2.1	—	23.7
Big Rock Nuclear Power Plant	4.0	1.8	—	26.0	1.2	—	4.5	37.5
San Onofre Generating Station	6.2	—	—	100.0	6.4	—	—	112.6
Malibu Nuclear Plant	2.1	—	(PROJECT CANCELLED)					2.1
Connecticut Yankee Atomic Power Station	6.0	—	—	97.0	7.1	—	12.3	122.4
Carolinas-Virginia Tube Reactor	11.2	1.0	—	23.0	0.6	—	1.9	37.7
Pathfinder Atomic Power Plant	7.9	0.4	—	29.7	1.8	—	3.2	43.0
Peach Bottom Atomic Power Station	14.5	7.8	—	31.6	2.6 (2.4)	—	1.0	57.5
Fort St. Vrain	27.9	21.6 (21.5)	8.0	231.0 (226.8)	10.4 (6.1)	5.0	21.5 (21.1)	325.4
Totals	$109.6	$71.2	$95.1	$689.4	$39.9	$20.0	$49.7	$1,074.9
Total AEC								264.6
Total Participant								810.3

a Costs incurred by participants for operation not included.

b All costs are through June 30, 1974. When two numbers are given, the top number is estimated cost and the bracketed number is cost through June 30, 1974.

c AEC shared costs of operation not included.

services required for the construction and operation of the reactor. Of the plants proposed, this reactor was recognized as the most advanced.[44] Its construction and operation, however, met with a number of legal and technical difficulties and it is no longer operating because of a lack of AEC or industry financial support. The Fermi reactor program was first to be attacked by outside "intervenors." Because of its significance in the evolution of public involvement in nuclear power issues, it will be discussed further in Chapter VI.

The second reactor listed in Table 10 was not actually contracted for until September 21, 1957. The conditions of its contract were similar to those of round-two proposals, which by then had been requested by the AEC. This contract was with Consumers Public Power District of Hallam, Nebraska. Because of the limited ability of the utility to assume risk for the plant, the contract provided for AEC ownership of the reactor, which was a sodium-cooled, graphite-moderated reactor supplied by Atomics International.

The privately financed Commonwealth Edison plant, Dresden 1, was a boiling-water reactor plant supplied by General Electric. This plant continues to operate successfully today.

A definite pattern among the AEC, utilities, and equipment manufacturers was established in these developments of demonstration reactors. All the reactor suppliers except APDA were involved with AEC R&D and prototype developments of the type they constructed, and thus were able to utilize government-funded technology. Round one represented an attempt by the AEC to speed up development with a minimum of direct government participation and costs. The financial support of the reactor projects was a fixed amount over a fixed time period, and thus provided the legal arrangement for the government to remove itself from the endeavor. By limiting AEC total support of the demonstrations, averaging about 20 percent per project, the government placed the greater risk—and therefore the greater incentive for cost-cutting—on the shoulders of industry. Because of these features, this subsidy approach can be considered advantageous from the standpoint of ultimate normalization of the atomic energy industry within the conventional framework of private industry.

THE POWER DEMONSTRATION REACTOR PROGRAM—ROUND TWO

None of the reactors under round one was for a small-scale plant. On September 21, 1955, the AEC issued a second request for proposals for relatively small reactor projects having generating capacity from 5 to 40 Mwe.[45] The criteria for selection of projects and the form of financial assistance were similar to those of round one with one important difference. This was that the AEC would consider proposals specifying that the commission finance and retain title to all or a portion of the reactor plant. By retaining title to that portion of the plant financed, the AEC circumvented the stipulations of section 169 of the 1954 Act prohibiting direct subsidy of reactor construction. The AEC also made explicit that the technological advancement represented by the proposed design was to be considered as a criterion for evaluation of proposals, as well as the contribution the project would make toward achieving economically competitive power.

The smaller size and particularly the financial arrangement were probably a response to criticism that because of the financial risk, round one effectively precluded participation by consumer-owned utilities.[46] Of the seven proposals received for round two, six were from municipally or cooperatively owned utilities and one was from a university. Four of the seven proposals were accepted for negotiation, but after more than a year of negotiations, agreements had still not been consummated. The principal difficulty was the inability of the utilities to make definitive long-term commitments and assume the financial risks required.[47]

Since second-round invitations called for small reactors, it was probable that responses would come from small utilities. At the time of the 1957 authorization hearings, the JCAE noted that after seventeen months of negotiations, no contracts had been signed with the second-round proposers; and that after more than twenty-seven months, a contract with Consumers Public Power District of Nebraska based on a first-round proposal had not been consummated.[48] The public power groups, being small, did not have the competence to design, construct, or manage the projects. Their costs and schedules were overly optimistic.[49] It was also recognized that large utilities would not be interested in the small reactors because of their higher unit power costs.

Recognizing these factors, the JCAE stated that developing small and intermediate reactors should be the AEC's primary interest and that negotiation with cooperatives and public utilities should take into consideration basic differences in their size, financial structures, and capacity for participation.[50] This concern with the PDRP second round was just one of several JCAE attempts at that time to influence the reactor programs.

The power development programs were not moving with sufficient speed to satisfy many members of the JCAE. Earlier, in 1956, an unsuccessful attempt had been made by the joint committee through the so-called "Gore-Holifield Bill" to have a major government reactor construction program (see section "The Gore-Holifield Bill," later in this chapter). In July 1957, the JCAE obtained authorization power over AEC cooperative reactor programs.[51] Using this power, in August of 1957 the committee revised the ground rules for the second-round projects. The new ground rules, incorporated in the 1958 authorization act, directed that second-round projects:

>   . . . shall be carried on by direct contract between the Commission and the equipment manufacturer or engineering organization with respect to the development, design, and construction of the reactor and related facilities, and by direct contract between the Commission and the cooperative or publicly owned organization with respect to the provision of a site and conventional turbo-generating facilities, the operation of the entire plant including training of personnel, the sale by the Commission of steam from the reactor complex to the cooperative or publicly owned organization, and other relevant matters. Sale of steam by the Commission under contract with the cooperative or publicly owned organization shall be at rates based upon the

present cost of, or the projected cost of, comparable steam from a plant using conventional fuels at such locations. Projects covered under this subsection shall be operated under contract with the Commission for such period of time as the Commission determines to be advisable for research and development purposes but in no event to exceed 10 years. Upon the expiration of such period the Commission shall offer the reactor and its appurtenances for sale to the cooperative or publicly owned agency at a price to reflect appropriate depreciation but not to include construction costs assignable to research and development. In the event the cooperative or publicly owned agency elects not to purchase the reactor and its appurtenances, the Commission shall dismantle them.[52]

Thereby, the JCAE established detailed policies and procedures for the AEC to follow. This interference, as well as others by the JCAE during the 1956–58 period, created considerable friction between the commission and the joint committee.

With regard to the second-round proposal, the JCAE essentially relieved the small utilities of many of the project responsibilities for which they did not have adequate staff or financial base. It also placed the financial risks on the government. Round two, as spelled out by the JCAE, was contrary in approach to the AEC's policy of limiting AEC commitments and involvement in demonstration programs. The final arrangement was a "forced fit" and probably contributed little to economic development except to confirm the higher costs of small projects.

Because of technical and economic feasibility problems, only two of the original seven proposals were accepted. These were the Elk River and the Piqua projects listed in Tables 10 and 11. The two other round-two projects listed were negotiated subsequently. The small reactors under round two not only were of interest to small U.S. utilities, but were of potential use for small or developing countries. However, because of their high costs and the greatly improved economics of large reactors, small systems are not competitive and consequently have not been sold commercially.

THE POWER DEMONSTRATION REACTOR PROGRAM—ROUND THREE

In the environment of tremendous JCAE pressure to expand the nuclear power reactor program, in January 1957 the AEC announced a third-round Power Demonstration Reactor Program.[53] The third-round proposal was apparently designed to forestall attempts by the JCAE to have the government build large power reactors.[54] The round-three program proposed AEC assistance similar to that of round one, but also considered the loan of heavy water to those projects requiring it. The program had no cut-off date for receiving proposals, but requested them as soon as possible. They were to be considered individually as soon as received, within the limits of the AEC's available funds. There was a cut-off date for construction completion, June 30, 1962, except for the homogeneous reactor type, which was later allowed an extension to June 30, 1963. A number of reactors were proposed, and several were constructed. On August 23, 1962, the commission announced a modified round-three program calling for proposals for projects of at least 400 Mw$_e$.[55] Only proven reactor concepts were eligible. All round-three reactor projects accepted by the AEC are listed in Tables 10 and 11. Except for the current LMFBR development, these were the last to receive direct subsidies from the government.

Many of the reactors built under the PDRP continue to operate, although others have been decommissioned. The importance of this program was in the subsidization of industry when nuclear power was under development and not economically competitive and in the introduction of nuclear power to the utilities. The program cost the AEC approximately $265 million and industry $810 million for research and development, plant construction, operator training, fuel fabrication, and fuel-use charges. The costs do not include facility operations. The AEC assisted in the operation of five of the plants. Most of the AEC financial support was in connection with the five AEC-owned reactors and the two high-temperature, gas-cooled reactors—approximately $140 million and $67 million, respectively.

The Power Demonstration Reactor Program provided a final mechanism for technology evaluation. It provided industry with valuable experience in designing, constructing, and operating progressively larger-scale plants. Since it led to the current commercial reactors, it can thus be considered a success. It was initiated in a time of delicate balance between JCAE forces wanting immediate construction of many large reactors and the AEC-industry forces desiring a more deliberate approach to reactor selection. Undoubtedly the JCAE pressures had significant bearing on the extent and timing of private industry involvement.

JOINT COMMITTEE INTERVENTION AND PRESSURES

Although by 1956 the AEC had initiated the five-year experimental reactor program and the Power Demonstration Reactor Program, the JCAE was still not satisfied with the progress being made. It was particularly concerned over the fact that few reactors of any substantial size were planned and none was operating. There were two major factors contributing to slow progress: first, essentially all technical data had been secret until 1955 and declassification was still in progress; second, although the AEC wanted private industry as a major participant in the development, industry was slow to commit major resources because of technical and economic uncertainties and financial risks. The JCAE saw foreign countries taking the nuclear power leadership away from the United States through their aggressive reactor construction programs. These events prompted the JCAE to intervene in the AEC planning process through legislative actions that called for a large construction program. These actions also brought into play the conflict between private and public power. Similar conflicts were evident in the 1954 Act debates on private ownership of reactors, patents, and so forth. There were indications that some joint committee members were motivated by a desire to establish the beginnings of a "nuclear TVA." There was a real threat that if industry could not or would not build the reactors, then the government would have to.

Although the JCAE's most ambitious plan, the Gore-Holifield bill, failed in Congress, subsequent scaled-down attempts met with some success. The most intense pressure by the JCAE on the AEC's reactor program took place during the period from 1956 to 1968. It was also during this period that the JCAE obtained authorization power over the AEC's programs. These actions were important not only from the standpoint of the results they produced, but also because they reinforced the position of the JCAE as a strong force in the nation's nuclear program.

THE GORE-HOLIFIELD BILL

The Gore-Holifield bill, referred to earlier, was the first bill specifically directing the AEC to initiate a more aggressive program and was the most ambitious of all legislative proposals to involve government in nuclear power reactor ownership. The bill was seen by many as a mechanism to put the government into the nuclear power business and to impede private utility investments. Holifield saw it as a "trial balloon" for a government nuclear power industry or at least a spur to get industry moving on construction of nuclear reactors.

The bill (S 2725, HR 10805) was introduced by Senator Albert Gore (D., Tennessee) and Representative Chet Holifield (D., California) early in 1956, and in their view was designed to accelerate the civilian reactor program.[56] The bill authorized and directed the AEC to construct six nuclear power facilities, of different designs and in different geographical areas of the United States. These reactors were to be in addition to the reactor development program carried out by private industry or public groups licensed under section 103 (research and development reactors) of the 1954 Act. Hearings were held in May 1956, and although the bill was never passed, it is worthy of consideration in the light of the various approaches suggested by people with conflicting viewpoints.

It will be remembered that under the strong leadership of Chairman Lewis Strauss, the AEC had interpreted the 1954 Act as a mandate to develop nuclear power through private industry. There were many proponents of nuclear power, however, who felt that development efforts were progressing too slowly despite the fact that the AEC had initiated several new reactor programs. In its *Semiannual Report to Congress, January–June 1956,* the AEC reported that "the Nation's program for development of nuclear reactors to generate electricity for civilian use went forward on a broad front during the last 6 months." [57] By the time of the hearings on the Gore-Holifield Bill, the AEC had initiated its five-year experimental reactors program in late 1953, the first round of the Power Demonstration Reactor Program in January 1955, and the second round of PDRP in September 1955. The AEC reported to the committee that there were planned or under consideration approximately twenty-five reactors covering eight different types in these three programs, with total electrical capacity of 1,182,000 kilowatts and at a total cost of $671 million—$313 million from the government and $358 million from industry.[58] They had three firm proposals for reactors to be financed completely through private funds. These were of the boiling- and pressurized-water types and two were large reactors having a combined electrical output of 320,000 kilowatts.

Since the AEC program was extremely diversified, the argument for the bill could not be based on the need for exploration of the six different reactor types proposed; instead the argument was based primarily on the need to decide which type of reactor should be chosen and how soon it ought to be carried to the large-scale demonstration stage. Proponents of the Gore-Holifield bill wanted the government to build the large reactors immediately; the AEC favored a more deliberate approach. As will be seen later, from the perspective of a technological delivery system, the latter approach may have proved more sound.

The AEC's approach at this time to orderly reactor development was spelled out to the committee by the AEC's director of reactor development, Mr. Kenneth Davis, as follows:

1. Exploratory phase, in which very preliminary work on fuel and other component materials is carried out and conceptual design studies are made, including reactor physics and engineering characteristics.
2. Developmental phase, in which conceptual ideas are tested on an expanded experimental basis and more detailed studies are made of fuel element design, control problems, heat transfer, and fluid mechanic problems.
3. Reactor experiment phase, in which design and construction of an operating reactor is undertaken to provide technological data on all basic questions, including performance of fuel elements, behavior of control systems, safety, and other physics and engineering characteristics.
4. Prototype phase, in which design and construction of prototype power reactors are undertaken with the aim of producing power on a continuing basis and to gain information on construction problems, operating problems, and unit costs.
5. Commercial phase, in which reactors are built as economically competitive power-plants.[59]

The question, according to the AEC, was not whether the United States could build the reactor, but what was the best way to achieve economic nuclear power. Mr. Strauss had the following to say about the AEC's policies and position:

The question is, however, at what cost will these plants work? It is because the primary problem in the United States is cost and no longer one of feasibility, that the Commission is actively engaged in exploring a large number of diverse reactor concepts. That exploration is proceeding primarily by the conduct of reactor experiments and associated research and development designed to develop necessary data with respect to the specific practicality, efficiency, and costs of a variety of systems.

We fully appreciate the importance of building full-scale reactors. Indeed there is a point at which only a full-scale reactor can provide the cost information and the engineering improvements that are necessary to achieve significantly lower costs.

But we believe that our present state of knowledge of some reactor concepts is short of the point where construction of full-scale reactors at this time is either necessary or advantageous.

In brief, our present goal is more scientific knowledge, not simply more kilowatts. While we advance on a broad front and with the vigor to achieve that knowledge, we believe we should continue to proceed toward that goal in an orderly and flexible manner.

This, in our view, means coordinating and timing both experimental and full-scale plants with the status of the particular areas of technology they are designed to explore and the nature of the information we can expect to get from them.

We believe that the enforced adoption of arbitrary goals of kilowatt capacity or numbers of full-scale reactors for an early date, such as 1960, is unwise because it would divert scarce technical skills from activities which promise greater results in subsequent years.[60]

A major argument used by Senator Gore and other proponents of the bill was that the United States was falling behind the foreign nations, particularly the United Kingdom, France, and Russia. The Russians had just recently announced a five-year program to build ten full-scale power plants, having a total capacity of approximately 2.5 million kilowatts. About one half of the total were dual purpose (plutonium producers for weapons plus some power), and about one half were optimized power stations. About 10 percent of the total was to be in pilot plants.[61] They were considering seven different types, similar to those of the United States. Dr. Walter Zinn, an early pioneer in reactor development and later director of Argonne National Laboratory, was serving as a consultant to the JCAE and had this to say about the British and Russian programs:

I think if you limit the amount of construction that is to be undertaken to the kind of program we now have, our choices are as good a bet as anybody. This can be seen by noting that we are being sincerely flattered by being imitated. Both the British and the Russians apparently are trying hard to come through with programs which imitate ours. . . . There is only one Russian reactor which is different from ours, and it is a gas-cooled heavy water moderated reactor. If we include the fact that we do have the Hanford type of reactor but not as a power reactor, the Russian program, their main program is really a graphite moderated pressurized water reactor which is a model of the Hanford type.[62]

The British had a much more limited program in terms of developmental scope and were concentrating primarily on a low-rated, gas-cooled, graphite-moderated reactor similar to the one built at Oak Ridge in 1942. They had two under construction and had proposed six additional ones, all dual purpose. In addition, a ten-year plan called for sixteen power-only reactors with a total capacity of 1.5 million to 2 million kilowatts.[63] The British, unlike the United States or the Soviet Union, had an urgent need for an alternative energy source. The Soviet objectives were weapons plutonium production, political prestige, and possible export interest. The Soviet developments were of most concern to Gore and Holifield and their supporters in proposing the accelerated U.S. program. For example, in support of the bill, Senator Pastore said that "if we are outdistanced by Russia in this race, it would be catastrophic. If we are outdistanced either by the United Kingdom or France, there would be a tremendous economic tragedy to our commerce and the international commerce of this great Nation of ours.'' [64] However, as indicated before, the AEC felt a kilowatt race at that time would be detrimental to the long-range goal of economic power. According to Strauss, the AEC policy was to design plutonium production reactors for a high-quality product at minimum unit (plutonium) cost, and its commercial reactor objective was to develop power reactors with minimum unit energy cost (mills/kwh). [65]

Commissioner Thomas Murray, a holdover from Truman's administration, was the only one of the five AEC commissioners to favor the Gore-Holifield bill. In a letter to the JCAE he expressed gloomy prospects of producing any substantial quantity of industrial nuclear power in the United States by 1960. He saw at "the root of the matter . . . the fact that the Government has prematurely abdicated to private industry the primary responsibility for building large power reactors.'' [66] His proposed action paralleled that of the bill.

The Rural Electric Cooperative Association had supported the ill-fated Johnson Amendment to the 1954 Act, which would have allowed the federal government to construct commercial atomic power plants. It now supported the Gore-Holifield bill. [67] TVA took the position that the federal government must take the initiative and bear the bulk of the tremendous expense to develop civilian nuclear power. However, they recognized that any rapidly expedited program would produce uneconomical power and, therefore, based their justification for early construction of a number of large power reactors on international reasons, not domestic requirements. [68]

The AFL-CIO saw the United States falling behind other countries and urged passage of the bill. [69] On the other hand, the Edison Electric Institute, representing 186 utilities serving 80 percent of all electric customers in the United States, was "unalterably opposed to this bill in particular and to legislation of this general type.'' [70] They gave the following reasons: (1) adequate progress was already being made; (2) industry projects already undertaken would demonstrate the practical value of commercial power; (3) the United States would be able to maintain leadership through quality and not crash quantity programs; and (4) the public power preference clause of the 1954 Act discriminated against the great majority of America's electric customers.

Francis McCune, General Electric, gave testimony on the broad scope of his company's effort and stated that the proposed government program would heavily tax the available manpower. The same point was made by several witnesses. At this time, General Electric was constructing the 180,000 kilowatt Dresden plant for Commonwealth Edison without direct government subsidy. [71] Manpower was a constraint and the AEC had initiated programs to help remove it.* Mr. McCune considered the company's need for long-range planning and

* These programs are summarized in Chapter VII.

spending based upon this need to be more important than the proposed construction program. He felt that the federal government as a customer versus the existing power industry would cause confusion in business planning and hence would weaken their efforts and make them ineffective.

In countering the diversification of reactor types for major demonstrations (as proposed in the Gore-Holifield bill), Mr. McCune, who had been a manager at the government's Hanford plutonium production plant, stated that General Electric had seriously considered two other reactor types before choosing the boiling-water reactor. One was a Hanford type, which was still being considered for a dual-purpose reactor by the AEC, and the other was the homogeneous type being developed at Oak Ridge. His judgment was that the latter type was not far enough along in development for any reasonable prospects of success.[72] Evidence later showed that selecting the boiling-light-water reactor over the other two was indeed a wise decision.

Westinghouse, which had three pressurized-water reactors and a homogeneous reactor under contract, also believed manpower could be a constraint on more rapid development. Both General Electric and Westinghouse had significant sources of manpower from other government nuclear programs. Mr. Charles Weaver, vice-president of Westinghouse, did not directly oppose the bill, but did say, "I vigorously support Admiral Strauss's statement that kilowatts should not be regarded as the measurement of accomplishment." By this statement and his review of the substantial progress being made by Westinghouse, opposition was implied.[73]

Although there were many other individuals representing various interest groups, the supporters were generally public power proponents and the opposition came mostly from the private manufacturers and utilities and from the AEC.

The Democrats had regained control of Congress in 1954, but while the bill passed the Senate, it was defeated in the more conservative House.

The record will show that the more deliberate approach pursued by the AEC was probably the best in the long run. The two reactors promoted by Westinghouse and General Electric, the pressurized- and boiling-water reactors, are now the backbone of the United States nuclear industry and are capturing much of the world market. Neither the French nor the British reactors being built at that time became economically successful, and indeed in 1970 the French abandoned their early concept in favor of the light-water reactors, as did the Swedes. The British, too, have gone to alternative concepts, and have considered but rejected the water reactors. Because of the British discovery of the North Sea oil, some of the pressures on their energy supplies have been reduced.

Table 12 presents data on nuclear power plants in operation, under construction, or planned in the European Community. The first category, graphite/gas, was the first type promoted by France and the United Kingdom; no additional reactors of this type are under construction or planned. Essentially, all reactors planned or under construction are either boiling-water or pressurized-water reactors. The fast reactor remains the type of the future. The high-temperature gas-cooled reactor (HTGR) developed by Gulf-General Atomic has recently breached the U.S. market and could be a significant factor in the future. It might be worthwhile to note that Japan is developing a major nuclear industry based primarily on the water reactor. The U.S. reactors are being purchased as being more economically competitive than the reactors developed by France, the United Kingdom, and Sweden. The Canadians, however, have not abandoned their heavy-water reactor type and it is being sold in a few instances.

TABLE 12

Net Electrical Capacity (Mw$_e$) of Nuclear Power Plants—
Actual or Projected—in the European Community, January 1973

Type of Reactor	Country	In Operation	Under Construction	Ordered and Planned	Total Mw$_e$
Graphite/gas	U.K.	5,165	—	—	5,165
	France	2,365	—	—	2,365
	Italy	200	—	—	200
Total		7,730			7,730
Advanced gas reactors	U.K.	34	6,200	—	6,234
Boiling light water	Germany	1,088	1,630	2,990	5,708
	Italy	150	783	—	933
	Netherlands	52	—	—	52
Total		1,290	2,413	2,990	6,693
Pressurized light water	Germany	958	3,099	2,430	6,487
	France	270	890	2,740	3,900
	Belgium	10	1,650	—	1,160
	Italy	247	—	—	247
	Netherlands	—	450	—	450
Total		1,485	6,089	5,170	12,244
Heavy water	Germany	151	—	—	151
	U.K.	100	—	—	100
	France	70	—	—	70
	Italy	—	—	32	32
Total		321		32	353
High temperature	Germany	13	300	—	313
Fast	Germany	19	—	282	301
	U.K.	14	250	—	264
	France	—	233	—	233
Total		33	483	282	798
Not yet determined	Germany	—	—	7,300	7,300
	U.K.	—	—	650	650
	Netherlands	—	—	600	600
	Italy	—	—	600	600
Total				9,150	9,150

Source: Nuclear News, 16, 4 (March 1973), p. 47.

Although the attempt by certain members of the JCAE to pass the Gore-Holifield bill did not succeed, many were not content to leave entirely up to the AEC the specifications of the types of reactors to be developed. Soon after the defeat of the Gore-Holifield bill, the AEC again took the initiative by requesting, in January 1957, third-round proposals under the Power Demonstration Reactor Program. This action was perhaps an attempt to take the initiative from the JCAE and possibly prevent further attempts of the Gore-Holifield type. If so, the AEC was not successful. Four proposals were received from industry, but none of these included a gas-cooled reactor of the type of particular interest to the JCAE.

Representative Holifield, who was chairman of the JCAE subcommittee on legislation, continued to push for AEC effort on the gas-cooled concept. Apparently he continued to be concerned about the kilowatt lead that the British were taking through construction of several dual-purpose natural uranium, graphite-moderated gas-cooled reactors.

On July 3, 1957, Public Law 85-79 was passed; this amended the 1954 Act to give the JCAE additional control over the civilian reactor program.[74] The amendment did three things: first, it required the AEC to obtain congressional authorization of funds for any nonmilitary reactor that had a thermal output greater than 10,000 kilowatts or that was to be used in electric power generation; second, it required the AEC to obtain congressional authorization for funds to be used in the Power Reactor Demonstration Program with industry; and third, it required the AEC to submit to the JCAE forty-five days in advance any plans to establish or revise prices for buy-back of special nuclear materials produced in power reactors, and any criteria for the waiver of any charge for the use of a special nuclear material. These amendments gave the JCAE considerably greater control over what projects would be undertaken by the AEC and under what conditions.

After this bill was passed, Holifield again took the initiative and proposed an expanded program, calling for four reactor projects over and above those the commission was requesting. One of these was dropped before the proposed legislation was sent to the floor and another, a dual-purpose production reactor, was reduced from a request of $95 million for construction to $3 million for study. The bill, S 2674 (HR 8996), did contain $15 million for an experimental plutonium-fueled reactor and $40 million for the gas-cooled reactor that Holifield had been pushing. The House passed an amendment by Representative Van Zandt which eliminated these two requests from the bill,[75] but later a similar amendment proposed by Senator Hickenlooper failed to pass the Senate.[76] Hickenlooper pointed out that, with respect to the natural uranium reactor, "that reactor is one which the Atomic Energy Commission does not want to build" and that the plutonium test reactor should be postponed.[77] He also took the opportunity to criticize the role the JCAE was taking: "It is interesting to note that leading reactor experts such as Dr. Smyth, Dr. Zinn, and Dr. Weinberg, have indicated very clearly they think it is unwise for the Congress to specify particular types of reactors for the AEC to build. . . ." [78] The conference bill that was finally accepted included $3 million for further study on the gas-cooled reactor. [79]

As directed by the JCAE, the AEC immediately initiated a study of a gas-cooled, graphite-moderated reactor, fueled with natural uranium. This study, conducted by Kaiser Engineers and ACF Industries, Inc., developed a conceptual design of a 22 Mw$_e$ plant with helium coolant and slightly enriched uranium, which gave better economic performance [80] than natural uranium fuel.

On April 22, 1958, the JCAE subcommittee on legislation held hearings on the gas-cooled reactor. [81] Holifield clearly indicated what he considered to be the role of the JCAE in power-reactor-program specifications and expressed his dissatisfaction with the AEC for not giving sufficient attention to the gas-cooled, graphite-moderated reactor:

> The joint committee's interest in gas-cooled reactors goes back several years. . . . I think it is important that the role of the joint committee in connection with this gas-cooled reactor report is clearly understood. The joint committee has construed its role as reviewing the objectives and scope of the atomic-power program and filling gaps where necessary in this program as well as in other aspects of the overall atomic energy program. In this connection, the joint committee does not necessarily believe that gas-cooled or natural uranium reactors are better than other reactor types, but merely, that these types have not received the attention they deserve. [82]

A summary report of the AEC findings from the gas-cooled reactor study was sent to the JCAE on April 1, 1958. Comments on the report were solicited by the JCAE from various reactor experts, manufacturers, and utilities. [83]

The responses were less than enthusiastic for the concept. This might have been expected, since the concept had not been proposed by any organization in the three rounds of PDRP. Most saw potential in the gas-cooled reactor, but not in the specific type that was being proposed. One such response was from A. B. Grenninger of the General Electric Company, who stated that "a development program is definitely in order. I question the justification for building something in a hurry. . . . Certainly we should not build a prototype reactor that represents little advance over what the British are now doing; our target should be an exit gas temperature of something like 1200°F." [84] In his reply to the committee, Alvin M. Weinberg, director of ORNL, took the opportunity to question the JCAE's role in deciding basically technical issues:

> Finally, before trying to answer your specific questions, I should like to question, as I have in communications with committee members in the past, the usefulness of your committee's raising in such detail extremely technical issues. It is unclear to me how the joint committee can formulate sound technical questions without having a staff somehow comparable to the staff of the Commission itself. The issue I touch upon is the very difficult one of the proper role of Congress in relation to administrative agencies whose jobs are highly technical. My own personal feeling is that the separation of function between Congress and the Commission would be much better

understood if the joint committee concerned itself primarily with setting forth the goals, and directed its probing toward the progress in achieving these goals, rather than trying to specify the means for achieving the goals. In particular, I think the joint committee would do very well to place on record what our goals in civilian nuclear power are. As my remarks show, I would consider the threefold goal:

(1) to make competitive nuclear energy in the United States as soon as possible;
(2) to develop reactor systems which are immediately competitive outside the United States;
(3) to develop power breeders;

to be sensible and valid. You will note that I set (3) forth as a separate and distinct goal in itself. Once the goals have been set, I would consider it the business of the committee to ascertain how much progress the Commission is making in achieving these aims.[85]

Weinberg favored the gas-cooled concept for inclusion in the U.S. program, but questioned the graphite reactor. Later, during oral testimony supported by the results from an Oak Ridge study, he favored development of a slightly enriched uranium-oxide-fueled reactor similar to that which was being studied.[86] The system was also very much like the advanced gas-cooled reactor of the British,[87] to which Grenninger from General Electric had objected.

In the authorization bill for fiscal year 1959 appropriations, the JCAE again included funds for the graphite-moderated, gas-cooled reactor, and the new plutonium-production reactor for Hanford. Funds requested were $51 million for the former and $145 million for the latter, which included $20 million to make the production reactor convertible to dual purpose.[88] The AEC had requested $120 million for a plutonium producer only (nonpower producing), which the Budget Bureau had eliminated.

The Bureau of the Budget had not requested the funds for the dual purpose production reactor. The JCAE had added it based on what they claimed was the need for plutonium for national defense and for replacement of old Hanford reactors, and not solely on economic grounds. Senator Leverett Saltonstall (R., Massachusetts) proposed an amendment to eliminate the reactor and was supported by Senator Hickenlooper, who stated that "no Defense Department requirements have been laid down for the plutonium which will be produced by means of this plant."[89] Senator Henry Jackson (D.) from the state of Washington, where the plant was to be located, tried to pacify Senator Saltonstall and other strong private power advocates by stating that the power from the reactor would be used at Hanford and that there was no provision in the bill for the sale of power to a public or private utility.[90] Senator Saltonstall's amendment failed to pass.

In the case of the gas-cooled reactor, the AEC had requested that it be part of the Power Demonstration Reactor Program. The JCAE allowed for this. An amendment by Senator Saltonstall, passed by the Senate [91] and later modified in conference, read as follows:

If the Commission determines, at any time within sixty days after the announcement provided for in subsection (a) that (i) any public, private, or cooperative power group, equipment manufacturer, or other person or organization has designed and is ready to construct and operate such a reactor at its own expense and not in conjunction with any cooperative arrangement with the Commission and (ii) the purposes of the gas-cooled reactor project 59-3-10 as a part of the Commission's reactor-development program would be substantially fulfilled by the construction and operation of the reactor by such group, equipment manufacturer or other person or organization, then the Commission shall not be obligated to proceed with such project under this section.[92]

A second amendment by Senator Saltonstall required that if the reactor were built by the government, the AEC would have to sell or dismantle the reactor after it had served its purpose for research and development and national defense. The amendment passed the Senate and was accepted in conference. The version initially reported out by the JCAE and accepted in the House allowed the AEC to continue to operate the reactor for generating electricity. Again, these moves were indicative of the private-public power conflicts existing at that time.

With the provision that the gas-cooled reactor could be built either under PDRP or as a private effort, Senator Clinton Anderson (D., New Mexico) apparently was suspicious that the AEC might allow another reactor to replace it, a possibility that was not specifically what the JCAE had in mind. Anderson stated that "any organization which makes a proposal to do this job solely to keep the Government out will have trouble qualifying getting Government assistance. . . . Since this is an experimental prototype, with provisions to test both natural as well as enriched uranium fuel rods, it is rather unlikely that any private utility group will wish to undertake it." [93] The bill for fiscal year 1959 appropriations was signed by the president on August 4, 1958, and immediately the AEC invited industry to submit proposals on a gas-cooled reactor. A bid was received from Philadelphia Electric Company and General Atomics Division of General Dynamics for a highly advanced, high-temperature, graphite-moderated, helium-cooled reactor. It was later to be designated the Peach Bottom Reactor and was fueled with a mixture of enriched uranium and thorium. The reactor was to be constructed under a fixed-price contract for $24.5 million and have a 28.5 Mw_e net output. The proposal requested the AEC to provide $14.5 million for research and development work, to waive fuel-use charges up to $500,000 for research and development and up to $2 million for the initial five years of operation.[94]

The proposal was the only one received. No proposals were received from private or public utilities for a gas-cooled reactor meeting the criteria spelled out by the JCAE.[95] The AEC, therefore, went ahead with plans of its own to construct the plant designated by the JCAE. It was called the Experimental Gas-Cooled Reactor (EGCR), and was to be built at Oak Ridge with completion scheduled for 1962.[96] The power output was to be fed into the Oak Ridge AEC facility. The power plant was to be operated for the commission by TVA.

A brief history of the three resulting reactors—the EGCR, the Hanford dual-purpose reactor, and the General Atomics high-temperature, gas-cooled reactor—points out the pitfalls Congress potentially encounters in going beyond broad policy issues and attempting to spell out technical details of programs.

First, two gas-cooled reactors were constructed and both experienced some difficulties and delays during construction.[97] Peach Bottom was completed in late 1964 [98] and continues to operate today. It is a prototype of the current commercial high-temperature graphite reactor (HTGR) sold by Gulf-General Atomic. A demonstration plant, Fort St. Vrain, under the AEC PDRP, followed Peach Bottom in construction before the HTGR's were accepted commercially. While the HTGR has not yet been fully demonstrated and has experienced setbacks, several large commercial-size HTGR's have been ordered by utilities.

The EGCR, on the other hand, did not lead to a commercial reactor. Construction was essentially complete by the end of 1965—about three years behind schedule. On January 7, 1966, the AEC announced it was terminating the project and cited the following factors as contributing to the decision: "(a) continuing design and engineering difficulties with corresponding delays and rising costs; (b) the diminishing potential of timely and significant contributions of the EGCR project to commercial development of high-temperature gas-cooled reactor technology in light of current industrial trends; and (c) competing demands for limited funds." [99] The reactor never operated.

It is also of interest to point out that the first British natural-uranium-reactor type was replaced with an advanced reactor: the AGR. This reactor is not unlike the EGCR, and its ability to compete economically is questionable. The British had hoped the fast breeder would be commercially available in 1975. That will not be the case. A synopsis of a British policy study on future reactors was recently reported as concluding that "although with important reservations, . . . light water reactors, the high temperature gas-cooled reactor (HTGR), and the steam generating heavy-water reactor (SGHWR) will all be somewhat more economic than the British AGR for power stations ordered during the late 1970's." [100] The first two are the current U.S.-developed commercial reactors; the SGHWR developed by the British has not been introduced commercially; and the AGR is the current British commercial reactor.

The third concept authorized in the 1958 legislation, the dual-purpose production reactor (N-reactor), dates back to around 1952, when the AEC was in the process of expanding its weapons production capability. Some companies, e.g., General Electric and Monsanto, proposed to build dual-purpose reactors with private funds and to sell the plutonium to the government. There were two reasons why this never occurred: private ownership of reactors was not allowed at that time, and the plutonium buy-back price was set too low to justify the dual-purpose approach.

The N-reactor has been a controversial project since inception. Originally the AEC supported the concept as a single-purpose (plutonium-production) reactor, but the General Electric Hanford management recommended the dual-purpose approach for at least two reasons: they felt that no new production reactor should use direct cooling from the Columbia River, because of potential contamination; and they thought that a dual-purpose reactor would place Hanford in a better competitive position with the newer Savannah River's single-purpose production reactors, which were more efficient plutonium producers.

Other G.E. management, however, did not support the concept. The project had a substantial private versus public power content. Up to that time, Bonneville had received its electric power from hydroelectric plants. The private utilities did not want the first thermal power plant tied to the Bonneville Power Authority system, thereby setting a precedent for such public power expansion in the electric power field as was occurring in the TVA system.[101]

Another factor that may have had some bearing was the possibility of a treaty with Russia to shut down all or part of the weapons production facilities. Russia had some dual-purpose reactors which they could claim were power producers; the United States had none. With these issues affecting the decisions, the fight on the project went on up through construction. It was resolved when the AEC decided to sell the steam generated to the Washington Public Power Supply System (WPPSS), a consortium of seventy-six utilities—five private and seventy-one public.

The N-reactor was built by Kaiser Engineers on a cost-plus-fixed-fee contract.[102] The $145 million authorized by Congress did not include the electrical generating plant. On April 11, 1963, the steam supply contract with WPPSS was signed.[103] WPPSS sold $122 million in bonds to provide funds for the 800 Mw_e electric generation part of the plant. The power was to be distributed over the Bonneville Power Authority transmission system and was to be split fifty-fifty between the private and public power utilities. It was estimated that the AEC would receive $125 million for the steam over a twenty-four-year period.

The reactor was completed at a final cost of $199.7 million, which included neither the $122 million for the generating plant nor the funding for supporting research and development.[104] It did include about $15 million for a fuel-fabrication facility and modification of the Hanford fuel-reprocessing plant. The plant reached its full design thermal power of 4,000 Mw_{th} in December 1965, three years behind schedule.[105] WPPSS completed its construction, and full power of 800 Mw_e was reached briefly on December 9, 1966 and then on a more sustained basis starting in May 1967.[106]

In the meantime, the AEC announced a substantial reduction in its special nuclear materials production: four reactors were shut down on December 30, 1964, and diffusion plant operations were curtailed by 25 percent.[107] There were nine production reactors at Hanford, location of the N-reactor, and five at Savannah River. On January 28, 1971, the last of the Hanford production reactors was shut down, including the N-reactor.[108] WPPSS negotiated a contract with the government for continued operation of the N-reactor to June 30, 1974.[109] WPPSS was to reimburse the AEC for operation up to $20 million per year for an amount of power up to 4 billion kilowatt hours. The $20 million was less than what was initially proposed by the AEC, but was negotiated as

reasonable when other factors were considered. There was no plant depreciation, normally the largest factor in power costs, considered in this charge.

WPPSS had until June 30, 1972, to exercise an option to assume responsibility for operating the reactor. A study determined that it would not be economically attractive to use the N-reactor as a steam producer. An important factor was that an oxide fuel, which was more suitable for a power-only operation,
had not been developed. Also, it would have cost a great deal, probably $40
million to $50 million, to bring it up to safety standards for commercial licens-
ing. In 1973, WPPSS announced that the reactor would not be used after June
30, 1975, and that it would be replaced with a 1,200 Mw_e water reactor.[110] An
added high-pressure turbine will produce 400 Mw_e, and the existing low-pres-
sure turbine will produce the remaining 800 Mw_e. The contract with the AEC
was later amended at WPPSS's request. Under the new agreement, the N-reactor will supply steam to WPPSS until October 31, 1977.[111]

In summary, the reactor was an inefficient producer of power ($\sim$ 20 percent
efficiency) and a poor producer of weapons-quality plutonium. Even so, the
plutonium that it has produced and still produces is useful in the weapons program. The total capital cost was approximately $340 million, which corre-
sponds to about $400 per kilowatt of installed electrical capacity. Approxi-
mately eight months after WPPSS had signed its contract with the AEC,
General Electric sold its first "turnkey" (fixed-price) boiling-water reactor
plant to Jersey Central Power and Light at a cost of $110 per kw_e, including
about $13 per kw_e chargeable to money interest during construction.[112] This
total was less than the $150 per kw_e for just the electrical generating equipment
alone supplied by WPPSS. While exact figures were never published, the reactor manufacturers did lose money on the first turnkey plants, of which several
were built by General Electric and Westinghouse.

Since the N-reactor was dual purpose, these costs, while interesting, cannot
be used as the sole criterion for judging the government's decision to proceed
with the project. As far as WPPSS is concerned, the agreement with the AEC
was designed to make the economics favorable if the reactor were to operate for
at least eight years.

The N-reactor was the world's largest power reactor and continued until
recently to hold the record for electrical energy (kilowatt hours) generation. It
still continues to help fill a gap in energy requirements in the Pacific Northwest.
While substantially different in concept from today's commercial reactors, it
did make some useful contribution to the technology in the areas of zirconium
cladding and the use of mild steel piping, which is more easily decontaminated
than the stainless steel being used at the time.

CONTINUED JCAE PRESSURE ON REACTOR DEVELOPMENT

Even after the JCAE authorized, through the 1957 legislation, additional reactors to the numerous reactors already proposed, the committee continued to
pressure the AEC for an expanded power reactor development program. On

November 27, 1957, the chairman of the JCAE sent a letter to Chairman Strauss of the AEC in which he emphasized the need for clarification of the country's policies and objectives in the nuclear power field and urged close cooperation between the JCAE and the AEC in formulating a realistic and well-balanced program.[113] After several meetings between the AEC and JCAE, the AEC prepared a plan for a long-range civilian nuclear power program. The AEC released a statement on the program for publication on June 3, 1958. At that time the chairman of the JCAE legislative subcommittee, Representative Holifield, said that the committee would consider the AEC's statement as a tentative proposal until the committee had completed its own independent statement. While the committee felt that "the AEC long-term-program statement represented a genuine step forward and attempted to be responsive to suggestions by the Joint Committee . . . it did not cover completely several aspects of the program reflecting committee views." [114] The JCAE soon released its own draft statement, called "Proposed Expanded Civilian Nuclear Power Program," for the purpose of obtaining the views of industry and the AEC.

It had been approximately four years since the commission had initiated its five-year experimental reactors program and the Power Demonstration Reactor Program. The year 1958 was a low point in optimism for nuclear power costs. While industry had initiated several independent or cooperative programs, the JCAE felt that "construction of prototype and full-scale power reactors have not been progressing as rapidly as desired due to difficult technical problems and unanticipated increases in costs." [115] The committee also continued to give considerable importance to both the implications of international competition and the domestic needs for nuclear power. The JCAE spelled out the following objectives for the U.S. nuclear power program:

- Achieve and demonstrate in the United States economically competitive nuclear power by 1970.
- Achieve and demonstrate in high-cost free world nations economically competitive nuclear power by 1968.
- Fortify the position of leadership of the United States in the eyes of the world in the peaceful applications of atomic energy, particularly with regard to electric power generation.[116]

The proposed expanded program included twenty-one reactors having a total capacity of one million electrical kilowatts at an estimated cost of $500 million for construction and $375 million for associated design and development costs.[117] The JCAE made it clear that this program was in addition to already planned projects: "It should be understood that the expanded program does not include reactors now under construction or already implemented. Nor does it include reactors constructed by private industry not specified in the list of reactor types for the expanded program." [118] To clarify the point further, two tables, reproduced here as Tables 13 and 14, were presented to identify clearly the type, size, and schedule of the reactors to be included in the expanded program and those already under way or proposed in the AEC program. The JCAE

TABLE 13

POWER REACTORS FOR NEW UNDERTAKINGS

Project	Approximate Electrical Rating (Mw_e)	1958 Status	Approximate Time Interval
Heavy-water-cooled and -moderated power components reactor	0 (60 thermal Mw_e)	Under study by contract with AEC	1956–60
Gas-cooled, graphite-moderated reactor	40	Under study by contract with AEC	1958–62
Boiling-water reactor with nuclear superheat	10 to 50	Proposal made to AEC	1958–62
Heavy-water-cooled and -moderated reactor	100 to 250	Under study by contract with AEC	1958–63
Aqueous homogeneous solution reactor	75 to 150		1959–65
Process-heat reactor	0 (45 Mw_th)		1959–62
Fused-salt-fueled reactor	10		1959–64
Steam-cooled, heavy-water-moderated reactor	10		1959–65
Intermediate-energy neutron breeder	10	Under study by Southwest Atomic Energy Associates	1958–67
Water-cooled, graphite-moderated, Hanford-type reactor	300	Under study by contract with AEC	1958–63
Pressurized-water, enriched-uranium-fueled reactor	200		1959–64
Boiling-water, enriched-uranium-fueled reactor	200		1960–65
Organic-cooled reactor	50		1960–64
Liquid-metal-fueled-reactor experiment	0 (5 Mw_th)		1959–63
Two small second-generation industrial plants	15 to 40		1961–65
High-temperature, gas-cooled, graphite- or heavy-water-moderated reactor	200		1961–66
High-temperature, sodium-cooled, graphite- or D_2O-moderated reactor	200		1961–66
Organic-cooled reactor	200		1962–67
Sodium-cooled fast or intermediate breeder	200		1963–68
Liquid-metal-fueled reactor	50		1963–68

Source: U.S., Congress, JCAE, *Expanded Program*, p. 16.

TABLE 14

STATUS OF POWER REACTORS UNDER WAY OR PROPOSED [a]

Project	Approximate Electrical Rating (Mw$_e$)	1958 Status	Approximate Completion Date
Boiling-water, enriched-uranium-fueled reactor	180.0	Under construction by Commonwealth Edison Co.	1959
Pressurized-water, enriched-uranium-fueled reactor	163.0 [b]	Under construction by Commonwealth Edison Co. of New York, Inc.	1960
Pressurized-water, enriched-uranium-fueled reactor	134.0	Under construction by Yankee Atomic Electric Co.	1960
Boiling-water, enriched-uranium-fueled reactor	16.5 [c]	Contract awarded to Elk River Electric Cooperative and ACF by AEC under power demonstration program	1961
Boiling-water, enriched-uranium-fueled reactor	50.0 [d]	Contract awarded to Northern States Power Co. & Associates by AEC under power demonstration program	1962
Sodium-cooled, fast breeder	100.0	Under construction by Power Reactor Development Co.	1960
Sodium-cooled, fast breeder	20.0	Under construction by Argonne National Laboratory	1960
Sodium-cooled, graphite-moderated reactor	75.0	Under construction by AEC and Consumers Public Power District of Nebraska as part of power demonstration program	1962
Sodium-cooled, D_2O-moderated reactor	10.0	R&D contract awarded by AEC to Chugach Electric Assn. and Nuclear Development Corporation of America under power demonstration program; letter of intent negotiated on construction	1963
Organic-cooled and -moderated reactor	12.5	Proposal of city of Piqua, Ohio, and Atomics International accepted by AEC under power demonstration program	1961
Homogeneous aqueous slurry	70–150.0	R&D proposal of Pennsylvania Power & Light Co., Baltimore Gas & Electric Co., and Westinghouse Electric Corporation accepted by AEC under power demonstration program	1964
D_2O-cooled and -moderated pressure tube	17.0	Proposal of Carolinas-Virginia Nuclear Power Association, Inc., accepted by AEC under power demonstration program	1962

TABLE 14 (*Continued*)

Project	Approximate Electrical Rating (Mw$_e$)	1958 Status	Approximate Completion Date
High-temperature, gas-cooled, D$_2$O-moderated, pressure tube	50.0	Proposal of East Central Nuclear Group & Florida West Nuclear Group accepted by AEC under power demonstration program	1963
Boiling-water, enriched-uranium-fueled reactor	60.0	Reactor announced February 1958 by Pacific Gas & Electric Co. and Bechtel	1962

Source: U.S., Congress, JCAE, *Expanded Program*, p. 17.
[a] Reactors in operation as of January 1958 omitted.
[b] Additional 112 electrical megawatts from oil-fired superheater.
[c] Additional 5.5 electrical megawatts from coal-fired superheater.
[d] Additional 16 electrical megawatts from oil-fired superheater.

also expected the base program of general reactor research and development to continue at a rate of $125 million to $150 million per year.[119]

Although Tables 13 and 14 indicate a program of extremely broad scope, they are misleading since they do not list many experimental reactors in the AEC program. A more comprehensive illustration of its program was published by the AEC in its 1958 annual report and is reproduced here as Figure 1.[120] Not only does it show the accomplishments not listed in Tables 13 and 14, but it also serves the purpose of illustrating the acceleration of the program after the passage of the 1954 Act. However, even this figure omits several pertinent reactors built, approved, or under study, such as the N-reactor, Peach Bottom, several experimental testing reactors (MTR, ETR, TREAT, GETR, WETR, SPERT, ATR, BORAX-5, etc.), Liquid Metal Fuel Reactor-1, and military and maritime reactors.

Possibly the JCAE's feeling that progress was insufficient stemmed from the fact that there was only one full-scale power plant in operation at that time, namely, Shippingport. Moreover, if the JCAE was interested in the total industry development it should have considered the experience gained in construction of the plutonium production reactors (thirteen large reactors in operation at that time) and navy propulsion reactors (five in operation and thirty-one planned), as well as over two hundred research, training, and test reactors and critical facilities.[121] Equally important at that stage of reactor development were the in-depth AEC base programs of research and development in such areas as metallurgy, chemistry, physics, fuels, waste management, reactor safety, and radiation effects. These were conducted by AEC contractors in AEC laboratories, in universities, and in industry laboratories.

In addition to the broad objectives of the program stated above, the JCAE stated as a basic policy that the AEC must provide "positive leadership to make

Figure 1

CHRONOLOGY OF CIVILIAN POWER REACTORS

TYPE OF REACTORS	Net kwe	PROJECTED TIME INTERVAL
essurized Light Water		
Shippingport Atomic Power Station	60,000	
Yankee Atomic Electric Company	110,000	
Consolidated Edison Thorium Reactor	255,000	
•iling Water		
Boiling Reactor Experiment No. 1	None	
Boiling Reactor Experiments Nos. 2-4	2,000	
Experimental Boiling Water Reactor	4,500	
Vallecitos Boiling Water Reactor	5,000	
Dresden Nuclear Power Station	180,000	
Northern States Power Company	62,000	
Rural Cooperative Power Association	22,000	
Humboldt Bay Project	50,000	
·ganic-Cooled		
Organic-Moderated Reactor Experiment	None	
City of Piqua	10,500	Design to start 1959
•dium-Cooled		
Sodium Reactor Experiment	6,000	
Hallum Nuclear Power Facility	75,000	
Chugach Electric Association, Inc.	10,000	Design to start 1960
st Breeder	Negli-gible	
Experimental Breeder Reactor No. 1		Mark I & II Cores — Mark III Core
Experimental Breeder Reactor No. 2	16,500	
Enrico Fermi Atomic Power Plant	90,000	
uid Fuel	Negli-gible	
Homogeneous Reactor Experiment No. 1		
Homogeneous Reactor Experiment No. 2	Negli-gible	
is-Cooled		
Gas-Cooled Power Reactor	26,000	
East Central / Fla. W. Coast } Nuclear Power Groups	58,000	Design to start 1960
•avy Water		
Plutonium Recycle Test Reactor	None	
Heavy Water Components Test Reactor	None	
Carolinas-Virginia Nuclear Power Assoc., Inc.	16,950	

1952 1953 1954 1955 1956 1957 1958

urce: U.S., AEC, Semiannual Report to •ngress, July-December 1958, p. 17.

═══DESIGN   ——OPERATION

--------CONSTRUCTION ——|SHUTDOWN

certain the objectives are achieved in terms of practical results." [122] It went on to spell out the ways this leadership should be accomplished:

(a) Continuance of responsibility by AEC for the conduct of the base program of research and development through its national laboratories, industrial contractors, universities and nonprofit institutions.

(b) Assumption by AEC of positive direction of the reactor development program from the stage of feasibility studies of promising reactor concepts, through the necessary reactor experiments, up through the construction and operation of experimental prototype reactors. Large-scale demonstration plants also would be constructed if not otherwise provided by industry.

(c) Provision of positive direction by AEC of the power demonstration program by the selection by AEC of the reactors to be designed and constructed and the setting of realistic dates for submission, approval, and negotiation of proposals for each project. In the event a satisfactory proposal is not received within the time limit specified in the invitation, or is not implemented within a reasonable time to be specified in the proposal, the AEC promptly would assume responsibility for construction of the project unless sufficient cause can be shown for the delay. [123]

With some modification of (c), these three policy statements accurately represented the government's position on its role in developing commercial nuclear power.

Although the JCAE said that projects wholly financed by private industry should be encouraged to the fullest extent possible, it was apparent that the JCAE wanted the AEC to take a greater leadership role in demonstration projects. The JCAE went on to spell out in considerable detail criteria for cooperative and government-owned projects. [124]

It also spelled out general technical objectives: cheaper components, cheaper field assembly, better fuel elements, higher temperature steam, cheaper reprocessing of irradiated fuel, cheaper waste processing and disposal, use of plutonium as a fuel, use of natural uranium as a fuel, and breeding.

The JCAE submitted the proposed expanded nuclear power program for comments to various sectors of industry, including equipment companies; reactor experts; private, public, and cooperative power organizations; architect-engineers; and consultants. There was general agreement on the objectives and scope of the program, with the AEC providing the leadership and using the participation of industry to the fullest extent possible.

The principal differences arose over the method of implementing the program. As one might expect, the private utilities and reactor equipment companies wanted the demonstration projects to be within the current utility system. This was succinctly stated by the Edison Electric Institute:

. . . as this new field of energy unfolds in the United States, it seems to us to be particularly important that at each stage of development of the new field, prime consideration be given to the maintenance of our normal business system. Whatever we have in the way of productive capacity in this country can be credited to that system, and as we enter this new field of energy, every effort should be made to protect and strengthen it. . . . Detailed Government controls and Government ownership of nuclear powerplants will not serve to create this environment (maximum use of industry's inventiveness and productive capacity) and will be detrimental to the achieve-ment of the program objectives.[125]

The American Public Power Association wanted more government partici-pation in the demonstration phase and stated that "a selected number of sec-ond- and third-generation plants should be scheduled definitely as Federal proj-ects." [126] The association also declared that a "truly economic industry be developed" and "built-in or hidden Federal subsidies be avoided to the extent possible." TVA objected, and rightly so, to a rather surprising statement in the proposed program that would have excluded TVA from participating in the pro-gram.*

Part of General Electric's submittal was an extensive program plan devel-oped by the company with the goal of reaching competitive nuclear power in seven years. The information provided was very specific in regard to the com-pany's goals. The statement is reproduced in part here in order to show what at least one company was planning at that stage of nuclear development:

Operation Sunrise is a program for the *development in depth* of boiling water reac-tor systems to reach competitive nuclear power in 7 years. It is a program that begins with the results of solid experience and proceeds in a straight line toward a reasonable and attainable goal.

Specifically, the program includes:

1. A group of small and medium "developmental" nuclear powerplants, to be in operation by 1962, which will provide technology leading to competitive nuclear power.

2. "Evolutionary" plants, to be in operation by 1965, which will be competitive in their locations. These plants will produce power for under 8½ mills per kilowatt-hour.

3. "Target" plants, to be in operation by 1970, which will be competitive with 25 percent of the conventional plants then being installed in the United States. The larger plants will produce power for approximately 6½ mills per kilowatt-hour.

4. Supporting research, development, and testing to make this possible.

The plan went on to set forth future technical objectives:

The boiling water reactor is now capable of attaining a series of five significant technical objectives, the proper blend of which will lead directly to competitive nuclear plants:

1. Increased power density: A doubling in the power output from the present 30 kilowatts per liter of reactor core volume to 60 kilowatts per liter.

2. Reduction in plant complexity; the nuclear steam supply system can be simpli-fied, the plant layout can be made more compact, and containment costs can be reduced.

3. Improvement in steam conditions to increase thermal efficiency from the present 28 percent to over 31 percent with saturated steam or to 35 percent with superheating.

4. Increased plant size from the present practical limit of 200,000 kilowatts for a saturated steam station to over 450,000 kilowatts for a superheated steam plant.

5. Improved fuel performance through the development of reliable fuel perfor-mance for exposures of up to 15,000 megawatt-days per ton.

---

* TVA has become one of the major users of commercial nuclear power and is directly involved with the current breeder demonstration program.

The presentation went into considerable detail on the basis for the plan, the reactors involved, costs, and utility participation. This might be considered a bold projection for the times. The 1958 United Nations Second International Conference on "The Peaceful Uses of Atomic Energy" had just been held in September in Geneva and had resulted in a sobering of industry's attitude toward the near-term prospects of competitive nuclear power.

The General Electric plan might have been a factor in stopping a push by certain members of the JCAE for the AEC to own and operate the large demonstration plants. The G.E. policy was strongly opposed to government ownership or involvement in industrial ventures. It had sold the Dresden plant to Commonwealth Edison at a considerable reduction in price on condition that the utility not accept any government subsidy.

The expanded program proposed by the JCAE was never incorporated into substantive legislation. It probably did have a significant effect, however, on prodding industry to develop a more aggressive program, such as General Electric's Operation Sunrise. It also resulted in the sponsoring of all future government-supported reactor projects through the JCAE's annual authorization legislation, and the incorporation of these into the AEC's Power Demonstration Reactor Program.

Another possible factor in lessening JCAE pressures for AEC-owned and -operated plants was a change in the chairmanship of the AEC. Mr. Strauss, who was frequently at odds with the JCAE, particularly on program management prerogatives, was replaced by John McCone on July 14, 1958, and relations between the AEC and JCAE improved greatly after this point. It must also be recognized that the 1956–58 period probably represented the extreme for JCAE intervention in detailed specifications of government nuclear power programs. However, the JCAE continues to be very much interested in and aware of the technical programs in depth, and derives much of its strength from its involvement at this level.

REMOVAL OF A ROADBLOCK—THE PRICE-ANDERSON INDEMNITY ACT

THE NEED FOR GOVERNMENT INDEMNIFICATION

The 1954 Atomic Energy Act allowed for private ownership and operation of nuclear reactors. This quickly raised the question of liability in the case of an accident. It was the highly improbable catastrophic accident that was of concern to the industry. Since no such accident had ever occurred and since, therefore, there was no way to predict the extent of its damage or the probability of its happening, the insurance industry had no actuarial experience for establishing coverage or premiums for coverage.

In March 1955, the AEC established a group from the insurance industry to study the problem of insurance coverage for peaceful uses of atomic energy.

The group concluded that they saw no difficulty in providing property insurance for nuclear facilities and that the primary problem was one of providing third-party liability insurance.[127] Following their report to the commission, the insurance companies formed three pools to cover atomic energy activities.[128] One, made up of stock companies, was to provide property damage insurance on the nuclear facilities; a second pool, also made up of stock companies, was to provide public liability insurance; and a third pool, consisting of mutual companies, was to provide both types of insurance. The total amount of insurance from the three pools was to be $60 million dollars for liability, and the same amount for property damage. Although this insurance was more than four times that heretofore provided any other industry, it was still viewed as inadequate coverage for catastrophic accidents, regardless of how remote the possibility of their occurrence.

The Atomic Industrial Forum, representing private industry, also reviewed the problem and arrived at conclusions similar to those of the government. At AIF's request, the Legislative Drafting Research Fund of Columbia University, under the direction of Arthur W. Murphy, conducted a comprehensive study on ways to give financial protection to reactor owners against atomic hazards. Their findings identified the major problems facing the government and industry in further nuclear development, with respect to both the risk to private companies and the inability of private insurance companies to provide adequate liability insurance. Their report stated:

1. The development of atomic energy, especially for power purposes, calls for operations involving substantial quantities of radioactive material. And there is, despite every safety precaution, a possibility, however, remote, of a catastrophic accident.
2. From the viewpoint of atomic industry, the primary financial protection problem is that posed by the threat of huge liability to the public arising from such an accident. Under existing legal rules, the operator of an atomic installation, and in some circumstances the suppliers, may in the event of a serious accident be subject to tort liability far beyond that ever previously imposed.
3. Although private insurers are expected to offer to atomic industry insurance coverage many times greater than that available in other industries, the magnitude of the risk is such that the potential liability cannot be covered by private insurance alone.
4. In the license program, the possibility of unprecedented liability for a catastrophic accident is a serious deterrent to the broad private participation that has been a major objective of the Atomic Energy Act of 1954. Although private industry is participating in atomic energy development under Government contract, many questions remain as to the adequacy of the financial protection now afforded contractors.
5. As matters now stand, one of the most significant results of a serious accident could be that members of the public in large numbers would have to bear a major share of the losses.
6. The National Government has a double responsibility: (a) to remove the major roadblock which the financial protection problem poses to broad, effective participation by private industry in the rapid development of atomic power; and (b) to

provide substantial assurance to the public that it will be compensated for losses that may result from that development. There is wide agreement among the interested parties that the financial-protection problem calls for the establishment of some program by the National Government.[129]

The study further stated that:

Given the need for some action by the National Government, there are two basic objectives which must be met by any program: first, the public should be given protection against financial loss because of personal injuries and property damage due to radiation; and second, atomic industry should be protected against the possibility of overwhelming losses from liability in the event of a catastrophic accident.[130]

At this time in the history of atomic energy, the very first steps were being taken to develop commercial nuclear power. It was far from competitive and industry could not foresee when it would become profitable. The suppliers and the operators of nuclear facilities were not willing to take on the additional financial risk of an accident, which, if it happened, would bankrupt the companies involved.

It became apparent that legislation was required to remove the roadblock presented by inadequate liability insurance. After further study, the AEC made proposals to the JCAE for legislation to provide for indemnification against liability of facility operators and suppliers of materials, equipment, or services to the facilities.

LEGISLATIVE ACTION

Legislative proposals for indemnity were introduced in the 84th Congress, second session, and hearings were held by the JCAE in May and June 1956.[131] During the session, a number of possible approaches were considered: HR 9701 provided for government liability coverage without a maximum limit; HR 9802 provided for a limited liability; HR 11242 provided for a voluntary system of government liability insurance in excess of the amount available from private insurance carriers; and HR 11523 provided for government indemnity in excess of private financial protection. The last was modified to cover any person who might be liable and was reported out by the JCAE as HR 12050 (S 4112); however, it was not brought up for debate on the floor in 1956.

The legislation proposed by the joint committee authorized the commission to determine the amount of liability protection which the licensee for reactors must have to protect the public against nuclear incidents. Beyond this amount it was up to the government to indemnify the reactor operator for sums up to $500 million. If a runaway reactor caused damage greater than the sum of the private protection and government indemnity, the way was left open for Federal contributions through additional congressional action, or for liability proceedings to provide a technique for apportioning the moneys available. The commission had authority to use this same approach for those doing work directly for the commission, not merely licensees. The coverage also applied to suppliers of the licensee if they were found liable.

The use of the indemnification approach rather than government insurance was explained by the JCAE as follows:

> A system of indemnification is established rather than an insurance system, since there is no way to establish any actuarial basis for the full protection required. The chance that a reactor will run away is too small and the foreseeable possible damages of the reactor are too great to allow the accumulation of a fund which would be adequate. If this unlikely event were to occur, the contributions of the companies protected are likely to be too small by far to protect the public so Federal action is going to be required anyway. If the payments are made large enough to insure that there is an adequate fund available, the operation of the reactors will be made even more uneconomic. On the other hand, if, as the Joint Committee anticipates, there never will be any call on the fund for payments, the funds will have been accumulated to no purpose. Hence, in this instance it seemed wisest to the Joint Committee not to treat this as an insurance problem but to treat it as an indemnification problem. There seems to be no real need for establishing all the technical mechanisms of an insurance fund in this situation.[132]

Thus, while private industry was saying that it needed the protection before it could proceed with further development, the government recognized that the cost of insurance would put a deterring economic burden on reactor costs. By stating that it would not require full insurance, the JCAE indicated that an indirect government subsidy to the reactor development program was intended. If no accident ever occurred, the approach would essentially cost the government nothing.

The 1956 Bill was reintroduced in the Senate by Senator Anderson (S 715) and in the House by Representative Price (HR 1981) early in 1957. Another bill, S 1684-HR 6604, was also introduced formally to require the AEC to maintain the existing Committee on Reactor Safeguards and to have public hearings and issue public reports. The JCAE held hearings on these bills in March 1957. With minor exceptions, S 715 (HR 1981) was identical with the committee bill reported out in 1956.

It was the view of the AEC, as expressed by Chairman Strauss, that the problem of indemnity was "one of our principle [sic] problems involved in the rapid development of nuclear power in the United States" and that the bills under consideration "offer a practical approach to the necessity of providing adequate protection against liability arising from atomic hazards, as well as a sound basis for compensating the public for any possible injury or damage arising from such hazards." [133]

The estimate of extent and probability continued to plague the committee. During the 1956 hearings, Dr. W. F. Libby, scientist and AEC commissioner, had presented some estimates. On July 6, 1956, the committee requested the AEC to perform additional studies on the problem. The study undertaken was performed by the AEC's Brookhaven National Laboratory and its results were reported by the AEC during the 1957 hearings. It has been cited as a classic study by those opposing nuclear power.

In his 1957 report, Strauss indicated the extreme difficulty, particularly at that time, in making such a study: "To produce such a study, it was necessary to stretch possibility far out toward its extreme limits. Some of the worst possible combinations of circumstances that might conceivably occur were conjoined in the hypothesis in order that we might assess their consequences. The study, therefore, ought to be regarded as an estimation of the consequences of unlikely, though imaginable, combinations of failure and error and weather conditions; it is not in any sense a prediction of any future condition." [134]

He also gave credit to the AEC and the JCAE for having the foresight to have such a study conducted: "We are not aware of such a study having been undertaken for any other industry. I venture to say that if a similar study were to be made for certain other industries, with the same free rein to imagination, we might be startled to learn what the consequences of conceivable major catastrophic accidents in those other industries could be. The actual safety experience of these industries stands on the record in marked contrast." [135]

In the three types of accidents investigated, the theoretical estimates reported ranged from no injuries to an upper limit, in the worst case, of 3,400 killed and 43,000 injured. The costs ranged from about $.5 million to $7 billion. The estimate of this happening was given: "If there were 100 large power reactors operating in the United States, the most pessimistic of the probabilities quoted above lead to the estimate that there would be less than 1 chance in 50 million of getting killed in any year in a reactor accident. By comparison, there is presently about 1 chance in 5,000 of getting killed in any one year by an automobile accident." [136]

This part of the finding is usually ignored when the 1957 study is used by opponents of nuclear power. However, the study's overall findings did point out a dysfunction in the development of nuclear power: the inability to predict reliably the probability and consequences of an accident. This uncertainty has been and remains a source of major controversy. Although major advances have been made in reactor safety engineering, the problem of how to achieve satisfactory prediction continues to exist and can be resolved only from the experience of operating a large number of reactors over a long period of time.

A representative of the mutual insurance companies gave testimony favoring the proposed legislation and was "convinced that in the public interest and to further the program of the peaceful development of atomic energy, some such legislation is necessary." [137] Like the AEC, the mutual companies had suggestions on particular details but not on the broader issues involved. The private pools similarly endorsed the intent and purposes of the proposed legislation.[138] The insurance companies had already developed policies providing up to $60 million coverage per accident, a figure they felt was ample for all foreseeable needs.

Of course, the reactor manufacturers were in favor of the legislation. Mr.

Francis K. McCune, vice-president of the General Electric Company, observed that:

> The need for legislation is generally recognized. It has the support not only of the members of this committee, but of the President and the Commission and I believe of almost every group in any way connected with atomic activities.[139]
>
> In testifying on this subject in the past 3 years, I have said, in effect, that failure to provide liability protection could constitute a major obstacle to private work in the atomic field. I have expressed concern that some projects might be delayed or halted if legislation were not enacted. In this connection, I believe all of you are aware that in a recent poll conducted by the Atomic Industrial Forum, the unresolved liability question was rated second only to the lack of economic incentives as a roadblock to further progress.[140]

Westinghouse presented a similar position, as did other manufacturing organizations. Component suppliers were equally eager for the passage of legislation covering not only reactor owners and operators but their own possible liabilities, which could exceed those covered by their private insurance. The utilities, both public and private, also favored the legislation and its overall objectives. The American Public Power Association wanted the $500-million limit removed and the government indemnity clearly identified as a subsidy to the industry.[141]

The most severe criticism, not so much of the legislation *per se* but of the AEC and its licensing practices, came from several unions.[142] These unions were embroiled in a fight with the AEC over the licensing of the Fermi fast reactor planned by the Power Reactor Development Corporation (PRDC). PRDC was a nonprofit corporation that had several utilities as members, among whom Detroit Edison Company had primary leadership. The unions' objection to the licensing of the reactor was that an unproven reactor was being located in a populated area. They saw the government indemnification acting as a force to reduce stringent safety criteria. They urged that the legislation not be passed until a thorough examination of the AEC licensing procedures had been made and the committee was satisfied that criteria and standards were satisfactory. They also asked that the Reactor Safeguards Committee consist of outstanding scientists and engineers from fields bearing on reactor safety, that a report be required from the Safeguards Committee and be made available to the public sixty days before issuance of a license, and that the committee maintain its independence from the AEC. In introducing the bill (S 1684) giving statutory requirements for a Reactor Safeguards Committee, Senator Anderson went to considerable length to point out explicitly the need for public disclosures: "We should establish procedures which are open to all, with a maximum of information disseminated as to the hazards and safety of each proposed design of a reactor, and as to the administrative considerations and actions taken on each application. The public has a substantial investment in the atomic energy program and has a right to know and analyze the steps being followed by administrative officials." [143]

The bill did not require the Safeguards Committee to review every facility, but only those referred to it by the AEC. Public hearings on license applications were required, an action that might be considered a forward-looking social responsibility for that time.

The bill (S 2051-HR 7383) that finally emerged from the joint committee was not substantially different from the one that had come out of the committee the previous year. It received approval from all its members except one, Representative Holifield, who stated:

> My objections to H.R. 7383 and S. 2051 may be summarized as follows:
> (1) It would provide another Government subsidy to atomic power development without any commensurate benefits to taxpayers and power consumers.
> (2) It would place upon the Federal Government an enormous potential liability that could reach several hundred billion dollars.
> (3) It would weaken congressional control over appropriations by transferring to the Atomic Energy Commission complete discretionary power to commit the Government to undetermined liabilities in advance of appropriations.
> (4) It would further weaken congressional control over appropriations by transferring to the district courts authority to allocate funds for the payment of claims indemnified by the Government.[144]

Some additional insights into his motives are obtained from his concluding remarks:

> In my view, this legislation is unnecessary and unwise. If the risks are negligible, as the proponents of this bill contend, there is no reason why the Government should assume potential liabilities of the magnitude indicated above. If the risks are real and substantial, then reactor development programs should continue to be developed under direct Government supervision and control at isolated locations, with the continued promise of safety exhibited in the record of Government performance.[145]

He wanted the reactor to be located at remote sites until proven safe and to be operated and controlled by the government. He had not completely given up on the idea of a government-operated nuclear power utility, and he carried his fight against the legislation to the floor of the House. His objections were similar in part to those raised by the unions.

The bill was first introduced in the House and was sponsored by Representative Price and Senator Anderson. Representative Price gave the following explanation of what the bill would provide:

> First as a condition for a license for a reactor, the Commission will require the licensee to take out and maintain financial protection. . . .
> Second, each licensee required to furnish financial protection is also required to maintain a contract of indemnification with the Federal Government by which the Government will indemnify the licensee up to $500 million. . . .
> Third, both the financial protection and the Government's indemnification are to be made for the benefit of any person who might be found liable for a reactor incident. . . .
> Fourth, the Commission is given the authority to use this indemnification procedure with its own contractors and subcontractors. . . .
> Fifth, in the more remote contingency that the possible damages might exceed the

amount of financial protection . . . the Commission or any person can apply to the district court having jurisdiction in bankruptcy over the site of the nuclear incident and have the funds available prorated among all those to whom liability is owed. . . .

Sixth, the Joint Committee recommends that the Commission charge $30 a year per thousand kilowatts of thermal energy. . . .[146]

Mr. Holifield was quick to identify himself as the lone dissenter on the JCAE, and gave his reasons for opposing the bill: government subsidy, government liability, and location of plants near cities (PRDC case).

Several congressmen supported the bill with statements; one was Representative Van Zandt, who had read into the record the strong testimony of Frank McCune, head of General Electric's Atomic Products Division:

At present I see no alternative but to recommend that work on the Dresden Station be halted as soon as practicable after the end of this session of Congress in case appropriate legislation has not been passed by that time.

Also, as I now see it, it is my view that General Electric should not take on any other comparable project if it appears that appropriate legislation will not be passed.[147]

General Electric indicated it could not proceed "with a cloud of bankruptcy hanging over its head." Van Zandt saw the problem as "the straw that broke the camel's back"; that is, the ultimate stumbling block in continued reactor development by private industry.

Representative Cole read into the record a letter from Dr. Smyth who was identified as "one of the foremost and best informed scientists in the field of atomic energy and former member of the Commission." The letter was addressed to Representative Holifield and stated: "Failure of this Congress to pass the insurance bill which has been approved by the joint committee and which everyone seems to feel is desirable and appropriate can seriously impede the program." [148]

Representative Price offered several relatively minor amendments to the legislation, including one adding the word "advisory" to the title of the Reactor Safeguards Committee. Representative Holifield offered amendments striking the word "advisory" and also making mandatory the approval of the Reactor Safeguards Committee before the AEC could issue a license. Holifield's amendments failed and Price's amendments passed. The bill was passed by the House on July 1, 1957.[149]

The amended House bill was then considered by the Senate. It was sponsored by Senator Anderson, who reviewed the purpose and features of the legislation, stating: "The probability of there ever being any necessity for using the provisions of this act is very very slight." He emphasized the safety history of the reactor field. There had been only three reactor accidents up to that time: one was in Canada, one was the EBR-1 meltdown, and the third was a deliberate power excursion with the BORAX experiments. Senator Anderson further testified that no one had been injured in any of the accidents, even though none of the reactors had had the containment feature now used on commercial reactors.[150]

Without mentioning Representative Holifield by name, Senator Anderson countered his opposition to the bill by stating:

> Some have claimed that this indemnity is an additional subsidy to the private industry. . . . If this bill should not pass, not only will the entire atomic energy program, the entire demonstration program, be immediately halted, but another Government program of complete Government ownership, complete Government construction, and complete Government operation would have to take its place with the only inherent powers in the Commission to grant indemnities which are presently subject to the availability of future funds. This is not a sound way to reach the problem. . . .[151]

He also read into the record a statement from President Eisenhower supporting the need for the legislation: "I should also state that the President, in his budget message said: 'As a further and necessary step to facilitate industry's investment in atomic powerplants, legislation will again be proposed to authorize the Government to supplement commercially available insurance against liability rising from possible nuclear accidents.' " [152]

The House bill was then passed by the Senate without further comment or amendment. It was signed by President Eisenhower on September 2, 1957.

FEATURES OF THE ACT [153]

The original Price-Anderson Act applied only to facilities for which a construction permit was issued between August 30, 1954, and August 1, 1967. The act required licensees to furnish financial protection to cover public liability claims up to an amount specified by the AEC, and provided government indemnity in the amount of $500 million for each nuclear incident over and above the amount of financial protection required. The act further specified that the maximum coverage available from private sources be required for all reactors rated above 100,000 kilowatts electrical. Based on data from the insurance industry, the AEC determined that the maximum amount of available private liability insurance was $60 million, of which $46.5 million was available from the stock companies' pool and $13.5 million from the mutual companies' pool. For reactors with a lower power rating, the act specified lesser amounts, depending on the power rating. These were spelled out in published regulations. For example, for power and test reactors authorized to operate above one megawatt, a minimum of $3.5 million and a maximum of $60 million were specified. The exact amount required was calculated by taking into consideration the populations around the reactor: for a reactor located in a densely populated area, the maximum amount would be required. The minimum private coverage for any activity was $250,000.

The act covered chemical processing and fuel fabrication plants and transportation between plants. The act authorized the AEC to collect a fee of $30 per year per thousand kilowatts of thermal capacity for research and development reactors and to reduce the fee for commercial reactors. The purpose of the fee was to cover administrative costs and was clearly identified as such by Representative Price during the debate on the bill in the House: "The fee for indemnification is not set by the Commission. The Committee was not seeking to go into the insurance business. It is not trying to establish an actuarily sound fund, and it is not trying to get into the rate-making business. The legislation calls for a minimal fee to cover administrative costs of this program." [154]

EXTENSION OF THE ACT

Provisions of the original Price-Anderson Act were effective for ten years. The act, as amended on September 29, 1965,[155] extended government indemnity for an additional ten years. In addition to providing for the extension, the amendment required that the amount of government indemnity would be reduced by the amount that the financial protection required. For example, when the maximum private insurance was increased from $60 million to $95 million, the government indemnity was reduced to $465 million. This allowed an automatic approach for the government to get out of the indemnification of licensees if the private insurance industry were able to provide the entire $560 million. The amount required of industry was increased to $74 million in 1965 and to $95 million in 1973.[156] Effective January 1, 1975, the total insurance available was increased to $300 million per plant. Of this total, the liability insurance was $125 million and represented a further decrease in the government's indemnity. In addition, property damage coverage was increased to $175 million. As seen by the insurance pool, these increases were an "expression of insurance industry confidence in the safety of nuclear installations and a recognition of increasing nuclear plant values." [157]

Another significant change in the act in 1965 required that anyone covered by the indemnity waive any defenses that he may have in the courts, so that anyone damaged can be compensated immediately by proving that he was damaged. This is a "no-fault"-type clause which does not require proof of negligence of the reactor owner before the injured person can be compensated. The government has thus established procedures whereby it can immediately make payments to the injured. These provisions are considered to be far superior to those covering injuries suffered by the public as a result of other types of disasters.

The major opponents to the extension were the union and company representatives of the coal industry.* Mr. Brice O'Brien, general counsel of the National Coal Association, suggested that "government insurance be made available, in any amount desired, to supplement the maximum amount of commercial insurance available" and "at rates reasonably commensurate with commercial rates." [158] In addition to these modifications, Mr. Joseph Moody, president of the National Coal Policy Committee, proposed that a nuclear liability fund be established by assessing the utility operators according to the

---

* Mr. Adolph J. Ackerman, consulting engineer, also gave extensive testimony opposing the legislation.

number of kilowatt hours generated.[159] The rates suggested were one to three mills per kilowatt hour, an increase in generating costs on the order of 15 to 50 percent. In an exchange between Mr. O'Brien and Representative Holifield on the subsidy matter, Representative Holifield suggested that oil, gas, and coal were being subsidized through depletion allowances and government mainte-nance of the Mississippi River for barge shipment of coal to New Orleans and Florida.[160] The testimony of the coal industry representatives had no impact on the legislation.

In summary, there was little opposition to the Price-Anderson Act. Essen-tially all of those supporting the original bill supported the amendment, includ-ing manufacturers, utilities, insurance companies, and the AEC. It removed the roadblock to continuing private involvement in nuclear power with a minimum of government interference, and the 1965 amendment provided an automatic way for government to disengage itself through the initiative of private en-terprise. Although the AEC was authorized to set the amount of private cover-age required of licensees up to the maximum available, it purposely stayed out of the rate-setting business, leaving that to the normal institutional structures: the insurance companies and the states.

By passing the Price-Anderson Act, Congress took another step toward ac-complishing one of the fundamental purposes of the 1954 Atomic Energy Act; namely, "to encourage widespread participation in the development and utiliza-tion of atomic energy for peaceful purposes." The Price-Anderson Act has been controversial, however; and opponents of nuclear power have suggested its repeal. They contend that: (1) it creates a government subsidy; (2) it encour-ages industry to be less safe; and (3) it provides inadequate coverage for some types of accidents that can be envisioned.

Because of the controversy, the AEC considered recommending a phasing out of the Price-Anderson Act, possibly in the 1980's.[161] It would be replaced with a contingency-fee system under which utilities would be assessed on a *pro rata* basis when a nuclear incident involving liability claims arose. The contin-gency fee would be based on a reactor's power capability. Total phase-out of the act would come when the contingency fees payable after the accident to-taled $560 million, or possibly more. If such a plan were put into effect, it would represent another step toward removing the government from the nuclear energy business.

THRESHOLD OF ECONOMIC COMPETITIVENESS

In 1958, John McCone replaced Admiral Strauss as chairman of the AEC. Although a strong leader, his relationship with the JCAE was one of coopera-tion. He thus reduced the level of controversy that had existed between the AEC and the JCAE when Strauss was chairman. Probably another significant factor in the reduction of JCAE pressure on the AEC to build large numbers of plants was the fact that many of the demonstration reactors were under con-struction in the 1958–60 period (see Table 10, presented earlier in this chapter), and the AEC had in operation a number of its experimental and prototype reactors. Table 15 summarizes the status of civilian reactor projects as of the end of 1961. In addition to these, there were many supporting reactor facilities in operation.

Significantly, a substantial number of privately financed reactors were planned by that time. Three of the seven private projects had power levels substantially higher than those of the cooperative demonstration reactors. This was a result of the recognized fact that one major way of reducing power costs of nuclear plants was to go to larger reactors.

By the end of 1962, seven more of the civilian power reactors became operable, including the large Consolidated Edison Thorium Reactor. Also by the end of that year, three reactors—Dresden, Yankee, and Shippingport—had each generated over one billion kilowatt hours of electricity; indeed, Dresden had produced over two billion.[162] Transition of the technology to industry was proceeding at a rapid pace.

In response to a request from President Kennedy, Glenn Seaborg, chairman of the AEC, submitted on November 20, 1962, a report summarizing the status of nuclear power development and its role in the U.S. economy. In view of the significant progress that had been made, the AEC concluded that "nuclear power is on the threshold of economic competitiveness and can soon be made competitive in areas consuming a significant fraction of the nation's electrical energy; relatively modest assistance by the AEC will assure the crossing of that threshold and bring about widespread acceptance by the utility industry." [163] Due to both advancing technology and increasing reactor size, great progress had been made in bringing down nuclear power costs. They had been reduced from more than 50 mills per kwh for the Shippingport reactor in 1958 to 10 mills per kwh for the then-existing full-scale plants, and were projected to be 5.5 mills to 6 mills per kwh for the large Bodega Bay plant, which was in the planning stage.[164] Fossil-fuel costs at that time ranged from $.15 to $.38 per million Btu. The AEC predicted that light-water reactors ordered at that time could compete with coal at $.30 per million Btu or higher.[165] Although there were a considerable number of electrical generating stations in the 300- to 500-Mw$_e$ range in the United States, still larger plants—up to 1,000 Mw$_e$— were being considered. The growing trend toward very large installations definitely favored nuclear plants, with high capital costs and low fuel costs. Size was to be a significant factor in giving nuclear power a competitive edge over fossil fuel, even in the middle of coal-producing regions of the United States. Also, because of the low-fuel-cost characteristic of nuclear plants, power costs would be reduced in high-cost-fossil-fuel areas. Thus, since fuel transportation is not a significant part of the cost of nuclear power, electric power costs would tend to be more uniform throughout the country.

Despite the optimism generated by the power cost reductions, the AEC saw that the development of a mature nuclear power technology and its utilization on an extensive scale would be a long process. There was still the need for

TABLE 15

Type and Status of Civilian Power Reactor Projects, 1961

Project	Type	Status	Power (Kw$_e$)
Private Industry			
Vallecitos Boiling Water Reactor	BWR	Operable	5,000
Dresden Nuclear Power Station	BWR	Operable	180,000
Saxton Nuclear Experimental Reactor	PWR	Construction	3,250
Consolidated Edison Thorium Reactor	PWR	Construction	255,000
Humboldt Bay Reactor	BWR	Construction	48,500
Vallecitos Experimental Superheat Reactor	BWR	Construction	0
Bodega Bay Reactor	BWR	Design	313,000
Government			
Experimental Breeder Reactor No. 1	Sodium/Fast	Operable	150
Experimental Boiling Water Reactor	BWR	Operable	4,500
Organic Moderated Reactor Experiment	Organic	Operable	0
Plutonium Recycle Test Reactor	D$_2$O	Operable	0
Los Alamos Molten Plutonium Reactor Experiment	Molten Fuel	Operable	0
Boiling Reactor Experiment No. 5	BWR	Construction	2,650
Heavy Water Components Test Reactor	D$_2$O	Construction	0
Experimental Breeder Reactor No. 2	Sodium/Fast	Construction	16,500
Experimental Organic-Cooled Reactor	Organic	Construction	0
Molten-Salt Reactor Experiment	Molten Salt	Design	0
Ultrahigh-Temperature Reactor Experiment	Graphite	Design	0
Experimental Beryllium-Oxide Reactor	BeO	Design	0
Government—with Utility Participation			
Shippingport Atomic Power Station	PWR	Operable	60,000
Sodium Reactor Experiment	Sodium/Graphite	Operable	6,000
Experimental Gas-Cooled Reactor	Graphite	Construction	23,200
Cooperative Power Demonstration Projects			
Second-Round-Type Arrangement			
Hallam Nuclear Power Facility [b]	Sodium/Graphite	Construction	75,000
Elk River Reactor	BWR	Construction	22,000
Piqua Nuclear Power Facility	Organic	Construction	11,400
Boiling Nuclear Superheat Reactor	BWR	Construction	16,300
La Crosse Boiling-Water Reactor	BWR	Design	50,000
Third-Round-Type Arrangement			
Yankee Atomic Power Station [b]	PWR	Operable	141,000
Enrico Fermi Atomic Power Plant [b]	Sodium/Fast	Construction	60,000
Pathfinder Atomic Power Plant	BWR	Construction	62,000
Carolinas-Virginia Tube Reactor	D$_2$O	Construction	17,000 [a]
Big Rock Point Plant	BWR	Construction	47,800
High-Temperature, Gas-Cooled Reactor	Graphite	Design	40,000

Source: U.S., AEC, *Annual Report to Congress, 1961*, p. 29.

[a] Includes some oil-fired superheat.

[b] Proposal submitted in response to first-round invitation.

proven and improved technology—e.g., increased core power densities and increased fuel life—if nuclear power was to be widely competitive and accepted. Because of the long lead time for constructing reactor plants, successive developments could still take decades. The commission also recognized the psychological factor retarding this new technology and stated that "before committing a substantial fraction of their installations to nuclear technology, utility executives will want to be convinced, themselves, that nuclear power is economical, reliable and safe." [166]

Recognizing the difficulties in forecasting the nation's energy requirements and nuclear power use, the AEC "crudely estimated" that by the year 2000, one half of the electric generation in the United States would be from nuclear plants and that by the middle of the twenty-first century, essentially all would be.[167] Under what was called "conservative assumptions," cumulative savings in generation costs by the year 2000 were estimated to be about $30 billion, and annual savings were estimated to be between $4 billion and $5 billion.[168] Because it was expected that there would be insufficient low-cost uranium available to sustain the number of converter-type reactors that would be needed, the use of nuclear power over the long term was seen to be possible only if breeders were developed.

The year 1963 became the turning point for both the government-supported developmental phase and the commercialization of nuclear power. Although the AEC could see a shifting in its development program to advanced converters and breeders that would better utilize nuclear fuel resources, it also saw the continuing need for assistance to industry in improving the design of the plants of increased size that were based on proven technical concepts. In August 1962, the AEC had called for proposals under the modified round-three Power Demonstration Reactor Program. Three proposals were received from industry: the Connecticut Yankee, 490 Mw_e; San Onofre, 395 Mw_e; and the Malibu plant.[169] It is interesting to note that all three plants involved Westinghouse Electric as the nuclear reactor supplier. The proposed AEC assistance on these projects was to be for fixed amounts of $13.2 million, $13.0 million, and $16.2 million, respectively.[170] Actual AEC expenditures were $13.1 million, $12.6 million, and $2.1 million (see Table 11), holding within the initial agreement. Because of technical difficulties in meeting the required fuel lifetime (previously discussed), the Malibu plant was not built. The Connecticut Yankee and San Onofre plants were built and operate today at power levels of 600 Mw_e and 450 Mw_e; they hold positions number one and three in the world for kilowatt hours generated from a single nuclear power reactor.[171]

In the JCAE hearings on the AEC's cooperative power reactor program, Representative Holifield stated that "two of the proposed projects are, in large measure, a direct outgrowth of the design assistance stimulus.* And now we hear reports of other large proposed plants which may follow and which ap-

* The JCAE had authorized this type of assistance in the previous year.

parently will not be dependent upon design assistance in order to proceed. I believe it can be said that nuclear power is on the move.'' [172]

Holifield was correct in his analysis. These projects became the last ones of the light-water reactor type to be approved for direct government assistance. They were considered to be ''substantially competitive.'' [173] Only one other project under the converter reactor type was approved later: the less advanced, high-temperature graphite Fort St. Vrain reactor. The primary factor was status of the technology, which was implied in announcements in late 1963 by two utilities, Jersey Central Power and Light Company and Niagara Mohawk Power Corporation, stating that they planned to purchase boiling-water reactors from General Electric Company.[174] These plants, which would not come under the Demonstration Program, were of a size similar to that of the three nuclear plants proposed by Westinghouse, and thus the two companies were in a similar competitive position with regard to the number and size of plants planned.

CHAPTER V

Toward Normalization of the Industry

CHANGING GOVERNMENT OBJECTIVES

As THE threshold of competitive nuclear power was approached, the AEC saw a need to review and change policy matters dealing with: (1) reactor development; (2) ownership of nuclear material, which was still a government monopoly; (3) the uranium supply industry, which had been fostered by the AEC and was heavily dependent on the weapons program; (4) uranium enrichment services, which also were a government monopoly; (5) the increasing quantity of radioactive waste to be generated by private industry; and (6) reactor safety, licensing, regulation, and siting.[1] These issues will be discussed in this chapter and in Chapter VI. The acceptance and growth of nuclear power in the United Sates will also be reviewed.

The reactor types that were "substantially competitive" in the early 1960's were the light-water-moderated and -cooled converter reactors. But these were competitive only on paper, since only small and medium-size reactors were actually in operation. As previously stated, several of the large commercial-size reactors had been sold in 1963, but these were not to be in operation until several years later. Competitive nuclear power, therefore, was still to be demonstrated. In recognition of this fact, the AEC stated in its 1962 report to the president that its program objective for the immediate future was to encourage full-scale application of the light-water reactors so as "to gain experience and knowledge from actual operations, to get a growing nuclear equipment industry really underway, and to convince utilities of the future economic benefits that they can gain from increasing use of nuclear power."[2] Thus, the commission continued to support, although with diminishing emphasis, the light-water reactors in the 1960's, not only through the broader base technology programs on reactor fuels, physics, and engineering, but also through those on safety, waste management, and demonstration projects. By 1970, except for safety and waste management, the AEC considered the light-water reactor technology to be sufficiently developed, and had phased out its direct support of the industry.

The changing emphasis on reactor types was clearly indicated by the AEC's stated objectives in 1962; these were summarized by the commission as follows:

1. The demonstration of economic nuclear power by assuring the construction of plants incorporating the presently most competitive reactors types;
2. The early establishment of a self-sufficient and growing nuclear power industry that will assume an increasing share of the development costs;
3. The development of improved converter and, later, breeder reactors to convert the fertile isotopes to fissionable ones, thus making available the full potential of the nuclear fuels.
4. The maintenance of U.S. technological leadership in the world by means of a vigorous domestic nuclear power program and appropriate cooperation with, and assistance to, our friends abroad.[3]

To make the transition was not a simple management task for the AEC, since there were still in its laboratories and in the demonstration program a large number of "vested interest" projects that had not been accepted commercially and had little chance of ultimate success (see Table 15, in Chapter IV, for a list of the many reactor types considered). The task of making the transition fell on the shoulders of Milton Shaw, who had become the director of the AEC's Division of Reactor Development and Technology in 1964.

On February 14, 1964, in support of its objective to shift emphasis to advanced converters for the intermediate term, the AEC solicited proposals from the nuclear industry for the cooperative design, construction, and operation of a spectral-shift * reactor nuclear power plant. On February 22, it then requested proposals for the cooperative design, construction, and operation of prototype advanced converter reactor plants incorporating (1) the heavy-water-moderated, (2) the high-temperature, gas-cooled, (3) the thorium seed-blanket, or (4) the sodium-cooled, graphite-moderated concepts. The AEC considered each of these five advanced concepts desirable and ready from a technology standpoint for prototype construction.[4] The major advantage of the advanced converters was in improved utilization of uranium and thorium. While the light-water reactors might use up 1.5 percent to 2.0 percent of the uranium, the advanced converters could use many times that amount. The consequence of this greater efficiency could be to delay or even possibly to eliminate the need for the breeder.

In response to the AEC requests, four proposals were received: a 260 Mw_e high-temperature, gas-cooled reactor, which would be the second stage of development for the HTGR's following the Peach Bottom Reactor; a 560 Mw_e thorium seed-blanket reactor being developed by Rickover's Naval Reactor group; a 150 Mw_e spectral-shift reactor employing both light (H_2O) and heavy

---

* Spectral shift was a method of controlling the reactor by modifying the neutron energy spectrum through the process of varying the ratio of heavy water to light water in the moderator.

(D_2O) water for control and conversion improvement; and a 200 Mw_e sodium-cooled, graphite-moderated reactor. Of these, only two were accepted: the seed-blanket reactor and the high-temperature, gas-cooled reactor.[5] While neither of these specific projects was constructed,* a reactor project similar to the last one was announced in 1965 and was constructed in Colorado by General Atomics [6] for Public Service Company of Colorado; it is referred to as the Fort St. Vrain plant in Tables 10 and 11 (Chapter IV). The Fort St. Vrain plant achieved criticality in January 1974, but equipment problems have delayed full power operations, which are scheduled for summer 1975.[7]

As noted in Chapter IV, the development of the seed-blanket reactor continues and is projected to be a breeder if successful. Except for the HTGR, which might now be called an intermediate converter,** the AEC's advanced converter developmental program was reduced to one concept in 1965: a concept which combined the heavy-water-moderator and organic-coolant technologies and was identified as the HWOCR.[8] The program was to be conducted for the AEC by Atomics International, a division of North American Aviation, and Combustion Engineering, and was to make use of certain Canadian facilities. A supporting HWOCR thorium-fuel-cycle development program was being carried out by Babcock and Wilcox Company.[9] Bringing in Combustion Engineering and Babcock and Wilcox was a further attempt on the part of the AEC to broaden the competitive base of the industry. The HTGR and HWOCR concepts continued to be the main developmental thrust of the AEC's advanced converter reactor program in 1966.

In 1967, the AEC published a supplement to the 1962 report to the president. While it stated that the objectives expressed in the 1962 report were still regarded as valid, it went on to say that the commission was conducting a "series of comprehensive reviews and assessments of reactor concepts." [10] Also at that time, the AEC declared that further government assistance to the development of light-water reactors under the demonstration program was not planned. The HWOCR program was also eliminated, leaving only the HTGR and the breeders as reactor developments still supported by the government. The AEC did, however, continue to support until about 1970 the joint U.S.-Euratom light-water reactor research and development on plutonium utilization in thermal reactors.[11] Also, light-water reactor safety and waste management still receive substantial support from the government.

ACCEPTANCE AND GROWTH OF COMMERCIAL NUCLEAR POWER

Despite the fact that nuclear technology represents a marked shift from the technology previously employed by the utility industry and that there has been much controversy surrounding its use, the nuclear reactor is rapidly gaining a major foothold in the field of electric power generation. A large industry is de-

---

* The reasons that the seed-blanket reactor has not been constructed are discussed in Chapter IV, in the section on the Pressurized-Water Reactor.

** Its conversion ratio had been projected to be 0.90 to 0.95, but is now closer to 0.80.

veloping to supply the equipment, materials, and services to maintain and expand this industry. Utilities are obtaining, at a rapidly increasing rate, badly needed operating data for demonstrating to the public and critics that reactors can be operated safely. One catastrophic accident would be a severe setback to the industry or might possibly destroy it, and could potentially do great harm to the public. The industry needs to demonstrate and establish firmly that the current reactors are safe, reliable, and competitive before it introduces a substantially different reactor concept. In that regard, the AEC's termination of its advanced converter reactors employing substantially different concepts was viewed favorably by some in industry. The following sections will discuss the nature of the industry, product acceptability, and product reliability.

THE NUCLEAR INDUSTRY

The industry consists of two major components: the suppliers of equipment, materials, and services; and the users—the electric utilities. It is a rapidly expanding industry, which is projected to be the major supplier of the nation's electrical energy requirements in the future. In addition to the projection that nuclear power will be an increasing fraction of the energy source for electrical generation, electrical generation will become a larger fraction of the total energy needs in the future, which in turn are themselves projected to continue to rise. The Federal Power Commission (FPC) points out that generation of electricity used about one fourth of the total energy consumed in the United States in 1970. The FPC expects this to be about one third by 1980, and to be approaching one half by 1990.[12] The FPC projects that total energy requirements for the nation will approximately double by 1990 and that nuclear plants will supply about one fourth of that total (50 percent of electrical power). This increase will require that nuclear additions to the utility systems in the 1970's equal fossil-fueled additions, and that they be about twice fossil-fueled plant additions in the 1980's.

This is very rapid expansion for a new, capital-intensive industry. Assuming that the environmental and safety issues can be resolved satisfactorily, some officials see two significant constraints on the ability of industry to absorb this rapid expansion: availability of trained manpower and availability of the large capital funds required. Eventually another constraint might be the availability of uranium ore, using environmentally acceptable mining techniques, at acceptable costs.

Reactor Industry

Initially, the major cost of the nuclear industry is plant construction. In 1971 the AEC projected that installed nuclear capacity would be approximately 300,000 Mw_e by 1985.* [13] Based on the 1971 projection, the cumulative

---

* In 1974, the AEC forecast for 1985 was revised downward to a range from 230,000 Mw_e.[14] The same AEC study forecast a foreign installed capacity for 1985 ranging from 290,000 Mw_e to 420,000 Mw_e.[15]

power-plant costs in the United States were expected to be about \$105 billion up to 1985, at which time the annual expenditures will be approximately \$11 billion.[16] Although the total costs for the power plants are quite high, the nuclear steam supply system (NSSS) makes up less than 8 percent of these costs, as shown in Table 16. It is seen from the table that the major costs are involved with construction, materials, labor, architect-engineers, construction cost escalation, and interest during construction. The last two items, escalation and interest during construction, account for almost 50 percent of the costs, and thus create an incentive for reducing the lead time for licensing and constructing a nuclear power plant.

TABLE 16

1,000 Mw$_e$ NUCLEAR PLANT INVESTMENT COST
(Est. Millions of Dollars)

Cost Account	Percentage of Total	For 1981 Operation (Estimate in 1972)	For 1983 Operation (Estimate in 1974)	Percentage of Total
Nuclear steam supply system	8.9	46.3	55.4	7.7
Turbine generator unit	6.4	33.2	44.6	6.2
Construction materials and equipment	13.8	71.6	77.0	10.7
Craft labor	16.3	84.8	106.2	14.7
Professional services	8.1	42.1	47.3	6.6
Construction equipment and temporary facilities	4.9	25.5	25.5	3.5
Contingency	2.7	14.1	23.1	3.2
Escalation during construction	22.7	118.4	218.0	30.3
Interest during construction	16.2	84.1	123.0	17.1
Totals	100.0	520.1	720.1	100.0

Source: Nuclear News Buyers Guide 18, 3 (1975), p. 29.

Until 1972, the NSSS industry was made up of four reactor vendors: General Electric, Westinghouse, Combustion Engineering, and Babcock and Wilcox. GE's product is the BWR; the others produce PWR's. In 1972, Gulf-General Atomic strengthened its position and had sold seven nuclear power plants by the end of the year, all of them high-temperature, gas-cooled reactors (HTGR's). Table 17 shows the number of reactors sold by the five reactor vendors as of December 31, 1974. General Electric and Westinghouse dominate the business. This dominance can be attributed to: (1) their head start in selling commercial reactors; (2) the depth of their nuclear expertise; (3) their experience and reputation as suppliers to utilities; (4) their large corporate financial resources; and (5) their leadership in producing and selling large units.[17] In fact, because of the late entry of Combustion Engineering, Babcock and Wilcox, and Gulf-General Atomic, as well as their comparative lack of demonstrated reactor operating performance, they have been excluded from some utilities' bidders' lists. The picture could change substantially as the products of these three companies become more acceptable to the utilities; such a trend has already been made apparent by Gulf-General Atomic's penetration of the market and by Combustion Engineering's sales performance in 1973 and 1974, when their percentage of reactors sold was higher than that of previous years.

TABLE 17

NUMBER OF REACTORS SOLD, BY VENDOR, AS OF
DECEMBER 31, 1974

Vendor	Number Sold	Percentage of Total
Allis-Chalmers [a]	1	—
General Electric	73	31.9
Westinghouse	82	36.3
Babcock and Wilcox	30	13.3
Combustion Engineering	32	15.5
Gulf-General Atomic	7	3.0
Total	225 [b]	100.0

Source: Nuclear News 18, 3 (February 1975), p. 17.
[a] Allis-Chalmers no longer offers reactors for sale.
[b] The electrical generating capacity of these plants totals 221,662 Mw_e.

In 1974, however, the utility industry was beset with many financial problems and uncertainties in projections of future electric power needs stemming from the rapid rise in costs of energy. These problems prompted cancellation or postponement of not only nuclear plants but also fossil-fueled ones. More nuclear plants were canceled than fossil because of the higher capital costs, greater lead time, and greater uncertainties in the licensing process. Even in view of these problems, twenty-two orders (or letters of intent) for a total of 26,264 Mw_e were placed in 1974. This compares with forty-six in 1973 and thirty-six in 1972. In the cutbacks, General Atomic was most severely affected. The company last to establish a commercial market, it has had all but two of its nuclear power plants canceled or delayed.[18]

When compared with the nonnuclear electric utility equipment industries, the nuclear reactor supply business appears to be at least equally competitive. Various major parts of the nonnuclear industry have historically been dominated by a few companies. General Electric and Westinghouse have long dominated the electric equipment business in such product areas as turbo-generators, transformers, and switchgear. Babcock and Wilcox and Combustion Engineering are prominent suppliers of fossil boilers and steam generators. Because these two companies supply approximately 80 percent of the fossil boilers, they have every reason to want to see these products remain in competition with nuclear equipment.[19] Thus, this factor could tend to reduce the nuclear competition but increase competition between nuclear and fossil plants.

All of the vendors had substantial AEC contracts for civilian reactor research and development, other areas of research, and government nuclear business. Two companies that participated in the AEC's Power Demonstration Reactor Program, Allis-Chalmers and Atomics International, have not established themselves in the commercial reactor market. Allis-Chalmers has dropped out and Atomics-International is now very active in the fast breeder program. Gulf-General Atomic was the only new entry in the utility equipment field. Despite the fact that the nuclear industry evolved from a highly secret, military-dominated development, and despite the fact that there was major government intervention in the development of the civilian reactor through base technology and reactor plant subsidies, the resulting reactor industry can be considered to fit the normal industry pattern from the standpoint of suppliers and users: the utilities' ownership was not changed by nuclear power, and the nuclear equipment vendors are the same companies that historically have been major suppliers to the electric utility market. Gulf-General Atomic is the exception.

Fuel-Cycle Industry

The next major cost of nuclear power is the fuel cycle. Table 18 gives the approximate distribution of the cumulative costs (except for mining costs), through 1985, associated with the components of the fuel-cycle business.

TABLE 18

CUMULATIVE NUCLEAR POWER FUEL CYCLE COSTS
THROUGH 1985
(Dollars in Billions)

Cost Component	Cost	Percent
Uranium ore concentrate	$ 6.5	28.9%
U_3O_8 conversion to UF_6	1.1	4.4
Uranium enrichment	8.5	37.8
Fuel fabrication	5.5	24.5
Fuel reprocessing	1.4	4.4
Total	$23.0	100.0%

Source: U.S., AEC, *The Nuclear Industry—1971,* p. 12.

The fuel cycle may be divided into five components. Uranium mining and processing, the first of these components, will be discussed later in this chapter in the section on "Uranium Supply and Enrichment Services." The second component, the conversion of U_3O_8 to UF_6, which is required for enriching the uranium in the diffusion plants, represents a cost of approximately $1.25 per pound of U_3O_8, in addition to the $6.00 to $8.00 for the initial U_3O8.* Two U.S. companies have the capability to conduct that conversion: Allied Chemical and Kerr-McGee.[20] Since foreign uranium is enriched in U.S. plants, it also must be converted to UF_6. Canada, the United Kingdom, and France compete

* Since these cost estimates were made, uranium oxide prices have escalated and are in the range of $15 to $25 per pound in 1975.

with the domestic facilities for the conversion business. In 1971, 24 percent of the normal uranium delivered to the diffusion plants was converted to UF_6 in foreign facilities.[21] The cumulative total cost through 1985 for UF_6 conversion is $1.075 billion for domestic fuel and $887 million for foreign.

The third component of the fuel cycle, uranium enrichment, will also be discussed later, in the section on "Uranium Supply and Enrichment Services." The fourth component is fuel fabrication. In 1974, the initial fuel for the reactor, which is supplied by the reactor vendor, made up almost all of the market. In the long term, however, the major fuel business will be supplying reload cores. After a reactor has gone into operation, approximately one fourth to one third of reactor fuel is replaced annually. In addition to the four light-water reactor vendors, there are three independent competitors for the fuel-fabrication business: a joint venture between Gulf Oil and United Nuclear; Nuclear Fuel Services; and Exxon Nuclear. Another company, Kerr-McGee, has large uranium holdings and supplies UO_2 pellets for the fuel, but has not yet decided to enter the fuel design and fabrication business. Except for the reactor vendors, the other competitors are associated with large oil companies who are establishing a position in the broader energy supply field.

As shown in Table 18, cumulative U.S. requirements for power reactor fuel fabrication are projected to total $5.5 billion by 1985, at an annual rate of approximately $700 million.[22] In 1985 the cost of replacement fuel will be almost twice the initial fuel business.

The last major part of the fuel cycle, irradiated fuel reprocessing, remains a small part of the total nuclear business, but with the operation of a substantial number of power plants (fifty-five at beginning of 1975), an appreciable amount of the spent fuel is being generated. By 1985 this market is projected to be about $250 million annually and will have a cumulative total of $1.4 billion.[23] However, considerable uncertainty in the availability of reprocessing facilities exists in 1975. The first facility is the Nuclear Fuel Services plant, located in New York. Constructed and operated for reprocessing of spent fuel, it has been shut down for modification and is not likely to be back on line until 1979.[24] The General Electric plant in Morris, Illinois, after being essentially completed, was determined to have process deficiencies. There has been no public announcement as to whether GE will make the costly modifications necessary to correct the deficiencies, but it is not likely that the facility could be available within five years in any event. The third facility under construction, located in South Carolina, is owned by Allied-Gulf Nuclear Services; although it has been delayed, it is likely to be placed in operation before the others are available.

It is possible that government-owned facilities could be used for fuel reprocessing. On May 20, 1971, the AEC announced plans to permit interested industrial companies to conduct feasibility studies on the commercial value of the Richland, Washington, Purex plant. This plant was built to reprocess fuel for weapons materials and was scheduled to be phased out in 1974.[25] Exxon Nuclear is actively studying the reprocessing area and has accepted the AEC's invitation to investigate the use of the Purex facility.[26] The AEC terminated its receipt of light-water reactor fuel for reprocessing as of January 1, 1971. It continued to process government fuel, however. The government will receive and process fuels from research and test reactors and other power reactors (HTGR's) through December 31, 1977.[27] In addition, Gulf-General Atomic is working with the AEC to develop the technology for uranium-thorium reprocessing and for refabrication of the HTGR fuels.

A wide range of other nuclear service-type activities is performed by industry; these include waste management, radiation dosimeter services, management of contaminated laundry, transportation, whole body counting, reactor servicing, decontamination, and reactor irradiation services.[28] Except for waste management, these services are performed by private companies. The government will probably remain the custodian of radioactive waste for the foreseeable future. Industry will pay the government a single fee designed to cover all costs of disposal and perpetual surveillance.[29] The cost is estimated to increase power cost by 0.03 to 0.05 mills per kilowatt hour, approximately one half of one percent.

PRODUCT ACCEPTANCE

Product acceptance can be most definitively measured by assessing the extent to which nuclear reactors are being purchased by the electric utility industry. The primary and essentially the only competitors of the nuclear power plant are the fossil-fueled plants, ones that burn coal, oil, or gas. In making a choice among the various power plant types, several factors must be taken into consideration. These include economics, environmental suitability, and the lead time required to put a power plant on line. Because of the long lead time and recent delays in constructing and licensing nuclear plants, utilities have gone in some instances to alternative solutions in order to reduce the risk of "brownouts." Even though power costs are considerably more, gas-turbine-driven generators that can be put on line in eighteen months, compared with five to seven years for coal or oil plants and seven to nine years for nuclear plants, have served the purpose of avoiding power shortages, although they are used primarily as peaking-plants. Even the large-base-load fossil plants are sometimes selected over nuclear plants on the basis of shorter lead time and lack of licensing uncertainties.

Two problems have contributed to the extended lead time required for nuclear plants: delays in construction and power plant licensing. Both have become a major cost factor in the construction of nuclear plants. As seen in Table 16, according to current estimates, the costs of escalation and interest during construction represent almost 50 percent of the total power plant cost. However, with the rapid rise in cost of fossil fuels because of environmental constraints (for example, low-sulfur fuel requirements) and because of the tightening of the supply/demand picture, nuclear power remains competitive despite the significant increase in plant costs.

In 1974, nuclear plants were producing electricity that was substantially cheaper than that produced by the fossil-fuel plants. According to a study by the Atomic Industrial Forum (AIF), twenty-one United States utilities produced electricity from nuclear power at an average cost, including capital costs and fuel, of 10.52 mills per kilowatt hour (mills/kwh), compared with fossil-fuel plant costs of 17.03 mills/kwh.[30] Fuel cost alone was 2.15 mills/kwh for nuclear compared with 11.25 mills/kwh for fossil fuels (up 77 percent from 6.35 mills/kwh in 1973). Northeast Utilities reported saving an estimated $106 million with nuclear plant operation in the first three quarters of 1974.[31] In 1974, there were 103,426,886 megawatt hours of nuclear electrical generation from 42 plants. Assuming an average savings of 7 mills per kwh as indicated by the AIF report, a total savings of over $700 million dollars was accrued by using nuclear energy. In addition to the 42 nuclear power plants that were operating in 1974, the United States had 183 plants under construction or on order. Assuming that the average savings from these plants will be similar to that of the 42 operating plants, the total savings to the nation could be approximately $14 billion annually. The fuel consumed by the 225 plants would be equivalent to burning 10 million barrels of oil per day—a quantity greater than the total U.S. oil production in 1974.

The reactors that are being sold in the United States are almost totally of the light-water reactor (LWR) type, either the pressurized-water reactor (PWR) or the boiling-water reactor (BWR). Recently, the high-temperature graphite reactor (HTGR) has entered the market and seven reactors of this type have been ordered.

As of December 31, 1974, most of the 225 U.S. nuclear power plants that were operable, under construction, or on order (see Tables 17 and 19) had a capacity of 800 Mw_e or higher. The total capacity of the 225 plants was 221,662

TABLE 19

GEOGRAPHICAL DISTRIBUTION OF OPERATING OR PLANNED
NUCLEAR POWER PLANTS AS OF DECEMBER 31, 1974

Region	Total Number of Units
Northeast	59
Midwest	53
South	81
Southwest	13
West and Northwest	19
Totals	225

Source: Nuclear News 18, 3 (February 1975), p. 51.

Mw$_e$, an average power level per reactor of almost 1,000 Mw$_e$. The acceptability of these large reactor sizes on utility electric distribution grids has been a significant factor in making nuclear plants competitive. Since plant costs are higher and fuel costs are lower for nuclear than for fossil plants, the nuclear plant becomes competitive only when it is large enough to produce comparatively high levels of power. As most recent utility purchases have been for between 1,000 and 1,200 Mw$_e$, with some approaching 1,300 Mw$_e$, the building and operation of the large-scale nuclear plants have been both justified and economically feasible.

The fact that large-scale nuclear systems are required in order to compete with fossil plants could be considered a negative factor in the utilization of these plants. It is true that for such large units to be acceptable, a utility system must itself be sufficiently large to handle the outage of one or more such units. In many areas of the country this problem is considerably mitigated by high-voltage-line interties and by the need to supply large demands.

Although small utilities are not likely to purchase large reactors, they are protected from unfair competition by features of the antitrust laws and by amendments to the Atomic Energy Act of 1954.[32] For example, in many states the antitrust laws provide that surrounding utilities can compete for supplying bulk electricity to a small utility even if the transmission intertie is owned by a single company. In the case of a nuclear reactor, review is required by the Department of Justice to determine "whether the activities under the license would create or maintain a situation inconsistent with the antitrust laws" before a license can be granted by the AEC.[33] This legislative requirement protects the smaller companies and allows them to reap the benefits of nuclear reactors and their economy of scale. In view of the licensing requirements, companies constructing large nuclear plants have entered into "procompetition arrangements" with other bulk power suppliers, including access to the nuclear units, coordination and sharing of reserves, unit power sales and purchases that would reduce costs for the parties, and transmission services using their facilities.[34]

At one time, economics would have been the most significant measure of product acceptability. More recently, however, the nation has become concerned with environmental and safety factors in our technological society, and therefore evaluation of a product or project must include assessment of these parameters. This important aspect of product acceptance is discussed in Chapter VI.

OPERATING RELIABILITY OF THE PRODUCT

No general survey of utilities that own reactors was made in order to obtain data on the subject of reactor reliability. Reliability is discussed here in terms of availability of the reactor as a power producer. Since there has never been a malfunction or accident inflicting personal injury due to nuclear causes, there exist no experimental data on this issue. The current period is one in which new power plants are coming on line frequently, but in which the total number in operation for several years is small; therefore, sustained reliability has not been demonstrated by a large number of reactors operating over a long period.

Several recent articles have discussed reliability and have indicated a mixed picture in terms of success. In a *Wall Street Journal* article, Louis Roddis, president of Consolidated Edison Company, was quoted as stating that "the 18 longest-running U.S. nuclear power plants averaged only 61.9 percent of their potential output through last September 30. Four came close to 80 percent, but three of these subsequently broke down. Eight of the 18 were delivering about 50 percent of the power they were theoretically capable of." [35] The article points out that utilities generally had assumed 80 percent reliable delivery in economic studies on plant selection. The article also quoted Virginia Electric Company as saying that "its latest coal-fired plant delivers only about 50 percent of its potential power." The two largest reactor vendors, General Electric and Westinghouse, indicated that their "nuclear plants perform as 'good or better than' comparable sized conventional units." This has also been the experience of Commonwealth Edison Company with two large plants, one nuclear and one coal fired, put on line in 1972.

In a rebuttal to the *Wall Street Journal* article, the Atomic Industrial Forum (AIF) presented some additional data. [36] It quoted Lelan F. Sillin, president and chairman of Northeast Utilities, who said:

> Despite the four-month down time associated with the outage of Millstone Unit 1 (a reactor extensively discussed in the article), the cost of electricity it produced in 1972 was about 8.5 mills per kilowatt hour. This includes all fixed charges and fuel costs. In our fossil plants the comparable costs were about 11 mills per kilowatt hour. Furthermore, the Millstone unit had generated in excess of 7 billion kilowatt hours of electricity prior to the shut-down and for a large new generating unit it performed well during the first 21 months of its operation. [37]

The AIF article stated that the Connecticut Yankee reactor, in its sixth year of operation, is the "lowest-cost producer of base load electric power in New England—about 5.4 mills per kilowatt hour." The plant availability factor during the last five years was given as 81 percent. This reactor also holds the world record for total electric energy generated—over 23 billion kilowatt hours. It is a 600 Mw$_e$ station.

The AIF article also gave some performance data it had collected. These data showed that from June 1 to September 30, 1972, nineteen nuclear plants reported an average reactor availability of 83 percent and a total plant availability of 78 percent, and from October 1 to December 31, 1972, twenty-one plants reported reactor availability of 73 percent and plant availability of 69 percent. The fact that plant availability is lower than reactor availability indicates that some nonnuclear problems are more serious than nuclear ones.

Commonwealth Edison Company gives an additional perspective to the reliability comparison. In 1973 Commonwealth operated about 20 percent of the nuclear capacity in the United States. In a letter to the editor of the *Wall Street*

Journal, the company's representative stated, "Our four big nuclear units rang up a 69 percent operating rate during the six months ended March." [38] This was a higher operating rate than that of their fossil plants. However, because of customer peak-to-average load demand, "all of our base load units (nuclear and fossil) tend to operate in the rough general area of 50 percent to 60 percent today." From September 1972 to February 1973, Commonwealth's four large fossil plants averaged 74 percent availability, and its four largest nuclear plants averaged 82 percent. These figures do not include the company's oldest and smallest (210 Mw$_e$) nuclear plant, Dresden 1, which had an availability record of 95 percent during this period.

The AIF article also quoted a 1972 American Nuclear Society review of operating experience: "Over the past four years, power reactor availability for the 100 Mw$_e$ and larger plants has ranged on an industry basis from 75 percent to 86 percent, with an average four-year availability of 81 percent."

In these comparisons, a point of confusion could arise: the low figures quoted by the *Wall Street Journal* were based on percent operation of theoretical capacity, while the industry figures were based on time availability. Both could be misleading. It is unknown, for example, how much the reactors were operated or available at power levels below rated capacity and how long the plants sat idle when actually available. The availability figure should be a better indication of reliability than the actual percent operation of the plant's theoretical capability. The Nuclear Regulatory Commission reported that the forty-two plants operating in 1974 were producing electricity 68.5 percent of the time. [39] The availability factor for December 1974 was reported to be 72.7 percent.

In any event, there have definitely been problems of reliability; some are common to large plants generally and others specifically to nuclear plants. It has been only recently that utilities were able to use large (500 to 1,000 Mw$_e$) plants of any kind on their systems. In the case of nuclear plants, reactor power densities and fuel life requirements in new plant designs are significantly higher than in earlier reactors, and are consequently not supported by extensive experience. Fuel quality has plagued a number of reactors and industry has initiated programs to solve the problems as they arise. There is a general feeling in the industry that a period of consolidation and demonstration is needed before the technology is pushed further. Bertram Wolfe, of General Electric, looks for better operating performance, higher than 70 percent to 80 percent, but stresses the need for feedback from operating experience. [40]

The AEC has taken specific actions to limit the size of licensable reactors to no more than 1,300 Mw$_e$, and has also proposed changes in the 1971 "Interim Acceptance Criteria for Emergency Core-Cooling Systems" that could cause an average derating of total nuclear generating capacity in the United States by about 5 percent. [41] If these changes were to be implemented, the AEC estimates that it would take about two and one half years to redesign the fuel and make other plant modifications necessary to permit affected plants to resume full-power operation.

THE WEANING OF THE INDUSTRY—PRIVATE
OWNERSHIP OF NUCLEAR FUELS

Although commercial breakthrough for nuclear power occurred in 1963, the government still retained a monopoly on the nuclear fuels necessary for operating the plants. Fuels were available to industry only through leasing arrangements with the AEC. Many interest groups believed the time had come to allow private ownership of the nuclear fuels so as to bring into play traditional marketplace forces and to eliminate a potential major subsidy from government to industry through the lease charges.

THE NEED FOR LEGISLATION

Neither the 1946 Act nor the 1954 Act allowed private ownership of special nuclear materials. The 1946 Act clearly stipulated that all fissionable materials be the property of the commission. There were several reasons for this tight control of fissionable material. Atomic energy was born as a weapon and the control of its frightfully destructive power was paramount. Little had been accomplished in developing peaceful uses and the uranium supply was scarce. A major hope of the government in the postwar era was that atomic energy would come under international control, and that mandatory government ownership of all fissionable material would provide a firmer position for accomplishing this goal.

By 1954, several important aspects of the situation had changed. International control of atomic energy had not been accomplished and the United States no longer had a world monopoly. Moreover, the U.S.S.R. had developed the atomic bomb and other countries were developing their own nuclear capabilities.

There were also several changes in peaceful developments. Several research and prototype reactors had been constructed. Although still in short supply, uranium availability was no longer an acute problem. In addition, industry had become considerably involved in the commission's programs and had gained greater insight into nuclear developments.

The 1954 Act provided a transition between a largely military operation and the complete opening of the door to peaceful developments. It moved closer to full private ownership by permitting private persons, under license from the AEC, to own and operate nuclear reactors and other facilities intended to produce and utilize special nuclear materials. It also permitted a greater degree of cooperation with our allies in the peaceful and military uses of atomic energy, and called for freer access to scientific and technical aspects of atomic energy. The requirement for mandatory government ownership of special nuclear materials was "retained by the Congress out of an abundance of caution rather than legal necessity." [42] Clandestine use of these materials was and still is a concern.

By 1963, great strides had been made in developing civilian nuclear power.

Through the AEC's Experimental Reactors Program and the Power Demonstration Reactor Program, the technology had been demonstrated and a close cooperative arrangement between industry and government had been developed. In addition, uranium was no longer in short supply. With the advent of commercial nuclear power appearing close at hand, the commission considered it an appropriate and opportune time to take the next major step in turning the nuclear business over to private enterprise.

THE AEC PROPOSES PRIVATE OWNERSHIP OF NUCLEAR FUEL

After discussion with groups concerned with the nuclear and electric utility industries, the commission concluded that it would be desirable to permit private ownership of nuclear fuels, provided that there was an adequate transition period between total government ownership and full private ownership. On March 15, 1963, the AEC submitted to Congress an amendment to the Atomic Energy Act of 1954 to allow private ownership; if passed, the amendment would:

1. Maintain government authority to control special nuclear material, as well as other materials and facilities under its jurisdiction.

2. Allow the AEC to provide, for a fee, enrichment services to domestic and foreign customers supplying their own uranium.

3. Make available services for reenriching depleted or enriched uranium recovered from irradiated fuels.

4. Repeal Section 52 of the 1954 Act, which stated: "All rights, title, and interest in and to any special nuclear material within or under the jurisdiction of the United States, now or hereafter produced, shall be the property of the United States and shall be administered and controlled by the Commission as agent of and on behalf of the United States by virtue of this Act." [43] Thus, private ownership of special nuclear materials was to be allowed.

The AEC expected the proposed legislation to have the following effects:

1. To avoid continued distortion of technology that had resulted from the policy of leasing rather than selling enriched uranium, and thus to put the power reactor business on a sounder long-term basis.

2. To allow and eventually to require utilities to obtain nuclear fuels under more nearly the same economic conditions that apply to other fuels, and thus to permit a more realistic comparison of commercial aspects of nuclear and conventional power.

3. Eventually to reduce, and then to eliminate, the AEC's investment in nuclear fuels used by utilities, which otherwise would grow to a multibillion-dollar investment.

4. To provide a guaranteed purchase price for plutonium and U-233 based on the AEC evaluation of their worth for power reactors, rather than maintaining the higher price based on weapons value. Accordingly, when the guaranteed fair price of $30 per gram expired on June 30, 1963, an interim price of $10 per gram of fissile plutonium was established by the AEC. The buy-back

period was to remain in effect only during the time required to develop and demonstrate power reactor utilization of these materials.

5. To authorize the AEC to enter into agreement with licensees for such periods of time as the commission deemed necessary or desirable for the enrichment of uranium owned by such licensees (toll enrichment), thereby encouraging a commercial market for uranium ore. The same services could be provided for foreign-owned uranium under an agreement for cooperation.

6. To require private ownership of nuclear fuels by July 1, 1973. The AEC estimated that for privately owned utilities, private ownership of fuels might increase power costs by 0.2 to 0.4 mills per kilowatt hour. The interim period would allow power reactor owners time to reduce the effect of this increase through other actions. The AEC stated, "The availability of enrichment services and the enlarged opportunity for operation of the competitive forces of private enterprise are expected to neutralize this effect in the 1970's." [44]

THE JCAE HEARINGS ON THE PROPOSED LEGISLATION

The private ownership legislation was introduced in Congress by Senator Pastore (S 1160) and Representative Holifield (HR 5035). Hearings were held by the JCAE in the summer of 1963 and again in June 1964. The key issues in the hearings were:

- The date of mandatory private ownership of uranium.
- Guaranteed AEC buy-back of plutonium and U-233.
- Importation and enrichment of foreign uranium.
- The terms and conditions of toll enrichment of uranium.

The interested industry parties testifying on the legislation were the reactor manufacturers, public and private utilities, nuclear fuel suppliers, uranium ore suppliers, and the coal industry. Other segments of industry, such as the oil and gas industry, did not participate in the hearing. Generally, the coal industry and its associated unions have been the most active of the "outsiders" in atomic energy legislation affecting electric power. A number of participating companies had overlapping interests; for example, reactor vendors or ore suppliers are in some cases also fuel suppliers.

Although there were a few instances of substantial disagreement, the industry generally agreed that the proposed legislation would be favorable. The major exception to the favorable response came from the AFL-CIO representative, Andrew J. Biemiller, director of the Department of Legislation. The AFL-CIO represented more than two thirds of the organized workers at AEC installations. Mr. Biemiller reiterated a position taken by the AFL-CIO in 1961: "We most strongly oppose the proposal by the Commission to amend the 1954 Atomic Energy Act to allow the Federal Government to divest itself of ownership of special nuclear material—the fuel of atomic powerplants—and pass the ownership to monopoly and large business." [45]

The AFL-CIO was not opposed to nuclear power, and in fact supported more rapid development. Nonetheless, the unions were quite concerned over a number of events affecting employment in the industry. First, they saw that top priority had been given to the space program by President Kennedy and that the "role of the atom in America's energy future is now relegated to the indefinite future file, the 'when and if' file of the President's scientific advisor." [46] Second, they were aware of AEC considerations to cut back weapons materials production severely. They were also concerned about possible negative effects of the legislation, such as a delay in the rapid introduction of nuclear power as a result of the higher costs of nuclear energy regulation and control of the materials; detrimental effects on small fuel fabricators and the monopolistic implications of those effects; and monopolistic pricing practices. In summary, the AFL-CIO's stated position was that it opposed the legislation proposals for two reasons: "because they endanger public ownership and public control and because they will assist and encourage big business monopoly." [47]

Other objections to the legislation were in regard to specifics and not against private ownership *per se*. Senator Thruston Morton (D., Kentucky) introduced a bill, S 2635, which differed from S 1160 and HR 5035 in two substantial ways.[48] First, it required private ownership of special nuclear materials upon enactment of the legislation; and second, it terminated guaranteed purchase by the government of plutonium and other byproducts from nuclear reactors. Senator Morton pointed out that the purchase of the Oyster Creek plant by Jersey Central Power Company was decided on a competitive basis, with coal selling at 26 cents per million Btu's. He argued that the average price of coal in 1963 was more than twenty-six cents in twenty-six states, and less in only sixteen states. He concluded, therefore, that since nuclear power was already competitive with coal, "there is no valid reason that henceforth the civilian nuclear power industry should be further coddled and nourished by the taxpayers of the Nation." Senator Morton also agreed with the AEC's revised position, which banned toll enrichment of foreign-purchased uranium to be used in domestic reactors until 1975, and he urged a careful look at the situation after that date.

In the long run, the AEC-supported bill would accomplish what Senator Morton was proposing, but it also provided a transition period. In addition, the AEC had early in 1964 received a proposal for a "spectral shift reactor" and had made a public announcement calling for proposals for design, construction, and operation of four advanced converter reactor concepts under the Power Demonstration Reactor Program, which provided governmental assistance in the form of the waiver of certain fuel costs. Senator Morton's bill would not permit this unless contracts were signed before the bill was passed. The AEC stated that "if S 2635 were enacted prior to the execution of contracts for such projects, the extra cost to the reactor operators arising out of the necessity for purchasing the reactor fuel could amount to 0.2 to 0.4 mills per kilowatt hour (even without considering any factor for waiver of use charges or payments for special nuclear materials produced in the reactors)." [49] The AEC believed this would have an adverse effect on its advanced converter reactor program.

The coal industry's interests were represented by Brice O'Brien, general counsel, National Coal Association (NCA), and by Joseph E. Moody, president, and George Weil, atomic consultant, National Coal Policy Conference, Inc. (NCPC). NCA's and NCPC's views were fully reflected in Senator Morton's S 2635; Kentucky is, after all, a major coal-producing state. Morton, in his testimony, had specifically endorsed the "official policy statement of the coal industry in regard to nuclear power." O'Brien's and Moody's testimonies were complementary. The positions of the two organizations can be summed up by two quotes from Moody's testimony. Mr. Moody stated, "I would like to emphasize that NCPC fully endorses Mr. O'Brien's contention that the Federal Government's guaranteed repurchase of plutonium, particularly that produced in reactors used to generate commercial power, should be ended immediately. . . . Mr. Chairman, there is no valid reason for any delay in making private ownership of all special nuclear material mandatory immediately upon enactment of this legislation." [50] The NCPC agreed with the AIF (Atomic Industrial Forum) that the AEC should toll enrich foreign uranium for use in domestic reactors only to the extent that it would not threaten preservation of the domestic uranium industry, but the NCPC took a much stronger position on this issue. Moody stated, "We think it is clearly not in the national interest, both from the economic and a security standpoint, to permit free or excessive imports of oil or gas, either by tanker or pipeline, of electric energy and of uranium, natural or enriched." [51]

In testimony at the 1963 hearings, Mr. Stephen Dunn, then president of NCA, pointed out that the lease-buy option increased the subsidy to Rural Electrification Administration (REA) utility groups without diminishing the subsidy to investor-owned utilities.[52] Since REA had government funds available at 2 percent interest, they would likely buy the uranium during the transition period, while the investor-owned utilities would likely lease the uranium at the favorable government interest rate of 4¾ percent, a figure substantially below the "customary commercial burden of carrying charges ranging from 10 to 15 percent." This low interest rate was estimated to reduce private utility generating costs by 0.50 to 0.98 mills per kilowatt hour. Therefore, it was expected that both private utilities and the REA would favor the proposed bill.

The utilities were in favor of the bill, and while they recognized the higher potential costs, they also were anxious for private ownership of nuclear materials so as to permit the competitive forces of the free market to come into play; they also felt that the legislation would remove one of the major uncertainties about future power costs.[53] The two major industry associations, the AIF and Edison Electric Institute (EEI) were likewise in favor of the proposed legislation.

The testimony by Sherman R. Knapp, president of Connecticut Yankee Power Company, is representative of the views of the private utilities. He stated his emphatic support both of the bill and of the position taken by the Edison Electric Institute and the Atomic Industrial Forum.[54] He thought the time had come to resolve the problems existing in the area, and proposed private ownership in the development of advanced reactor types; he felt that government subsidies in this area could be provided in some other way. His company was at that time receiving substantial government subsidy for the Connecticut Yankee power plant, a 490 Mw_e PWR, a subsidy which he stated to be "for design assistance up to a maximum of $6,050,000 and a waiver-of-use charge which is presently estimated at $7,145,000." [55] The waiver-of-use charge was to terminate in April 1972.

The spokesman for Consolidated Edison Company, M. L. Warning, senior vice-president, was even more specific, particularly concerning imports. He testified that, "from our standpoint, we do not believe there should be restrictions imposed on the importation of either foreign uranium concentrates or foreign-enriched uranium. Complete flexibility to purchase from whichever supplier can best meet the utility's nuclear fuel needs should result in maximum competition at lowest practicable prices." [56]

The import issue was probably the most controversial of all the bill's provisions. There were two questions: (1) could foreign uranium be enriched in the U.S. diffusion plants? and (2) could foreign ore be used in domestic power plants? The AEC had stated that its intent was not to allow foreign uranium to be used in U.S. reactors before July 1, 1973 (revised later to 1975), but that it would provide enrichment services for import uranium that would be reexported. This latter provision was very crucial to the U.S. reactor manufacturers. Enrichment of foreign uranium for foreign consumption was aimed at accomplishing two goals: encouraging the construction of U.S.-type enriched uranium reactors in foreign countries; and providing foreign countries that have a supply of U_3O_8 with the chance to enrich their concentrate for ultimate use within their own country, thus improving their balance of payment with the United States. The United Kingdom and the U.S.S.R. were potential competitors for providing enrichment services and for supplying nuclear power plants. The position taken by the AEC with regard to import and utilization of foreign ore was aimed not only at helping the U.S. ore and reactor manufacturing industries, but also at aiding the U.S. balance-of-payment problem. In 1974, ERDA announced plans to gradually lift the uranium embargo, starting in 1977; the embargo is to be totally lifted by 1984.[57]

The disposition of the AEC's large uranium stockpile was also seen as a major question in regard to imports. This uranium had been purchased at $8 per pound of U_3O_8, whereas the market at that time was closer to $6 per pound. Also, the AEC had agreements to continue to purchase reduced quantities of uranium at reduced prices from the domestic ore industry until 1968. During this transition period, the commercial requirements would hopefully grow and help fill the gap in demand. There was fear that foreign ore would be dumped on the U.S. market at low prices during this period of a "soft" market. This concern is illustrated in the testimony of D. A. McGee, president of the Kerr-McGee Oil Company, a large holder of domestic uranium ore. He felt that the government should "not permit substantial importation of foreign uranium, except for re-export, until such time as the AEC determines that the domestic market has grown sufficiently to support a competitive domestic industry, taking into account the ability of the domestic market to absorb, in addition to supplies from private domestic sources, any excess AEC inventory." [58] One small domestic uranium ore company testified that it believed it could compete with foreign ore, but asked only that the government defer unloading its stockpile.

THE JCAE-SPONSORED BILL

In an attempt to satisfy both interest groups—the holders of domestic ore as well as the utilities—the JCAE retained the enrichment of foreign ore for reexport in the AEC's proposal, but it proposed that toll enrichment of uranium of foreign origin for domestic use would not be permitted until after July 1, 1975.

The bill sponsored by the JCAE differed from the original AEC proposal in the following ways:

1. The commission was prevented from distributing special nuclear materials except by sale (i.e., not by lease) after December 31, 1970. The AEC had proposed that it be permitted to distribute the material by sale, lease, and lease with option to buy until 1973. The new provision shortened the period during which the AEC could lease its uranium, a change that helped the ore industry. The date to terminate all uranium lease arrangements for power reactors remained as proposed, June 30, 1973, unless otherwise authorized by Congress.

2. Under the original 1954 Act, the AEC was required to pay a fair price for all special nuclear materials produced in nuclear reactors, since the AEC had the sole right to own such material. In the 1964 JCAE-proposed bill, the AEC was authorized to purchase plutonium produced in reactors licensed under section 104 of the 1954 Act. Reactors licensed under this section are for research and development. The AEC was not authorized under the amendment to purchase plutonium produced in reactors licensed under Section 103, commercial reactors. In the JCAE's view, such a reactor "should by definition, 'stand on its own feet' as a commercial enterprise." [59] The original AEC-proposed bill would have authorized AEC to establish guaranteed buy-back prices from both types of reactors. However, at that time no reactors were licensed under section 103, since a finding of "practical value" of the reactors, which was required for such licensing, had not been made. The commission was at that time considering such findings for the light-water reactors, which were starting to be sold on a commercial basis.

3. The AEC had proposed the option of buying back all special nuclear materials produced in a nuclear reactor for a period up to seven years.[60] The JCAE separated the time periods for plutonium and U-233 buy-back, the guaranteed buy-back period of the former extending until January 1, 1971, and that of the latter lasting a maximum of ten years. In addition, the JCAE limited the materials to be purchased to those produced from utilization of AEC uranium, either from lease or sale. This limitation gave industry some incentive to use AEC

uranium, and did not require the government to buy plutonium and U-233 produced from privately owned special nuclear material.

4. The joint committee required that proposed guaranteed purchase price and periods for special nuclear material, as well as criteria for waiver of any use charge, be submitted to the JCAE, and that a period of forty-five days elapse while Congress is in session before putting these in effect. The JCAE could, however, by resolution in writing, waive these conditions. Thus, the JCAE maintained control of the AEC's actions in these matters.

5. The AEC proposed that toll enrichment services commence immediately on enactment of legislation. The final bill stated that toll enrichment services for privately owned uranium would not be allowed until after December 31, 1968. This delay would allow the AEC to dispose of a part of its uranium stockpile. The joint committee also specified that the commission, taking into consideration the desired viability of the domestic uranium industry, would not provide toll enrichment of foreign uranium for domestic use without submitting the criteria for such action to the JCAE for the forty-five-day review period. This constraint also applied to charges to be made for all toll enrichment services. The AEC charges were to be sufficient to assure reasonable compensation to the government.

6. The commission's bill would have required mandatory private ownership of material intended for use in facilities licensed under section 103 or 104. The final bill applied the requirement only to those persons possessing or operating a nuclear reactor, if the material is intended for use in such reactor. This modification allowed the AEC to continue leasing special nuclear material to persons engaged in conversion or fabrication of such material. This provision was in response to a problem, brought out during the hearings, involving the small fuel processors, who might not have had sufficient capital for the material inventory required by private ownership.[61]

ENACTMENT OF THE LEGISLATION

The bill passed in the Senate without discussion. The identical bill was introduced in the House by Representative Holifield. Several congressmen rose to give support to the bill, praising the JCAE and particularly Congressman Holifield for the fine work that had been done in formulating the bill.

Representative Jack Westland, from the state of Washington, stated, "This is truly enlightened legislation. In an era where the trend is toward increasing the Government's role in business, here we have a striking example of a step in the other direction. . . . Mr. Speaker, S 3075 is a triumph of good sense and vision. It will assure that nuclear power will take its rightful place in our free enterprise economy." [62]

Representative John Anderson of Illinois summarized the significant features of the bill and spoke in favor of it, calling it

a rare bill in this day and age of expanding Federal power and authority. . . . It sets an example which could be well followed in other fields.

For the taxpayer, S 3075 means freedom from the heavy responsibility of financing a multibillion dollar nuclear fuel inventory.

For the utility company, it means a new ability to make long-term commitments for nuclear fuel under economic conditions comparable to alternate sources of energy.

For the uranium industry, we will open a new range of commercial dealings in uranium and eliminate the complete dependence of this industry on U.S. Government contracts.

In the international area, this bill creates new opportunities to improve our balance of trade by encouraging the sale abroad of American nuclear reactors, materials and services.[63]

Representative Thomas Morris, as a representative of New Mexico, one of the major uranium-producing states, stated,

I am particularly pleased with the careful attention which has been given to the problems of the domestic uranium industry by this committee. Although our uranium industry has a guaranteed market from the Government through 1970, the prospects after 1970 depend, almost entirely on the civilian nuclear power market. . . . I am particularly pleased that the committee has taken special care to provide protection to our domestic uranium producers against the competition of cheap foreign uranium. . . . Our uranium industry is a vital link in the national defense and security.[64]

These statements indicate that there was a genuine interest in Congress to reduce government involvement as the industry became competitive. One congressman pointed out that the two remaining subsidies, enriching service and indemnity by government, should eventually be eliminated.[65] The bill was passed by the House with little further discussion. It was then signed into law by President Johnson on August 26, 1964.

In summary, through the passage of the Private Ownership of Special Nuclear Materials Act, the government took another step in turning over the "commercial" reactor industry to private enterprise. The act's features are summarized as follows:

1. Private ownership of special nuclear materials (nuclear fuels) permitted, August 26, 1964.

2. Toll enrichment of privately owned uranium begun January 1, 1969. Enrichment of uranium for foreign countries allowed.

3. AEC distribution of power reactor fuel under lease agreement terminated December 31, 1970.

4. AEC guarantee to purchase plutonium terminated December 31, 1970. Guarantee prices for U-233 extended to ten years beyond origination of the act.

5. Private ownership of power reactor fuel made mandatory—all lease arrangements for such fuel terminated July 1, 1973.[66]

The act allowed for a substantial period for effecting a smooth transition from full government ownership to private ownership. Except for a position of caution, this action could have taken place ten years earlier, when private ownership of nuclear reactors was allowed by the 1954 Atomic Anergy Act. However, since nuclear power was not commercial during the ten years, this delay probably had little negative effect on commercial development, and did allow flexibility for government subsidies in fuel-cost waivers during the developmental period.

Generally, the government's planned actions during the transition period were well defined in the act, giving industry a firm basis for planning. Specific items that remained to be settled included the buy-back price of plutonium and U-233, toll charges, policies toward foreign uranium after 1975, and unloading of the AEC stockpile.

The act in no way reduced the responsibility and the authority of the AEC regulatory control over the possession of special nuclear materials; such regulatory control was necessary to protect the common defense and security, as well as the public health and safety. The JCAE pointed out that "the elimination of the statutory requirement for mandatory Government ownership of special nuclear material is not intended, in any way, to detract from the Commission's jurisdiction or authority under the Act to issue licenses, rules, regulations or orders to protect the public health and safety and the common defense and security, or to guard against the loss or diversion or unlawful possession and use of special nuclear material." [67] In view of the current controversy over nuclear materials safeguards, AEC retention of control is an important feature of the act.

Another important aspect of the act is that it gave domestic and foreign industries access to the government diffusion plants for toll enriching of uranium, thus providing them with the enriched uranium necessary for plants based on U.S.-developed technology. It left open the question of future ownership of these plants and ownership of additional enriching plants that will be required in the early 1980's.

Although there were substantial objections during the hearings, with opinions ranging from support of continued government monopoly of ownership and no imports to advocation of immediate private ownership and complete freedom of use of foreign uranium, the final bill as enacted differed only in relatively minor ways from that originally proposed by the AEC. Pressure groups opposing the legislation were very limited. Except for one, the AFL-CIO, all the interest groups' objections focused on details only, and not on the broader philosophical question of private versus public ownership of atomic energy resources.

URANIUM SUPPLY AND ENRICHMENT SERVICES

POSTWAR SHORTAGE OF URANIUM

In the early postwar years, uranium shortage, along with weapons production priority and secrecy, was an important deterrent to commercial reactor development. In 1947, the United States ore supply came from one mine in the then Belgian Congo and another small source in the sub-Arctic regions of Canada. [68] Even the Congo supply was controlled by the Combined Development Trust, established during World War II to allocate production among the United

States, the United Kingdom, and Canada.[69] The United States had obtained small quantities of uranium concentrates produced in vanadium mills on the Colorado plateau, but these operations had ended with the war effort.[70]

Potential shortage was somewhat relieved by an agreement with the British that the United States would receive all uranium concentrates available in 1948 and 1949 through the Combined Development Agency; this was to provide about two thousand tons of uranium concentrate annually through 1950.[71]

The Canadian supply was no more than 150 tons per year; but even though the supply from the Colorado plateau was only about 300 tons per year in 1948, additional ore bodies had been located and inferred reserves had increased sharply. Some bodies were of low grade, however, and it appeared that making uranium available in the United States at that time was more a matter of cost than of supply.[72]

David Lilienthal, chairman of the AEC, believed the problem of uranium shortage was temporary, and at a press conference in 1948 stated: "The potential of the atomic age has been sold short several times in recent weeks. Statements have been made and widely publicized, that there is only enough uranium ore to last a relatively brief period and so the prospects of benefit from atomic power must go glimmering. This is simply not so. It appears clear that atomic energy is on a sound basis for an indefinite period in the future." [73] He based his position on his knowledge of recent discoveries of ore; the belief that reserves of uranium, like those of other minerals, would increase as the need and economic incentives expanded; and his faith in the intensive and extensive AEC program for uranium discovery and production.

Since the government was encouraging uranium supply development primarily for the weapons program, another problem facing the industry, particularly the mining industry, was the question of how long there would be a market for uranium. Specifically, the mining community wanted to know how long the demand for weapons would exist and how soon uranium demands for power would be significant. Nuclear-powered ships and aircraft were under active development in the late forties and fifties; but even if these were successful, their demand for uranium would hardly match that required by the weapons program. In a speech before the Western Division of the American Mining Congress in Denver, September 25, 1952, Commissioner Smyth attempted to predict the future of uranium.[74] Smyth stated, "It is my own belief that the use of uranium for power purposes will become economically feasible before the need of uranium for military purposes begins to slack off." [75] As will be seen later in this chapter, this prediction did not quite come true.

Soon after the war, it became obvious to the AEC that a government program was required to assure an adequate supply of uranium for its weapons program in order to maintain national security. The program developed for this need and its results provided assurance to the power industry that uranium supply was not a roadblock to nuclear energy use. The gaseous diffusion plants constructed to provide enriched uranium for the weapons program also opened up the prospects of using enriched uranium in power reactors, a finding that resulted in considerably broadened reactor design choices and made the current commercial reactors possible. Meanwhile, the increased ore supply reduced the pressure to develop the breeder. Because of the importance of the uranium ore and enrichment programs to power reactor development and application, they will be described briefly in the next sections.

THE AEC'S URANIUM ORE PROGRAM

As previously discussed, it was not until 1964 that private ownership of special nuclear materials was allowed. Until that time, the government bought and owned all uranium as soon as it was mined, at prices set by the government. It was in this context that the uranium mining industry developed.

Recognizing the shortage of uranium and the United States' dependence on foreign ore, the AEC set out soon after the war to establish a program that would provide sufficient uranium for both weapons production and research needs. John Gustafson, director of the AEC's raw materials division and a mining engineer, and his staff developed plans to provide incentives for increased exploration and production by private industry, to reactivate Colorado mills at three locations, and to develop improved processes for extraction of uranium from the low-grade ore of the Colorado plateau.[76]

In connection with the first of those goals, on April 9, 1948, the AEC initiated an incentive program that offered domestic producers (1) a ten-year guaranteed minimum price for certain high-grade uranium ores or mechanical concentrates (assaying 10 percent or more by weight U_3O_8); (2) a \$10,000 bonus for the discovery and production of high-grade ore or mechanical concentrates (assaying 20 percent or more by weight U_3O_8); and (3) a guaranteed three-year minimum price for uranium-bearing carnotite-type or Roscoelite-type ores of the Colorado plateau. These offers were made to stimulate production and exploration.[77]

The government also carried out an extensive domestic exploration program between 1948 and 1955. This program consisted of airborne radiometric surveys, geological investigations, and exploration drilling.[78] These activities were conducted by the AEC's geological staff, by private contractors, and by the U.S. Geological Survey and the U.S. Bureau of Mines, under contract with the commission. The AEC's efforts in exploration were greatly curtailed in 1956 after a substantial increase in activities by private industry. In addition, the AEC constructed and operated ore-buying stations, which were later phased out,[79] and built numerous access roads to mine areas.

The need for improved ore process methods became obvious because of the low grade and chemical complexity of the domestic ore deposits. Through contractors and its own laboratories, the AEC developed new processes to reduce costs and improve recoveries.[80] The AEC terminated its process development program in 1958, and left private industry to continue to improve extraction methods as conditions warranted.

In July 1955, the AEC announced that the United States had become the world's leading producer of uranium ore.[81] Table 20 shows the rapid rise in postwar uranium production in the United States, but in 1952 the amount of uranium produced in the United States still represented less than 25 percent of the United States total procurement. By 1957, U.S. annual production had grown to 8,600 tons of U_3O_8, and mill capacity under contract was expected to double by 1959.

TABLE 20

U.S. PROCUREMENT OF URANIUM CONCENTRATES, FISCAL YEARS
1947–52 (U_3O_8 in Tons)

Fiscal Year	Domestic	Canada	Overseas	Total
1947 (½ year)	0	137	1,440	1,577
1948	116	206	1,689	2,011
1949	115	217	1,909	2,241
1950	323	235	2,505	3,063
1951	639	255	2,792	3,686
1952	824	210	2,623	3,657

Source: Hewlett and Duncan, The Atomic Shield, p. 674.

The AEC program had been successful in developing a viable industry. Despite the increase in domestic supplies, however, the United States continued to receive a substantial portion of its uranium from South Africa, the Belgian Congo, Portugal, and Australia. Foreign reserves had also grown rapidly; developed or partially developed reserves were estimated to be one million tons and would be twice that with full development.[82]

The government's direct purchase of uranium ore was to continue until March 31, 1962, when the program would end as planned. In May of 1956, in anticipation of a transition from a government-controlled market to a commercial market, and to provide a basis for long-range planning by the mining and milling companies, the AEC announced a new procurement program for the period April 1, 1962, through December 31, 1966; this program provided a guaranteed market, subject to certain conditions such as quality, for domestic uranium concentrates. The basic price established was $8 per pound of U_3O_8.[83] By the time the new program was initiated in 1962, twenty-four ore processing mills had negotiated contracts. In 1962, U.S. receipts of U_3O_8 totaled 28,690 tons, of which domestic sources accounted for 59 percent; Canadian, 26 percent; and overseas, 15 percent.[84]

It was evident to the AEC in 1962 that by 1966, which was the termination date of the AEC's purchase program, the commercial market for uranium would not be sufficient to absorb the production from the uranium industry. With the objective of maintaining a viable industry, the AEC announced a stretchout program on November 17, 1962. The program was to run from December 31, 1966, to December 31, 1970.[85] The new program consisted of deferral of a portion of the material then contracted for delivery to the AEC before 1967. The deferred material would be purchased by the AEC during the period from January 1, 1967, through December 31, 1968, at prices previously established. An additional quantity equal to the deferred quantity would be purchased from January 1, 1969, to December 31, 1970. The fixed price would be 85 percent of production cost plus $1.60 per pound of U_3O_8, with a maximum of $6.70 per pound.[86]

In 1966, when the new program went into effect, the AEC projected a rapidly rising commercial market. The free-world production in 1966 was about 18,000 tons (U_3O_8); it was projected to double by 1975, and triple by 1980.[87] The first direct sales of uranium to industry for nuclear power installations were announced in 1966, and amounted to 20,000 tons over a period through 1975.

In 1971, the AEC terminated its uranium purchase program. The domestic uranium-producing industry became entirely dependent on the commercial market. Commercial production in 1971 was 12,400 tons of U_3O_8; commercial requirements were projected to be 10,200 tons in 1972, 20,100 tons in 1975, and 34,300 tons in 1980.[88]

From 1947 to 1970 the AEC's purchases of uranium (tons of U_3O_8) had been: [89]

Domestic	—	174,500 tons (55%)
Canada	—	73,800 tons (24%)
Overseas	—	67,600 tons (21%)
Total	—	315,900 tons

After making allowances for government requirements, the AEC estimated that it had 50,000 tons of surplus U_3O_8 on hand.[90] On October 31, 1971, the AEC sought public comment on plans to dispose of its surplus, beginning in 1974.[91] The plan called for deliveries in any one year not to exceed either one half the projected cumulative growth in domestic requirements beyond 1973, or one fourth the total domestic requirement in any one year. Also, the AEC asked comment on a plan to defer until the later part of the 1970's any relaxation on enrichment of foreign ore for domestic use. These moves would help maintain a viable industry while ore demands increased.

In the early 1970's, the government operated the diffusion plants on what they called a "split tails" basis. The plants are operated with actual uranium "tail" of 0.3 percent U-235, but industry supplies U_3O_8 quantities on the basis of a lower tail, 0.2 percent, which would require less uranium. The additional uranium required for the 0.3 percent tail is made up from the government stockpile. The customer, however, pays the higher cost based on 0.2 percent tail. If this method were to continue, the government stockpile would be depleted by 1976.

Even with the government-dominated program, the uranium industry developed along a not unexpected path. Table 21 lists companies with uranium

TABLE 21

URANIUM MILLING COMPANIES AND PLANTS

Company	Plant Location	Nominal Capacity (Tons Ore Per Day)
The Anaconda Company	Bluewater, New Mexico	3,000
Atlas Corporation	Moab, Utah	1,500
Continental Oil Company, Pioneer Nuclear, Inc.	Karnes County, Texas	1,750
Cotter Corporation	Canon City, Colorado	450
Dawn Mining Company	Ford, Washington	500
Federal-American Partners	Gas Hills, Wyoming	950
Humble Oil and Refining Company	Near Douglas, Wyoming	2,000
Kerr-McGee Corporation	Grants, New Mexico	7,000
Mines Development	Edgemont, South Dakota	650
Petrotomics Company	Shirley Basin, Wyoming	1,500
Rio Algom Mines, Ltd.	Near La Sal, Utah	500
Susquehanna-Western, Inc.	Falls City, Texas	1,000
Susquehanna-Western, Inc.	Ray Point, Texas	1,000
Union Carbide Corporation	Uravan, Colorado	2,000
Union Carbide Corporation	Rifle, Colorado	2,000
Union Carbide Corporation	Gas Hills, Wyoming	1,000
United Nuclear-Homestake Partners	Grants, New Mexico	3,500
Utah Construction and Mining Co.	Gas Hills, Wyoming	1,200
Utah Construction and Mining Co.	Shirley Basin, Wyoming	1,200
Western Nuclear, Inc.	Jeffrey City, Wyoming	1,200
Total		33,900

Source: U.S., AEC, *The Nuclear Industry—1971,* p. 20.

plants and their capacities. Many are mining companies and three are "energy" (oil, for example) companies.

URANIUM AVAILABILITY

Uranium availability is critical to the continued viability of the light-water (converter) reactor industry. There are many difficult questions surrounding this issue, with major uncertainties in the answers. Some of the important questions are: How much energy will be used in the next twenty-five to fifty years? How much energy will be supplied by electricity, and of that, how much will be generated by nuclear power? How soon, if at all, will the breeder reactors take over from the converter reactors? Will breeder reactors be supplanted by another energy source such as fusion? If so, when? How much uranium exists, and how much can be mined in an economical and environmentally safe way?

Insight on uranium supply is obtained from a study performed by Battelle Memorial Institute for the National Science Foundation.[92] The study concludes that:

1. Reasonably assured uranium reserves recoverable at a 1974 forward cost of $15/lb U_3O_8 should be adequate at least through 1985.

2. Uranium resources from conventional sandstone deposits recoverable at a 1974 forward cost of $30/lb U_3O_8 should be adequate to the year 2000.

3. Thorium * resources should be adequate to supply all conceivable needs through the year 2000.

The study assumes that LWR's, HTGR's, LMFBR's, and fossil fuel plants are or will become available over the period. Based on the probability that higher electricity cost to the consumer will reduce demand, the study estimates that the cumulative uranium demand through the year 2000 will be approximately 2.1 million tons. This compares with AEC's estimated reserves of 2.4 million tons recoverable at forward costs of $30/lb U_3O_8. The AEC reserves figure includes only uranium estimated or known to exist in known ore deposits or extensions of known uranium districts. It does not include the vast uranium potential that lies outside the conventional sandstone-type deposits. Enormous quantities of uranium have been identified in marine black shale (e.g., Chattanooga shale in eastern Tennessee), marine phosphorites, granites, seawater, and other unconventional resources. It is estimated that over 4 billion tons of U_3O_8 exist in seawater alone. Various researchers have estimated the cost of production from seawater to range from $30 to $1000/lb of U_3O_8.

Table 22 summarizes the Battelle study estimates of various uranium resources. As can be seen in the table, much of the potentially available uranium is of low-grade quality, and would require considerable mining and handling. Consequently, before many of these resources can be made available at reasonable costs, it will be necessary to conduct research and development on exploration, mining, and milling techniques.

It was concluded in the Battelle study that the energy balance and environ-

TABLE 22

Estimated U.S. Uranium Resource Availability

Source	Approximate % U_3O_8	Estimated Cost of U_3O_8 Recovery—$/lb	Estimated Short Tons—U_3O_8
Conventional Sandstone and Vein Deposits	0.2	10	1,000,000
By-Product from Copper Leach	0.001–0.0012	10	30,000
By-Product from Phosphoric Acid Production	0.015	12	70,000
Conventional Sandstone Deposits	<0.1	30	200,000
Unconventional 0.0X Deposits	0.0X	40	1,000,000
Bearpaw Mountain Syenite	0.05	50	85,000
Chattanooga Shale	0.007	80	2,600,000
Marine Phosphorites	<0.006–0.012	100	7,100,000
Additional Marine Beach Shales	0.005–0.007	120	23,000,000
Conway Granite	0.001–0.003	150	7,500,000
Sea Water	0.0000334	300	4,500,000,000

Source: Battelle Pacific Northwest Laboratories, "Assessment of Uranium and Thorium Resources in the United States and the Effect of Policy Alternatives." Richland, Washington: the Laboratories, December 1974.

* Thorium is used as the fertile material in the HTGR's and some breeders under development.

mental impact of mining low-grade deposits need not be fundamental constraints to the production of such resources. For example, various studies have been made by the U.S. Bureau of Mines and others on mining the Chattanooga shale. Holdren of the California Institute of Technology has compared the environmental impact of surface mining eastern coals with that of underground mining the Chattanooga shale uranium. From this study it would appear that the coal mining presents a greater potential environmental insult than does the mining of low-grade uranium. It is also interesting to compare energy available from the Chattanooga shale with that available from coal. Allowing for all energy costs in producing electricity—costs such as mining, enriching, processing, fabricating, thermal to electric conversion—Battelle calculated that the net energy from one ton of shale is 1,850 kwh, which is about equivalent to the net energy attainable from a ton of coal. The net energy from the uranium included recycling of plutonium in converter reactors. If a breeder reactor had been assumed, the energy available would have been as much as fifty or sixty times higher.

The Electric Power Research Institute (EPRI) conducted another study to assess the probable availability of uranium resources and the requirements for their use.[93] This study is based on several assumptions. First, it assumed that nuclear power would provide the base load for electric utilities, and that the LMFBR would be introduced at a relatively slow rate; that is, once introduced, it would take ten years for the LMFBR to capture 20 percent of the then current market for new base-load additions, and another sixteen years for it to take over 100 percent of the new base-load market. Second, the study assumed that fission power would fulfill all base-load conditions; consequently, any use of other energy sources for this purpose—such as coal, solar energy, or fusion—would reduce the uranium requirements. Third, it assumed several possible electric power and population growth rates. For example, in the EPRI "reference" case, the per capita electric energy consumption increased from 8,937 kwh per capita in 1972 to 50,000 kwh per capita by 2040. Using this reference case as a base, and assuming that the breeder is introduced in 2040, the EPRI study stated that there is a 50 percent probability that the uranium requirement will be less than 7.9 million tons of U_3O_8 by that year. Given that 7.9 million tons will be required, the study then indicated that there is a 10 percent probability that resources available from known producing areas at a cost of less than $100 per pound of U_3O_8 will be greater than this amount. This probability goes to about 73 percent if other likely United States producing areas are included. The study did not include low-grade ore in either known or potential areas—Chattanooga shale, for example. The study did point out, however, that the volume of low-grade ore that must be mined in order to produce a given amount of energy approaches that of coal (a conclusion similar to the one reached by the Battelle study). The mining of low-grade ores, then, cannot have the economic and environmental advantages associated with mining and transporting relatively small volumes of material. If lower grade ores with uranium content from 0.05 percent to 0.20 percent are included, the study concludes that there is a 50 percent probability that the uranium resources are greater than 21 million tons. Much of this uranium, however, probably would not be recoverable at a cost below $100 per pound.

Although utilization of the low-grade ores might result in high-cost uranium, a major advantage of nuclear power is that the cost of electric power generation is relatively insensitive to changes in uranium cost. The fuel cost for nuclear energy is roughly 2 to 3 mills per kilowatt hour ($.002 to $.003), compared with electricity delivered to the home at $.03 to $.08 or more. There are three major components of nuclear fuel costs: uranium, enrichment of the uranium, and fabrication of the uranium into fuel assemblies used in the reactor. Of the fuel cost, the natural uranium (U_3O_8) represents about one third of the total and produces an increase of no more than one tenth of a mill per kilowatt hour for each dollar increase per pound of uranium. Uranium has increased in price in the early 1970's from $6 per pound to $25 per pound. This represents an increased electric energy cost of less than one mill per kilowatt hour. If uranium costs were to increase to $100 per pound, this increase alone would represent an electric energy generation cost increase of less than one cent per kilowatt hour. Therefore, unlike power produced by fossil fuels, nuclear power is relatively insensitive to the energy resource cost. The major part of nuclear power cost is the capital investment, which has inflated dramatically since General Electric sold the first commercial reactor.

There are various factors which can affect the total uranium resource requirement. Plutonium recycling can reduce the overall uranium resource requirement by as much as 15 percent or more. The tails assay from uranium enrichment plants can also have a significant impact on the total uranium required. Uranium enters the enrichment plant with 0.7 percent U-235, unless it is recycled uranium, and leaves at some depleted value. The projected cumulative requirement of 2.1 million tons to the year 2000 is based on tails assay of 0.3 percent U-235. Lowering the tails assay to 0.2 percent would reduce the total uranium requirement by 400,000 tons. Technically, the diffusion plants are capable of operating at a tails assay as low as 0.1 percent, but the plant capacity for producing enriched uranium would be considerably reduced. The implication of improved enrichment efficiency for U.S. uranium availability is obvious.

In summary, there are many factors affecting the availability of uranium, of which only a few have been discussed here. A number of these will be determined by government policies and society's choices. From a technical and fundamental availability viewpoint, it would appear that sufficient uranium to fuel the present converter reactors could be made available for many decades, until the development of the breeder or other alternative energy sources.

URANIUM ENRICHMENT FACILITIES

The availability of enriched uranium has made possible more economically efficient nuclear power reactors. The current United States commercial reactors utilize this type of uranium as a fuel. The light-water reactor (LWR) uses slightly enriched uranium (2 percent to 4 percent U-235), while the high-temperature graphite reactor (HTGR), which has recently been accepted commercially, uses highly enriched uranium (93 percent U-235) with thorium.

Although several techniques have been explored for concentrating the U-235 isotope in uranium—e.g., electromagnetic separation, gas diffusion, gas centrifuge—gas diffusion is the only method that has been developed and used on a large scale. All diffusion plants were built initially to provide highly enriched uranium for weapons. Five countries have such plants and could compete for supplying the world enriched uranium market: France, the United States, the Soviet Union, the People's Republic of China, and Great Britain.[94] The plants in both France and Great Britain are small in relation to U.S. enrichment capabilities [95] and their capacity to compete will likely be limited by those countries' domestic demands.

Today, all enriching facilities (diffusion plants) in the United States are government-owned. This is the last area in the power reactor manufacturing industry that remains as a government monopoly. Some consideration has been given to selling the government plants and/or to industry's constructing privately owned plants.

On the assumption that foreign enrichment facilities will provide 5 percent of the free-world foreign requirements in 1975, and that this amount will increase to 35 percent in 1985, the AEC has estimated that the United States must have new enriching plants on line around 1983 in order to meet the U.S. and the remaining free-world requirements.[96] Several companies are actively looking at the possibility of supplying these facilities. Until they actually do so, however, the government will remain the sole source for enriching services, enriching privately owned uranium as allowed under the 1964 Private Ownership of Special Nuclear Materials Act.[97]

There are at present three government diffusion plants: Oak Ridge, Tennessee; Paducah, Kentucky; and Portsmouth, Ohio. Their total annual capacity, operating at a power level of 6,000 megawatts, is 17.1 million kilogram separative work units (SWU).* [98] The original costs totaled about $2.4 billion, and had a depreciated vlaue as of June 30, 1968, of $1.1 billion.[99] The first plant, located at Oak Ridge, was completed at the end of World War II.[100] Major expansion of facilities at Oak Ridge and construction of new facilities at Paducah and Portsmouth occurred in the late forties and early fifties.[101] The costs of the facilities were: Oak Ridge, $832 million; Paducah, $787 million; and Portsmouth, $767 million, with capacities in terms of millions of kilograms of

---

* A separative work unit is not a measure of the quantity of material processed, but rather of the effort expended in separating the uranium into two streams, one enriched and the other depleted. For example, assuming the depleted stream to be 0.2 percent U-235 (natural uranium is 0.71 percent U-235), 17.1 separative work units would produce 7.79 million kilograms (kg) of 2.0 percent enriched uranium from 27.5 million kg of natural uranium; or 3.97 kg of 3.0 percent enriched uranium from 21.8 kg of natural uranium.

separative work units per year of 4.86, 7.34, and 4.86, respectively.[102] By comparison, the British Capenhurst plant has a capacity of 400,000 kilograms of separative work units, and the French Pierrelatte plant is said to be about the same size.[103]

The AEC has announced two programs which, if completed, would increase the cumulative capacity of its facilities to 26.5 million separative work units.[104] One is the Cascade Improvement Program (CIP), which would provide for incorporating the most recent advances in gaseous diffusion technology into the existing plants. The second program, the Cascade Power Uprating Program (CUP), would allow higher power levels to be used.[105] The costs of these improvements would be $975 million.[106]

MEETING FUTURE ENRICHMENT REQUIREMENTS

As stated in the previous section, additional uranium enrichment facilities will be needed by 1983; that is, assuming that the two programs for upgrading current facilities are completed and that stockpiling of enriched uranium will occur during the interim when the full capacity of the plants is not needed to meet current industry demands. It is estimated that government requirements will be less than 10 percent of total requirements by the mid-1970's.[107]

In planning for meeting future requirements for enrichment services, three questions are pertinent: How much? When? By Whom? In predicting when and at what rate additional United States enrichment capacity will be needed, the AEC takes into consideration the following factors: (1) the tails assay at which existing plants are operated, (2) the portion of added enriching requirements that will be met by countries other than the United States, (3) the timing of the CIP and CUP, (4) the extent to which plutonium recycle is utilized in light-water reactors, (5) the determination of how soon and at what rate commercial breeders will be built, and (6) the rate at which nuclear power will grow.[108]

W. E. Johnson, former AEC commissioner, has estimated that the peak demand will be about 75 million SWU per year and will occur in the early 1990's, assuming the commercial breeder is introduced in 1986 [109] (which is not likely to occur). He further suggests that projected requirements might be met with additional capacity of 25 million to 40 million SWU per year by preproduction. The total cost of plants plus the required power stations would range between $5 billion and $10 billion dollars. Since reactor plants have a thirty- to forty-year life and since breeders are not likely to take over the complete power reactor market initially, enriching facilities will be needed beyond 2020. The question under study now is who will supply the capability.

First, consideration has been given to the possibility of private industry's taking ownership of the AEC's gaseous diffusion plants.[110] During the 1969 JCAE hearings, Dr. Seaborg, chairman of the AEC, testified that:

> The Atomic Energy Commission believes that any plan of future responsibility for uranium enriching must make adequate provision for the national defense and security, must assure that the amount of capacity available to meet requirements is not a

deterrent to continued growth of this newly emerging source of power, must provide adequate compensation to the Government for its equity in the enterprise, must provide for the fulfillment of Government supply commitments, and must otherwise be in the public interest. Establishment of a Government corporation is one alternative vehicle for satisfying these criteria which deserves careful consideration.

Any decision to transfer responsibility for uranium reenrichment from the Government to the private sector must identify in some detail a course of action upon which policy, technical and economic determinations have been made to assure that the above criteria would be satisfied. Political and technical developments may substantially affect the manner in which transfer to private enterprise might best be accomplished.[111]

The AEC's tentative conclusion was that the uranium enrichment service should be established on a "business-type basis," which could be accomplished through a government corporation "with authority to reapply revenues and to obtain financing by borrowing either from the Treasury or by issuing revenue bonds to the public, or both." [112] An alternative to an AEC government corporation would be one similar to TVA.[113]

In August 1969 a White House Task Force on Uranium Enriching Facilities, headed by Paul W. McCraken, chairman of the Council of Economic Advisers, presented the results of their study to President Nixon.[114] They did not arrive at a specific recommendation, but instead presented advantages and disadvantages of several alternative courses of action: selling government facilities to private industry, either to a single firm or to a multifirm oligopoly; establishing a government corporation; or maintaining the current system.[115] It was concluded that any private ownership arrangement would require some government price regulation, since there would be no competitive industry until late in the 1980's. Sale of plants to private industry was seen as increasing the risk of both dissemination of enrichment technology to unauthorized persons and diversion of enriched uranium for unauthorized uses.[116] Because of national security reasons, enrichment technology had remained classified and industry had not been allowed to do private research in that area.[117]

On November 10, 1969, the president announced that he had asked the AEC to operate the diffusion plants as a separate organization in a manner which would approach "more closely a commercial enterprise." [118] The president expressed belief that eventually the federal government's responsibility as owner-operator of the facilities should be ended. In the same year, the AEC considered setting up a new entity—an AEC directorate[119]—but later in 1970 discarded this plan [120] because the plants were operating at a relatively small fraction of their capacity and were not producing enough to make such a step worthwhile.

Also, in 1969 the Atomic Industrial Forum submitted its report to the JCAE on the subject of ownership.[121] The report concluded that transfer of the gaseous diffusion plants to private ownership was both feasible and desirable. However, it stated that industry would demand as a prerequisite the assurance of adequate production of enriched uranium at reasonable prices.[122] Because of several other problems associated with immediate transfer of plants to private industry—e.g., security, competition, antitrust problems—AIF suggested as an interim solution a government corporation wholly separate from the AEC, whose objective would be to solve these problems and to develop the necessary procedures for transferring the plants to private industry no later than 1974.[123]

At the request of the JCAE, the General Accounting Office conducted a detailed study on the government's investment, economic worth of plants, transfer to industry, the government corporation approach, and financial return to the government. While the GAO did not make any specific recommendation regarding government versus private ownership, it did conclude that early transfer to private industry was less favorable than government retention, from the standpoint of ensuring that additional enrichment capacity would be available when needed.[124]

The Edison Electric Institute, representing the private utilities, did not recommend a specific mode of ownership and took the position that the JCAE and the AEC were most qualified to determine the future mode of ownership that would best serve the public interest.[125] While EEI favored ultimate private ownership, it recommended that any transitional government corporation should "make adequate payments to government in lieu of taxes in order to bring expenses in line with those of an investor-owned enterprise and thus: (1) facilitate transition to private ownership at some time in the future, (2) make any 'yardstick' comparison realistic, and (3) avoid any implication of subsidy for nuclear power." [126] This approach, requiring payments in lieu of taxes, would have been similar to that of the TVA.[127]

The American Public Power Association supported continued government ownership.[128] With the objective of eliminating government subsidy of nuclear power, the National Coal Association recommended the formation of a "Government-Consumers Co-op," owned on a *pro rata* basis by the users.[129]

The solution to the problem of ultimate ownership of existing government plants has not yet been found. Steps were taken by the AEC, however, to provide private industry with access to enrichment technology. The AEC announced on June 21, 1971, that it would grant access to this technology to a limited number of U.S. companies desiring to carry out independent development work. Access was to be allowed both to gaseous diffusion and to gas centrifuge technology, the most promising competing process.[130] The AEC considered this to be an approach that would encourage private industry to enter the enrichment equipment field, as well as that of enrichment service. As of November 30, 1971, twenty-two companies had applied for security clearance in order to obtain the classified information necessary for them to submit a proposal to enter the restricted field.[131] Seven ultimately submitted proposals before November 30, 1972, and all seven were accepted by the AEC.[132] Six of the proposals were concerned primarily with gas centrifuge technology.[133] The seventh proposal was from Reynolds Metal Company for access to gaseous diffusion technology. In May 1973, the commission expanded its uranium enrichment access program by publishing amendments to Title 10, Part 25 of the Code of Federal Regulations.[134] These amendments permit participants to receive the technical and economic information required for evaluation and eventual construction of uranium facilities. By 1974, ten industrial organizations were participating in the program, which had been broadened to allow participants to use AEC equipment test stands at Oak Ridge, Tennessee. By September 1975, these facilities will be available for testing centrifuges manufactured by industrial companies.[135]

The government enrichment service has become a major business and is destined to become even larger. As of June 30, 1974, the AEC had 252 active contracts covering supply periods of up to thirty years; 165 contracts were with domestic firms and eighty-eight were with foreign entities.[136] These contracts cover 205,000 megawatts of domestic nuclear power capacity and 69,000 megawatts of foreign capacity. The value of these contracts amounts to over $27 billion, compared with $10 billion as of June 30, 1973.[137] The revenues in 1974 for enrichment services were $541 million.

Several private companies have made proposals to enter the enrichment service business. In March of 1972, Reynolds Metal proposed that it organize a consortium to own and operate a gaseous diffusion plant near Buffalo, Wyoming, where the company owns more than 2 billion tons of low-sulfur coal.[138,139] This proposal has not culminated in specific plans to build the plant.

The Uranium Enrichment Associates (UEA) are considering building a gaseous diffusion plant in Alabama at an estimated cost of $2.75 billion.[140] The plant is planned to have a capacity of 9 million separative work units. It was originally proposed by Bechtel Corporation, Union Carbide, and Westinghouse. The latter two dropped out in 1974, but Goodyear Tire and Rubber Company decided to join Bechtel in the venture.[141] UEA has requested that the government provide seals and barriers for the plant, technical assistance, and a guarantee of plant completion in the event that UEA is unable to do so. According to plans, the plant will be in operation by 1983. About 40 percent of its output will serve the U.S. market; the remainder, the foreign market.[142] A number of other companies, including General Electric, Exxon, Arco, and Electro Nucleonic, have also expressed interest in the possibility of entering the field.

Several European countries are likewise taking an interest in expanding their enrichment capacity. Erodiff, to be owned by France (42.8 percent), Iran (10 percent), Italy (25 percent), Spain (11.1 percent), and Belgium (11.1 percent), plans to build an enrichment facility in southern France.[143] In addition, Iran and France are considering building a second plant employing centrifuge technology.[144] Another group, Urenco/Centec, also plans to employ centrifuge technology to perform enrichment services in Almelo, the Netherlands; and Capenhurst, England. This project is a joint venture between Great Britain, Germany, and the Netherlands.[145] South Africa, too, has announced an enrichment pilot plant employing a new process.[146]

The ultimate total need for uranium and enrichment services will depend on a number of factors: (1) degree of acceptance and growth of nuclear power; (2) timing of the introduction of the liquid-metal fast breeder reactor; (3) availability of other energy sources; and (4) growth of electric power requirements. In addition, the extent to which private industry will provide the service is influenced by government policies and the extent to which foreign governments and companies enter the enrichment field. Because of the uncertainty in these factors, as well as the very large investment required, private industry has been and is likely to continue to be reluctant to enter the field until the direction of nuclear power is better defined.

At present, the United States and the world are in a state of transition on energy issues in general. Although major energy questions, such as availability and cost, have gradually been becoming serious over many years, the problem associated with these issues were brought to "crisis" magnitude with the 1973 oil embargo and with the extreme acceleration of energy costs since then. It will take several years for the direction of national policies to be better defined; it will also be several years before we can see the degree to which the greatly expanded research and development on alternative energy sources will lead to solutions having a significant impact on energy supply. Regardless of the outcome of this research, however, it is clear that nuclear power, if properly managed, can make a very significant contribution to the world's energy needs.

CHAPTER VI

Regulation of Nuclear Power

SINCE its establishment by Congress through the Atomic Energy Act of 1946, the AEC has had responsibility both for protecting the health and safety of the public with regard to use of nuclear energy, and for regulating the control and use of source, byproduct, and special nuclear materials. The spectrum of problems in fulfilling this responsibility continues to widen as the nuclear industry grows.

During the period when all nuclear materials and reactors were owned by the government, control was relatively simple. With the expanding spheres of private ownership allowed since 1954, the task has become increasingly difficult. First nuclear reactors and then, ten years later, fuels, had to be licensed and regulated as private property. Now with significant numbers of power reactors in operation for more than a year, the entire nuclear fuel cycle has begun to command the attention of concerned organizations. Waste storage, nuclear materials transport, and special nuclear material (SNM) safeguards, all are in the spotlight. Plutonium is of particular concern, as it becomes available from reprocessed irradiated fuels and owners seek AEC approval to recycle it back into the reactors. This issue could have considerable impact on the future of the liquid-metal fast breeder reactors, whose viability will depend on a major plutonium fuel cycle industry. The current commercial light-water reactors operate with slightly enriched uranium, but could use the generated plutonium as partial fulfillment of subsequent fuel reloads. This would increase the utilization of uranium. Thus the question of recycling of plutonium involves balancing the trade-offs among uranium conservation, energy costs, and SNM safeguard risks.

Since all phases of the fuel cycle have been active to some degree for many years, the AEC established many requirements for protecting the public safety and the environment. These have become more comprehensive, exacting, and demanding as the industry has grown and as concerned organizations have interjected their views and rights into the licensing and regulatory processes.

As the industry grew and matured during the 1960's and 1970's, the AEC phased out its promotional development effort on current commercial light-water reactors. By 1971, the only significant governmental support for the light-water reactor industry was in the areas of safety and waste management research and uranium enrichment. The AEC's major efforts became development of advance systems—the breeders—and the regulation of the light-water reactor industry.

REGULATORY ORGANIZATION

In order to focus greater management attention on its growing regulatory role and to separate the promotional and regulatory efforts, the AEC made several major organizational changes during the years of commercial reactor introduction. In late 1959, it created a Division of Compliance, made up of five regional offices, to inspect licensees for compliance with applicable regulations. In 1961, the commission further separated the regulatory and promotional functions by placing all regulatory divisions under a director of regulation, reporting directly to the commissioners. Previously, all AEC divisions, both statutory (e.g., Military Applications) and AEC-created (e.g., Compliance), had been grouped under one of the assistant general managers, who in turn was under the general manager. Divisions placed under the director of regulation were Compliance, Reactor Standards, and Reactor Licensing. Until 1972, this structure remained essentially unchanged: although the regulatory functions were not totally severed from the promotional part of the AEC until 1974, the separation of regulatory and promotional functions within the AEC was effectively completed by these early administrative changes. On April 25, 1972, AEC Chairman Schlesinger announced that the regulatory staff was again being reorganized, this time under three directorates: Regulatory Standards, Licensing, and Regulatory Operations. It was felt that these better reflected and separated the three different types of functions of a regulating agency.[1]

In its regulatory role in the new industry, the AEC's duties were similar in scope to those of other "traditional" federal agencies, like the Federal Trade Commission or the Federal Communications Commission. The regulatory system encompasses three aspects or functions, analogous to the three branches of government. First, rule making—the issuance of requirements of generalized applicability—is a *quasi-legislative* function, amplifying and clarifying the general words of the authorizing statute (here, the Atomic Energy Act and its amendments). Second, licensing is a *quasi-judicial* function, through which the determination of facts necessary to grant or deny a license application is conducted before an impartial tribunal in a setting that is partly adversary in character. Third, the coordination of policy, enforcement of determinations, and administration of the agency itself make up a *quasi-executive* function.

The Division of Reactor Standards and others performed the quasi-legislative rule-making function for the commercial power reactor industry by developing detailed regulations governing plant construction, licensing, and operation.

Together with AEC procedural regulations and regulations applicable to all other areas of atomic energy, these standards are codified and published as Title 10 of the U.S. Code of Federal Regulations (10 CFR). The continuing process of developing standards is handled by the Directorate of Regulatory Standards.

The Division of Reactor Licensing (DRL) handled the quasi-judicial function of facility licensing. The Atomic Safety and Licensing Boards (ASLB's), created by statute in 1962, are composed of three memebers each, appointed by the commissioners. These boards actually conduct the hearings and make the licensing decisions, with input from the Advisory Committee on Reactor Safeguards (ACRS). The functions of the DRL were placed under the Directorate of Licensing by the 1972 reorganization.

The Division of Compliance handled the quasi-executive inspection and enforcement functions until these functions were assigned to the Directorate of Regulatory Operations in 1972. Quasi-executive policy determinations have since been made by the commissioners. Differences of policy and coordination of policy between separate functions (e.g., rule making and licensing) are resolved by the director of regulation or, ultimately, by the commissioners. Similarly, the commissioners allocate priorities and resolve conflicts between AEC regulatory functions and promotional or operational functions.

NUCLEAR POWER PLANT LICENSING

ORIGIN

As early as the 1940's, it was recognized that the operation of nuclear energy utilization facilities posed grave threats to the safety of nearby citizens and employees. Since radiation in the form of fission products is a necessary consequence of the operation of reactors, the dangers inherent in both "regular," low-level releases and catastrophic, high-level accident releases had to be evaluated. Faced with an expanding program of research, test, and production reactors, the AEC became concerned about the siting process; now site safety had to be considered along with available manpower and laboratory expertise.

In 1947, on the advice of Robert Oppenheimer and its General Advisory Committee, the AEC established the Advisory Committee on Reactor Safeguards (ACRS) under the chairmanship of Edward Teller. This committee was responsible for overseeing the safety aspects of the nuclear program, and in this capacity reviewed the suitability of locating reactors at specific sites. To aid in this assessment, the committee developed the first formula for restricted zones around a plant. Reflecting the lack of a structural containment vessel in the early test and production reactors, this formula scaled the zones in proportion to the power output of the reactor. In the 1954 Atomic Energy Act, which allowed private nuclear energy utilization and which created the AEC licensing authority, there are no fewer than twenty-five references to "the health and safety of the public." [2] Shortly after passage of the 1954 Act, the AEC affirmed that hazard evaluation would receive a substantial part of AEC staff attention and that the test for issuance of construction permits would be whether the AEC was convinced that, following completion, the proposed reactor would be capable of operating safely at the selected location.[3] The 1954 Act specified only that the AEC find the activity to "provide adequate protection to the health and safety of the public." [4] The AEC regulations released in 1959–62 were equally vague in requiring that the applicant show a "reasonable assurance" that the facility could be operated without unreasonable risk to the public health and safety.[5] AEC rules on reactor site criteria used to evaluate the safety of operation at a given site indicate that the commission weighed the reactor design and safeguards against the location of the site, in terms of both nearby population density and the physical characteristics of the site. Population exclusion zones and low-population zones are delineated as the area beyond which a projected catastrophic accident would result in less than a specified radiation dose.[6]

Early AEC test and production reactors were placed in remote locations in order to minimize public hazards, and reactors constructed under the Power Demonstration Reactor Program were designed with structural containment vessels surrounding them. Any releases, including those generating the high pressures likely to occur in major accidents, would be contained by these vessels, and could thus be subsequently recovered and disposed of. As reactors grew in size, the use of a containment vessel was supplemented by design features to absorb the pressure surges in accidents. Some leakage was always assumed, however, and the effect of this leakage on the surrounding area then became the focus of the siting problem. The ACRS maintained that the resolution of this problem lay in remote siting of reactors. As a result of this concept, unfavorable ACRS reports led to delay or rejection of reactors proposed at Piqua, Ohio; Jamestown, New York; and La Crosse, Wisconsin. In a case discussed later in this chapter, an unfavorable ACRS report touched off the storm of protest over the PRDC Fermi plant.*

The reactor site criteria adopted by the AEC in 1962 set down a procedure for relating plant size to distance from specified population densities—the larger the plant, the further the distance from population centers—and thus formalized the "remote location" concept, subject to modification through use of engineered safeguards. In 1963, the AEC deputy director of regulation, Clifford Beck, left the way open for future proposals utilizing this trade-off.[7]

The licensing process affords a review of various reactor protection and accident safety features. Other information about the application, such as security, operators' qualifications, and applicants' financial soundness, is required by the AEC, but reactor safety has been essentially the most crucial issue in determining acceptability of a proposal. In recent years, determination of reactor safety has been joined by the need to take account of other issues, typically raised under various federal environmental protection statutes in licensing hearings.

---

* The Fermi reactor history is recounted in a later section of this chapter.

The AEC Licensing Structure

As discussed previously, the basic requirements and structure of the facility licensing system were established by 1962. The significant features are summarized below:

- The Atomic Energy Act of 1954 created a two-step licensing requirement, consisting of a construction permit and an operating license (1954).[8]
- Provision was made for the regulatory staff to be assisted by other outside organizations, notably the Federal Radiation Council in establishing permissible radiation doses (1959) [9] and the U.S. attorney general on antitrust matters in commercial licensing (1954).[10]
- The Advisory Committee on Reactor Safeguards (ACRS) was given statutory force and was required to make a public report on each application (1957).[11]
- Public hearings on all construction permit, operating license, and license amendment applications were required (1957); [12] later, uncontested operating license and license amendment hearings were exempted (1962).[13]
- The AEC was authorized to create Atomic Safety and Licensing Boards (ASLB's) to conduct licensing hearings (1962).[14]

The ACRS is composed of fifteen persons, appointed by the commission to four-year terms. Committee members are chosen from industry, the national laboratories, private practice, and universities, in order to provide a balanced, broad range of experience pertaining to reactor safety. The ACRS is independent of all subdivisions of the AEC; its duties are prescribed by the 1957 legislation: "The Committee shall review safety studies and facility license applications referred to it and shall make reports thereon, shall advise the Commission with regard to the hazards of proposed or existing reactor facilities and the adequacy of proposed reactor safety standards, and shall perform other duties as the Commission requests." [15]

The ASLB's are composed of three members, one of whom must be qualified in administrative procedure (usually a lawyer or federal hearing examiner). The other two must be qualified in technical matters,[16] and normally are selected by the commission on an *ad hoc* basis from a panel of qualified persons from private industry and universities.[17] Like the ACRS, each ASLB is independent of other AEC divisions. Within the regulatory apparatus, AEC staff members participate in the promulgation of standards and regulations (the quasi-legislative function), assist individual licensing applicants, and evaluate applications in preparation for licensing decisions (the quasi-judicial function).*

---

* See earlier discussions in this chapter of the three functions of the regulatory apparatus: legislative, judicial, and executive.

The staff supervised by the director of regulation regulates licenses of reactors and other facilities that produce and use atomic energy; it also regulates and licenses the possession, use, and transfer of enriched uranium, plutonium, natural uranium, thorium, and byproduct materials. It also regulates the health and safety features of licensee activities. Regional offices monitor and audit the operation of power plants and other facilities.

The maximum doses of radiation permissible for humans and the permissible levels of nuclides derived from these doses are evaluated continuously by regulating agencies and certain scientific bodies outside the AEC, which were established for the express purpose of establishing standards or permissible radiation exposure for human beings. These scientific bodies include the U.S. National Committee on Radiation Protection and Measurements (NCRP); the Committees on the Biological Effects of Atomic Radiation, under the auspices of the National Academy of Sciences, National Research Council; the United Nations Scientific Committee on the Effect of Atomic Radiation; and the Federal (U.S.) Radiation Council (FRC), which was established to provide protection policy on exposures of radiation workers and members of the public. This responsibility is now held by the Environmental Protection Agency (EPA).

The maximum permissible concentrations and doses established by the International Commission on Radiological Protection (ICRP) and the NCRP form the basis for the regulations pertaining to the discharge of radioactive wastes by nuclear establishments.

PROCEDURAL STEPS

The AEC discharges its responsibility for protecting the health and safety of the general public vis-à-vis nuclear energy in three ways:
- It establishes standards and regulations governing the construction, licensing, and operation of nuclear plants. These must be adhered to by industry, and are published in the Code of Federal Regulations.
- It conducts detailed safety reviews prior to the issuance of a construction permit, and again prior to the issuance of an operating permit. The purpose of these reviews is to ensure that the facility is located, designed, engineered, and constructed in strict accordance with AEC regulations and with well-disciplined quality assurance and engineering practices, and that it will be operated in accordance with these rules and practices.
- It inspects the licensed project after it is in operation to assure compliance with AEC regulations.

The Codes of Federal Regulations which spell out these rules and procedures are:
- 10 CFR 20—standards for radiation protection.
- 10 CFR 50—reactor licensing.
- 10 CFR 100—site evaluation.

Many steps must be taken and many requirements met between the time a utility decides to install a nuclear power plant at a given location and the time the plant actually begins operation. The utility normally approaches the AEC with a definite site and reactor system already in the planning stage.

1. The utility assembles data on the proposed site and reactor system and submits it to the Division of Reactor Licensing (Directorate of Licensing) for informal review. The licensing staff either accepts the application or, more commonly, requests more information.

2. When the application is made acceptable through informal consultation, it is docketed by the licensing staff as a formal application for a construction permit.

3. An ACRS subcommittee and the licensing staff undertake simultaneous studies, characterized at this point by free contact between the staff, the ACRS, and the applicant in order to gain all the relevant information.

4. The staff prepares a final report to the ACRS; the entire ACRS meets to consider the report.

5. The ACRS issues its recommendation as a letter to the AEC. Typically only two or three pages, the letter does not detail ACRS findings, but indicates areas that the ACRS wants to review, and usually concludes that remaining questions can be resolved during the construction of the facility. The staff submits its detailed report to the commission at the same time. Until recently, these reports were concerned solely with site and facility safety questions (as well as the required findings as to the applicant's financial status, etc.). Legislation passed in 1970 now requires that an environmental impact report and an opinion of the Attorney General on antitrust issues be submitted to the AEC at the same time.

6. The commission appoints three members to an Atomic Safety and Licensing Board that will hold the required construction permit hearing. Notice is given to parties who may be interested. The ASLB often holds prehearing conferences to clarify procedures and issues.

7. If the attorney general has indicated possible antitrust problems, a hearing on this issue is conducted separately from the safety/environmental hearing.

8. At the hearings, persons desiring to intervene or speak are given a chance to do so. The AEC has very liberal rules as to who is allowed to participate. If there is no intervention, the ASLB reviews the applicant's record, often spot-checking the work. In contested hearings, the ASLB must hear and decide every contested issue.

9. The parties then submit proposed findings of fact and law (those contentions that each party wants the ASLB to decide). The board then issues an initial decision, which is a written statement deciding each issue that the applicant is required to answer as well as each issue that was contested. The permit decisions must also contain a description of the reactor, a discussion of significant safety questions, etc., whether or not the hearing is contested.

10. The hearing record and the ASLB initial decision are sent to the com-

mission for review. An Atomic Safety and Licensing Appeal Board (ASLB) is delegated the responsibility for performing all commission reviews on facility license decisions. The ASLB may adopt the initial decision, may request more information, or may modify the decision. The commission will not normally review ASLB actions unless the ASLB requests a determination of a unique policy or legal problem, or unless the commission reviews on its own motion.

11. If the decision is to issue the applicant a construction permit, adverse parties may initiate court action (in a U.S. Circuit Court of Appeals). Similarly, the applicant can appeal a denial of a construction permit. If a permit is issued, the applicant can proceed with construction of the facility.

12. The procedures for obtaining an operating license are similar. Informal contact between applicant and staff prior to application is encouraged. The AEC need not hold a public hearing if the application is uncontested. The operating license decision is concerned with applicant compliance with all previous requirements, including resolution of questions left unresolved at the construction permit stage. Usually a more detailed safety review is made, and new issues and conditions may be initiated and decided.

13. In a hearing on a contested operating license, procedures identical to those of the construction permit hearings are followed. If possible, the same ASLB is convened.

14. The first operating license is usually a provisional license, allowing fuel loading and low-power testing. Subsequent applications are necessary to obtain a full-power operating license. As in the case of the first operating license, hearings on uncontested applications are discretionary. The same is true of all uncontested applications to amend an existing operating license.

Licensing has become a big business for the AEC. As of January 1, 1975, the commission had granted operating licenses for 53 power plants, totaling 36,297 Mw_e, and 63 plant construction permits; of the latter, 25 operating licenses were under review. In addition, 74 construction permits were under review; of these, 10 applicants had been given authorization for preliminary site work.[18] Under licensing procedures currently employed, nine to ten years are required to bring a custom-designed nuclear plant into service. This time is divided approximately as follows: two years for concurrent site selection, plant design, and filing of construction permit application; two years for AEC construction permit review; and five to six years for construction (the operating permit review takes place during the latter part of this period).

Since almost one half the cost of a nuclear plant is for interest and escalation during the licensing review and construction phases, major incentives exist for reducing the long lead time. The AEC believes that the lead time could be shortened by as much as two years through plant standardization, and another two years by use of predesignated sites.[19] A substantial reduction in the construction permit review process took place as the AEC gained licensing experience and developed procedures, and as major licensing and environmental policies and jurisdictional issues were resolved, often through court actions.

For example, in 1970 the safety and environmental reviews took 23 and 31 months, respectively; in 1973, these had been reduced to 15 and 13 months.

While policy and jurisdictional issues were being resolved in the early 1970's, there were considerable delays in obtaining a reactor license. According to industry analyses, environmental problems caused the licensing of nuclear plants to grind almost to a halt in 1971. The logjam was broken in May 1972, ending a "17-month hiatus in AEC decisions on full-power operating licenses and a similar interruption in construction permit decisions for nuclear power plants." [20] The first full-power operating license to go into effect after January 1971 was issued on May 24, 1972, and by the end of that year, 7 full-power and 2 partial-power operating licenses had been granted—the most in any single year. In addition, 8 construction permits were issued. [21] By the end of 1972, there were 29 central-station power reactors operating in the United States and approximately 100 in the "free world." [22] By the end of 1974, the number operating in the United States had increased to 55.

In November 1972, AEC Commissioner William O. Doub stated at an industry meeting that "the system today is once again functioning." [23] Indeed, the government has continued to issue licenses since 1973, but many problems still face the industry that must be resolved before the public will fully accept nuclear power. In 1972, the president of Atomic Industrial Forum stated that "public attitudes will probably continue to be more important to nuclear power than to any comparable industry, and we believe it is to the benefit of all to take steps now to insure that the public will be properly and fully informed." [24] In 1972 and early 1973 the AEC did take steps designed to improve licensing procedures, to increase assurance of reactor safety, and to improve public participation in regulatory functions. These may have helped speed up the licensing process in 1973. [25]

Consideration of Environmental Quality

Early siting problems and conflicts centered almost entirely on safety of the proposed reactors. The AEC's interpretation of its responsibilities in reactor licensing was restricted solely to the safety of the public from radiation. In the late 1960's, however, the environmental issue became firmly injected into siting considerations. The problem of thermal pollution from nuclear plants arose as a point of contention between citizens and the AEC at siting hearings conducted by the ASLB for the nuclear plants at Shoreham, Monticello, and Calvert Cliffs, among others. In each case it was disallowed as a pertinent issue. Because of their significance and influence on the licensing process, the Monticello and Calvert Cliffs cases will be discussed further later in this chapter.

The issue of the scope of AEC environmental considerations was resolved by events following the passage of the National Environmental Policy Act of 1969. [26] NEPA contains both a general statement of congressional intent with respect to the relationship between man and the environment and a series of specific requirements with which federal agencies must comply. This act has become tremendously important in the licensing and regulation of nuclear power plants. A summary of its principal features follows:

- The purposes of NEPA, stated in section 2, are:

  To declare a national policy which will encourage productive and enjoyable harmony between man and his environment; to promote efforts which will prevent or eliminate damage to the environment and biosphere and stimulate the health and welfare of man; to enrich the understanding of the ecological systems and natural resources important to the Nation; and to establish a Council on Environmental Quality.

- Section 101 declares it to be congressional policy that federal agencies use "all practicable means, including financial and technical assistance," to protect and enhance the environment consistent with present and future beneficial use of the environment.
- Section 102 contains directions that federal agencies, "to the fullest extent possible," should:
  1. Utilize an interdisciplinary decision-making process, specifically by developing procedures to assure that unquantified environmental values be given appropriate consideration.
  2. Issue a public, detailed environmental impact statement (EIS) with any recommended "major" action or proposed legislation. The act specified information to be included in the EIS, particularly short- and long-term effects of the action, and alternatives to the action.
  3. Consult with other federal agencies, both in the preparation of the EIS and following the EIS.
- Section 103 requires that agencies review all of their statutory authority, regulations, and policies, and report areas which may be in conflict with NEPA purposes and provisions within six months.
- The final provisions of NEPA created the Council on Environmental Quality, consisting of three members "highly qualified" to analyze and interpret environmental information. The function of the council is to assist and advise the president in preparing an annual Environmental Quality Report; gather environmental information; review federal programs for achievement of national environmental policy goals; develop and recommend new environmental quality policies; conduct research, studies, and investigations; and make policy recommendations.

The intent of Congress that all segments of the government comply with NEPA was explicit: "The policies, regulations and public laws of the United States shall be interpreted and administered in accordance with the policies set forth in this chapter. . . ."

A series of executive actions gave effect to the NEPA policies. Executive Order 111514 (3/29/70) required the existing Citizens' Advisory Committee to advise the new Council on Environmental Quality, and elaborated on the duties of federal agencies under NEPA.[27] Reorganization Plan No. 3 (effective 12/2/70) created the Environmental Protection Agency (EPA) and transferred to it the functions of the Federal Radiation Council (FRC) and the functions of the AEC's Radiation Protection Standards Division, which set limits on exposure levels, concentrations, or quantities outside the boundaries of areas controlled by persons lawfully possessing or using radioactive material. The AEC retained its authority for implementing and enforcing on-site radiation standards. The EPA also assumed functions previously conducted by the Departments of the Interior, Agriculture, HEW, and others.

In 1970, in response to NEPA, the AEC established regulations that outlined its interpretation of its responsibilities under the act. The regulations included the steps necessary to produce an Environmental Impact Statement for a proposed reactor:

- Submission to AEC of "Applicant's Environmental Report—Construction Permit Stage."
- Preparation of a draft statement by AEC staff for circulation to appropriate federal and state agencies.
- Collection by the AEC of comments made by other governmental bodies on AEC draft statements.
- Issuance to the Council on Environmental Quality of a final statement as well as the applicant's report, the draft statement, and all comments received.
- For matters other than those considered in the construction permit stage,[28] adherence to the same procedures followed for the operating license stage.

The AEC implemented measures requiring each license applicant to submit the "Applicant's Environmental Report—Construction Permit Stage" at the time of application. To meet NEPA specifications, these reports had to address the following:

- The environmental impact of the proposed action.
- Any adverse environmental effects that could not be avoided if the proposal were implemented.
- Alternatives to the proposed action.
- The relationship between local short-term uses of man's environment and the maintenance and enhancement of long-term productivity.
- Any irreversible and irretrievable commitments of resources that would be involved if the proposed action were implemented.

The AEC maintained that issues to be considered under the provisions of NEPA did not include radiological effects, since relevant procedures already existed within AEC regulations. Water quality matters were excluded by the AEC's interpretation of the provisions of the Water Quality Improvement Act of 1970.[29] The AEC required only that the applicant produce certification of compliance with water quality standards by an appropriate agency; the ASLB's were not required to judge the matter further.

During the construction permit hearings for the Calvert Cliffs reactors, the ASLB rejected matters relating to water quality. This decision was taken to court by the intervenors, the Calvert Cliffs Coordinating Committee. The

AEC's position was overruled by the court. The case had considerable significance in upholding the intent of NEPA.

INSPECTION AND ENFORCEMENT

To date, most of the public attention and nuclear power controversies have dealt with construction and operating licensing reviews, review of highly technical generic problems, and the question of nuclear energy as an acceptable risk to society. Little attention has yet been paid to the significant segment of the AEC's regulatory activities involved with inspection and enforcement. Undoubtedly, these will gain in importance as more reactors and supporting fuel-cycle facilities (fuel fabrication, reprocessing, and waste storage) are built and put into operation. The critical value of the inspection role was vividly brought to the public's attention in early 1975, when newspapers carried major headlines stating that twenty-three boiling-water reactors were to be shut down for comprehensive examination after cracks had been discovered in a BWR pipe associated with the emergency core cooling system.

The AEC inspection and enforcement program consists of three distinct but related functions, each essential in determining the safety of a nuclear plant:
- To ascertain whether the nuclear power plants are constructed and operated in accordance with AEC regulations and license conditions.
- To enforce compliance with regulations and license conditions.
- To appraise construction and operating experience and feed back the findings to provide a basis for improved standards and technical reviews.[30]

According to the AEC, the program involves the planned, systematic examination by AEC field inspectors of all aspects of each nuclear plant; these inspections are carried out on a sampling basis throughout the life of the plant. The program is based on the premise that each applicant or licensee is responsible for the quality of design and construction and for the safe operation of its facility. AEC inspections evaluate the licensee's efforts to meet these responsibilities, and prepare the way for corrective action where necessary.

Regulatory inspections cover four phases of a nuclear power plant's life:
- Preconstruction—Before the AEC will docket a construction permit application, an acceptable program of quality assurance for design and procurement must be implemented by the electric utility, its suppliers, and other contractors.
- Construction—Shop and site inspections are made on equipment fabrication and plant erection to verify the suitability of materials used and the quality of fabrication; various tests are also carried out and their results recorded.
- Preoperation and startup—The purpose of this phase is to verify the adequacy of the design, the quality of individual components, and the performance of the many safety-related systems. Other areas examined during this period include the operating organizational structure, personnel training and performance, the results of monitoring and sampling programs for

radiation and effluent control, the results of environmental monitoring, plans and training for emergencies, security provisions, and administrative controls for safety.

• Operation—Inspections are made to determine whether the licensee is operating in a safe and responsible manner and in conformance with AEC requirements. The staff follows closely the control and release of radioactive effluents. Likewise they evaluate testing and preventive maintenance programs and determine whether plant management is taking timely corrective action when abnormal events occur.

When a licensee is found in noncompliance with an AEC regulation or condition in the license, civil fines and suspension of operations or amendment of license can be imposed. The licensee is also obligated to investigate and evaluate each abnormal occurrence and to report the findings to the AEC and other relevant agencies such as the Council on Environmental Quality, the U.S. Coast Guard, the Forest Service, and the Soil Conservation Service.

LICENSING OF OTHER FUEL-CYCLE PROCESSES

The discussion in this book has been concerned primarily with the nuclear reactor power plant. However, the reactor is only one of several process steps in the production of nuclear energy. The supply of nuclear fuel to the reactor and disposal of the waste products require a sequence of complex operations, all of which come under the regulation of the AEC. The sequence of the nuclear fuel cycle includes the mining and milling of uranium, refining of uranium and conversion to uranium hexafluoride, enrichment of the uranium in the isotope U-235, conversion of the enriched uranium to fuel material, fabrication of reactor fuel elements, use of fuel elements in nuclear power plants, chemical reprocessing of spent fuel to obtain reusable fuel material, recovery and marketing of plutonium and other byproducts, and disposal of radioactive wastes. Table 23

TABLE 23

FUEL CYCLE PLANTS
(As of June 30, 1973)

Type	In Operation	Planned or Under Construction
Uranium Mills	20	5
UF$_6$ Production Plants	2	—
Enriched Uranium Processing and Fabrication Plants	19	6
Plutonium Processing and Fabrication Plants	11	6
Fuel Reprocessing Plants	1	4
Waste Burial Grounds	6	—
Total	59	21

lists the number of fuel-cycle plants either in operation or planned as of June 30, 1973.[31] Missing from the list are the uranium enrichment plants; these are totally government-owned and were discussed in Chapter V.

The magnitude of present and future materials handling and processing can be estimated from data given by the AEC in its 1973 annual report to Congress.[32] A typical 1,000 Mw_e pressurized-water reactor requires an initial fuel loading of about 81 metric tons of slightly enriched uranium. An additional 26 metric tons per year must be supplied to replace spent fuel. For each of these nuclear power plants, over 240,000 short tons of uranium ore must be mined; about 500 short tons of uranium oxide must be processed into feed for the U-235 enrichment plants; and, based on manufacturing yield, 92 metric tons of enriched uranium oxide must be available for fabrication into reactor fuel elements for the initial core loading, which is valued at about $23 million. Approximately one third of these amounts is required each year thereafter to replace the fuel consumed.

After being "used up" in the reactor, the fuel elements from a year's operation still contain about $2 million worth of unconsumed uranium and fissionable plutonium as well as large amounts of highly radioactive fission products, which require careful handling. These spent fuel elements are transported to fuel-reprocessing plants by highway and rail in massive, shielded containers designed to withstand the effects of accidents without releasing the radioactive cargo.

The fuel-reprocessing plants separate the unconsumed uranium and the plutonium from the other highly radioactive fission products. These heavily shielded facilities purify the uranium and plutonium for reuse in other reactors and concentrate the radioactive wastes into small volumes for storage on-site pending transfer to the government for disposition.

As with nuclear power plants, fuel-cycle activities and facilities are regulated via safety, environmental, and safeguards evaluations and periodic plant inspections during construction, start-up, and operation. In all of these areas, the AEC requires adherence to standards established for the protection of the public health and safety, security, and the environment.

The licensees must demonstrate that the fuel cycle process in question can be carried out within acceptable health and safety limits. Of major concern is the exposure of the industrial worker and the public to radiation. As with the nuclear reactor, a controlled and acceptable exposure occurs during normal operation. Overexposures can occur either from such accidents as spills of highly radioactive materials or from improper operation of the process. Where enriched uranium or plutonium is involved, a nuclear chain reaction is possible and must be guarded against. Such "criticality" accidents have occurred in the past, and are most likely to happen in cases where the enriched uranium or plutonium has been concentrated. The greatest risk from such accidents is to the industrial worker in experimental, process, or storage facilities. However, the risks are minimized by remote handling of materials and regulations that require the nuclear material concentrations to be well below those which could sustain a neutron chain reaction.

The AEC's nuclear materials regulatory responsibilities cover not only the licensing of fuel-cycle activities, but also the licensing of byproduct materials (radioisotopes) applications in medicine, industry, agriculture, research, education, and national defense.

Another set of serious problems concerns the safeguarding of "special nuclear materials" from theft or diversion and the physical protection of nuclear facilities from industrial sabotage. Of all the problems facing the nuclear industry, the most difficult may be to demonstrate that an acceptable level of risk can be reached in these areas.

Regulations are contained in 10 CFR 50, 70, and 73 for safeguarding nuclear facilities and materials. These regulations require that any person licensed to operate a "production or utilization" facility, such as a power reactor or fuel-reprocessing plant, must have in place an AEC-approved security plan that provides physical protection at the licensed facility.

These regulations apply to operators of fuel-reprocessing plants and other licensees (such as operators of fuel-fabrication plants) who use highly enriched uranium, U-233, or plutonium—alone or in combinations exceeding 5,000 grams. These people are required:

- To equip and train guards and watchmen to protect against industrial sabotage.
- To establish a "protected area," enclosed by a physical barrier.
- To control access by individuals, vehicles, and packages to the protected area.
- To install lighting along the perimeter of the area.
- To develop a response capability to intrusion.
- To establish a liaison with law enforcement authorities for assistance when necessary.
- To establish an emergency, two-way communication link with law enforcement authorities.

Materials accountability procedures at nuclear facilities are required as another means of providing safeguards. These involve frequent physical inventories, double-entry accounting records, recording of all material transfers, and system audits.

Shipments of special nuclear materials must also be safeguarded. Additional protection is required when the shipment contains U-235 (in uranium enriched by U-235 to concentrations of 20 percent or more), plutonium, or U-233, in amounts exceeding 5,000 grams. The following AEC statements summarize these requirements.[33]

When cargo aircraft are used, the number of en route transfers must be minimized and the transfers must be observed by armed monitoring personnel. Unarmed escorts must accompany air and sea movements from the last terminal in the United States to the point where the shipment is unloaded at a foreign terminal. Shipments of all but small quantities of these materials on passenger aircraft were banned in February 1973.

Truck or trailer shipments must be accompanied by an armed escort traveling in a separate vehicle, unless trucks or trailers specially designed to protect against theft or diversion are used. In addition, shipments must be made on a point-to-point basis with no loading or unloading of other cargo between these points.

Other safeguard measures include use of preferential routing to avoid trouble areas, continuous surveillance of truck transport and transfer points, and pre-planning of shipments to assure delivery at a time when the receiver is available to accept the material.

When rail transportation is used, the shipment must be escorted by two armed individuals in the shipment car or in an escort car of the train. These persons must keep the shipment cars under observation and must detrain at stops when practicable in order to guard the shipment cars and check car or container locks and seals.

Scheduled ship-to-ship transfers are not permitted. Transfer at domestic ports from other modes of transportation must be observed by armed monitors. In order to assure that import shipments of strategic quantities of special nuclear material are adequately protected, importers must provide the same level of protection as that given to domestic shipments.

At the present time, the licensee is required to provide the protection for safeguarding materials in transit or at nuclear facilities. Because of the potential seriousness of the consequences of illegal diversion, safeguarding of nuclear materials is a highly controversial subject and constitutes one more problem that must be resolved to the satisfaction of the industry and the public before nuclear power can be considered an acceptable risk.

ROLE OF THE STATES

In a 1959 amendment to the Atomic Energy Act, Congress authorized the AEC to enter into agreements by which individual states would assume AEC's regulatory responsibility over nuclear source and byproduct materials and, to a somewhat lesser extent, over special nuclear materials.[34] However, the statute specifically precluded such agreements in connection with facility licensing or waste disposal. Implicit in the legislation was the notion that Congress had intended to preempt all state control over the entire field of radiation safety, since AEC approval was required before states could assume regulatory responsibility. The U.S. Supreme Court ruled on April 3, 1972, that the states were preempted from regulating radiation emissions from nuclear power plants.[35] (See discussion in a later section of this chapter of hearings on the Monticello reactor.)

Despite the emission regulation decision, the states now have substantial authority with respect to water quality. In 1965, Congress amended the Federal

Water Pollution Control Act (FWPCA) to require the states to establish water quality standards for federal (interstate) waters. By 1971, only about half of the states had standards fully approved by the Environmental Protection Agency (EPA), and enforcement of the standards was lagging. In June of 1971, President Nixon ordered the Army Corps of Engineers to begin enforcement of an 1899 statute which required anyone discharging refuse into U.S. navigable waters to obtain a permit from the corps. Previously, the corps had issued permits only for discharges that might affect the navigability of the water.[36] Enforcement of the new permit program created a crushing administrative burden for the Army, because under the National Environmental Policy Act (NEPA), it had to issue environmental impact statements before it could issue permits to discharge waste. The Army had as many as 20,000 permit applications pending review.

On October 18, 1972, however, the entire structure of water pollution law and responsibility for its enforcement was changed by passage, over President Nixon's veto, of the Federal Water Pollution Control Act Amendments.[37] Under these amendments, states were made responsible for preparation and enforcement of effluent discharge limits for each pollution source for both inter- and intrastate waters. If the states do not establish such discharge limits, or if the limits set are "inconsistent" with federal (EPA) requirements, the administrator of the Environmental Protection Agency will establish the limits.[38]

The 1972 amendments make the states once again responsible for issuing permits for the discharge of effluent into waters, except where an interstate agency, created by interstate compact, has the responsibility.[39] If a state has no provision for issuing permits, the administrator of the EPA has the responsibility. Discharges without a permit are illegal. The secretary of the Army, acting through the chief of Army engineers, again has the responsibility for issuing permits only in the case of discharge of fill or dredged materials into navigable waters.[40]

The 1972 amendments also require the creation of national standards of performance for specific industries. In line with these, and subject to EPA approval, the states may then promulgate their own standards for the discharge of thermal and other pollution, including hazardous substances. Steam electric power plants are specifically included as an industry subject to state regulation. So long as state standards are at least as stringent as those required by section 306 of the 1972 amendments, the states are authorized to apply and enforce them. The only pollution sources exempt from state-established standards are new sources owned or operated by the United States.

It is noteworthy that low-level radiation discharge is never specifically mentioned in the amendments to the act. They merely state that the discharge of "hazardous substances," and of radiological, chemical, or biological warfare agents can be regulated by the states.[41] "Hazardous substances" are defined by section 311b (2a) as "elements and compounds which, when discharged in any quantity into or upon the navigable waters of the United States or adjoining shorelines or the waters of the contiguous zone, present an imminent and substantial danger to the public health or welfare, including, but not limited to, fish, shellfish, wildlife, shorelines and beaches.'' Nuclear fuel reprocessing plants were temporarily left out of the list of new sources for which standards of performance are to be developed, but as soon as the EPA is able to establish the level of controls possible in such plants, they are to be added to the list. Discharges from these plants will then be brought into the sphere of substances that may be regulated by states technically and administratively competent to do so.

States may enforce their requirements with respect to effluent limits, compliance schedules, new point sources of pollution, hazardous substances, and thermal discharges, as long as the requirements are at least as stringent as the federal requirements.

The states have other legitimate and recognized interests in the siting of power plants from environmental and land-use perspectives. In the last few years, the states of Arizona, Connecticut, Maine, Maryland, New Hampshire, New Mexico, New York, Oregon, South Carolina, Vermont, and Washington have passed legislation dealing with power plant siting. For example, in February 1970, the state of Washington enacted legislation to create the Thermal Power Plant Site Evaluation Council.[42] Formed from members of relevant state and local agencies, the council was designed to provide a unified review process at the state level.

ROLE OF THE INTERVENORS

While each reactor proposal is subject to an involved and lengthy review by the AEC, ACRS, and in some cases by state agencies, many encounter no serious objections and proceed in a routine fashion. Some, however, meet with great resistance from outside intervenors. While most early interventions focused on details of the licensing procedure—often on whether the plant was a development prototype or a commercial facility—most recent interventions have concentrated on radiological and environmental matters. Intervention in an ASLB hearing requires both knowledge of hearing procedures and technical knowledge of the proposed reactor. A great deal of time is required to attend the prolonged series of sessions, which may recess and resume unpredictably. Intervention is thus only likely to occur when there are individuals who have great objections to a plant and who have the requisite expertise and time. Widespread public opposition to a plant is often insufficient to bring about intervention; on the other hand, sometimes a single individual can intervene effectively in the absence of public concern. Thus, the occurrence or nonoccurrence of a contested hearing is not an exact measure of public response to a proposed reactor.

The first major intervention (Fermi) and a number of subsequent ones (e.g., Quad Cities) were conducted by labor unions and union leaders. Later in the 1960's, intervention against some reactors was attempted by potential competitors of the applicant utility (e.g., the Duke and Vermont Yankee plants). The interventions on environmental issues were mounted by states (e.g., New Hampshire against Vermont Yankee, Illinois against Quad Cities) and by a number of citizen environmental groups.

Usually the organizational umbrella for citizen intervention is a local group, sometimes *ad hoc*. In order for it to be granted standing to sue, an organization often has to prove to the court that it has interests in the locality of a proposed plant. National organizations are becoming involved in increasing numbers; for example, the Sierra Club has attempted to prevent California reactors at Bodega Bay, Diablo Canyon, and Mendocino. Moreover, local chapters of such organizations sometimes intervene independently of their national leadership—the Sierra Club on the Midland plant, and the National Audubon Society on the Pilgrim plant. Quasinational organizations have developed, which intervene in regional areas. Businessmen for the Public Interest in Chicago, and Union of Concerned Scientists in Cambridge, Massachusetts, are two examples.

As the number of interventions has increased in recent years, so has the number of individuals equipped to intervene. The amassed pool of expertise has become generally available to local groups and national organizations, and as a result, more recent cases have had to be handled more thoroughly. While the motives of intervenors vary and are often questioned, intervention is an established part of the review process and has had a substantial impact on the plant siting process. Discussion of three cases of intervention—the Fermi, Monticello, and Calvert Cliffs reactors—will demonstrate the impact which intervenors have had and continue to have on the licensing process.

THE FERMI CASE

After passage of the 1954 Act, the regulations issued by the AEC governing the licensing of nuclear facilities were quite general in scope and thus provided flexible control. The Hazards Evaluation Branch of the Division of Civilian Applications worked informally with applicants in the preparation of hazards reports, which were then usually presented to the Advisory Committee on Reactor Safeguards (ACRS). The ACRS, in turn, made recommendations to be acted upon by the AEC commissioners in issuing or denying a construction permit.[43] The entire process was carried out essentially in secrecy,[44] and the only formal notice made was an announcement in the Federal Register that a construction permit had been issued.[45] Although the license applications, including the hazards reports submitted by the applicant, were placed in the AEC's public document room, the interested public did not have available the AEC or ACRS appraisal of the safety of a proposed power plant.[46] The AEC approach to licensing was soon to be challenged, however. The intervention by third-party organizations in connection with the licensing of the Fermi reactor represented the first major challenge of the licensing process and had great impact on subsequent licensing procedures.

In January 1956, the twenty-five-company Power Reactor Development Company (PRDC), made up of equipment manufacturers and utility companies, applied for a license to design, construct, and operate a 100 Mw$_e$ fast breeder power plant (later called the Fermi plant) at Lagoona Beach, Michigan, about thirty miles from Detroit.[47] On June 6, 1956, the ACRS issued a report to the AEC stating that it was not sure that the Fermi plant could be operated safely at the Lagoona Beach site.[48] In August 1956, the AEC nonetheless issued a construction permit, subject to intervention within thirty days,[49] with the stipulation that certain problems would have to be solved prior to operation. The reaction was swift: the JCAE chairman, Senator Clinton P. Anderson, incensed by the secrecy and the fact that the AEC invoked executive privilege to keep the ACRS report from even the JCAE,[50] called the AEC's action a "star chamber proceeding" and expressed his desire to separate the AEC's regulatory functions from its research, production, and promotion functions.[51] Five days later he notified AEC Chairman Lewis L. Strauss that the JCAE was undertaking a study of the problem, specifying the possibility of legislation to require open hearings prior to construction permit issuance, to require publication of ACRS reports, and to separate the hearing functions of the AEC.[52] The same month, three international labor unions, all AFL-CIO members, formally intervened in the licensing proceedings;[53] Senator Anderson told an AFL-CIO convention in October that he had requested that the unions (and the governor of Michigan) intervene.[54] JCAE member Holifield and AEC Commissioner Murray also opposed the plant.[55]

The AEC responded by beginning to give advance notice of proposed licensing actions and by making public the reports of its own hazards evaluation staff (but not reports of the ACRS). These reforms did not satisfy the JCAE, however; the 1957 Price-Anderson Act, along with the indemnification measures discussed previously, established the ACRS as a statutory body and required that the ACRS review every license application and issue a public report upon each. In addition, a public hearing was required for all application proceedings, whether or not they were contested.[56] The question of separation of AEC functions was not approached. Berman and Hydeman in an exhaustive study of AEC regulatory performance, urged in 1961 that this subject be reopened, and recommended that the AEC be split into two independent agencies, an Atomic Energy Administration (operations and promotion) and an Atomic Energy Board (regulation, standards, program evaluation, licensing).[57]

The AEC-required "Hazards Summary Report," prepared by PRDC, stated that the maximum credible accident would be the melting of the fuel in one subassembly, automatic reactor shutdown, and no radiation leaching. A report by the University of Michigan Engineering Research Institute, received by PRDC in 1957, estimated that a release of all radioactive material from Fermi could result in as many as 133,000 deaths, 181,000 immediate injuries from radiation, and 245,000 long-term injuries. The AEC's widely quoted Brookhaven

Report on possible effects of large reactor accidents, also issued in 1957 and using various accident assumptions, estimated up to 3,400 deaths and 43,000 injuries.[58]

The AEC affirmed its issuance of the Fermi construction permit in 1958 and 1959. The unions appealed, but the U.S. Supreme Court held that the AEC could issue construction permits while leaving resolution of some technical matters until a later stage, and that nothing in the 1954 Act precluded location of reactors near large population centers.[59]

In July 1961, PRDC submitted its application for an operating license. After numerous delays centering around fuel fabrication, and after low-power testing, a full-power license was issued in January 1966. The first generation of electricity was achieved in August 1966, but a partial fuel melt-down caused by blockage of sodium coolant closed the plant in October. Fortunately, the accident did not result in a large-scale release of radioactivity and no one was injured.

After extensive testing to determine the melt-down cause, the reactor was issued a new operating permit in May 1968. In December 1969, the ACRS issued a favorable letter on restart of the reactor, and in February 1970, the commission authorized restart. The plant was operated briefly at 200 Mw_{th} in late 1970. Since there were no redesigned fuel elements available, PRDC then cut back power to conserve the original fuel elements. The reactor was operated on a limited basis as a research and development facility from October 1970 until November 27, 1972, when it was announced that it would be dismantled.[60] Although the Fermi reactor was unsuccessful as a demonstration plant that would lead the way to a commercial fast breeder, the controversy stirred by its construction had significant and constructive effects on the AEC regulatory process.

MONTICELLO

Fermi was atypical in that it was a sodium-cooled fast reactor rather than one of the light-water-moderated reactors that have become the mainstay of the industry. On the other hand, the Monticello reactor, built by Northern States Power Company of Minnesota, represents a typical boiling-water reactor, sharing its basic design with many other modern plants. It was proposed a decade after Fermi and experienced intervention at both the construction and operating license stages; the intervention was on environmental as well as safety issues. The case was also important in that it presented a challenge to the AEC's sole jurisdiction over radiological matters. The newly formed Pollution Control Agency of the state of Minnesota attempted to impose radiological emission standards, stricter than those of the AEC, on the plant. This attempt was challenged in court and eventually the U.S. Supreme Court ruled in favor of the AEC's preemption of the field.[61]

In 1966 Northern States Power awarded a contract to the General Electric Company to supply a boiling-water reactor for a proposed 545 Mw_e power plant. In January of 1966, the utility began planning for the new plant, and in February of that year, it applied for a permit from the state agency charged with the regulation of water quality, the Minnesota Water Pollution Control Commission. Application for a waste permit from the commission was made in October.[62]

In line with the company's policy of ringing the urban area with plants to provide an efficient and reliable network of power supply, the plant was to be located on the Mississippi River in open rural country about thirty-five miles northwest of Minneapolis–Saint Paul.

Previous experience with nuclear power in the region consisted of two small research-and-development prototype boiling-water reactors constructed for rural electrical cooperatives. A 22 Mw_e PDRP plant at Elk River, Minnesota, only about a dozen miles down river from the Monticello site, had begun operation in 1964; it was not a success and was shut down in February 1968. The other, located 140 miles southeast of Minneapolis-Saint Paul at LaCrosse, Wisconsin, began operations in 1967, as consideration of the Monticello plant was under way. Monticello was the first major nuclear plant to be located in the region.

In the spring of 1967, the public review process began. The AEC held a hearing on a construction permit for the plant. The hearing was contested on both environmental and radiological grounds, with intervenors in this hearing continuing to play an active role in the process of review through final granting of the operating license. No more than one or two construction license hearings had previously been contested on environmental grounds. The construction permit was granted in June 1967.

In May, a new state environmental agency, the Minnesota Pollution Control Agency (MPCA), was created to replace the old Water Pollution Control Commission. Organization of this agency continued through the summer, with an executive director being appointed in November. Since this agency now had jurisdiction over water discharge permits, Northern States Power Company (NSP) reapplied for a permit for Monticello in July 1967.[63]

Early in 1968, the MPCA started to assert jurisdiction over radioactive emissions from the plant. In an effort to write a waste discharge permit, the agency engaged Dr. Ernest C. Tsivaglou of the Georgia Institute of Technology to study the problem. On the basis of his report, the agency drafted a permit regulating both conventional and radioactive discharges from the plant.[64]

There was at the time correspondence with the AEC over the legality of the state permit. The AEC claimed sole jurisdiction over the regulation of radioactive discharges from nuclear power plants, and the special assistant attorney general of the state of Minnesota concurred with the AEC's jurisdictional claim. The AEC also took issue with the content of the permit, maintaining that it would be difficult to meet and achieve plant operating reliability. Nevertheless, in May 1969, the MPCA issued the permit.[65] It differed from a conventional AEC operating permit in that it set emission limits on an isotope-by-isotope basis rather than on a gross level of activity. It also required extensive monitoring and other precautions to reduce the activity released. In general, it represented limits thirty to fifty times more restrictive than those recommended by the AEC.

Later in 1969, Northern States Power Company brought two suits against the MPCA. Its suit in Federal District Court argued that the state did not have the power to regulate radioactive emissions and that the permit was unreasonable; the second issue was later dropped from the suit. The other suit was brought in the state court in Wright County, where the plant was located. This suit contended that the conditions required of the plant were unreasonable.[66]

Public sentiment and controversy were growing. Local environmental groups had taken up the issue and had come out both against the plant and, in some cases, against the MPCA permit as too loose. In the fall of 1969, a symposium on Nuclear Power and the Public was held at the University of Minnesota.[67] The panels were filled with personages nationally known in the nuclear power controversy. The local press noted that at a similar forum held in Vermont a few months earlier the AEC had been embarrassed by adverse presentations and that they were sending their "first team" to Minnesota, including Representative Craig Hosmer of the JCAE and AEC Commissioner James Ramey. Also present were Dr. Arthur R. Tamplin, the nuclear power critic from Lawrence Radiation Laboratory, and Dr. Barry Commoner, director of the Center for the Biology of Natural Systems at Washington University, who is an outspoken environmental advocate.

In January 1970, the state of Minnesota gave testimony at the JCAE hearing on the Environmental Effects of Producing Electric Power. A delegation led by Governor Harold Levander presented Minnesota's case. He noted that the states of Michigan, Illinois, Vermont, and Wisconsin had petitioned the court to file *amicus curiae* briefs, and the states of Hawaii, Kentucky, Maine, North Dakota, Pennsylvania, Utah, Virginia, and the territory of Guam had advised the Minnesota attorney general that they wished their names attached to the state's brief.[68]

In mid-March 1970, the AEC broke from its usual procedure and announced it would hold a public hearing on a provisional operating license for the plant. Such hearings had been mandatory until 1962, after which they were held only in contested cases. The AEC stated that intense public interest was the reason for this move. Three parties petitioned and were granted leave to intervene in the hearings as full participants.[69] One was a local environmental group, the Minnesota Environmental Control Citizens' Association (MECCA), that had been active in the controversy for some time. The second was a group of three graduate students in physics at the University of Minnesota, who had been following the issue and had given advice to people in the MPCA on occasion. The third was the state, which was automatically a party in the hearings, but played a minor role. A high school student from a school near the plant also intervened to learn more about the process of citizen involvement in environmental affairs.

Before the hearings got under way, NSP filed for a provisional operating license for fuel loading and low-power testing to get the plant ready for summer operation, in the event the usual provisional operating license would be granted subsequently. This was argued before the ASLB and denied on the basis that operation might prejudice the final decision, in the event changes might be desired in the plant.

At this point in the decision-making process, there existed several positions or points of view among the participants. MECCA had been opposed to the plant all along and viewed the hearing as another chance to stop the plant by whatever means appeared useful. They were resolved to bring up issues they thought relevant, even though the ASLB might rule them not germane. This happened with the problem of thermal pollution. Although this hearing followed the passage of NEPA and the publication of Appendix D to 10 CFR 50, the decision on Calvert Cliffs had not been handed down and the ASLB ruled that evaluating thermal pollution was not an AEC responsibility. Greater familiarity with NEPA within MECCA might have generated a challenge on this matter prior to Calvert Cliffs. MECCA also raised the question of plant safety and the safety of the public both in the case of routine emissions and in the case of accidents.

The three physics graduate students approached the matter differently. They based their contentions on technical matters regarding plant safety. They did not attempt to bring up policy questions related to the desirability of allowing a certain population dose, but instead criticized the AEC's and NSP's calculations in attempting to limit the dose. They also sought to explore the ability of the plant to meet the more restrictive Minnesota standards. In their view the hearing was an opportunity in an adversary situation to gain access to information denied them by NSP and others in their study of the plant.

The state of Minnesota was included in the hearings by the ASLB, although it was not willing to take a full part. There were two reasons for this hesitation. First, the state maintained that since its jurisdiction over the operation of the plant was before the courts, it could not recognize the authority of the AEC in this matter and could not act as a party in the AEC hearings. Secondly, the state was represented by counsel from the state attorney general's office, rather than by the Pollution Control Agency. He was not supported with staff and testimony, and was in no position to make technical arguments. This limitation typified the ambiguous posture of the state. It firmly maintained its right to regulate the plant, but was not willing to consider seriously the use of that right.

Northern States Power Company approached the hearing with a good-faith effort to present their case according to conventional guidelines with the expectation that the board would grant them an operating license at an early date. Their view of the hearing was that it was a procedural and informational undertaking, rather than a decision-making step.

The AEC staff shared with NSP the burden of proving that an operating license should be granted, but they were sensitive to the broader issues being raised both by NEPA and by safety questions. They were also concerned with a timely resolution of the matter, as the proceedings cut into their capabilities for handling other reactors around the country.

The Atomic Safety and Licensing Board was comprised, as usual, of three members—one with legal background, and two with technical expertise. They were constrained by published AEC policy, but made an attempt to hear fairly all issues they could consider relevant, and allowed great latitude to the intervenors in the interest of uncovering important issues. They viewed their role seriously, as real decision makers, and required substantial efforts from the AEC staff and the NSP. It is interesting to note that two of the members of this board were on the board that subsequently rejected an operating license for Columbia University's Triga research reactor, the only example of the rejection of an operating license. The rejection was later overruled in an appeal to the AEC.

As in the case of Fermi, public access to documents became an issue. The board expressed an interest in seeing field inspection reports on the plant to help them assess the quality control in the plant. The AEC staff balked, contending these reports were privileged information. The intervenors then subpoenaed the documents to force the issue. Eventually, censored reports were provided to all parties.[70] This conflict marks another example of the divergence between practices intended to insure the smooth internal functioning of a government agency and those needed to guarantee the public's right to technical information.

The hearings started in April 1970, were recessed, and continued in the summer. Finally, in September 1970, a provisional operating license was granted for fuel loading and low-power testing. A full power license followed in March 1971.

The federal suit was decided against the state and upheld the AEC's jurisdiction over radiological matters. Minnesota appealed to the U.S. Supreme Court which, on April 3, 1972, upheld the district court, noting that it was proper in this technical field for federal regulation to preempt state control.[71] The rulings were based largely on the wording of the 1959 amendments to the Atomic Energy Act, which permitted delegation of certain AEC regulatory powers to the states, but which prohibited delegation of other AEC functions, including regulation of radioactive discharges from nuclear power plants. It was further based on comments by the JCAE, in support of the 1959 amendments, which indicated the committee's intent that reactor regulation remain solely on AEC function.[72] The ruling was not based on the fact that Minnesota's regulations were more stringent than those of the AEC.

CALVERT CLIFFS

The Fermi and Monticello cases were among the few isolated instances of public concern over nuclear power plant siting in the late 1950's and early 1960's. Large-scale public intervention did not become a significant factor in the licensing process until the late 1960's, when large numbers of nuclear reactors were in the process of being constructed or operated and there was a general increase in concern over environmental poblems.

This rising public concern was reflected in the Congress and produced a landmark piece of legislation, the National Environmental Policy Act of 1969 (NEPA), previously discussed in this chapter. The substantive policy statement of NEPA is that the federal government "use all practicable means and measures" to protect environmental values. Congress did not establish environmental protection as an exclusive goal; rather, it desired a reordering of priorities, so that environmental costs and benefits could assume their proper place along with other considerations.

It took more than eleven months for the AEC to modify its licensing procedures in response to the new requirements of NEPA. The AEC added Appendix D to Part 50, Licensing of Production and Utilization Facilities, of Title 10, CFR. This outlined the AEC's policy and how it viewed its responsibilities under NEPA. As described earlier in this chapter, it included the steps necessary to produce an environmental impact statement for a proposed reactor.

However, in the appendix, the AEC maintained that issues to be considered under the provisions of NEPA did not include radiological effects, since procedures for treating these already existed within AEC regulations. Water quality matters were excluded by the AEC's interpretation of the provisions of the Water Quality Improvement Act of 1970 (PL 91-224). The AEC required that certification of compliance with water quality standards by an appropriate agency be produced by the applicant. This was then sufficient consideration of water quality matters, and the commission and ASLB's were not required to judge the matter further.

In hearings on the issuance of a construction permit for the Baltimore Gas and Electric Company's Calvert Cliffs reactor, the Atomic Safety and Licensing Board rejected matters relating to water quality. This decision was taken to court by intervenors, the Calvert Cliffs Coordinating Committee. The U.S. Court of Appeals, District of Columbia Circuit, overruled the ASLB and the AEC on July 23, 1971, and required the AEC to take a much more complete view of the environmental effects of proposed reactors.[73] This single decision was to have resounding effects throughout the nuclear industry; not only did it cause reactor delays costing many millions of dollars but it had a marked effect on the AEC's approach to licensing. Probably of more importance, the court decision gave teeth to the National Environmental Policy Act. It also gave firm precedence for intervenors to challenge the industry on a broad range of environmental issues.

The court issued a blistering denunciation of the AEC's interpretation of NEPA. Excerpts from the court opinion indicate the tenor:

Our duty . . . is to see that important legislative purposes, heralded in the halls of Congress, are not lost or misdirected in the vast hallways of the federal bureaucracy.

We find the policies embodied in NEPA to be a good deal clearer and more demanding than does the Commission.

[NEPA] duties are qualified by the phrase "to the fullest extent possible." . . .
This language does not provide an escape hatch for footdragging agencies. . . .
Congress did not intend the act to be such a paper tiger.

[The AEC's] responsibility is not simply to sit back, like an umpire. . . .

[The AEC's] approach to statutory interpretation is strange indeed—so strange
that it seems to reveal a rather thoroughgoing reluctance to meet the NEPA
obligations. . . .

The Commission's crabbed interpretation of NEPA makes a mockery of the Act.[74]

Specifically, the court held that NEPA contained both substantive and procedural duties, each with a different effect on the agencies. NEPA Section 101,
requiring that agencies use "all practicable means" to assure and enhance environmental quality, was seen by the court as a flexible policy, open to exercise
of agency discretion (with a consequent limitation on ability to force an agency
to take some action). NEPA Sections 102 and 103, however, specified mandatory procedural duties incumbent upon all agencies without discretion. Measured by this yardstick, the AEC's regulations were deficient in four respects:

- The ASLB reviewed AEC staff environmental reports only in contested
  cases. The court held that agencies must conduct an independent review at
  each stage, regardless of contest.
- An AEC rule that put off consideration of environmental issues until
  March 1971 violated the immediate (January 1970) effect given by
  Congress to NEPA. All licensing actions after January 1970 were required
  to be rereviewed.
- The AEC's practice of accepting water quality compliance reports from
  other agencies under the Federal Water Pollution Control Act (FWPCA)
  and compliance reports in other areas was termed an abdication of the
  AEC's duty to conduct a meaningful balancing of all costs and benefits
  required by NEPA on a project-by-project basis.
- The AEC's refusal even to consider halting construction on plants in order
  to weigh the desirability of technical alterations for environmental improvements and its refusal to consider "backfitting" extant facilities with
  such technological improvements violated the spirit of NEPA, which
  required the agency to consider the costs, benefits, or alternatives of each
  project at every significant stage. Obviously, the further along the construction process is, the greater will be the economic cost of changes, and
  the environmental considerations would thus eventually be outweighed.
  The court's view of this approach was that it "hardly amounts to consideration . . . 'to the fullest extent possible.' " The AEC was thus required
  to consider all plants that had not received operating licenses, even prior to
  the application for operating license.[75]

The AEC responded quickly to the Calvert Cliffs decision by issuing, on
August 4, 1971, interim guidance to affected license applicants (sixty-one
applicants and post-1970 licensees, eighty-eight reactors total) [76] and, without

notice or hearing, by releasing regulations on September 9, 1971, effective on that date.[77]

The new AEC requirement was made retroactive to January 1, 1970, when NEPA took effect. The effect of the regulation was to make the AEC directly responsible for evaluating the total environmental impact of nuclear power, including thermal effects, which it had previously rejected. This required preparation of a large number of detailed environmental impact statements on the facilities involved and caused considerable delay in licensing.

With the industry facing this problem, the AEC's regulations instructed Atomic Safety and Licensing Boards to proceed expeditiously with pending hearings and those in progress. During the review period, the AEC also provided for possible authorization of fuel loading and limited operation of power reactors, consistent with appropriate regard for environmental values. Also in revising the regulations, the AEC noted its intention to be responsive to the conservation and environmental concerns of the public, but added that it was also examining steps that could be taken to reconcile a proper regard for the environment with the necessity of meeting the nation's growing requirements for electric power on a timely basis. Thus, it assured the industry that balanced considerations would be given to both issues.

Some felt the AEC overreacted to the court decision. In testimony to the Senate Committee on Interior and Insular Affairs, Charles F. Luce, chairman and chief executive officer of Consolidated Edison Company of New York, stated, ". . . AEC did not utilize the full measure of discretion available to it under the court's opinion when it amended its licensing regulations. On the contrary, it subjected to substantially the same kind of preoperational environmental review all nuclear plants which did not have an operating license on January 1, 1970, the date NEPA became effective." [78]

The utility industry was already plagued by other problems and was concerned that the AEC's actions would bring about further delays in reactor start-ups, thus causing power shortages in the country. Luce went on to say,

> . . . this procedure is rife with opportunities for delay from applicants whose engineers and scientists are already overloaded with work, litigious intervenors, overworked AEC staff and counsel, and overscheduled hearing examiners and AEC commissioners. Such delays could well mean the difference between adequate power and blackouts. And I use that term advisedly, for the people of a city, state, or region. Most assuredly, they will mean higher cost electricity. For example, every day's delay in the start-up of Indian Point No. 2 ultimately will cost electric consumers about $130,000. One year's delay could cost them about $48 million.[79]

Mr. Luce's testimony typified the concern expressed by the utility industry and others who feared a power shortage and delays caused by the new procedures. In a letter to James Schlesinger, the new chairman of the AEC, Nelson Rockefeller, then governor of New York, wrote, "A serious danger of a power supply emergency in New York City during the summer of 1972 impels me to urge your Commission to invoke with all possible speed whatever extraordinary procedures may be available in handling the application of Consolidated Edison for an operating license for its Indian Point No. 2 plant.'' [80] This is characteristic of the type of pressure brought to bear on the AEC on behalf of a single plant; yet, many plants were involved in similar problems and each was applying its own pressure in its own way.

There were also fears in the AEC that the government could be sued for the costs of plant delays since the industry had followed procedures set down by the AEC and was not to blame for the situation in which it found itself. Possible solutions to the problems caused by the new procedures were recommended. The Edison Electric Institute, representing the private utility sector, recommended several possible remedies including interim licensing. Its representatives stated in their testimony, "If the provisions in the AEC regulations authorizing provisional operation prove to be ineffective, we believe Congress should consider the desirability of affirmative legislation to authorize operation of needed nuclear generating capacity on an interim basis. . . ." [81] After the Calvert Cliffs decision the AEC then (fall 1971) began granting licenses for plants to operate on partial capacity, thereby reducing the environmental effects and, hopefully, complying with the Calvert Cliffs decision.

The environmentalists, however, continued to attack the licensing of power plants that lacked thorough evaluation of thermal pollution problems. In the court case of *Isaac Walton League* v. *Schlesinger,* a decision was reached by the court on December 13, 1971, that a partial-power license could not be issued without the environmental impact statement required by NEPA. The AEC's appeal was not ruled on because a private compromise was reached between the intervenors and the power company involved. The compromise required the utility to construct a $30 million cooling system that would effectively discharge the heat into the atmosphere instead of into the river. But the utility was allowed to operate the power plant as initially constructed, discharging heat to the river, until the new cooling system was completed.

AEC licensing on an interim basis was further restricted in the Kalur case, December 21, 1971. Under the little-known Refuse Act of 1899, it was ruled that an impact statement must be filed prior to the licensing of a plant. The case was appealed by the administration, but it was evident that legislative action was required if licensing relief were to be given the utilities. Several approaches to legislation were considered. The one finally enacted (HR 14655) was proposed by JCAE member, Congressman Hosmer, and gave the AEC authority to issue interim licenses to nuclear power plants pending compliance with NEPA requirements.

Opposition to the proposed bill arose through a coalition called the National Intervenors (it included the Sierra Club, Friends of the Earth, Environmental Action, Inc., and the Environmental Policy Center). The coalition's grounds were that the bill would set a precedent for gutting NEPA. It felt that once the

AEC was given authority to ease the NEPA restrictions, other federal agencies would follow suit.

Another major controversy arose over the fact that the AEC would not be required to hold public hearings on site construction. JCAE member Senator Howard Baker (R., Tennessee) offered an acceptable compromise: hearings on site construction would be required, but the nature of the hearings was left to the AEC. Also the temporary licenses were to be valid only up to October 30, 1973, the end of the period in which there were likely to be acute power shortages. HR 14655 passed the House on May 17, 1972, by voice vote; the Senate passed it 80–0; and President Nixon signed it into law on June 2, 1972. While the bill gave the industry the relief it wanted, it also kept intact the basic tenets of NEPA in the long term.

Another procedural change instituted by the AEC in 1972 dealt with the handling of plant safety, radioactive emissions, waste disposal, and other like issues that pertained to the nuclear program as a whole. The AEC proposed to cover these issues together in a series of general hearings, rather than deal with them in detail at individual licensing hearings. The aspects of each issue common to all plants would be investigated and regulations would be proposed as a result. Consideration of these issues would thus be removed from the licensing process and repetition of arguments would be avoided. Early in 1972 two general hearings were begun. The one on the subject of routine radioactive emissions from plants was designed to remove ambiguity from the existing AEC regulations requiring these emissions to be kept "as low as practicable." Simultaneously, a rule-making hearing was scheduled on the safety aspects of the emergency core cooling system (ECCS) installed in all reactors and designed to limit the consequences of a reactor accident's resulting in the loss of the primary coolant from the reactor core. This controversial hearing continued through the entire year. In 1973, hearings were also begun on the nuclear fuel cycle and on the handling and transportation of high-level radioactive wastes. While it appears logical to attempt to settle these issues once and for all by a general hearing and thus to streamline the plant licensing procedure, the success of the venture is still not apparent. Final evaluation must await the outcome of rule making by the AEC on each of these issues and the impact of these rules on the licensing process.

NUCLEAR SAFETY ISSUES

For the most part, current controversies surrounding nuclear power no longer focus primarily on problems of individual power plant siting; in these areas, resolutions are accomplished either through concessions by the AEC and the affected utility or through the courts. The area of controversy first expanded to include highly technical generic issues such as emergency core cooling, fuel densification, and seismic design requirements. More recently, Congress has raised not only the question of energy development priorities but also the question of whether the advantages of nuclear power are outweighed by its disadvantages. Although the formation of the Energy Research and Development Administration and Nuclear Regulatory Commission was designed to separate the promotion of nuclear power from its regulation, another goal was to have ERDA place the priorities of alternative energy developments more on a par with those of nuclear power. This reordering of priorities is still in transition and the first ERDA budget to Congress is still dominated by nuclear power expenditures.

The environmental issues associated with nuclear power are many, and include the views that (1) nuclear power plants are potentially so hazardous that they should not be allowed on earth under any circumstances; (2) nuclear plant safety features are inadequate and there should be a moratorium on nuclear plant use until these problems are solved; (3) radiation releases are too large and should be reduced; (4) alternative methods must be employed to reduce thermal pollution of cooling water sources; (5) the problems of handling, shipment, and storage of nuclear waste have not been solved; and (6) the possibility of diverting plutonium and highly enriched uranium for clandestine purposes presents an unacceptable risk to the public. These objections show up at regulatory hearings on licensing, at JCAE hearings on nuclear power, during Congressional and state reviews of nuclear power, and in the press. In many cases, objections to a particular plant have been resolved. Licensing objections do not show up in all reactor plant proposals, and despite those that do, many utilities still believe that, when both costs and environmental impact are considered, nuclear power is a better alternative to meeting the nation's electrical energy needs than are the available fossil fuels. Natural gas, a highly clean fuel, is in short supply and not available in sufficiently expanding quantities to meet demands. Likewise, conservation and high cost of oil are legitimate concerns for the nation and the world. Although coal is in ample supply, there are many enviromental problems associated with its use. Technology for other alternative energy sources for electrical power generation—e.g., solar energy and nuclear fusion—is not at a stage of development where these sources can be used in the near future.

Even with the uncertainties in the nation's energy supplies, however, the question of a nuclear power moratorium is receiving attention in many states. The Sierra Club, which once considered nuclear power as having environmental advantages over other energy alternatives, passed a resolution in 1974 calling for such a moratorium. The organization opposes the licensing, construction, and operation of new nuclear power plants pending: (1) development of adequate national and global policies to resolve problems resulting from energy overuse and unnecessary energy growth; (2) resolution of the significant safety problems inherent in reactor operation, in disposal of spent fuel, and in the possible diversion of nuclear materials capable of being used in weapons manufacture; and (3) establishment of adequate regulatory machinery to guarantee adherence to these conditions. These issues also represent the focus of growing general public concern about nuclear power.

Congress is also raising questions both about specific aspects of the nuclear program and about a possible moratorium. Huge cost overruns in the liquid-metal fast breeder program are causing questions to be raised about this high-priority project. Some view the possibility of the LMFBR's going the route of the supersonic transport (SST); in any case, it will be carefully scrutinized during ERDA budget hearings. Plutonium recycling, which would normally be considered a generic technical problem, is being questioned in connection with broader societal and international issues because of the enormous potential hazards of plutonium. These issues are being raised in Congress at a time when there are few of the old guard, like Hosmer and Holifield, left on the JCAE. Nuclear technology itself is highly complex and is rightly the arena of the scientists and engineers. However, in the broadest sense, value judgments on the trade-offs between the benefits and risks of a technology must be made in the political arena, namely, by the Congress and the president, who represent the public.

Although the national commitment to nuclear power was for many years accepted as a public policy, the evidence indicates that the development and regulation was a closed loop made up of the nuclear industry, the AEC, and JCAE. Although Congress was supposedly representing the public, it was itself totally dominated by the members of the JCAE. It is time that Congress reaffirm the national commitment or offer an alternative course to be followed.

There has been much written and said by the opponents and proponents of nuclear power. Because of the complexity of these issues, both technical and political, a brief discussion here can only hope to list some of the major risk issues.

There are many points in the nuclear fuel cycle where measures must be taken to assure protection of the health and safety of the nuclear industrial worker and the public. Reactors routinely release some radioactivity during normal operation. The release can be increased many orders of magnitude during abnormal operation. Transport of nuclear materials can endanger the public through accidental release of radioactive materials or theft of special nuclear materials. Chemical reprocessing, fuel fabrication, and uranium enrichment plants are sources of radioactivity and provide opportunities for theft of special nuclear materials. Uranium ore mining exposes the workers to radiation; the tailings from mining operations have also been sources of problems. Many of these problems can be and have been alleviated through application of additional technology or through new or modified procedures. The problems which could ultimately decide the future of nuclear power are the ones for which answers cannot be absolutely demonstrated except by actual deployment of nuclear power over a long period of time. Of the problems in this category, three problems of major proportions are nuclear reactor accidents, special nuclear materials safeguards, and long-term waste management.

RISKS DURING ROUTINE OPERATIONS

Nuclear Reactors

Routine release of radioactivity from nuclear plants was a major issue in the late 1960's and early 1970's. The maximum permissible doses are based primarily on recommendations of the International Commission on Radiation Protection (ICRP). They recommend that the maximum doses be set at 5 rems per year for nuclear workers, 500 millirems for any individual in the general population, and 170 millirems for the total population.

The natural background level of radiation ranges from 100 to 250 millirems per year. In a study by the National Academy of Science, it was estimated that exposing the entire U.S. population to an additional 170 millirems per year, the maximum recommended by ICRP, would increase the number of cancer deaths by six thousand.[82] Although the 170-millirem level has been accepted as a standard, AEC regulations call for a very much reduced level. Guidelines call for a maximum dose to an individual at the power plant fence boundary of 5 millirems per year. This figure is a factor of 100 below the ICRP recommendation of 500 millirems per year for any individual. The 5-millirem exposure assumes the individual remains at the plant boundary at all times. The AEC guideline of levels of radiation that are "as low as practicable" is expected to keep annual doses to sizable population groups at less than one millirem per year. According to the commission, most pressurized-water reactors in operation meet the 5-millirem guidelines, but several of the boiling reactors do not.[83] Those not meeting the guidelines are being required to install improved radwaste systems.

The entire population would not receive the 5-millirem exposure. The AEC estimates that the average annual dose to the population would be 0.2 millirems from all of the projected nuclear plants (approximately one thousand) by the year 2000.* This quantity can be compared with the amounts of radiation coming from natural and other man-produced sources (see Table 24). Assuming the hypothesis that the genetic and somatic effects of low-level radiation on humans are linearly proportional to dose (a hypothesis accepted by ICRP), then 0.2 millirems exposure to the population in the year 2000 would increase cancer deaths in the United States by about seven, a number so low that it is statistically undetectable. As seen in Table 24, man voluntarily subjects himself to a much wider range of radiation by such factors as where he chooses to live. For example, a person living in Colorado will receive a radiation dose of approximately 250 millirems from natural sources; this dose is over one thousand times the average exposure expected from steady-state operation of all nuclear power plants in the year 2000. Table 25 lists the causes of projected cancer deaths in the United States.

In addition to being exposed to radiation from natural sources, the general

---

* The National Academy of Sciences prediction is 0.17 millirems.

TABLE 24

1970 AVERAGE WHOLE-BODY EXPOSURE OF
U.S. POPULATION
(Millirems)

Radiation Source	Average	Range
Environmental		
Natural	130	100–250
Fallout	4	
Medical		
Diagnostic	72	
Therapeutic		200–400,000
Radiopharmaceutic		44–279
Miscellaneous		
Television	0.1	
Commercial products	1.9	
Air transport		1–3
Commercial nuclear power		
facilities	0.003	

Source: U.S., Congress, JCAE, *Nuclear Reactor Safety,*
Hearings, 93rd Cong., 1st sess., January 23, September
25–27, and October 1, 1973, p. 365.

population is also exposed to radiation from weapons-testing fallout. This exposure, which has existed for the past two decades, far exceeds that expected from nuclear power. France and China continue to perform atmospheric nuclear weapons testing, which is the source of this radiation.

Eisenbud has compared the radiation exposure resulting from fallout with that coming from the Indian Point reactor. At the time of the comparison,[84] the reactor had been in operation for about ten years. Data concerning its radioactive discharges come from a 1971 EPA study on radioactive surveillance. Table 26 shows the comparative data. It can be seen from this comparison that the fallout on the Hudson River watershed alone far exceeds the total emission of several important radionuclides from Indian Point. The exposure to the total

TABLE 25

CAUSES OF CANCER DEATHS IN
U.S. POPULATION—YEAR 2000

Cause	Number
Nonradiation causes	486,000
Background radiation	5,310
Medical X-rays	3,720
Nuclear effluents	0–10

Source: U.S., AEC, *Annual Report to Congress, 1973,* Vol. 2, Regulatory Activities, p. 43.

TABLE 26

Comparison of Discharges of the Principal Radionuclides
from Indian Point I and Fallout from Weapons Tests [a]
(Curies)

Source of Discharge	Sr-90	Mn-54	Cs-137	H-3 (tritium)
Annual discharge from Indian Point I (1968)	<0.01	10.2	22.5	725
Fallout from weapons On Hudson River watershed (35,000 km^2)	825.0	1236.0	1320.0	205,000.0
On Hudson River surface	3.7	5.5	5.9	920.0
On mixing zone of river, 16 km above and below plant	0.58	0.87	0.93	144.0

[a] For purposes of comparison, the year of heaviest fallout (1963) is compared to the year of maximum reactor discharge (1971). These data have been assembled from several sources by my associate, M. E. Wrenn.

population from fallout (see Table 24) is 4 millirems per year, and is projected by the EPA to remain at this level through the year 2000.

Eisenbud points out that gaseous releases from PWR's are so insignificant as to be relatively less than the atmospheric discharges from fossil-fuel plants. The burning of coal or oil releases several radionuclides to the atmosphere, including radium-226, radium-228, uranium, thorium, and potassium-40. As in the case of nuclear plants, these quantities are too low to represent a significant public health hazard.

There are many complex factors involved in determing the amount of exposure man receives from nuclear plants. For example, it is necessary to study how various radioisotopes get in the food chain, and what effects they have on different parts of the body. These complications have been examined by the AEC and are taken into account in their predictions and setting of exposure standards.

It would appear that, in adopting the AEC guideline for radiation levels that are "as low as practicable," we can apply available technology to the operation of nuclear reactors to reduce the average exposure of the general population to acceptable levels. This conclusion is arrived at from comparison of the expected exposure resulting from the operation of reactors with other radiation exposures readily acceptable to man, and from currently demonstrated technology.

Other Fuel-Cycle Processes

Routine releases of damaging radiation also occur in other parts of the fuel cycle. The most important of these are releases from fuel reprocessing plants, where fission products are separated from the uranium and plutonium. Krypton and tritium, both gaseous fission products, have been routinely released from such plants. The one small commercial reprocessing plant that operated in the United States was closed in 1972 for expansion purposes. This plant was able to achieve annual release rates of 22 percent of maximum permissible values for liquid effluent and 7 percent for gaseous effluent.[85] Although releases from reprocessing plants have been held within permissible limits so far, they constitute a problem which must be given careful attention in the design and construction of new reprocessing facilities. Solutions to this problem, like those to questions of reactor design, should use the "low as practicable" approach, rather than allowing releases based on internationally accepted permissible rates.

Although miners represent a small part of the total population, the radiation exposure that they receive is another problem in the fuel cycle. The primary problem is from radon gas accumulation in underground mines. This accumulation can be monitored and controlled. The waste from mining and ore processing is another source of radiation. Although mismanagement of this material has occurred in the past, there is no inherent problem in managing this waste in such a manner as to eliminate the problem of exposure to the general population.

REACTOR ACCIDENTS

The core of a nuclear reactor which has operated for any significant time is a vast storehouse of radioactive fission products. Under normal operation, these products are contained in long, cylindrical, metal-clad fuel rods. The total core is contained in a thick-walled pressure vessel, which in turn is housed in a containment vessel. These systems are capable of containing fission products to acceptable levels under normal—and even abnormal—conditions, except in extreme cases.

A 1,000 megawatt light-water reactor will contain about 12 billion curies of fission products after sustained operation. Of these, iodine and strontium represent the greatest hazard if released to the atmosphere. It has been estimated that one fourth of the stored iodine-131, if released, would result in twice the maximum permissible concentrations for this isotope in the atmosphere over the forty-eight coterminous United States, up to an altitude of ten thousand meters. Half of the strontium-90 in the reactor is sufficient to contaminate the annual freshwater runoff of the forty-eight states with six times the maximum permissible concentration.[86] This is not to suggest that the material would be dispersed this way. Such a dispersion would be highly unlikely, if not impossible. The numbers, however, suggest the potential enormity of the hazard of an accidental release of these materials.

The hazards to the population from a reactor accident would depend on the severity of the accident, the degree to which the safety containment systems perform successfully, the population distribution in the immediate vicinity and downwind of the plant, and meteorological conditions.

There are likely to be many malfunctions during reactor operations, due either to equipment failures or personnel errors. The approach to the design, construction, and operation of reactors is to reduce the effects of these malfunctions on the worker and the public to acceptable levels, and to reduce their probabilities of occurrence.

In the prelicensing phase of construction and operation, an in-depth technical review is made of design, fabrication, construction, testing, and expected performance of all plant structures, systems, and components important to safety. All features must meet formalized AEC regulations and specifications. Nuclear plants are required to have safety features designed to control or reduce the consequences of certain postulated accidents. Some of these accidents, which are projected to have a very low probability of occurrence, could lead to radiological consequences outside the plant boundary that would exceed AEC regulations. These are the so-called "class 9" accidents. Since no accident of this type has ever occurred, it is very difficult to calculate the probability for such events.

In 1974 the most comprehensive study undertaken of nuclear accident risks was performed by the AEC.[87] The objective of the study was to "make a realistic estimate" of public risks that could be involved in potential "class 9" accidents. Although not stated by the AEC, another objective of the study was to supplant a much earlier study conducted in 1957, a study which had predicted the possibility of very serious consequences in terms of deaths, injuries, and property damage from reactor accidents.

How valid is the study? Some have objected to the methodology, which was based on that developed by the Department of Defense and the National Aeronautics and Space Administration. The study was supported by the AEC at a cost of $3 million, and involved fifty man-years of effort. While it was headed by Professor Norman C. Rasmussen of the Massachusetts Institute of Technology, it was staffed to a large degree by AEC personnel and AEC contractors. All of the staff, including Professor Rasmussen, were closely aligned with the nuclear industry. The day-to-day responsibility for the project belonged to Mr. Saul Levine of the AEC. Although one might criticize the approach of the study, and even the results, the results are comprehensive and the bases for the predictions are available for study. It is unfortunate that such an extensive study has not been made by the opponents of nuclear power or by a third party. Available technical and financial resources, however, would certainly limit the depth of any study that such a group could make. The AEC could have called on an unbiased third party to do the study, but both the complexity of the problem and the required technical understanding essentially necessitate that such an in-depth analysis be done by members of the nuclear community.

The Rasmussen study deals with the probability of occurrence and consequences of accidents from use of large commercial reactors of the pressurized-water and boiling-water types. It does not consider hazards associated with other parts of the fuel cycle.

How can "class 9" accidents occur? No attempt will be made in this discussion to explain the complex functions of the nuclear reactor or its many redundant safety mechanisms. But first, to dispel a myth formed during the public discussions of nuclear power that were held by early opponents, it should be pointed out that reactors *cannot* explode like a nuclear bomb. In fact, the ultimate problem, release of radioactive material, occurs after the energy release rate (power level) of the reactor is only a very small fraction of the normal operating power level. According to the Rasmussen study, the release of radioactive material (other than the controlled release during normal operation, discussed in the previous section) is most likely to occur when the nuclear-fueled core melts and makes its way through the concrete floor of the containment vessel into the ground below. While most of the radioactive material would be trapped in the soil, some would escape to the surface. Other less likely release routes—e.g., through a break in containment vessel—were also included in the study.

The most likely cause of a core meltdown is either a loss of primary coolant flow, or a power transient, followed by failure of the emergency core cooling systems (ECCS) or other backup cooling systems. The emergency systems are designed to be redundant, so that if some components fail to operate, the core can still be cooled. During any such accident, the reactor is automatically shut down by the control systems. Even if all normal or emergency systems fail and the water boils away, allowing the core to melt, the chain reaction cannot continue without the coolant water, which serves as a "neutron moderator."

The Rasmussen study estimates that the *most likely* core meltdown accident could occur once every 17,000 years per plant. If, for example, 1,000 plants are built by the year 2000, we could expect such an accident to occur once every 17 years. The estimated consequences of such an accident are shown in Table 27. However, since operating experience is likely to result in improved reactor designs and safety measures, this estimate, based on today's reactors, is not really valid.

In addition to determining the consequences of the most likely core melt ac-

TABLE 27

CONSEQUENCES OF THE MOST LIKELY
CORE MELT ACCIDENT

Type of Consequence	Size of Consequence
Fatalities	<1
Injuries	<1
Latent fatalities	<1
Thyroid nodules	~4
Genetic defects	<1
Property damage [a]	$100,000

[a] This does not include damage that might occur to the plant.

TABLE 28

Probability of Major Man-Caused and Natural Events

Types of Events	Probability of 100 or More Fatalities	Probability of 1,000 or More Fatalities
Man-caused		
Airplane crash	1 in 2 years	1 in 2,000 years
Fire	1 in 7 years	1 in 200 years
Explosion	1 in 16 years	1 in 120 years
Toxic gas	1 in 100 years	1 in 1,000 years
Natural		
Tornado	1 in 5 years	very small
Hurricanes	1 in 5 years	1 in 25 years
Earthquake	1 in 20 years	1 in 50 years
Meteorite impact	1 in 100,000 years	1 in 1,000,000 years
Reactors		
100 plants	1 in 10,000 years	1 in 1,000,000 years

cident, the Rasmussen study calculated the health effects and probability of oc-currence for 4,800 possible combinations of radioactive release magnitudes, weather types, and populations exposed. Estimates of these factors were ob-tained from evaluating failure probabilities of reactor systems, probabilities of various weather conditions, and population densities around present and planned reactor sites. Table 28 gives representative data covering the probabil-ities of 100 and 1,000 or more fatalities occurring from the operation of 100 nuclear power plants and from other man-caused or natural events. The data show, for example, that an accident causing 100 or more deaths could occur once every 10,000 years from the operation of 100 nuclear plants. The most severe accident calculated was predicted to have a probability of occurrence of once in a billion years and to produce 2,300 fatalities. The consequences of the most likely core meltdown accident would be far less than this. Table 29 com-pares fatalities caused by reactor accidents with other annual fatalities and inju-ries to which the U.S. population living near reactor sites are subjected.

The Union of Concerned Scientists (UCS) does not agree with the estimates

TABLE 29

Annual Fatalities and Injuries Expected Among the 15 Million People Living Within 20 Miles of U.S. Reactor Sites

Accident Type	Fatalities	Injuries
Automobile	4,200	375,000
Falls	1,500	75,000
Fire	560	22,000
Electrocution	90	—
Lightning	8	—
Reactors (100 plants)	0.3	6

made by the Rasmussen group. Their appraisal is that the number of fatalities for each accident would be much larger. While the Rasmussen study predicts that the most likely core melt would result in less than a single fatality per year per 100 reactors, the UCS believes that losses could be on the order of 10 lives per year for 100 operating reactors.[88] In a November 1974 news release, the UCS was highly critical of the Rasmussen study, pointing out a number of serious defects. These included using discredited safety analysis methods to estimate the chances of an accident, assuming that all important design errors and accident sequences have been identified, assuming that population living in the vicinity of nuclear plants can be swiftly evacuated in the event of an accident, and underestimating the consequences to public health and property by a factor that may be as much as sixteen times too low. According to the UCS, the largest accident considered by the AEC, when corrected for these errors, would result in 36,800 fatalities, rather than the 2,300 predicted by the AEC. However, such an accident would be highly unlikely to occur. According to UCS calculations, the more likely accidents would result in the loss of 10 lives per year per 100 operating reactors. This figure is still far below the number of fatalities due to other types of accidents, as can be seen from data presented in Tables 28 and 29.

It is impossible to determine from actual data which analysis is correct, since there have been no accidents of the magnitude and type contemplated here. Gast, using historical data on dam failures, has compared the nuclear accident rate with that of major dam disasters, and has concluded that "the risk-benefit situation for hydroplants is seen to be generally the same as for nuclear plants." [89] On the basis of past experience, one would have to conclude that the nuclear industry safety record has been outstanding. In the first thirty-two years of nuclear power (1943–75), there have been only seven deaths resulting from radiation exposure accidents. All but one of the fatal accidents were associated with experimental programs, and none was associated with commercial power reactors. Furthermore, the last of the fatal accidents occurred in January 1961, more than fourteen years ago.

In addition to the seven fatalities caused by radiation accidents, there have been only twelve cases of clinically observable radiation injuries to employees during the nuclear energy history.[90]

The excellent safety record undoubtedly is due not only to the design and procedural requirements placed on the reactor industry, but also to backup research and development on safety questions. Although the AEC safety R&D program has received much criticism, safety has been a major part of the AEC development effort from the beginning. AEC reactor safety programs have encompassed all aspects of reactor development: fuels, materials, physics, components. The AEC programs have dealt both with simulated reactor accident tests—for example, tests of sudden loss of the primary coolant, or of fission product containment systems—and with actual small-scale reactor tests. The BORAX experiments, which started in 1953 [91] and continued into the sixties, were crucial to the understanding of the operational stability of the water reactors, particularly with respect to the boiling-water reactor. A Special Power Excursion Reactor Test (SPERT) series was conducted at the National Reactor Testing Station (NRTS) [92] starting in 1955 and continuing for many years. The objective of the SPERT reactors was to investigate and obtain an understanding of reactor kinetic behavior with various fuels, moderator and coolant types, and conditions. Fast-reactor safety was partially studied in the Transient Reactor Test (TREAT), which was for the most part directed toward the study of fuel meltdown.[93] More recent reactor facilities designed for safety studies include the Power Burst Facility (PBF) and Loss of Fluid Test Facility (LOFT).[94] PBF was built to conduct research on fuel behavior under simulated accident conditions. LOFT is the "only integral test facility in the world in which major loss-of-coolant accident experiments will be conducted." [95] For several years the AEC conducted simulated tests on loss of primary coolant. One of the objectives of these tests was to develop a satisfactory "emergency core cooling system" in case of a severe reactor accident. Present commercial reactors have elaborate backup cooling and containment systems to assure the safety of the public from external release of radioactive materials.[96] Design codes and standards and quality assurance programs conducted by the AEC and industry are also important to the successful design of the nuclear reactor.

Critics have charged that the AEC has deemphasized light-water reactor

TABLE 30

DISTRIBUTION OF NUCLEAR SAFETY BUDGET,
FISCAL YEARS 1964–74
(Dollars in Millions)

Year	Light-Water Reactor	Fast-Breeder Reactor	Other [a]	Total
1964	$ 7.3	—	$9.0	$16.3
1965	10.6	—	8.4	19.0
1966	12.9	—	8.7	21.6
1967	20.1	—	8.5	28.6
1968	24.1	—	8.7	32.8
1969	21.0	$ 5.3	7.4	33.7
1970	22.1	7.7	7.3	37.1
1971	19.0	9.6	7.1	35.7
1972	22.4	16.8	2.4	41.6
1973 [b]	29.8	20.4	2.4	52.6
1974 [c]	30.3	30.3	3.6	66.0

Source: Private Communications with John Abbadesa, AEC Controller, June 28, 1973.

[a] Detail for FBR not available for FY 1964 through FY 1968. Shown under "Other."

[b] Estimated expenditures as obtained from John Abbadesa. Actual budget was $55.4 million.

[c] Initial budget to Congress. The budget was increased to approximately $72.2 million. The proposed budget for FY 1975 was $93.0 million.

safety while promoting the new LMFBR. Budget data obtained from the AEC show a slight downtrend in LWR safety support between 1968 and 1971 and, more recently, a rather rapid rise in both the LWR and LMFBR safety budgets—a rise that may indicate a positive response to AEC critics (see Table 30).

There have been major delays in obtaining timely answers to crucial reactor safety questions. For a comprehensive discussion of the issues, the reader is referred to a series of articles published in 1972 in *Science*.[97]

One of the major issues has been the reliability of the emergency core cooling system (ECCS) during a loss of coolant accident (LOCA). LOFT has been planned as the key facility for investigating the ECCS response to LOCA. Started in 1964, this program has undergone many delays and revisions. Other programs on reactor safety, such as reactor core blowdown tests relating to LOCA and fission product containment tests, were cancelled in the late sixties and early seventies, in order to increase the support of the higher priority (according to AEC policy) LMFBR program. Now, with the recent public and Congressional pressures and the increasing safety budget, a number of safety programs are being initiated or expanded. These include the LOCA program at LOFT and other test facilities; they also include tests on blowdown heat transfer, core reflooding heat transfer, piping and pressure vessel integrity, and other aspects of reactor safety.[98]

MATERIALS SAFEGUARD

As was previously pointed out, at the end of 1974 there were 225 nuclear plants planned for or operating in the United States, and about an equal number in the rest of the world. By the end of this century, expansion of nuclear power could increase the number in the United States by three to four times, with a comparable or greater expansion in the rest of the world. This will require a concomitant expansion of enrichment plants, fuel fabrication and reprocessing plants, and waste storage in all parts of the world. The possibility of diversion and improper use of fissionable material, sabotage, and terrorist activities will enlarge enormously. These problems require extreme administrative controls and are likely to be the most difficult ones for the nuclear industry to solve with predictable degrees of risk.

The problems stem from two generally accepted facts. First, a group of qualified persons without unduly large resources can make a crude bomb from six kilograms of plutonium (approximately thirteen pounds) or seventeen kilograms of highly enriched uranium. Second, plutonium is one of the most toxic substances known to man. Because of its biologically damaging, radioactive alpha particle, the maximum allowable amount of plutonium in the human is approximately one-billionth of a pound. Man-made U-233, a material from the thorium fuel cycle, is another potential weapons material.

These problems of safeguarding materials are not new to the industry, but they are expanding rapidly. Nuclear reactors have been extensively used to produce plutonium for weapons. The first atomic bomb exploded in New Mexico and the second bomb dropped on Japan were plutonium bombs. Nine reactors at Hanford and five reactors at Savannah River have been used to produce millions of pounds of plutonium. This material has been separated from the uranium and fission products, and has been processed, machined, shipped, stored, and assembled into bombs. Plutonium has been used in experimental facilities, fabricated into experimental fuels, and tested in civilian light-water reactors. All of these activities have required handling, storing, and shipping. To date, the safeguards system has worked. It might have worked because of relatively little public knowledge of its extensive existence. Today, with the nuclear power issue receiving so much public attention, and the widespread dissemination of information on plutonium as a dangerous and potential blackmail material, the controls of previous years are no longer acceptable. The AEC has estimated that the annual domestic requirement for plutonium will exceed two million pounds by 1980.[99] In a study in 1971, the AEC concluded:

> As long as significant quantities of nuclear materials are in active use by the government, by government contractors and by licensed commercial and other interests, there will be a distinct probability that some of those materials will be stolen, unexplainably or accidentally lost, diverted from authorized use or used or disposed of in unauthorized ways. The probability of such happenings is increased by the sheer volume of materials being processed and transferred, the number of licensees and contractors involved, and the technical difficulties of measuring quantities and verifying inventories.[100]

Large amounts of plutonium have been shipped internationally for many years—sometimes in secrecy as part of the weapons program, sometimes as part of programs for development of nuclear power. In March of 1975, the Nuclear Regulatory Commission (NRC) temporarily stopped licensing the importing or exporting of nuclear reactors and fuels while its safety regulations were being reviewed. This action came after Representative L. Aspin (D., Wisconsin) protested shipments of 200 pounds of plutonium oxide flown into New York's Kennedy Airport on commercial jets. Again, the commission was reactive, but on the other hand, there is no known case in which plutonium was diverted from authorized uses.

Plutonium has been mistakenly associated by some people with only the LMFBR, which has been attacked because of its plutonium hazard. It is true that more plutonium would be produced during LMFBR operations than during operations of other reactors, and that the quality of this plutonium for weapons purposes is likely to be better than that produced by LWR's. Light-water reactors, however, also produce large quantities of plutonium. Some of this is burned *in situ* and is responsible for a substantial amount of the energy generated in the LWR's, particularly during the last half of the life of a reactor fuel assembly. In addition, substantial quantities of plutonium are discharged in the used fuel. As was previously pointed out, one third of the fuel assemblies in an operating reactor are replaced each year. This represents about thirty tons of fuel, of which, depending on operating history, approximately one half of one percent could be plutonium. Therefore, approximately 150 kilograms of plutonium are available from each operating reactor each year. This plutonium has a market value of about $1.5 million. Because of its high Pu-240 content—about 20 percent, which is several times higher than that used for military purposes—it is not a good weapons material.

The points in the fuel cycle where plutonium becomes most available for weapons purposes are (1) after its separation from the uranium and fission products at the reprocessing plant, (2) during its shipment from the reprocessing plant to the fuel fabrication plant, and (3) during the fabrication of new fuel assemblies, at which time it is combined with fresh uranium. The plutonium could be reseparated after this last step, but to do so would require chemical facilities. However, the mixed uranium and plutonium, while unsuitable for weapons use, would be a highly toxic material and could be used in threats or for contamination purposes.

Light-water reactors employ slightly enriched uranium, which is not useful for weapons purposes. However, two other materials in commercial reactors are useful for weapons purposes: highly enriched uranium and U-233. These are available in the high-temperature, gas-cooled reactor fuel cycle. Some of the advanced reactors based on the thorium cycle, if developed, could also be a source of U-233. While not as toxic as plutonium, highly enriched uranium and U-233 are hazardous and require careful handling.

The Atomic Energy Act clearly places the responsibility on the AEC (now NRC) for developing regulations to protect special nuclear materials against loss or diversion. The system used by the AEC was briefly described in a previous section of this chapter. An important part of the system is a guard force. Even if there were no hazards associated with the materials, the economic value (plutonium has a market value of approximately $5,000 per pound) requires some protective system. In view of the extreme hazards of the materials, a system employing a special guard force is required to protect the materials not only during transit but also while they are being processed or stored.

The proposed use of a special guard force immediately draws the cry of police-statism from antinuclear critics. However, this approach is not without precedent. We have several examples of such guard forces in existence. Our societal laws are maintained by a combination of local, state, and federal law enforcement officials. A primary duty of the state highway patrol involves the safety of the public. In the recent past, special guard forces and procedures have been established to prevent hijacking of airplanes. And, of course, in order to safeguard our money, we employ both a special guard force and a special storage and transportation system.

The Atomic Energy Act already provides fines up to $10,000, imprisonment up to ten years, or both, for anyone possessing, acquiring, or receiving special nuclear materials (SNM) without a license. If the intent of the person is to injure the United States or obtain an advantage for a foreign nation, the maximum penalties are $20,000, life imprisonment, or both. The Atomic Weapons Rewards Act provides for payment of up to $500,000 to anyone furnishing information leading to discovery of an SNM or atomic weapon unlawfully located within the United States. Unfortunately, the threat of fines, imprisonment, and even death is not likely to deter terrorists or mentally deranged individuals.

In a study of the problem of safeguarding nuclear materials, Roger C. Cramton, dean of Cornell University Law School, concludes that Congress has the power to legislate a wide variety of possible approaches to establishing guard forces.[101] He sees the selection process as being determined not so much by legal issues as by economic, social, and political issues, along with issues of law enforcement efficiency.

It is obvious that, since plutonium is such a hazardous material, it will be equally hazardous to those attempting to divert it and fabricate it into a weapon. Those familiar with plutonium know of the extreme care which must be taken and the elaborate facilities which are required to protect the plutonium worker. It would require a very sophisticated operation to provide the same kind of life-saving protection for those attempting to make a bomb. Of course, for some terrorists, their life is not an issue. Nevertheless, because of plutonium's radioactivity, the slightest release which would be likely to occur during diversion and processing would enhance immensely the detection of its whereabouts.

One method of safeguarding plutonium would be to make it unavailable except under extremely hazardous, deadly conditions. If, for example, plutonium were not separated from all of the fission products, it would have sufficient radioactivity to cause certain death for those handling it. Of course, this method would require remote handling of recycled plutonium in all phases of the fuel cycle—a rather costly requirement. For metallurgical reasons, such an approach was considered in the 1950's and early 1960's for the LMFBR fuel designs. The metal fuel known as fissium (because it contained fission products) was supposed to be more stable under irradiation than fuel not containing fission products. The capability to produce such a fuel was designed into the EBR-2 facility.

The ultimate of this type of protection is the "throw away" fuel cycle, i.e., a cycle in which the used fuel from the LWR's would never be reused. No attempt would be made to separate the materials; rather, the entire fuel would be stored as highly radioactive waste material. This method, however, would increase the volume of waste to be stored; furthermore, it would not permit the reuse of the valuable uranium and plutonium contained in the spent fuel. The "throw away" fuel cycle has been considered by the Canadians on economic grounds. It might also be the most economic method for handling LWR plutonium, if elaborate protection measures turn out to be too costly. Of course, the "throw away" cycle does not solve the LMFBR plutonium problem, since the plutonium must be recycled if we are to reap the benefits of the breeders. However, the protection method discussed above, involving the retention of fission products in the newly fabricated fuel, could be employed for the LMFBR.

Another solution which would reduce the likelihood of both diversion and sabotage is to locate all fuel cycle facilities, except for enrichment and mining facilities, in nuclear parks. From an economic standpoint this could require a concentration of five to ten reactors, since fuel fabrication and fuel reprocessing facilities are generally capable of handling fuel for a substantial number of reactors. The nuclear park would be easier to guard than an equivalent number of separate plants, and would eliminate the need for transporting materials to other parts of the country. It has the major disadvantage, however, of being a concentrated target in case of war. Also, it may require the construction of electric transmission systems to bring large blocks of power to areas far removed from the electric generation site.

Dr. Theodore Taylor, an expert on the subject of weapons and coauthor of the book *Nuclear Theft: Risks and Safeguards,*[102] has publicly stated that while there is a pressing need for improved safeguards, both in the United States and internationally, he does not believe nuclear power ought to be stopped. According to Dr. Taylor, it would be "whistling in the wind" to seek a nuclear moratorium now. Dr. Taylor also has stated in testimony to Congress that a high level of security can be attained.

The question of international safeguards is also important. Because of the availability of air transport, a nuclear moratorium in the United States alone will not eliminate our risks from terrorists. It is not likely, however, that a world moratorium, even if desirable, could be accomplished. Although the United States might be blessed with other energy resources, particularly coal, other parts of the free world are not. Western Europe and Japan are highly dependent on imported oil. Nuclear power is an important alternative fuel for those areas, as well as for many other areas of the world. Such countries would not be eager to agree to a nuclear moratorium. Therefore, any solution to the problem will have to be international in scope. The International Atomic Energy Agency has had an active program on diversion detection but does not have one on safeguarding the material. This organization would have to be substantially strengthened if it were to take the leadership in providing an effective international safeguards system. Since the United States, regardless of its position toward nuclear power, cannot isolate itself from the dangers resulting from the lack of an effective safeguards system, it should be a leader in finding a solution to this international problem.

WASTE DISPOSAL

For each day a 1,000 megawatt plant operates, it generates approximately 3 kilograms of fission products. Thus, allowing for nonoperating periods, each plant produces about 800 to 900 kilograms of fission products per year, or slightly less than one ton. Some of these products decay very rapidly and are of little consequence after a few days, months, or years. Others will remain hazardous for centuries. Also, while better than 99 percent of the plutonium is re-covered, trace amounts remain in quantities large enough to represent a health hazard. The most plentiful of the plutonium isotopes, Pu-239, has a half-life of 24,400 years. Two important fission products which produce a large portion of the intermediate-term radioactivity are strontium-90 and cesium-137, with half-lives of approximately thirty years. Other fission products, such as iodine-129 and cesium-135, have half-lives in the millions of years. Because of the long half-lives of plutonium and some of the fission products, ways must be devel-oped to manage these materials for many centuries.

While radioactive wastes are generated in most of the steps of the fuel cycle, accumulating as liquids, solids, or gases at varying radiation levels, it is the so-called high-level waste that is the major problem. This material is a product of the purification stage of the irradiated fuel reprocessing. Most of the existing high-level waste has come from plutonium production programs for govern-ment weapons; a relatively small amount has come from commercial reactors, since there have only recently been substantial numbers of these in operation. High-level wastes are currently stored as liquids in large underground tanks.

The long-term storage of high-level waste remains as one of the major con-troversies surrounding nuclear power. In February 1971, the AEC decided to go to a retrievable surface storage system, requiring that commercial waste be converted to solid form, sealed in canisters, and shipped to a federal repository. The casks, which are about one foot in diameter and ten feet long, are designed to withstand tornadoes, earthquakes, and floods, as well as accidents such as fire or aircraft impacts. They will be stored either above ground, allowing natu-ral convection air cooling, or in water storage pools.

The process for converting the high-level radioactive liquid waste to a solid form was developed by the AEC. Two processes—pot calcination (phosphate glass) and spray solidification—have been used successfully to convert liquid waste to solid form.

Current regulations require that commercial high-level waste be converted to solid form and sealed in canisters within five years, and shipped to the reposi-tory no later than ten years after its separation from the irradiated fuel. The number of canisters required is approximately ten per year for each 1,000 Mw_e reactor in operation. The AEC estimated that some 500,000 cubic feet of waste will be generated through the remainder of the century; this waste will occupy a volume that is 100 feet square and 50 feet high. The first canisters will proba-bly be delivered to the government by 1983; by 2010, approximately 80,000 will have been shipped.

ERDA believes that their "engineered storage"—i.e., retrievable, solid-waste surface storage—is a satisfactory solution for the present, and plans to use it at least for the short term. Although this approach could be continued in-definitely, the government believes other more permanent waste storage methods would be better.

A major problem with the surface-storage method is the long-term requirement for human surveillance and maintenance. Storage in stable, geological formations, such as salt beds, would avoid this problem. The AEC has considered storage in geological salt formations to be an excellent long-term solution, and would probably implement it if it were publicly acceptable. With this storage method, the wastes could be sealed off from the biosphere and remain in the salt formation forever with a minimum of monitoring. The salt beds in Kansas have been essentially undisturbed for 200 million years, except for intrusion by man, and have not been in contact with circulating groundwater during this period. Thus, the only monitoring requirements would be to see that man does not drill holes in the formation, since to do so would allow surface water to enter.

Another approach to solving the waste management problem that is currently under study is to take a small fraction of the total waste—i.e., the fission products having relatively long half-lives—and shoot it to the sun. The advantage of this method is that the waste is totally removed from the earth. The cost of sending such long-lived fission products out of the solar system has been estimated to be about $150,000 per kilogram.[103] This would increase power costs by 2 mills per kilowatt hour or less, depending on what fraction is sent into space. While this method is much more costly than earth storage, it is not prohibitively high.

Other long-term methods are also being considered. These incude storage in basalt and in ice formations.

Waste management has begun to receive increased emphasis in the government's civilian reactor program. Prior to 1971, the responsibility for direction of long-term radioactive waste management, as well as development activities related to transportation of radioactive materials, had been carried out under several programs. These were then consolidated in a new AEC division in order to place greater emphasis on waste management and to improve the integration of relevant activities.[104] Budgets for waste management research have been substantially higher in recent years; these increases are indicative of the increased emphasis by the government on this problem area.

In summary, the major problem associated with waste storage is the long-term need to control the long-lived radioactive material. It is this problem that is the most difficult to guarantee. Nuclear opponents see difficulties in relying on society's institutions over such a long period. On the other hand, individuals like Alvin Weinberg, former director of Oak Ridge National Laboratories, believe that the problem can be adequately dealt with by employing the methods that the AEC proposed.[105] The problem of short-term storage safety is solved primarily through available technology and reasonable administrative procedures. The long-term question cannot be answered in absolute terms, but there do appear to be reasonable alternatives—either indefinite continuation of the currently planned engineered storage, or the adoption of a new approach that has been thoroughly evaluated. The former should suffice until the latter is found.

CHAPTER VII

Analysis and Evaluation of the Technological Delivery System Performance

THE material in this chapter is presented with the hope that it will yield a better understanding of the strengths and weaknesses of the system used in the development and deployment of commercial nuclear power, so that the system's weaknesses may be corrected and its strengths considered for application to other technological delivery systems. It is also hoped that the systematic approach presented will be of educational value to students of public administration, public policy, and political science, and to managers of technological developments.

DESCRIPTION OF THE TECHNOLOGICAL DELIVERY SYSTEM

The concept of a technological delivery system (t.d.s.) is used as a model to describe the complex processes of integrating inputs to the system of reactor development and commercialization in order to achieve inputs. It is a useful tool for visualizing the interactive components of dynamic processes. The use of a technological delivery system model has been proposed by Dr. Edward Wenk, Jr.:

> The notion of a "technological delivery system" represents the complex processes by which knowledge in natural and social sciences is deliberately applied to achieve desired outputs of consumer amenities and social values. It is more than hardware, in that the system involves an ensemble of practices and institutions to blend inputs of technical information, capital, natural resources and manpower with inputs of our society's value preferences. The institutional components of such a system include universities, profit and nonprofit research organizations, political components that serve to interpret value preferences through incentives or regulation, public delivery systems at the Federal, State and local levels, and a wide spectrum of private industry components from banking and production to the service sector. While the interrela-

tionships of these system components are represented by nominal legal, economic, social, political and institutional processes, the structure and conduct of the institutions are animated by and differentiated for each special output desired.[1]

The technological delivery system concept has been used as the focus of a methodology developed at the University of Washington in a research project on the "Social Management of Technology" (SMT).[2] The concept is presented here as a means by which to analyze and evaluate the performance of the nuclear development t.d.s.

The general model of the technological delivery system as proposed by Wenk is shown in Figure 2. The model contains four elements, whose interactions comprise the social management of technology:

1. *Inputs* to the system: scientific and environmental knowledge, capital, specialized manpower, natural resources and tools, and the orthogonal inputs of human values.
2. *Institutional structures,* public and private, that are organized within the system, each with management that mobilizes and manipulates inputs to produce desired outputs.
3. *System processes* whereby institutional structures act and react through information linkages, involving market, political, legal, and social processes within various constraints.
4. *Outputs* of the system, exhibiting both intended and unintended effects on the social and physical environments.

The t.d.s. that produced as its intended output the commercial nuclear reactor embraces all the components listed above.

The principal institutional components specifically pertinent to the nuclear power t.d.s. are shown in Figure 3. Several of the groups shown were expected to have a substantial influence on the operation, but had little or no influence in fact. For example, the full House and Senate had a relatively small overall and continuing influence compared with that of the Joint Committee on Atomic Energy. In a few important cases, however, the House and/or the Senate did have influence in altering specific parts of legislation and in conciliating differing views of bills proposed by the JCAE. Also, while this study did examine both total and individual nuclear program funding in order to establish government priorities and emphasis in the nuclear field, it did not examine the details of the federal government's budgeting process, except in special cases where institutional components of the budgeting process (the AEC, the Office of Management and Budgeting, and congressional appropriation committees) interjected significant differences from normal behavior.

A schematic of the AEC organizational structure is given in Figure 4. One of the purposes of the schematic is to define the components of the AEC organization that were active in the system. The arrangement shown in Figure 4 is essentially that of the AEC as of July 1972,[3] except insofar as it reflects part of a reorganization effective May 1973; at that time, the safety research and development function for the light-water reactor was placed directly under the general manager.[4]

All groups operating under the AEC general manager had either a direct or an indirect effect on the technological delivery system operation. The Division of Reactor Research and Development had primary responsibility for the AEC's management of its civilian reactors program. Water reactor safety was in this division until the May 1973 reorganization. At the next level of influence on reactor development were the Naval Reactors Division and the Division of Production and Management of Nuclear Materials. The former was important to the system because of its technical input; the latter was influential for several reasons: its technical input; its wartime facilities, manpower, and policies; and its supply of uranium. The Regulation Division had its major impact during the stage of commercial deployment of the nuclear power. Other organizations shown—e.g., the Division of Research—had either a relatively small or an indirect input to the system.

The two major industrial components within the institutional structure are the suppliers and the users. Although opportunities have arisen to influence the user structure, it has remained constant over the development period, and consists of the private and public utilities, essentially as they existed at the outset. The supply industry has evolved with the development of the t.d.s. and can be divided into two basic categories: equipment manufacturers, and the fuel-cycle industry. Although the first category involves a broad range of equipment, the nuclear reactor, sometimes called the nuclear steam supply system, is of primary interest here. Other important pieces of equipment include pressure ves-

---

Legend for Figure 2

1. To visualize the technological delivery system, it may be helpful to consider it in several steps:

   a. Producers of basic knowledge can exert a pressure toward the delivery of technological outputs via new discoveries, and social needs can exert a suction for such products; the resulting actions result in technological coupling of the *knowledge producers* (left edge of the technological delivery system) with the *knowledge consumers* (right edge).

   b. This technological coupling comes about through the integration of *applied research,* the establishment and operation of a *technological enterprise,* and viable *management,* thus overcoming *impediments* to satisfy explicit *social goals.*

   c. Government plays widespread and important roles in the *management* of technology in translating value preferences from special interests and the body politic into policies and public programs, including involvement with the private sector through instruments of regulation, subsidy, manpower training, and sponsorship of R&D.

2. Each technological delivery system is specialized in relation to the intended outputs, and usually also deals with a specialized body of knowledge.

3. *Environments,* social and physical, can only be vaguely defined but have a significant influence on the system. Also, the physical includes natural, man-modified, and man-made.

4. These impediments to delivery of intended outputs result from such causes as conflicting social value preferences, inadequate information and its flow, bureaucratic inertia, etc., and may occur anywhere within the system.

5. *Outcomes* (performance) refer to the external effects of system outputs (how well they match goals, at what costs to whom, with what secondary impacts) and also to the internal functioning of the system itself (how effectively the technological enterprise conserves resources, its efficiency, participant satisfaction).

Figure 2

THE TECHNOLOGICAL DELIVERY SYSTEM[1,2]

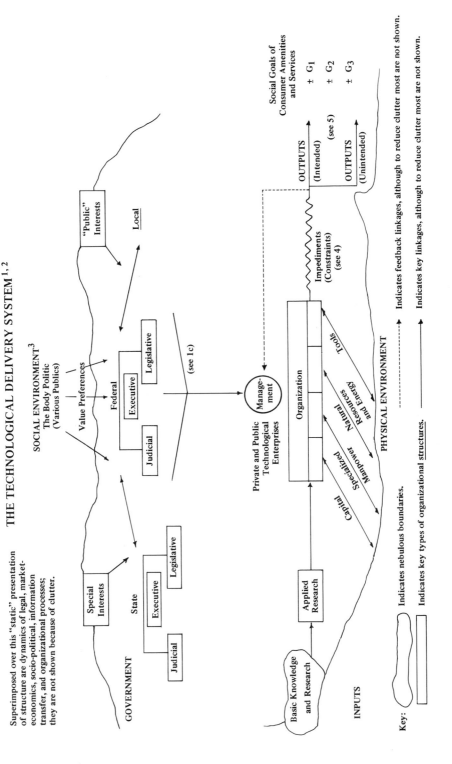

Superimposed over this "static" presentation of structure are dynamics of legal, market-economics, socio-political, information transfer, and organizational processes; they are not shown because of clutter.

SOCIAL ENVIRONMENT[3]
The Body Politic
(Various Publics)

"Public" Interests

Local

Value Preferences

Federal

Executive

Legislative

Judicial

(see 1c)

Special Interests

State

Executive

Legislative

Judicial

GOVERNMENT

Private and Public Technological Enterprises

Management

Organization

Tools

Natural Resources and Energy

Specialized Manpower

Capital

PHYSICAL ENVIRONMENT

Applied Research

Basic Knowledge and Research

INPUTS

Impediments (Constraints) (see 4)

OUTPUTS (Intended)

(see 5)

OUTPUTS (Unintended)

Social Goals of Consumer Amenities and Services

± G₁

± G₂

± G₃

Key:

Indicates nebulous boundaries.

Indicates key types of organizational structures.

Indicates feedback linkages, although to reduce clutter most are not shown.

Indicates key linkages, although to reduce clutter most are not shown.

Figure 3

MAJOR INSTITUTIONAL STRUCTURE COMPONENTS
INFLUENCING THE NUCLEAR POWER DEVELOPMENT

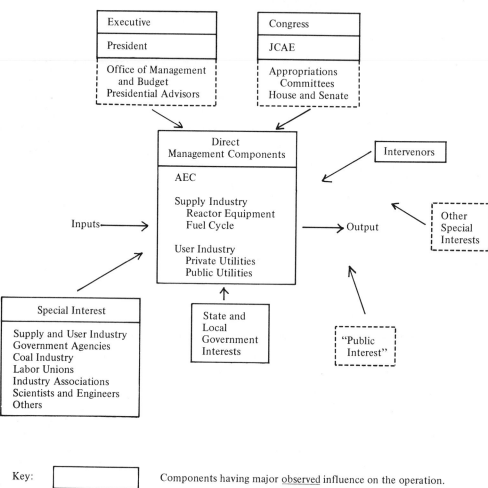

Key:

Components having major <u>observed</u> influence on the operation.

Components that might be expected to have an influence on the operation, but that in fact had little or no influence.

Figure 4

ORGANIZATIONAL STRUCTURE OF THE ATOMIC ENERGY COMMISSION

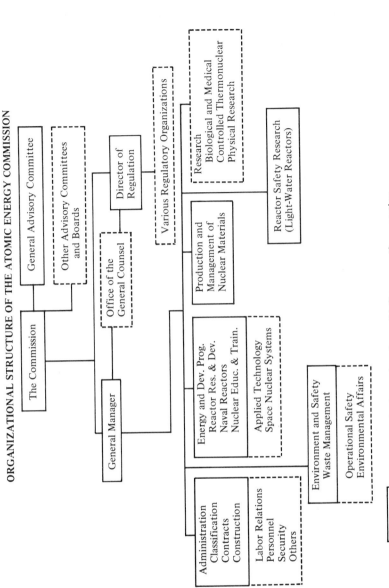

Key: ☐ Components having major <u>observed</u> influence on the operation.

☐ Components that might be expected to have an influence on the operation, but whose influence was <u>not</u> observed or was observed to be <u>relatively small.</u>

Source: <u>U.S. Government Organization Manual 1972/73</u> (Washington D.C.: GPO, 1973). Reflects some organizational changes implemented in 1973.

sels, controls, heat exchangers, pumps, valves, condensers, turbines, and electric generators. The significant components of the fuel-cycle industry are: uranium mining and milling, uranium conversion, uranium enrichment, fuel element fabrication, fuel reprocessing, waste management, and transportation. The chief fuel-cycle companies include the reactor vendors; the mining, oil, and chemical companies; and the government. With one exception—Gulf-General Atomic—the reactor vendors who have emerged are heavy equipment manufacturers who have historically been major suppliers to the utilities. Although emphasis in this study is on development and commercialization of the nuclear reactor, the above review of the institutional structure should help make comprehensible the operation of the technological delivery system and the interaction and motivations of institutional components.

The data base for analysis and evaluation of the nuclear power t.d.s. is taken from the case study material presented in Chapters I through VI and from interviews discussed in Chapter I. The analysis focuses on the t.d.s. institutions and policy-making processes, and the evaluation of the system's performance is made on this basis.

The analysis consists of two parts. The first is a set of process questions established to assist in identifying determinants of the system's outcomes, as well as to focus explicitly on presumed key aspects of the decision-making and policy-formulation and -implementation processes. The second part of the analysis examines a set of outcome variables for the purpose of evaluating the system's performance.

Central to the discussion about process questions and outcome variables are a number of key issues that arose during the system operations. These issues can be summarized as follows:

- Government monopoly of the technology.
- Government institutional framework for control of technology and its uses.
- Government program priorities.
- Technical and economic feasibility.
- Government contracting policies.
- Method of technology evaluation.
- Roles of government and industry in development, risk taking, and use of the product.
- Information, material resources, and manpower constraints.
- Technology introduction in the society.
- "Suction force" for the product, such as market forces, national energy resource needs, social and political forces.

The evaluation of the system's performance and possible application hinges on the answers to questions regarding how these issues arose, to what extent and how they were resolved, and what effect they had on the performance of the system. The discussion of the issues is interwoven with the answers to the process questions and the discussion of the outcome variables.

From the data developed in answering the process questions and in discussing the outcome variables, conclusions are drawn as to the system's performance and possible applications. The process questions are particularly useful in identifying what policies, institutions, and other factors had a favorable impact on the outcome. These are examined for possible application to other technological delivery systems. The outcome variables are helpful in identifying which outcomes from the system were favorable and which unfavorable, thereby providing a basis for a qualitative conclusion on the overall performance of the system.

PROCESS QUESTIONS

PROBLEM IDENTIFICATION

1. How was the problem identified and by whom?

The problem central to this study is the development of nuclear power as an energy source for the commercial generation of electricity. Although the potential of nuclear energy was undoubtedly recognized by a number of scientists—e.g., Fermi and Szilard, who were performing research on fission and on the feasibility of a nuclear chain reaction—it was Albert Einstein who, after encouragement from Szilard and with the assistance of Sachs, first brought this potential to the attention of the United States government. He did this by means of a letter to President Roosevelt, written on August 2, 1939—the letter in which he also pointed out fission's potential for weapons and as an energy resource.

The problem was further considered by individuals associated with the Manhattan Engineer District (MED) nuclear bomb development effort, after Fermi and MED had proved the technical feasibility of the fission chain reaction as a large source of controlled energy. The problem was implicitly acknowledged in the policy statements of the Atomic Energy Act of 1946, which established the governmental structure for the postwar management of nuclear energy matters.[5] While industrial organizations involved in the nuclear weapons program participated actively in the formulation of the 1946 Act, commercial interest groups were largely silent. The 1946 Act, first proposed by President Truman and then significantly altered by Congress through the leadership of Senator McMahon, was signed into law August 1, 1946. It was recognized even then that postwar control of nuclear energy, a central issue of the act, might have a significant effect on the approach to the problem. Among the many persons who felt this concern were: the military, scientists, members of Congress, and the president.

2. What stake did those identifying the problem have in the outcome?

The 1946 Act states: "The significance of the atomic bomb for military purposes is evident. The effect of the use of atomic energy for civilian purposes upon the social, economic, and political structures of today cannot now be determined."

Because atomic energy was still so new, no positions on it had been taken by labor, management, public and private power, and other interest groups. Thus, Congress was deprived of one of the sources of information and opinion upon which it traditionally based policy decisions.[6] The power vacuum that resulted was filled to a considerable degree by an array of political unknowns—the scientists,[7] many of whom had been party to the development of the atomic bomb. Another significant element was the military, which had just won a great war and which had managed the atomic bomb project. Discussion of the patent rights proposed for inclusion in the first atomic energy legislation led to the usual debate concerning the inroads socialism was making on private enterprise.

The stakes of individuals and groups concerned with the problem were associated for the most part with the control of atomic energy. Opinions ranged from wanting internationalization to wanting strict military control. The military wanted to assure weapons development with military access and control. To them, military control meant military preparedness against Russia and the only effective means of keeping military secrets. The Congress and the president, while considering national security to be of great importance, also favored the development and utilization of atomic energy for "improving the public welfare, increasing the standard of living, strengthening free competition in private enterprise, and promoting world peace." [8] The scientists wanted civilian control, which they viewed as necessary to provide the best conditions for conducting scientific research and exchanging information. All groups debating the issues wanted peaceful benefits to result from the technology which had produced such a devastating weapon.

As nuclear energy technology became of greater interest for commercial exploitation, industry interest groups began to play a more prominent role. The questions that concerned these groups involved ownership of nuclear reactors and materials, their control, and the extent to which nuclear power could be made safe and economical.

Later, at the stage of commercial introduction of nuclear power plants, other groups began to express their interest. These groups, believing that the health and safety of the public are endangered by the use of nuclear power, are influencing legislation and seeking means by which to reduce the apparent risks.

3. What were the social climate, historical patterns, and forcing or inhibiting functions?

A major war had ended, with nuclear energy playing a key role in the war's climax. After the debate had been settled as to whether the control of atomic energy should be military or civilian, there remained a conflict over whether the control should be international, and therefore open, or national, and therefore secret. Satisfactory relations with the other major world power, the Soviet

Union, had not come about and, as a consequence, absolute government control continued for almost a decade after the first nuclear bomb explosion.

Development, almost from the day of the discovery of the fission process, became a federal government monopoly, and was one of the most tightly held government secrets ever kept. Large government laboratories, production facilities, and towns were established whose mission was completely unknown to the public until the end of the war. The war effort accelerated the development effort and major strides were made in a few years. The technical feasibility of nuclear energy as a large source of thermal power was firmly established during this period.

There appeared to be a great sense of need by all groups to use this awesome force for the betterment of mankind. The public had an image of limitless available energy, although scientists were under no such illusion. The availability of uranium resources was a major question. There were, moreover, many technical questions about producing a safe, reliable, and economic nuclear reactor. The government's tight control was seen as a major inhibiting force in this area. In the 1950's, the secrecy surrounding nuclear energy and government monopoly was reduced significantly; in 1975, uranium enrichment is the only major area thus circumscribed.

The development of nuclear power paralleled the increasing role of government in supporting research and development on a broad scientific and engineering front after World War II. Price has referred to the approach that the government improvised to support R&D as a "new kind of federalism for the conduct of research." [9] The approach has been based on various types of relationships with private institutions and generally involves contracts by which institutions conduct R&D for, and at the expense of, the government. In the case of nuclear power, a commercial product—the nuclear power plant—was a specified goal.

The 1950's was a decade of rapid technological advances in many areas and science was viewed as an endless frontier to be explored; its benefits for mankind were seldom questioned. [10] It was not until the early 1960's that the benefits of rapid technological expansion in general came to be questioned. Nuclear power utilization has not been spared this questioning, and indeed is under close scrutiny by many interest groups. Both the broad issues of technology's impact on society and specific questions regarding public health and safety are being raised and, in 1975, remain unresolved.

GOAL AND POLICY FORMULATION

4. As policy proposals were formulated, what were the original goals and by whom were they formulated?

Broad goals were implicit in the policy statements made in the 1946 Act. (The policy statement and purposes are discussed in Chapter II; see section on the Atomic Energy Act of 1946.) The general goal of the act was to develop nuclear energy in such a way as to make the maximum contribution to the general welfare of the nation. A subset of goals in the 1946 Act was given in the policy statement, partially quoted above under Question 2. These goals were: improving the public welfare, increasing the standard of living, strengthening free competition in private enterprise, and promoting world peace. It was felt that use of nuclear power for electrical energy generation was one of many possible developments that might contribute to meeting these goals.

5. Were goals revised or reviewed?

The goals were reviewed and generally became more specific with time. The 1946 Act had put major constraints on reaching the desired goals. The principal constraints were scientific and technical secrecy and the government's monopoly of both necessary materials and nuclear reactors.

At the time of the passage of the 1954 Atomic Energy Act, market forces were not a major source of demand for the nuclear power plant, even though private industry was interested in it as a long-term energy source. The chief goal of United States policy at that time had broader international implications; generally stated, it was to establish and maintain the United States position of world leadership in the technology of nuclear power for civilian use. Within the United States, the symbol of that goal was the demonstration of safe and economically competitive electrical power generation from a nuclear station. Development of a nuclear industry in the private enterprise sector was another goal generally identified by the AEC, although it was not necessarily universally accepted. A third goal was the creation of a new energy supply to replace the diminishing supply from conventional sources.

Within the developmental programs, goals were established in much more narrow terms and therefore were more specific than those given above. For example, in the five-year experimental reactor program announced in 1954, specific types of reactors were projected with cost estimates, sizes, and time schedules. In 1958 the JCAE identified the goals of the program as being: (1) to achieve and demonstrate economically competitive nuclear power by 1970 in the United States; (2) to achieve and demonstrate economically competitive nuclear power by 1968 in free-world nations with high power costs; and (3) to fortify the position of the United States in the eyes of the world with respect to the peaceful application of atomic energy, particularly regarding electric power generation. Private companies also establish goals for specific programs, including program schedules, technical objectives, and power costs.

As nuclear power became "substantially competitive" in the early 1960's, the AEC again revised its goals, which became: (1) to assist in establishing a viable supplier and user industry; (2) to phase out government support of several reactor types as the industry became established; and (3) to set new development objectives for the AEC.

Other government goals overlapping those given above included: (1) to retain control of atomic energy programs under civilian rather than military direction; (2) to safeguard the interest of national defense and national security; (3) to protect the general public health and safety; and (4) to avoid the establishment of a monopoly in any sector of the nuclear industry.

6. Were estimates made of resources (funds, manpower, natural resources, institutions) needed for accomplishment?

No total estimates of resources needed for these developments were found in the literature examined. Estimates of costs for specific projects and major programs were made, some on a total and some on an annual basis. Shortages of manpower, natural resources, and institutional capabilities were recognized, and the government established long-range programs and policies either to overcome these shortages or to minimize their effect. These included: (1) creating an incentive program for exploration and development of uranium ore; (2) making available to industry and universities scarce materials, equipment, and facilities; (3) establishing education and training programs that utilized the special expertise and facilities within the government laboratories; and (4) providing research and training grants to universities.

7. What role did scientific information play in creating needs and opportunities, or in facilitating decisions?

The scientific discovery of fission was central to the technology. It was a fixed constraint on the system, holding promise as a new energy source and, at the same time, posing serious potential public health and safety problems. Basic principles of physics provided the framework of technological constraints and options. Research, development, and engineering in materials and components provided the basis for technological innovation. Because of the many possible combinations of moderator materials, coolants, and fuel designs, there were a large number of reactor concepts; these presented opportunities for engineering design optimization but made final selection difficult. Careful evaluation was required, involving management decisions on the extent to which materials and components should be studied and tested, which types should be carried through the expensive stage of prototype testing, and how many of the prototypes should be further evaluated through large-scale demonstrations. Inadequacy of the technological base and limited available resources—finances, materials, and manpower—were factors complicating the programmatic decisions. The long and extensive process of technical evaluation was the basis of controversy between the JCAE, on the one hand, and the AEC and industry, on the other; this controversy centered around the approach to be taken in performing the evaluations and in attaining the ultimate objective of economical nuclear power. Although the controversy had its political aspects, the paramount concern of all parties was the rate of technological progress.

8. What were the uncertainties in the factual base?

Nuclear energy was an entirely new technology. The technical feasibility of a nuclear chain reaction had to be demonstrated. The severe radiation environment to which materials would be exposed in a nuclear reactor caused great uncertainty about their performance characteristics and usable life, both of which would have a significant effect on power costs. Materials for fuel, moderator, coolant, and other reactor components had to have special nuclear characteristics compatible not only with the chain reaction requirements but also with physical and chemical requirements for high-power operation. This prerequisite necessitated new developments and extensive testing. The cost of commercial scale-up of the manufacturing and application of these new materials, as well as of the scale-up of prototype reactors, was a major unknown. A new industry had to be fostered, and extensive costly experimental and demonstration reactor programs were required for removing these uncertainties. Fabricability of new materials, such as zirconium, had to be demonstrated. Scientists' understanding of nuclear physics and neutron scattering—the interaction of the neutron with fuel and other reactor materials—was still incomplete. A thorough understanding of these phenomena was necessary in order to evaluate the details of system design for optimizing desired characteristics such as breeding, uranium enrichment, coolant flow, fuel life, safety, and costs.

Early uncertainties about the uranium supply cast some doubt on the long-term potential of nuclear power as an important energy source. This doubt, which placed a significant constraint on the system in the early postwar years, had two effects: it was a restraining influence on the breadth of the reactor types initially considered, and it raised questions as to whether there would be sufficient uranium for a viable power reactor industry. Because of the shortage of uranium existing after the war and because of the requirements for uranium in the weapons program, dual-purpose breeder reactors were considered necessary. The AEC initiated a uranium exploration and procurement program to alleviate this material shortage, and the the early 1950's the availability of uranium no longer appeared to be a constraint. This allowed the AEC laboratories and industry to widen the range of reactor types to be considered. It also encouraged industry to consider this new source of energy. However, if the breeder is not ultimately developed, within thirty to fifty years the uranium supply could again become a limitation on the size of the nuclear industry.

9. What were the constraints—technical, legal, social, political, institutional, and fiscal—to policy development and implementation?

In addition to the technical data constraints discussed under Question 8, the lack of available, qualified manpower presented another constraint on resolution of technical problems. Because the central technology of nuclear reactors was totally new, the scientific and engineering community was not able to supply the needed manpower. Some of the persons interviewed in 1973 stated that lack of available manpower remained a restricting factor on the growth of the industry. Initially, the government laboratories had essentially all of the know-how, and the universities were ill-prepared to train needed personnel. The AEC was successful in partially alleviating this constraint by (1) establishing reactor technology schools within its laboratories, for which it used its experienced staff as instructors; (2) allowing personnel from industry to take "on-the-job training" assignments within the laboratories; (3) supporting university research and fellowship programs; (4) allowing graduate work in its laboratories; (5) providing materials and equipment to universities; and (6) developing information and other programs.[11]

Legal constraints to private industry involvement in the development of commercial nuclear power were imposed by the Atomic Energy Act of 1946. The act prevented private ownership of nuclear power reactors and nuclear materials. The Atomic Energy Act of 1954 removed the reactor ownership constraints, but private ownership of nuclear fuels was not allowed until 1964.

Some JCAE members saw the AEC's proposed legislation for modifying the 1946 Act—which resulted in the 1954 Act—as a major "giveaway" to private enterprise of government-funded research and development. They believed nuclear power should remain under government ownership. As a compromise, not only was private ownership of nuclear fuels not allowed, but compulsory licensing of patents obtained by industry was required, regardless of who funded the development. This was seen as a mechanism to prevent the development of monopoly in private industry from patents that had as their basis government-funded R&D. According to some of those interviewed, this clause had little real effect on the industry.

Another constraint was the severe secrecy placed on the technology for national security reasons. In the mid-1950's, a major AEC effort to declassify information held by the government resulted in the removal of much of the secret classification of technology pertinent to commercial reactors. Uranium enrichment technology remains classified, but industry has been given access to the data.

Still another constraint was the legal liability of a reactor owner in case of injury to the public from a nuclear accident. The potential financial liability was greater than the amount of available insurance and greater than the risk industry was willing to take. The Price-Anderson Act, passed in 1957, removed this constraint by instituting government indemnification of the reactor owner. This act remains a controversial issue in 1975.

Social constraints during nuclear power development essentially did not exist; these did not become a significant factor until the commercial phase began. At the outset, society saw nuclear energy as having major potential benefits to mankind. At that time there also existed a desire to show the world that the United States wanted to convert to peaceful purposes the source of energy of the devastating nuclear weapon.

In recent years, however, special interest groups, segments of the public,

Congress, and state governments have all questioned the safety and environmental compatibility of the nuclear power plant. Intervention by these groups has caused delays and restrictions on power plant construction and operation. The issues they have raised have not been fully resolved, although nuclear power plants continue to be purchased by the user utilities in large numbers.

Except for the legal constraints on private industry discussed above, there were no other major institutional constraints. The Atomic Energy Act of 1946 clearly spelled out the organization, authority, and responsibilities of the congressional and executive institutions, the JCAE, and the AEC. Except for additional powers given later to the JCAE and some internal changes in the AEC, the two organizations have been highly stable.* The industry, while evolving with the technological development of nuclear power, has essentially encompassed existing institutions, and has joined with government in an informed government-industry nuclear complex.

In the early postwar years, a much higher priority was given to military reactors and weapons than to civilian development. Funding for civilian reactor development was relatively small, and a fiscal constraint probably existed. With the passage of the Atomic Energy Act of 1954 and the fulfillment of some of the weapons program needs, civilian reactor development funding expanded rapidly in the 1950's, remained fairly stable in the early 1960's, and then expanded further in the early 1970's. Nuclear development continues to receive the support of both the president and Congress, and funding has probably not been a significant constraint since the mid-1950's. However, the high priority given to nuclear energy has been seriously questioned in Congress, with the consequence that most of the expansion in the government's energy budget has gone for development of nonnuclear energy sources.

10. Were alternative implementation strategies considered? What mechanism existed for analysis and option identification?

The first alternatives considered for implementation were military versus civilian public control. Although the result was largely a civilian effort, the program has benefited substantially from work on military and defense materials production. It also has had direct assistance from the Navy, both in the development of the commercial light-water reactor and in the pressurized-water reactor program through the large-scale demonstration phase. Navy developments also had a major influence on the selection of the commercial reactor types that emerged from the system. The Navy was seriously considered by the JCAE as the most appropriate organization for building another reactor concept prototype, the Experimental Gas-Cooled Reactor, which was finally given to the civilian reactor program organization in the AEC. In 1975, the Navy was continuing work on a light-water breeder reactor concept for the commercial market.

---

* The AEC was split in 1974 into two parts; this change is discussed in Chapter II.

Completely private development was never seriously considered. However, there was concern about how program responsibilities were to be shared between government and private industry. The issue arose out of a difference of opinion between the AEC and the JCAE as to the amount of development progress being made. Development progress was measured in terms of numbers of reactors planned, built, and operating. The size of foreign programs was frequently used as a measuring stick. During the 1950's, there was a good deal of controversy on this question between the AEC and private industry on one side, and the JCAE and some public utilities on the other. The AEC tended to want to leave more of the development, particularly the demonstration phase, to private industry, while certain members of the JCAE wanted the government to build and operate a substantial number of large reactors. There was also concern on the part of the JCAE that the United States maintain world leadership. Resolution of the problem came about in two ways: (1) by congressional action approving or disapproving specific reactor programs, and (2) by expansion of the proposed AEC demonstration program. A third possible factor in the resolution was the expansion, starting in the late 1950's, of the privately funded parts of the program.

During the controversy just discussed, there was one possible deployment alternative to the existing utility institutional structure. Some people thought that a legislative proposal that was initiated in the JCAE for government construction and operation of several large power reactors represented the seeds of a "nuclear TVA." If such a system had been established, the government could have remained the sole or primary owner of power reactors, a situation that would have resulted in an entirely different system for nuclear energy utilization. The legislation, however, was defeated in Congress. Nevertheless, private industry's fear of government takeover of the field probably influenced its acceleration of development in the late 1950's.

Implementation of the R&D prototype reactors and demonstration reactor programs presented several alternatives. As with the question of development, the alternatives came about primarily through consideration of what the financial roles of government and private industry should be. In general terms, the government assumed primary financial responsibility for developing the base technology and for prototype reactors. Most of the work was performed in government laboratories operated by contractors, but substantial government-funded R&D was performed in private industry and university laboratories. Although the demonstration phase was primarily the responsibility of joint teams of equipment manufacturers and utilities, the AEC provided leadership and financial assistance; in some cases, it also constructed and owned demonstration reactors.

Technical alternatives were many. Alternatives existed for reactor materials, components, and concepts. These alternatives were evaluated by extensive testing programs for materials, components, and systems. Many reactor concepts were tested through the prototype and demonstration phase. Performance was measured in terms of operational behavior of materials and components, reactor safety factors, and power costs; all of these aspects interrelated. Final selection for commercial exploitation was made by the nuclear reactor manufacturers.

Other technical alternatives had to do with the efficiency of uranium utilization. Because of the uranium shortages in the early post-World War II years, primary emphasis was given to the breeder reactor, which would theoretically use almost all of the uranium. The development of this concept proved difficult and, as uranium supplies became more plentiful, nonbreeder (converter) reactors were given increasingly greater attention. The final selections were the converter reactor types. The breeder remains a goal to be reached and, again, is the primary objective for the AEC's nuclear power program.

Technical alternatives were further increased by the availability of enriched uranium from government plants built initially for weapons materials. Commercial nuclear plants employed in the United States and in many other countries are only technically feasible through the use of enriched uranium.

11. Who were participants in the decision process? Advocates? Opponents?

Government—namely the president, AEC, and JCAE—provided the leadership in decision making on policy issues.

In the early and middle stages of research and development, the AEC was the dominant decision maker, with input coming from the JCAE and outside interest groups. The supply industry and utilities were the primary decision makers in selecting specific reactor plants and in determining the rate of nuclear power utilization. However, because of the partnership that evolved between the government and industry, all four groups—the AEC, JCAE, supply industry, and the utilities—participated extensively in all policy and programmatic decision making. Opportunities for participation came about through R&D contractual arrangements between the AEC, industry, and the utilities; through frequent AEC and JCAE solicitation of opinions of interest groups; and through hearings held by the JCAE.

The chief advocates of nuclear development included the four groups mentioned above, plus scientists and engineers, educators, and some affected union organizations. There was no significant opposition to nuclear power during the developmental stage. There was, however, opposition to specific actions taken by the government during that time. Controversial issues included government versus private ownership of nuclear reactors and fuels; patents; accident liability; and government subsidies. In the utilization phase, considerable opposition has developed, both from individuals and from environmental, conservation, and other organized groups. Initially, opposition was most pronounced in regard to the AEC's licensing of reactor construction and operation; the opposition most often articulated at AEC and JCAE hearings has dealt with these subjects. More recently, serious objections have been raised concerning not only reactor safety, but also waste disposal, nulear materials safeguards, and other issues concerning the health and safety of the public.

In 1975, the acceptability of nuclear energy from the standpoint of public health and safety is being seriously questioned, at both state and federal levels. The views of opponents to nuclear power are having a substantial impact on the government in its resolution of the issues involved. Moratorium is a distinct possibility, particularly for individual states.

12. What were the interactions (collaboration, conflict) among the actors?

Major participants were identified in the answer to Question 11. The presidents holding office during the period under discussion have all been advocates of nuclear power; in several instances they have proposed major legislative actions on its development. They have also had the responsibility of appointing members of the AEC. In most periods the president was not a continuing activist for nuclear development; rather, he left most of the decisions on programmatic and policy matters to the AEC and the JCAE.

The nature of the interactions between the AEC and the JCAE was established to a large degree by the 1946 Act and later legislation. The AEC was directed to keep the JCAE fully and currently informed of the commission's activities. The JCAE was directed to make continuing studies both on these specific activities and on problems relating to the development, use, and control of atomic energy. These responsibilities, as spelled out in the 1946 Act, set the stage for close and continuing interaction between these two government bodies. The interaction of the JCAE with the rest of Congress was also determined to a large degree by the 1946 Act, which required that all legislation pertaining to nuclear matters be referred to the JCAE. The JCAE's position was further strengthened when Congress granted it authorization powers. The JCAE maintained a close surveillance of the various aspects of the atomic energy program and the work of the AEC, with a view to insuring that adequate progress was made and that public funds appropriated were spent wisely and efficiently.

Finally, a partnership was formed by the AEC, the JCAE, and industry. Industry became involved through operating contracts for R&D and production facilities and through government-industry cooperative programs. Other less prominent actors identified above became involved, not as direct participants in the program, but as opponents or proponents of specific issues brought up by the AEC, the JCAE, or industry, usually at the time of legislative activities on a major bill or program. As indicated above, the major conflicts regarding opposition to nuclear power did not occur until the commercialization stage. This stage has brought into play intervenors who have had and are continuing to have a major influence on the deployment of nuclear power.

13. How were conflicts resolved?

During the development period, discussions of controversial issues came about through informal and formal meetings and through memoranda between two or more of the interested groups. Opportunities for discussions existed because of the contractual relationships between the AEC and industry, the special relationship required by law between the AEC and the JCAE (discussed above), the JCAE's hearings on particular issues, and specific requests for information and opinions on issues. Resolution of major conflicts usually came about through legislative actions and/or AEC administrative or policy changes; in many cases these involved compromises on the issues. Compromises were reached through either bargaining or conciliating actions between opposing groups. Many significant examples can be found in the public record, particularly regarding legislative actions. For example, during the debate on the 1946 Atomic Energy Act, a compromise was reached between the forces proposing and opposing military control of atomic energy. This was achieved by the establishment of a civilian commission that received input from the military through the Military Liaison Committee. In working out the Atomic Energy Act of 1954, there were opposing views on private ownership of nuclear reactors and the "giveaway" to private industry of a technology developed largely through public funding. Three significant compromises were made: (1) not allowing private ownership of nuclear fuels at that time; (2) compulsory licensing of patents; and (3) the inclusion of the public power preference clause. The final version of the 1964 Private Ownership of Nuclear Materials Act also came about through compromises. Some of the areas in which compromises were reached included conditions of government uranium stockpile disposal, toll enrichment of foreign and domestic uranium in government facilities, government leasing of uranium, and government buy-back of plutonium and U-233. There were also significant power interplays between the JCAE and the AEC on reactor programs and projects: in some cases these ended in compromises; others ended with directives from the JCAE to the AEC for specific actions.

Except for a brief period in the mid-1950's, a cooperative partnership existed between the JCAE and the AEC and between government and industry in most policy matters. Generally, attempts were made to resolve conflicts by giving due consideration to differing viewpoints. However, there was little indication that the government actively sought truly adversary opinions except from a very limited number of interest groups, nor were there any significant adversary groups opposing nuclear power until after it was developed.

Conflicts and their resolutions during the deployment stage were substantially different from those of the development stage. The early conflicts during deployment were generally over specific reactor siting questions. These were initially aired in public hearings held by the Atomic Safety and Licensing Board. Resolution came about through compromises made by the affected parties—the intervenors, the AEC, and the electric utilities—or through court action. Broader issues have surfaced during licensing of a power plant—issues such as the authority of the AEC versus that of the states—and have been frequently resolved in the courts. The AEC and Congress have held public hearings on generic problems, with testimony being given by the interested parties. These hearings have affected safety criteria established by the AEC and have influenced safety R&D programs and management arrangements. Some issues have been settled by state referendums or other state actions; however, the broader question of whether the benefits of nuclear power justify the risks is essentially political and must be resolved by state and federal governments.

14. What were the effects of the power structure and organization on decisions?

Power structure and organization have been and continue to be particularly important factors in the development of nuclear energy. The organization of the JCAE and its responsibilities and authorities give it unprecedented powers within Congress. First, the JCAE has full jurisdiction over all legislative matters pertaining to atomic energy; second, it has authorization power on atomic energy legislation; and third, it has the statutory right to be fully and currently informed and to make continuing studies of all nuclear activities, a prerogative that gives it strong investigative powers. Thus the committee became the only source of expertise on nuclear matters in Congress, and has played a primary role in resolving disputes between parties prior to floor debates and in conference. It has traditionally supported nuclear power development, both within Congress and elsewhere.

The AEC also had a substantial amount of power. Given the sole responsibility in the executive branch for nuclear development, it exercised its control with monopolistic powers. The criteria for removal of members of the commission—inefficiency, neglect of duty, or malfeasance in office—limited the political pressure that could be applied by the president. With these powers and strong fiscal support from Congress and the president, the AEC was able to maintain a position of leadership in nuclear power development. It used this position to control programs and to pressure industry.

Some segments of industry, however, also had a certain amount of power. The practice of having the AEC's programs performed by operating contractors in AEC facilities, or, in many instances, performed in the same contractor's private facilities, gave a few companies an advantage that placed them in a favorable position for commercial use of atomic energy. These companies were also in a favorable position to influence governmental decision making.

For most of the development period, the structure produced by the three parties—the AEC, JCAE, and industry—was essentially a closed system. There was little interest on the part of these three parties in seeking outside input, nor was there much interest on the part of outside groups—i.e., "outsiders" in Congress, state government, and the public—in affecting the decisions made by this system. In recent years, however, this situation has changed dramatically. Congressional committees other than the JCAE, intervenors, and state governments are now taking an active role in decision making. Also, regulation of nuclear power has been separated from the development and now resides in the Nuclear Regulatory Commission.

Another recent change was the formation of ERDA by Congress in 1974. One objective of Congress in developing the new organization was to reduce the overall influence of the AEC on energy policy and programmatic matters. The government's nuclear organization no longer reports directly to the president. Placing the former AEC functions on the same organizational level with other energy development areas had the effect of upgrading the priorities of the latter. Other recent actions of Congress support this same intent: for example, it has markedly increased the budget of nonnuclear energy developments in the past few years, while maintaining the nuclear budget at a relatively constant level.

15. What was the distribution of risk, cost, and benefit; i.e., who were the winners and the losers?

The total cost of the development of the present commercial reactors was approximately $3 billion. The public costs expended by the AEC were approximately two thirds of this amount, or $2 billion. This figure does not include military reactor development, enrichment plants, uranium ore, and part of fuel reprocessing development expenditures, all of which benefited the civilian reactor program. Industry spent approximately $1 billion for research and development facilities and for equipment between 1954 and 1967, a time span that includes most of the development period. Industry costs do not include major reactor installations or manufacturing facilities.

Another potentially large financial risk was accepted by the government through the Price-Anderson Act of 1957. By this act the government indemnified owners and operators of nuclear facilities against accidents causing injury to the public. The total liability allowed per accident is limited to $560 million, with the government providing the difference between that maximum and the amount provided by private insurance. In 1957 the private insurance available was $60 million; in 1975, it was $95 million. The government coverage, therefore, was $500 million initially and $465 million in 1975. To date there have been no accidents requiring compensation to the public.

The potential benefits of nuclear power to the public are lower electricity costs and possibly lower environmental costs; the benefits to equipment manufacturers and fuel-cycle companies are profits from sales. The utilities' benefits are similar to those gained by the public. In addition, nuclear power provides the utilities with an alternative energy source, a benefit that could be a long-term boon to society in general. Benefits are also accruing to the nation, in terms of improved international balance-of-payments and profits to private industry through sales and services to foreign markets.

The exact benefits in terms of dollar savings or profits are difficult to determine, as most are still in the future. But with the large increases in fossil fuel costs since 1973, the cost of electric power produced by nuclear energy is substantially lower than that of electric power generated from coal or oil.

In 1962 the AEC's estimated cumulative electricity cost savings by the year 2000 were given as about $30 billion, at an annual rate of $4 billion to $5 billion. Assuming that the AEC's projection of an installed capacity of 1 million Mw$_e$ by the year 2000 is correct, this savings amounts to approximately 0.5 to 0.7 mills per kwh of electric energy generated, or less than 10 percent of power generation costs. In a 1973 study for Northeast Utilities, a utility located in a high-cost region, S. M. Stoller Corporation estimated that in the 1981–85 period nuclear power costs would average 5 mills per kwh less than coal, nuclear power's nearest competitor.[12] This estimate was made before the recent large increases in oil and coal prices. The 1973 Stoller estimate is about ten times the national average estimated in 1962, and would represent an annual savings of $40 million for a single 1,150 Mw$_e$ plant. The Stoller study recommended nuclear power over oil and coal for Northeast Utilities on the basis of cost savings, as well as for other reasons. AIF reported that the actual average savings of electricity produced in nuclear power plants in 1974 was approximately 6.5 mills per kwh. Northeast Utilities reported savings of $106 million for the first three quarters of 1974 as a result of using nuclear power.

Profits on nuclear sales are generally not reported separately by companies. Sales of nuclear plants, however, have grown rapidly. The annual rate of such sales is projected to be approximately $11 billion, with a cumulative total of $105 billion by 1985. The cumulative total sales of fuel-cycle services are estimated to be $22 billion by 1985.

Those who might stand to lose from the development of nuclear power were industries and labor groups providing alternative energy sources and equipment to the electric utilities. However, there is considerable overlap in the make-up of the potential winner and loser groups since, in many cases, such suppliers are also suppliers in the nuclear field. Other losers could be the public and utilities, if the claims of environmental and safety risks made by opponents to nuclear power are realistic. (For further discussion of costs and benefits, see presentation of Item One under "Outcome Variables" in the next section.)

16. Were the winners and losers participants in the decision-making process?

The decision to develop nuclear power reactors was made publicly by the president and Congress; to that extent, all parties—including the public—were participants. Both the AEC and the JCAE actively solicited differing points of view from potential winner and loser groups. All interest groups were given the opportunity to participate in legislative matters and frequently were formally requested to supply information to the JCAE. Because of the interactions among participants (described under Question 12), considerable opportunities existed for interested parties to review and provide feedback on AEC decisions with respect to policy matters and technical programs. The AEC was required by law to put the scope of major decisions before the JCAE for a definite period—thirty to forty-five days in most cases—before making such decisions. This time period afforded the JCAE opportunities to review and comment on the proposed actions.

During the period of nuclear power development, the most active potential winners in the decision-making process were the reactor and equipment manufacturers, the fuel-cycle suppliers, and the electric utilities. Other potential beneficiaries who had lesser input included such groups as the construction industry, transportation companies, banks, insurance companies, architect-engineering firms, and labor groups.

In the loser-group category, the most vocal group was the coal industry. This group, which was given considerable opportunity to be heard, was not against nuclear power *per se,* but rather against various subsidies, which, in its opinion, gave nuclear power an unfair advantage.

Those who feel that use of nuclear power in its current state of development presents an unacceptable risk to the public did not participate in decision making during most of the period of reactor development. Essentially, there was no articulated opposition to nuclear power during that time. The opposition appeared during the commercial deployment phase, and critics have since had an influential voice in decision making. They have become an active and important force in the AEC's and industry's reactor safety considerations.

SYSTEM PERFORMANCE

17. What were the implementation mechanics?

Government funding was obtained in much the same way as in other agencies, except for the special nature of the JCAE. Nuclear development budget requests were submitted to the Office of Management and Budget (OMB). After OMB and White House review, the president would submit a possibly revised budget request to Congress. Since the JCAE has jurisdiction and authorization power over all nuclear matters, the president's request would be considered first by the committee. Because of the relationship that had built up between the AEC and JCAE, the JCAE generally knew of the content of the AEC's request to OMB. After committee review, which generally involved the AEC and other interest groups, and after authorization, the appropriation bill would go to the Senate and House appropriation committees where it again would be reviewed and possibly modified within the JCAE authorization. It then would be acted upon by both houses of Congress, a process sometimes requiring conference resolution of differences. If passed, the appropriation bill would be submitted to the president for his approval and for distribution of funds.

Since the AEC elected not to conduct its own research and development, funds provided to the AEC were spent through the operating contractors of AEC facilities and through contracts with private and public institutions. In this way, the AEC has supported large R&D programs. Programs have included both those funded entirely by the government and cooperative efforts with industry. The most prominent example of the latter was the Power Reactor Demonstration Program (PRDP). In this program, demonstration reactors were constructed and operated on utility systems. Some of the reactors involving public utilities were totally funded by the AEC; others were funded primarily by the utilities with financial assistance from the commission.

In addition to the AEC-funded programs, private industry conducted its own R&D programs, which in some instances were supported by a utility or a group of utilities. Utility combines frequently were organized to fund R&D and reactor projects and to gain experience in reactor utilization.

The ways in which the AEC and industry conducted the R&D programs are summarized under Outcome Variable 8.

Decisions on final deployment of commercial reactors were and are the prerogative of the utilities. The mechanics take the form of competitive bids from reactor vendors and fossil-fuel plant suppliers; the utility then selects the supplier submitting the most advantageous bid. Cost is the most important parameter, with environmental issues and scheduling also entering into the decision. Power plant engineering and construction are carried out by architect-engineers, by others normally employed by the utility, and by the utility itself. A few of the first commercial reactors were supplied and the plant constructed by the reactor vendors; these were called "turnkey projects." In this type of project, the reactor plant was completed for operation by the vendor at a fixed cost to the utilities. That method was beneficial to the utilities in that it reduced their risks; in this way, it was important in opening up the commercial market. But, at the same time, it increased the financial risk to the reactor vendors, who lost money on these first projects. This method is no longer practiced.

Before a nuclear reactor can be employed, a construction permit and an operating license must be obtained from NRC (formerly the AEC's regulatory division). These involve detailed analyses of the safety and environmental impact of the nuclear plant. Public hearings are conducted by the Atomic Safety and Licensing Board. The operation of the plant continues to be monitored by NRC after it is licensed, to determine the degree of compliance with the agreed-upon operating specifications.

18. What significant events were triggered by information generation, transfer, and use?

The first event was the discovery of fission and its energy-releasing power. This event, when brought to the attention of President Roosevelt, triggered a mammoth government program which proved the technical feasibility of a nuclear chain reaction and of nuclear reactors as a large power source. Because of the military application of the results of this program, control of the new energy source was placed in the hands of government. This led to major government intervention in the development of the commercial reactor.

Many technical events in the late 1940's and 1950's combined to make possible nuclear power plants that were competitive with other energy sources. Since many of these events occurred in government laboratories, technology transfer to industry was important. This transfer was carried out in several ways: technical meetings and documentation, contracts with industry, and co-operative programs.

Table 1 (Chapter I) lists significant events in the development and deployment of the nuclear reactor.

19. Was performance assessed? Corrected?

Relationships within the whole system (composed of the AEC, Congress, utilities, contractors, and reactor manufacturers) were assessed by the JCAE and by the AEC over the years in terms of seeking the best way to perfect and deliver the technology. The JCAE played a major role in evaluating specific AEC and industry programs and in making recommendations for changes. It was particularly aggressive in proposing major changes in AEC programs based on the JCAE's reviews. Similarly, there was a two-way assessment and feedback between the AEC and industry on both government and private programs. Substantial changes occurred because of these assessments.

After assessing the AEC's progress in developing nuclear power, the JCAE determined it to be inadequate, and requested a more definitive reactor program from the AEC. This resulted in the five-year experimental reactor program of the early 1950's. The JCAE's assessment and continued evaluation of progress, as well as the AEC's own assessment, led to the important Power Demonstration Reactor Program and its several expanded phases. In addition, as a result of JCAE assessment, the second round of PDRP was significantly modified. Many specific reactor projects were initiated or terminated based on assessment by either government or industry of their potential contribution to nuclear power development. Significant realignment occurred in reactor development and uranium supply programs as the commercial phase was approached in the 1960's. These are but a few examples of changes made in policy, programs, and objectives as a result of frequent assessments initiated by the AEC, JCAE, the president, and industry.

An important part of the assessment process is now under way. First, the economic and environmental competitiveness of the product is being determined in the marketplace by the user utilities. Also, at this stage a significant segment of the regulation comes under the close scrutiny of state and local governments and of intervenors in licensing matters. This feedback is having a substantial effect on power-plant designs and on administrative procedures in licensing and operating reactors.

20. What were the intended outputs?

The intended outputs from atomic energy development and utilization were expressed in a broad sense in the policy statement from the Atomic Energy Act of 1946; they included: "improving the public welfare, increasing the standard of living, strengthening free competition in private enterprise, and promoting world peace.'' The specific intended outputs were safe and economic nuclear power reactors as major sources of energy for the generation of electricity.

21. What were the actual outputs? Externalities?

The actual outputs from the systems were safe and economic nuclear power plants—that is, safe and economic from the perspective of the users, the electric utilities. The nuclear reactor is being purchased in substantial numbers by the utilities. By the end of 1974 a total of 225 nuclear plants had been purchased. Their combined capacity of 222,000 Mw_e was equal to more than half of the U.S. generating capacity in that year. In many areas of the country, nuclear power plants are thought to be more economically and environmentally attractive than fossil-fuel plants.

The question of safety is still under discussion. Although the AEC, in deciding to license the operating nuclear power plants, judged them to have an acceptable level of risk to the public, a significant number of individuals and groups have questioned both the safety of reactor operations and the handling and storage of radioactive waste and nuclear materials. The government and industry recognize that safety questions remain sufficiently important to justify continued improvement in safety by means of further R&D and design changes.

External effects of nuclear reactors include waste heat discharge in cooling waters; small amounts (below maximum levels considered safe by AEC) of radioactive discharge in the plant vicinity; aesthetic effects of the plants and, in some cases, of the large cooling towers and ponds; the risks inherent in operation of the plants; the risks encountered in handling, transporting, processing, and storing highly radioactive products for many generations; and the risk of diversion of special nuclear materials for clandestine purposes. Other external effects result from the mining and milling of uranium ore and from the societal impact of an alternative energy source that will reduce the impact of shortages of other energy sources. Nuclear energy will also assist in conserving fossil fuels for other future uses.

Economic externalities include the improvement in balance-of-payments (discussed in answer to Question 15), and the utilization of a major national asset—the surplus uranium-enrichment facilities. There are also the economic benefits to the nuclear industry, and the concomitant costs to the competitor industries that supply alternative energy resources and equipment.

INSTITUTIONAL BEHAVIOR

22. Was the institutional base adequate to make and implement decisions?

Although some decisions made by the JCAE were overridden by Congress, and some decisions made by the AEC were substantially altered by the JCAE, their power base appears to have been sufficiently ample to permit them to initiate and conduct aggressive programs. The two governmental bodies were given clear responsibilities and authority for decision making and for implementing programs. It is true that a joint congressional committee with the type of jurisdiction given to the JCAE tends to present the decision makers with only one point of view, as opposed to the two different points of view they receive when jurisdiction over legislation is held by two separate committees, one from each house. On the other hand, a joint committee centralizes program and policy reviews in Congress and, as happened in the case of the JCAE, may become expert in the areas for which it is responsible. In some instances, however, the JCAE used this expertise and power to intervene in AEC administrative matters which might have been considered the purview of the agency. Moreover, the extensive use of such powerful joint committees probably would not be tolerated, as it would greatly undermine the two-house system.

The other institutions, reactor manufacturers, fuel-cycle supply companies, and utilities, had an adequate industrial base but initially were placed under severe restrictions regarding the degree of their participation. These restrictions were removed as the development evolved. All institutions were novices in the early years of nuclear development and each had to learn the necessary technical skills. In general, the overall institutional structure appeared to perform satisfactorily when evaluated in terms of the problem solved and in view of constraints inherently associated with it.

23. What problems existed in institutional coupling, i.e., communication and cooperation?

From the beginning, both the government's monopolistic control of all aspects of the technology and the secrecy placed on it put serious roadblocks in the way of industry participation. These problems and their resolution were reviewed in answer to Question 12. In addition, the newness of the technology and uncertainties about the uranium supply were factors retarding industry's interest in committing funds in the early development period. During this period, the AEC had to propose incentive plans in order to promote an aggressive program with industry.

In the mid-1950's there were serious problems of communication and cooperation between the AEC and the JCAE. To some extent these reflected a basic conflict between the chairman of the AEC and a few members of the JCAE. Although personalities undoubtedly played a role in the problem, the policy conflict centered around the rate of progress of nuclear power development and the approach to be used to expedite it. The AEC wanted to rely heavily on industry in the demonstration phase, while a few members of the JCAE wanted the government to undertake construction of several large reactors. The solution was to employ both approaches and to make compromises on the degree of each approach. Those members of the JCAE promoting large numbers of government reactors did not have sufficient political power in Congress to have the legislation enacted to provide for these reactors, but they were able to have passed legislation calling for a limited number of these plants. Such threats or specific actions by a member of the polity can be quite influential in the technology management process; in fact, these pressures undoubtedly influenced concurrent expansion of both private projects and cooperative projects between the AEC and industry.

The AEC, the JCAE, and participating industries were not under any illusion as to the ultimate benefits to mankind to be derived from uses of nuclear energy. However, the public, parts of industry, and other institutions were probably misled in the late 1940's and early 1950's regarding the potential benefits from using nuclear energy for purposes other than the generation of electric power. In the late 1950's, when the nuclear institutions became more aware of the complex problems involved in developing an economically feasible nuclear power plant, even they became discouraged. These problems were resolved in the late 1950's and the early 1960's through large cooperative programs between government and industry and through major risk taking by industry on large privately funded reactor projects.

Another communications problem was the need to educate the public as to the potential health and safety risks of nuclear power. This process has had a negative effect on the willingness of some segments of the public to accept nuclear power. Several of the individuals interviewed, however, believed that the AEC had not performed adequately in informing the public on the risks versus benefits of nuclear power.

24. Did institutions malfunction? How?

The answer to the question has to be somewhat subjective, since it is impossible to know what the outcome of alternative courses of action might have been. Government secrecy and control of the technology were definitely deterrents to nuclear development; consequently, some feel that the president and Congress erred both in placing such strict controls on nuclear matters in the first place, and in waiting so long to remove them. Even so, some secrecy on pertinent technology still exists today. If one were to consider just civilian power development, there might be grounds to conclude that the government malfunctioned in this area. It must be remembered, however, that national security was the overriding issue at the time.

A second possible area of government malfunctioning was in the total number of prototype and demonstration reactors constructed. It is likely that some of these were not backed by adequate supporting technology, nor could they be justified on the basis of their probable contribution to civilian reactor development. However, this approach did result in a competitive product in the United States, one that is being selected in the world markets over reactor concepts developed in other countries. So the error, if it occurred, was one of overtesting rather than undertesting of different concepts.

The problem of public education on nuclear power was mentioned in the previous question. A related area in which the AEC may have malfunctioned is that of R&D in the areas of reactor safety and waste management. Reactor safety programs have been extensively delayed and their scope has probably been inadequate. According to government and industry analyses, the inadequacy has not resulted in an unacceptable risk to the public. On the other hand, as judged by a significant number of interest groups, the risk levels indicated by the AEC are not backed by conclusive evidence. Such evidence should include extensive experimental findings, which could be derived at least in part from delayed programs and from additional programs. The expansion of the AEC's reactor safety budget in the past three years and the reorganization of the light-water reactor safety division indicated recognition by the AEC that reactor safety was still a problem, and a willingness on its part to devote greater management attention to the problem than it had in the past. In addition, in 1974 the promotional and regulatory functions of the AEC were separated; one reason for this separation was to reduce the influence of promotional groups on the regulatory process.

Waste management is not a pressing problem for the utilities at this time since relatively little waste has been generated so far. The engineered-storage approach proposed by the AEC is probably adequate until a more permanent approach—e.g., salt-mine storage—is demonstrated to be acceptable. At present, waste storage problems are more significant in the area of the nuclear weapons program. However, better and earlier planning and implementation of certain waste demonstration programs—e.g., the Lyons, Kansas, salt-mine demonstration—and better public education and public relations would probably have reduced the controversy over this area of risk to society.

Another area that has not been dealt with adequately is that of special nuclear materials safeguards. Both a national and international problem, it requires international solutions. Although the International Atomic Energy Agency has a role in detecting diversion, it is not authorized to protect nuclear materials. New initiatives are needed for developing an acceptable safeguards system.

Still other problems were caused by delays in planning for new facilities or bringing them into operation. As a consequence of these delays, fuel reprocessing and enrichment services may not be adequate in the next five to ten years.

25. What were the key policy uncertainties and did they have any effect?

There were undoubtedly uncertainties about the projected outcome of all major policies that were developed and implemented. The effects of several of these policies have been discussed in answer to previous policy process questions. The areas of uncertainty had to do with government control, secrecy, technical programs, and industry involvement, among other factors. In most instances, an innovative approach to policy development was used. Policies were continually altered to reflect the needs of the program based on its rate of development and the institutional pressures for change. Some examples can be seen in the evolution of the Power Reactor Demonstration Program; major pieces of legislation, such as the Atomic Energy Acts of 1946 and 1954, the Price-Anderson Act of 1957, and the Private Ownership of Nuclear Fuels Act of 1964; and the uranium ore exploration and development program.

26. At the top policy levels, what were the perceptions of societal value preferences, territorial imperatives, political realities, etc.?

Perceptions at the top policy levels may be inferred from testimonies given and actions taken, but there is no means by which to validate these inferences.

Perceptions of societal value preferences pertained to two major issues: national security, and utilization of nuclear energy for the betterment of mankind. Because of the destructive potential of nuclear energy, society wanted it carefully controlled by government. When international control was found not to be feasible, the government perceived that the public wanted the United States to maintain leadership in weapons development. It must be remembered that this was a period when there was considerable public concern over the spread of international communism. The controls and priorities established by the government to maintain its leadership in weapons development delayed its implementation of an aggressive program to develop peaceful uses of atomic energy—the second desire of the public. With regard to such uses of nuclear power, societal preference—almost without any articulated opposition—was that nuclear power should be developed as a safe and economic energy source to serve the consumer public.

Initial public acceptance of nuclear power stemmed from the optimistic forecasts that many of the problems of mankind could be solved by nuclear power reactors' providing low-cost electricity to the nation and to the world. There was also growing concern among knowledgeable people that conventional energy sources were limited, and a perception that new energy sources would be required in the twentieth century. Nuclear power was projected to have the potential to be a substantial substitute for fossil fuels. This potential was actively discussed in the early formulation of government policies on nuclear development.

Perception of territorial imperatives involved both international and intranational issues. The paramount international issue was the cold war with the Soviet Union and that nation's rapid development of nuclear weapons. This placed great urgency on the expansion of the U.S. weapons program. There was also concern over world leadership in nuclear power development. The major competition included the U.S.S.R. and two free-world nations, the United Kingdom and France. Other nations, including Canada, Sweden, West Germany, Italy, Belgium, and later Japan, were also actively involved in the nuclear field. Maintaining world leadership over the Soviet Union was seen as part of "the battle for men's minds" during the cold-war period, and was also regarded as important to our international trade position. These arguments were frequently used in justifying new or expanded programs.

The intranational territorial issues involved the proper respective roles of government and private industry in the development and use of nuclear power. Industry was particularly concerned with government dominance in the development. While industry undoubtedly approved of some government assistance, they did not want the AEC to be a "nuclear TVA," owning and operating large nuclear facilities for the purpose of generating electricity. Although government secrecy and controls of nuclear materials and reactors affected the pace of reactor development, the deployment of the reactor as an electric power generation facility has taken place within the existing utility institutions. Compulsory licensing of private patents, imposed in 1954 and still required in 1975, was another major issue involving government versus private rights.

Political realities were recognized in a number of decisions made by government and industry. The first major issue requiring a political compromise was in regard to military versus civilian control. As a result of pressures brought on the president and Congress by scientists and other individuals, and because of the initiative of Senator McMahon, a compromise McMahon Bill was formulated to replace the May-Johnson Bill that had been supported initially by President Truman. The McMahon Bill reduced military control and increased civilian control, but recognized the needs of the military by establishing the Military Liaison Committee.

The JCAE positions on several issues that arose during the hearings on the Atomic Energy Act of 1954 were split down political party lines. Political realities required the JCAE to reach compromises on these issues in order to get a bill passed that would allow greater private participation. Industry pressure groups (particularly public and private utilities), reactor developers, fuel-cycle companies, and the coal industry were active in pressing for legislation and programs favorable to their cause. Scientists and engineers from government laboratories and other institutions were also influential in government policy and decision making. All of these interest groups were active and vocal during the entire development period.

The tug-of-war between the AEC and JCAE on the Power Reactor Demonstration Program and on projects proposed by JCAE members, such as the Gore-Holifield Bill, produced considerable political infighting. The Price-Anderson Act was the direct result of political pressures from industry and, to a lesser degree, from the AEC. The 1964 Private Ownership of Nuclear Fuels Act showed signs of many compromises that had resulted from pressures by various interest groups with different objectives. Thus, the political subsystem of the AEC, the JCAE, and industry institutions proved to be rather stable and, in general, operated effectively throughout the period under review. The one significant exception was the failure to recognize the effect that the inherent nature of fission energy would have on its acceptability, and the consequent failure to anticipate the controversy that was to develop regarding this new energy source.

ANALYSIS OF OUTPUT—OUTCOME VARIABLES

The primary output of the technological delivery system is the commercial nuclear power plant. The following discussion of outcome variables should be considered in the context of two facts: (1) deployment of the product is still in its early stages, and (2) fission and its attendant radioactive products are fixed constraints on the system. Because of the first limitation, any discussion of the product's long-term impact (economic, environmental, social) must be considered to be speculative. It should also be noted that AEC performance in development of the liquid-metal fast breeder reactor has not been reviewed in this study, and consequently will not be assessed here.

THE DISTRIBUTION AND VARIANCE OF COSTS AND BENEFITS (PRIVATE AND SOCIAL) OF THE SYSTEM

A review of costs and benefits is given in Question 15 in the previous section. Other costs not presented there include opportunity costs of resources used (fiscal resources, materials, land, water) and environmental costs. These costs are generally considered in the context of alternatives—and, essentially, the only alternatives to nuclear power in the United States in 1975 are either fossil-fueled plants or no plants at all. Some of these costs and benefits are discussed below.

The National Environmental Policy Act (NEPA) of 1969 (PL 91-190) requires that for each power plant project a detailed statement be prepared on: (1) the environmental impact of the proposed action, (2) any adverse environmental effects that could not be avoided should the proposal be implemented, (3) alternatives to the proposed action, (4) the relationship between local short-term uses of man's environment and the maintenance and enhancement of long-term productivity, and (5) any irreversible and irretrievable commitments of resources that would be involved in the proposed action should it be implemented. In response to NEPA's requirement, both economic and environmental cost-benefit analyses are made.[13] The results of a completed study will depend on the particular plant considered.

Local, regional, and national economic impacts of the construction and operation of specific nuclear power generation facilities include the following:

Benefits—employment generated, value of power generated, resources utilization, direct and secondary effect on economy.

Costs—community services required, loss of alternative uses of land and other resources, and losses resulting from not using alternative resources (e.g., coal mining).

Environmental impacts are:

Benefits—reduction or elimination of gaseous and particulate matter from outdated or alternative fossil-fueled plants; use of electricity instead of fossil fuels for heat, transportation, etc.; recreational sites if large cooling ponds are used; reduction of coal mining, transportation, and storage.

Costs—increased thermal pollution; discharge of radioactive products to the atmosphere and water bodies; and risks resulting from reactor operation and from the storing, processing, and transporting of radioactive material.

There is no generally accepted methodology for quantifying environmental impacts that provides a common base for comparison with economic issues.[14] Therefore, the environmental impact analyses are generally performed on a relative basis with alternatives. Economic impacts are quantified in dollars and the net benefits of alternatives are compared. The final judgment as to whether or not a plant will be built is dependent on the interactions of many interest groups: the pertinent utility; the AEC; the Environmental Protection Agency; the courts; other local, state, and federal agencies; influential special interest groups; and the public.

The acceptance of a commercial product by the consumer is an important measure of its success. Thus, from the fact that the U.S.-developed nuclear reactor plant is being purchased, constructed, and operated in large numbers, it may be concluded that, in many areas of the United States and the world, such plants have been judged to be more economically and environmentally attractive than fossil-fuel plants.

IMPACTS ON SOCIAL VALUES

With the advent of any major new technology, the possibility exists of a great change in the economic and social environment. The automobile, television, and the computer are noteworthy examples. The primary output of nuclear power has not produced such dramatic changes, nor does it appear that it will. Application of this new energy source has been carried out in such a manner that the user cannot directly identify the source of the energy. Kilowatt hours of electric energy generated from nuclear energy are no different from those generated by other means. Although in many respects the nuclear reactor is much more complex and potentially more hazardous than a fossil-fuel boiler feeding steam to the turbo-generator, conceptually it has simply replaced the fossil-fuel boiler. Consequently, unlike the automobile, television, and the computer, the user of its output is totally unaffected by the utilization of the new technological development in the utility system. The transition is made by the electric utility.

There was a time during the period of development when some thought that nuclear energy would be extremely cheap and would solve many of the welfare problems facing much of the world's population. Unfortunately, this has not proved to be the case. In fact, the complex technology associated with nuclear power requires large industrial and technical capabilities. Many countries, particularly those with the greatest social needs, do not have these capabilities and must import them if they are to use nuclear power. In the long term, however, nuclear power may serve society by reducing the impact of fossil-fuel depletion. (See section on "Present and Future Range of Choices Available to Users/Consumers" for a further discussion of this point.)

Although electricity from nuclear power does not appear to be having any significant direct impact on social values, nuclear power is being introduced at a time when societal values regarding the uses and benefits of technology appear to be in transition. Nuclear power is just one of the many developments being questioned. The desirability and extent of the expansion of energy utilization in general is being publicly debated in 1975. The issue of total costs versus benefits to society is being raised, and environmental costs, a factor not previously considered in many areas of technology, are being included in the evaluation. Radiation from fission byproducts and the potential danger of nuclear materials, however, because of their characteristics of long-term import to society, fall in a unique category, and are being questioned apart from the general issue of technology.

POLITICAL POWER DISTRIBUTION

Nuclear power technology emerged from a highly secret and awesome military development totally controlled by the government, and the potential paths for its emergence from this military control to peaceful uses were many. From the end of World War II, political forces inside and outside of government have exerted pressures on both the government and industry. These pressures led to legislative and policy actions that resulted in the gradual normalization of the new technology within the traditional framework of the nation's institutions. While this normalization is not yet complete, almost all of the major steps have been taken.

The first major step was in determining the early postwar control. The overriding issue was that of military versus civilian control. Through the efforts of concerned scientists—particularly members of the newly formed Federation of Atomic Scientists—and with the legislative assistance of Senator McMahon, most of the control of the new energy source was removed from the military and placed in the hands of civilians. This was accomplished through the enactment of the McMahon Bill—the Atomic Energy Act of 1946. Unlike the initially proposed legislation (the May-Johnson Bill), the McMahon Bill provided civilian supremacy in the integration of national and international policy. It explicitly defined the proper military participation in atomic energy matters. Although it gave great powers to the Atomic Energy Commission for controlling nuclear energy matters, its establishment of civilian control permitted potentially greater freedom for scientific research. The "interest in maintaining the kind of professional environment necessary to the practice of science and a deep sense of urgency that the atom be used for peaceful ends" [15] was the factor that motivated the scientists to enter the political arena for the purpose of influencing the shape of government policy. It was a major concern of Senator McMahon that greater emphasis be placed on the civilian application of this new energy source. While one can only speculate on what might have been the path of development under military control, it is not unreasonable to assume that a system more closed to private investment and involvement would have existed. The opportunities for a totally government-owned and -controlled enterprise would probably have been greater. Certainly, tradition in the United States emphasizes civilian control of all aspects of our society, and military control and development of nuclear power would have made serious inroads on this tradition.

The Atomic Energy Act of 1946, discussed above, established two components of the political structure that have had great influence on nuclear matters: the AEC in the Executive Branch, and the JCAE in the Congress. Concurrent with, and to some degree as a result of, AEC contracting arrangements and development programs, a third component of the policy-making subsystem emerged. This component included the industrial suppliers, the user utility industry, and other special interest groups. Up to the end of 1974, the composition of this political subsystem (the AEC, the JCAE, and the special interest groups) was stable.* The term, "political subsystem," is derived from Redford, who defines subsystem (or intermediary) politics as "the politics of function, involving the interrelations of bureaus and other administrative operating agencies, the counterpart congressional committee structure, and the interest organizations, trade press, and lobbyists concerned with a particular area of program specialization." [16] This definition adequately describes the political structure of the technological delivery system in which much of the decision making and policy development takes place. The structure was shown in Figure 3 (this chapter).

Redford has concluded that there is probably some kind of subsystem for every major activity of government. He proposes that:

> (1) Subsystems provide stability for existing equilibrium among interests; (2) subsystems provide continuous access and superior opportunities for influence to high-quantity, aggregated interests; (3) subsystems provide some access and representation to interests that are not dominant. Occasional victories are won by even the normally excluded; and (4) substantial changes in the balances among interests served by the subsystems can be expected to occur only through macropolitical, e.g., the President, intervention that modifies the rules and roles operating in the systems. [17]

To a remarkable degree these propositions are borne out in this study of the nuclear power development. Because the subsystem operated effectively, stability of programs through government support was maintained; legislative actions, policies, and programs were developed to the mutual benefit and satisfaction of the interested parties; and mutually agreed-upon goals were established. The manner in which the commissioners can be removed—namely, only for neglect of duty or malfeasance in office—further strengthens the subsystem and

---

* In 1974, the AEC component was divided into two parts: NRC and one division of ERDA. This reorganization was discussed in Chapter II.

removes it somewhat from the influence of the president, although the desirability of this insulation could be debated.

Because of the JCAE's close relationship with the AEC and the statutory requirements that it be kept currently informed, the JCAE became a competent, knowledgeable, and respected body, capable of making well-founded decisions. While at times it appeared to usurp the management prerogatives of the AEC, one AEC official expressed the opinion that it is far better to have a strong, competent committee in Congress that does push the agency, than to have no truly interested and concerned representation. He saw the JCAE pressures on the AEC as a key ingredient in the successful development of atomic energy. Certainly, considerable program guidance and leadership has come from the JCAE. To paraphrase Robert Hollingsworth, general manager of the AEC, the JCAE is both a "Godmother" and a "Godfather," both a protector and a prodder. The success of the development, according to Hollingsworth, can be partly credited to the "incestuous" relationship that exists in this subsystem.

Another basis for the strength of the JCAE and the AEC is the clearly defined responsibilities of these two governmental bodies with respect to atomic energy matters, particularly on the developmental side. They were the recognized and accepted leaders in the government and had the nuclear development field as their sole domain. They were also new organizations with a sense of purpose.

There is indication from committee attendance records and from information presented by interviewees that the interest of Senate members of the JCAE in committee activities has waned since about 1964. They are purported to give higher priorities to other committee assignments and to attend JCAE meetings only when matters of particular interest to them are presented. Part of the problem was attributed to the fact that a smaller number of senators must carry out essentially the same congressional responsibilities as a much larger number of representatives. This tends to result in an abdication of JCAE responsibilities to the House members, which in turn leads to a redistribution of political power in Congress. There may also be a reduction of prestige from being a member of the JCAE as the nuclear industry has both matured and become controversial.

The political power of the utility industry was tested during the development stages. The conflict centered around the private versus public power controversy, which had existed for a considerable time and was not unique to nuclear energy. This political issue did affect various legislative matters, which in turn influenced programs and industry rights to some extent. However, there was no significant redistribution of the private and public components of the electric power industry because of the development of nuclear power.

Other components of the political subsystem have come into play with the deployment of the nuclear power plant. These groups are primarily concerned with plant siting and operating issues, and include the Environmental Protection

Agency, the Nuclear Regulatory Commission, other federal agencies, state and local governments, and special interest groups concerned with matters affecting the health and safety of the public.

PRESENT AND FUTURE RANGE OF CHOICES AVAILABLE TO USERS/CONSUMERS

Nuclear power presents electric utilities with an alternative energy source for both the present and the future. As indicated above, the plants are being judged initially on the merits of their economic and environmental competitiveness. In the long term, some fossil fuels—or all of them, depending on time frame—will become short in supply, and the alternative provided by nuclear energy could become more important in supplying the energy needs of society. The present commercial converter-reactor types probably will not be able to meet the long-term needs; either the breeder reactor or other energy sources will be needed. (See section on "Amount and Rate of Resource Conservation" for further elaboration of this point.)

There are other political and economic advantages of having an alternative energy source to fossil fuels, not only for the United States, but for foreign countries that are highly dependent on imported fuels. The supply of uranium, whether domestic or imported, may be more stable than fossil fuels—e.g., oil from the Middle East. Japan and many European countries are already very much dependent on importing their energy fuels, and the United States could become more so in the future.

PARTICIPANTS' SATISFACTION/FRUSTRATION IN REGARD TO SYSTEM PROCESSES AND SYSTEMS OUTPUT

The first frustration was seen when scientists and others objected to the dominance of the military in the proposed legislation for post-World War II control of nuclear matters. Satisfaction was obtained through passage of a modified bill, the McMahon Bill, that placed control in the hands of a full-time, five-member civilian commission.

However, even with civilian control, nuclear technology still remained under tight secrecy wraps, and was completely controlled and "owned" by the government until 1954. This frustrated attempts of industry and scientists to conduct research on atomic energy. While industry was allowed to begin study of the peaceful uses of atomic energy, it was only permitted to do so through government-controlled access to classified data. Industry was not allowed to own either the nuclear power plants for generating electric energy or the nuclear fuel required for their operation. The opportunity for a totally government-owned nuclear utility still existed. As discussed under Policy Process Question 9, the Atomic Energy Act of 1954 relieved part of industry's frustrations by allowing private ownership of nuclear reactors and by permitting greater freedom of participation in their development. But there were opponents to this action, and thus other frustrations were generated. Some members of the

JCAE saw the legislation as providing a major "giveaway" to private enterprise and believed that nuclear power should remain a government industry. Compulsory licensing of patents was provided in the 1954 Atomic Energy Act as a conciliatory move. This was seen as a mechanism for preventing the development of monopolies in private industry based on government-funded R&D. Even though compulsory licensing still persists today, the view obtained in interviews is that the patent clause has had little real effect on the industry. In summary, the 1954 Act was another significant step in normalizing the utilization of atomic energy in that it eliminated the sole right of ownership by the government.

Although the AEC had recommended otherwise, the 1954 Act barred private ownership of nuclear fuels. Nevertheless, continued government ownership of these materials probably did not have a deterring effect on reactor development. In fact, government waiver of fuel-use charges was used as part of a program designed for subsidizing nuclear power demonstration. However, as it became apparent that nuclear power would be "substantially competitive," the law was changed in 1964 and private ownership of the nuclear fuel used in civilian power plants was allowed. Effective December 31, 1970, government leasing of nuclear fuels was terminated and private ownership was required. This legislation was the last major step the government took to remove itself from areas normally considered to be the purview of private interprise.

In 1975, government ownership of the uranium enrichment facilities represents the only major exception to private industry's supplying the nuclear power market. This ownership stems from the government's weapons program, but the facilities are now mostly in excess of military needs. Although private ownership of these government facilities has been considered by the AEC and industry, no decision has been reached. Private ownership would require a large investment by private industry; also, national security issues are still involved. The capacity of the government's enrichment facilities, after about $1 billion worth of modifications to increase their output capability, would be sufficient to supply the market requirement only until the early 1980's. The decision will have to be made soon as to who—government, private industry, or a combine—is to build the next plant to increase that capacity. The Nixon Administration, wanting to partially remove the government from this aspect of the commercial field, stated that private industry should have the opportunity to do the job. In order to encourage industry to move into this area, the government has allowed industry access to enrichment technology data, even though such data are still classified. Because of competing technologies under development and the large capital investment required, however, the decision is difficult for industry to make. Another factor is the government's desire that the United States continue to supply the foreign market at competitive prices. One member of the JCAE considers this to be of major importance, and believes that the national interest requires that future structuring of the enrichment service keep this factor as a primary consideration, whether it leads to continued government ownership, a semi-public ownership without profits, or to private ownership. His reason is the projection of $1 billion to $1.5 billion per year in foreign exchange for at least 20 to 30 years.

The problem is complex and has foreign policy as well as national policy overtones. At this juncture, that fate of this part of the industry is very uncertain. The government could well remain in this commercial service for many years to come, a state of affairs that would result in an anomaly in the United States private enterprise system.

Interest in the promotion of a government-owned, nuclear-fueled electric utility, referred to by some as a "nuclear TVA," may have been part of the motivation for the proposed Gore-Holifield Bill of 1956, which called for large-scale construction of power plants by the government. This bill, which passed in the Senate but failed in the House, was opposed by both the AEC and private industry. To paraphrase a statement made by Representative Holifield during an interview, the introduction of the Gore-Holifield Bill caused private industry to fear that government was in effect going to take over the function of making electricity; i.e., that the country was taking a step toward nationalization—that the TVA principle was spreading. Some saw it as precisely that. The JCAE had become concerned (frustrated) over the progress being made on nuclear power by the AEC and industry. Representative Holifield believed that the introduction of the Gore-Holifield Bill, together with similar pressures exerted over the next few years by some members of the JCAE, including Representative Price, did push industry into taking a more active role in the development. He feels that the bill also pressured the AEC, which was against this type of legislation, to push the Power Demonstration Reactor Program more aggressively. The PDRP, by design, included major participation by industry. The pressure from the Joint Committee probably was thus partly responsible for potential reactor vendors' initiating more aggressive programs.

The years from 1954 to 1958 were a time when potential government take-over was a concern to industry; at the same time, however, private industry was hesitant to invest heavily in an area where profits, if any, appeared to be in the distant future. Because of program initiatives taken first by the AEC and later by industry, the deployment of the development has been within the existing framework of the industry—namely, the existing private and public utilities and private manufacturers. Reactors were built by the government, but the 1954 Act forbade the AEC from distributing or selling electric energy except that produced as a byproduct in its research and development facilities. Therefore, it would have been necessary to amend this clause if the government were to become a supplier of electric energy from nuclear power. The Hanford N-Reactor is one case in which the thermal energy of a government-owned reactor is indeed sold to a utility. This required special legislation and was probably the last vestige of the public-versus-private-power battle.

The opposition to nuclear energy has been discussed previously. There was essentially no opposition during the development stage; even the coal industry, which saw nuclear energy as a government-subsidized competitor, did not object to nuclear energy *per se*. It has been only at the stage of deployment that certain interest groups have opposed it. A number of the interviewees indicated that the problem was more one of public relations or the fundamental nature of fission than of AEC technology development performance.

CONFLICT—SPECIFICALLY THE CHANGE IN DEGREE
OF CONFLICT ARISING FROM THE SYSTEM

The major conflict arising from the system output involves the question of health and safety risks to the public. The points of controversy surrounding the use of the nuclear reactor have been listed by Alvin Weinberg as:

- Safety of reactors.
- Transport of radioactive fuels.
- Ultimate disposal of radioactive wastes.
- Clandestine diversion of fissile materials.
- Disposal of old reactor sites.
- Waste heat.
- Waste byproducts of mining uranium.[18]

The first five of these stem from the fundamental nature of the fission process, a given and fixed constraint on the system. The AEC's original charter, as stated by law, was not to look at alternative energy sources, but to develop the utilization of *fission energy*. Therefore, any evaluation of the performance of the technological delivery system must recognize this constraint.

Although some do not agree, the AEC, the reactor supply manufacturers, and the users have concluded that these problems have been or can be adequately solved so as to warrant a major commitment by the utility industry to nuclear power. Since the nuclear industry is still young and relatively small, the demonstration of whether adequate solutions have been or can be developed lies ahead and therefore cannot be evaluated with any absolute certainty. Some of the questions raised will not be finally answered for a very long time— thousands of years, if ever. Consequently, as Weinberg points out, resolution of these questions today "is a matter of opinion, not a matter of scientific fact—these questions transcend science, belong to transscience not science." [19]

Partial solutions to some of the problems listed above involve establishing adequate administrative and regulatory procedures. The two areas requiring significant technological developments—reactor safety and waste management—represent continued R&D costs to the system.

Concern with the health and safety of the public in general and of nuclear employees in particular has been an integral part of the AEC's research and development programs. Some of the first experiments performed on light-water reactors were safety experiments. While the safety of the reactors is sufficiently assured to justify AEC licensing for their deployment, it is likely that R&D on safety will continue for the foreseeable future. There were some signs, indicated by budget data, that the AEC reduced the priority of this research in the late 1960's, and this has been a criticism of the AEC. There has also been poor performance of management in conducting some recent safety programs. The AEC did become concerned, however, about the criticism it was receiving. As a result of the pressures applied by its critics, the water-reactor safety program is now being substantially expanded. Furthermore, in recognition of a need for greater emphasis on resolving safety questions, in 1973 the AEC placed the light-water-reactor safety program directly under the AEC's general manager.

Safety R&D should remain a part of the government's program, both as a support to its regulatory activities and as a responsibility to the public. To date there have been no serious reactor accidents involving a utility reactor that caused harm to the public. In fact, there have been only seven deaths attributable to nuclear accidents during the thirty-year history of nuclear reactors. A catastrophic accident, however, although judged to be an extremely remote possibility, could change the acceptability of the product overnight. This problem will be with the industry always, since it can never be proven that a major accident cannot happen. Only sustained satisfactory reactor operating experience and diligent response by government and industry to any operating problems can reduce the anxiety over the possibility.

In addition to reactor safety, another important area of concern has to do with the disposal of radioactive wastes. This is not yet a major problem, since utility reactors have not operated long enough to generate large quantities of waste. Of course, solutions should be in hand before such large quantities are generated. Two AEC solutions are: (1) engineered storage of solid waste in tanks and (2) permanent storage in salt formations. Weinberg, former director of the Oak Ridge National Laboratory, where much research on this subject has been conducted, concurs with the AEC's position on salt mines: ". . . solidification and disposal in salt seems to be a rational approach. . . . Aside from man-made holes, I know of no really basic question that has been raised as to the adequacy of disposal in salt." [20] The man-made holes discovered at a test site were produced by earlier nonnuclear explorations and were sources of concern regarding water leaking into the storage area.

Much of the current nuclear waste stems from the production of weapons materials. Although government management of nuclear waste from weapons production facilities is not a part of the development considered here, its mismanagement could have serious repercussions regarding the credibility of the AEC as a custodian of nuclear waste. Individuals in the AEC have indicated that waste storage was given second priority in the weapons materials production. The storage arrangements employed do not meet present-day requirements. Radioactive waste leaks that have occurred at Hanford have placed a stigma on the nuclear power reactor industry which is not necessarily justified.[21]

In recent years the AEC has placed greater emphasis on waste-management R&D through management reorganization and increased funding. This has been done in an effort to alleviate technical constraints and to demonstrate convincingly adequate solutions for waste storage, which in turn should assist in gaining public acceptance of waste storage methods proposed.

It appears that the AEC has fallen short in solving these problems in a timely manner, satisfactory to the public and to opponents of nuclear power. Although part of the problem is due to shortcomings in the AEC's public relations program, and although some of the AEC's critics give it high marks for its safety record and its concern over safety, both the AEC and the rest of the nuclear industry agree that continued research in reactor safety and waste storage is needed.

Initiative is also needed in the area of nuclear materials safeguards, including both technological and administrative solutions (see Question 24 for further discussion).

AMOUNT AND RATE OF RESOURCE CONSERVATION

The amount and rate of resource conservation will depend on the growth rate of energy use and the acceptability of nuclear power. There have been many projections of energy uses and sources. Table 31, prepared by the Department of the Interior, projects that the use of each energy source except nuclear power will double between 1970 and the year 2000, for a growth rate of approximately 2.3 percent per year. Nuclear power, representing only a small energy source in 1970, is projected to increase by almost 300 times by 2000 and will represent about 23 percent of the total United States energy requirements by the turn of the century; this is equivalent to almost 8 billion barrels of oil annually.

It has been estimated that the United States gas, oil, and coal resources are 0.7Q (where $Q = 10^{18}$ Btu.), 1.5Q, and 30Q respectively, and that the U.S. cumulative consumption of energy to the year 2060 would amount to 30Q.[22,23] The U.S. uranium reserves have been estimated to have an energy content of 615Q, assuming that all the uranium—both the U-235 and U-238 isotopes—is consumed.[24] However, the commercial light-water reactor is not an efficient utilizer of uranium and burns less than 2 percent of the total. While this amount still represents a sizable energy source, equal to about eight times the oil reserves, the breeder reactor would be necessary if a large percentage (60 percent to 70 percent) of the uranium is to be consumed.

Since the breeder is the advanced system now under development, one might question why the light-water reactor should have been developed. Was it a wise decision? During the technology evaluation period leading to the final selections of the first commercial reactors, major consideration was given to the breeder. However, the development of the breeder reactor has proved to be a much more difficult and complex task than the current converter reactors. Even though more than ten years have passed since the AEC assigned it the highest priority of advance reactor development, it is still far from a commercially acceptable power plant. There are two basic problems involved: first, when will it be economical? and second, will it be safe enough for use? Some projections indicate that it may not be acceptable until the 1990's, while other industry

TABLE 31

PRESENT AND FUTURE U.S. DEMAND FOR ENERGY RESOURCES

Energy Source	1970	1975	1985	2000
Petroleum (includes natural gas liquids):				
Million barrels	5,367	6,500	8,600	12,000
Million barrels per day	14.70	17.9	23.56	32.79
Trillion Btu.	29,617	36,145	47,455	66,216
Percent of gross energy inputs	43.0%	40.8%	35.6%	34.6%
Natural gas (includes gaseous fuels):				
Billion cubic feet	21,847	27,800	38,200	49,000
Trillion Btu.	22,546	28,690	39,422	50,568
Percent of gross energy inputs	32.8%	32.4%	29.5%	26.4%
Coal (bituminous, anthracite, lignite):				
Thousand short tons	526,650	615,000	850,000	1,000,000
Trillion Btu.	13,792	16,106	22,260	26,188
Percent of gross energy inputs	20.1%	18.2%	16.7%	13.7%
Hydropower, utility:				
Billion kilowatt hours	246	282	363	632
Trillion Btu.	2,647	2,820	3,448	5,056
Percent of gross energy inputs	3.8%	3.2%	2.6%	2.6%
Nuclear power:				
Billion kilowatt hours	19.3	462	1,982	5,441
Trillion Btu.	208	4,851	20,811	43,528
Percent of gross energy inputs	.3%	5.4%	15.6%	22.7%
Total gross energy inputs, trillion Btu.	68,810	88,612	133,396	191,556

Source: U.S. Congress, Senate. Committee on Interior and Insular Affairs, Hearings. 92nd Congress, 2nd Session (February 8, 1972), p. 104.

sources question whether it will ever be an acceptable plant for some utility systems.

The experience gained in manufacturing, constructing, siting, and operating current commercial power plants will be of considerable value for the introduction of any future nuclear power plant. When and if the breeder reactor is introduced, it is not likely to capture the entire nuclear power plant market. Studies have indicated, moreover, that the amount of plutonium from the breeders will eventually exceed that required for fueling new breeders and that the excess will then be used in the converter reactors.[25] Thus, the current converter reactors could continue as a viable market product for the foreseeable future. They will serve as an important interim and possibly continuing energy source for the nation and the world, relieving some of the pressures on the world's fossil-fuel supplies. In addition, if breeders are developed, they can utilize the uranium discarded from the converter-reactor fuel cycle; consequently, this uranium will not be wasted. On these bases, one could conclude that the initial selection of the converter reactors by the system was sound.

Availability of uranium has been used by critics of nuclear power to oppose both the current light-water reactors and the breeder. One argument is that the high-grade uranium ores should be saved in order to initiate the breeder program. Those advancing this argument thus oppose the present use of nuclear power. The other argument is that there is sufficient long-term availability of uranium that the breeders are not needed. Those proclaiming the first point of view do not recognize that uranium discarded from light-water reactors can be used in breeders, as discussed above. The second argument would place a much shortened life on *fission* power, since, without breeders, the uranium supply will eventually run out. Fission would then be replaced by fusion, solar energy, coal, or some other energy source. To the extent that this approach would place a lower limit on the size and duration of the problems associated with fission, the argument has merit.

While there have been considerations of other uses of commercial nuclear power—e.g., process heat and desalinization—the major civilian use of nuclear power for the near future will be for electrical power generation. Even though energy consumption for generating electrical power is projected to be about 50 percent of total energy uses by 1990 (in 1970 it was approximately 25 percent),* nuclear energy cannot supply all energy needs unless there are other developments as well. For example, before nuclear energy could replace fossil fuel for transportation, it would be necessary to convert electrical or nuclear process heat to a form suitable for mobile use. The extent to which such developments occur will determine the extent to which nuclear power can replace fossil fuels as an energy source, and, consequently, the extent to which fossil-fuel conservation will be affected by nuclear power in the near future.

INNOVATION AND PROGRESSIVENESS IN THE PRODUCTION
AND DELIVERY OF OUTPUTS

Within the constraints placed on the t.d.s. by its limitation to nuclear energy, the system has shown considerable innovation on its policy formulation and implementation. Some counterproductive policies were placed on systems performance, however, as a result of national security considerations.

Removing the control of nuclear energy matters from the military and placing it in the hands of a new five-member civilian commission and a special committee in Congress constituted the first significant step in assuring attention to peaceful uses after the war. However, secrecy, government monopoly, and military priorities slowed civilian development for almost a decade.

Starting in 1954, the government showed considerable innovation in policy formulation: it removed roadblocks when they became important to progress, but maintained control as dictated by other considerations. Examples of such actions are:

- Allowing private ownership of nuclear reactors but maintaining strict regulatory control to protect the health and safety of the public.

* See section entitled, ''The Nuclear Industry'' (Chapter V).

- Indemnifying reactor owners, an action that removed an unacceptable risk to industry.
- Controlling, but allowing, leases of nuclear fuels when they were in short supply and needed for the military.
- Providing enriched uranium so as to remove reactor design constraints of natural uranium.
- Assisting industry through AEC-funded R&D programs and cooperative demonstration programs.
- Providing industry with government services and materials when unavailable elsewhere.
- Contracting with industry to conduct government programs, thus giving industry firsthand experience with the technology.

The government showed considerable innovation and progressiveness in its approach to technical problems and in the partnership it formed with industry to solve them. Because of the great importance of technical solutions to the operation of the technological delivery system, the approaches will be summarized here.

The AEC practiced a policy and approach to technology development that were comprised of the following steps:

- Development of a broadly based supporting technology.
- Analysis of the characteristics of conceptual designs of reactors.
- Conduct of experimental studies on component development.
- Construction and testing of prototype reactor experiments.
- Performance of large-scale demonstration experiments.
- Commercial introduction on a basis competitive with alternative systems.

The AEC took primary programmatic and financial responsibility for the first four areas, with some exceptions, and industry took the major responsibility for the last two. Government laboratories can successfully develop the basic technology, but as the technology comes closer to application to a specific power plant concept, it becomes more important to have industry input. Early in the development, the AEC received this input from industrial analysis of various conceptual designs, analyses which were in many cases funded by the AEC. The AEC laboratories conducted similar analyses. These studies, along with component development, led the way to further technology evaluation through prototype construction and operation. The 1950's were a period of innovation, one which allowed great freedom in the government laboratories for exploring a variety of concepts. Many alternatives were allowed to be carried through the prototype stage and a substantial number of these became part of the demonstration program. While the AEC may have erred in allowing some prototypes to be built that did not have adequate technology bases, it was correct in deciding that, during the selection process, it was better to err in that direction than to be left with too narrow a choice. Some governments selected only one concept at an early stage because of conflicting objectives (e.g., early postwar needs for both weapons and power production) or because of lack of finances to support multiple approaches; the result of such a decision frequently was a non-competitive power system.

In most cases the reactor demonstration projects were carried out by industry. The AEC took the initiative in establishing its Power Demonstration Reactor Program, calling for industry to build nuclear plants on utility grids. Although the government's role provided a direct subsidy to industry, it had one important feature: the government's financial risk was fixed in both time and quantity. This limitation was important in that it provided industry with the incentive to apply its know-how in cost cutting, a major objective at that stage of the development. Power costs were reduced from over 50 mills per kwh for the first large-scale plant owned by the AEC (Shippingport), to around 13 mills for the first major demonstration reactors, and finally to around 5 mills for the first commercial reactor. Another important aspect of the closed-end risk feature of the government's role was that it automatically disengaged government from the program and its subsidization.

Although all reactor vendors did not participate equally in the government demonstration program—some of the demonstration plants were financed entirely from private sources—on the whole, the demonstration program was a very important phase for the utilities. It provided industry with the opportunity to gain the experience with nuclear power plants necessary for users to assess these plants as a competitive and reliable system. The financial risk to individual utilities was reduced both by government assistance and by the establishment of utility combines for funding individual reactor projects.

Although several different systems were still being considered in the early 1960's, once the reactor vendors made their selections the die was cast regarding the product. There might have been a potentially small incremental advantage in some of the advanced converters considered later, but it is the opinion of many of those interviewed that what the industry needs at present is a period of consolidation, product standardization, and demonstration. Therefore, AEC management probably made the right decision in terminating in the 1960's the advanced converter programs and other projects left over from the technology evaluation program. In their stead, it has established the breeder as the government's highest priority program.

With regard to policy development, there was a common innovative approach built into many of the government actions and policies. The disengagement feature was designed either to allow a transition period or to limit the involvement of government. The transition-period approach provided a smooth transfer from government to industry and gave sufficient advance notice regarding the termination of a particular subsidy or program to allow industry time for planning; on the other hand, it kept government involved so that it would not have to reinsert itself if the situation warranted its continued involvement. To stop the disengagement required positive action by the AEC or Congress and, with a few exceptions, the involvements were terminated as planned and not renewed.

Examples of this disengagement policy were seen in:
- The transition to private ownership of nuclear fuels.
- Government leasing of nuclear fuels.
- The guaranteed government buy-back of plutonium and U-233 produced in privately owned reactors.
- The uranium ore purchase program.
- Government reprocessing of irradiated fuels.
- Compulsory licensing of patents.
- Government indemnification of reactor owners.

The last two are cases in which the government did enact new legislation to continue their existence. In addition, because of recent difficulties arising with fuel reprocessing plants, some modification of government policy may be necessary.

EFFICIENCY—DEGREE TO WHICH THE SYSTEM AND SUBSYSTEM (A) CAPTURE AVAILABLE ECONOMIES OF SCALE, (B) EFFICIENTLY UTILIZE CURRENT CAPACITY, AND (C) EARN ONLY NORMAL PROFIT IN THE LONG RUN

From the beginning the system was built on the manpower, facilities, and contracting policies left over from World War II, and on those assembled primarily for military purposes after the war. The excitement and optimistic promise of nuclear energy and the desire of many people after the war to apply this new energy source to peaceful purposes attracted many outstanding scientists, engineers, administrators, educators, and legislators to the development; many of these people had been involved in the weapons program. The quality and motivation of these participants undoubtedly played an important role in the development and may indeed have created a unique atmosphere unlikely to be repeated.

One way in which efficiency was achieved was through the sharing of facilities and personnel between military and civilian programs. The national laboratories were important to both programs. In addition, laboratories built and staffed primarily for weapons work have contributed to civilian reactor developments in significant ways, and in some cases have been reassigned to civilian projects altogether.

Military production facilities and associated developments have also been important to the commercial development. Without the uranium-enrichment facilities built for weapons purposes, the current commercial reactors would not be feasible. This large national asset is now mostly surplus to military needs and is being utilized primarily by the commercial market.

The contracting policy that continued after the war was also efficient, allowing industry to become knowledgeable about nuclear technology even while it was still under heavy secrecy. This policy also provided a cadre of trained manpower readily accessible to the operating contractors for commercial programs. In general, contracting policy has assisted in accomplishing technology transfer from government to industry, thereby allowing industry use of government technology.

Because of the complexity of the technology, a company's entry into the field as a reactor vendor requires a highly competent technical staff. With one exception, the companies previously supplying large equipment to the electric utility industry are now supplying the nuclear reactors. Many of the other parts of the supply industry are likewise made up of companies supplying somewhat related materials and services—e.g., architect-engineering firms, and mining, chemical, and oil companies. The use of the reactor has also taken place within the previously existing industry framework—the existing private and public utilities.

Large reactors have been necessary in order to compete with fossil-fuel plants. When the development was initiated, 100 to 200 Mw_e power plants were large for most utility systems. In 1975, nuclear plants range up to 1,300 Mw_e. Even fossil-fuel plants have become large in some utility grids. While the big reactors capture economy of scale, their utilization is limited to relatively large utility grids. However, this limitation should pose no major problems; with the growth of electrical energy use, large grids, formed through power transmission interties, are found throughout most of the United States.

Economies of scale in the nuclear supply industry will come about as general acceptability of the product by the utilities and the rapid growth of purchases permit higher production rates of standardized designs in large automated production facilities. Many parts of the fuel-cycle industry are still in their infancy, and the supply industry in general is in the early stages of product introduction; consequently, profits have not existed for many companies. The first commercial nuclear plants, the "turnkey" plants (i.e., plants completely constructed by the reactor vendor), were unprofitable.[26] Because of the delay of approximately nine years from actual orders of nuclear plants to operation, profit patterns of the industry cannot be expected to be established at this early stage of product introduction. This is even more applicable to the fuel-cycle industry than to the reactor plant industry. Much of the fuel-cycle industry market will come only after sustained operation of the nuclear plants, which will then require reload fuels and the reprocessing of spent fuels.*

Because the industry structure appears to be at least as competitive as the industry traditionally serving the utilities, its profit margins should be expected to be no greater than those on other equipment, materials, and services provided to the utility industry. A meaningful evaluation of profits, however, can be made only after the industry has reached a more mature state than it has achieved as of 1975.

* For further discussion of this point see "The Market for Uranium and Plutonium" (*Nuclear News* 15, 5 [May 1972], p. 36) and "Industry Report: 1972–73" (*Nuclear News* 16, 3 [mid-February 1973], p. 16).

EVALUATION SUMMARY OF SYSTEM PERFORMANCE AND POTENTIAL ADAPTATION

SYSTEM PERFORMANCE

The principal thesis of this book is that the commercial nuclear power technological delivery system was, within the constraints placed on it by fission, a successful operating process—a successful government-industry partnership in the development of a major, technologically complex, commerical product.

The overall performance of the system—its outcomes—are summarized and evaluated below, on the basis of the data presented in the above analyses. The general criterion for judging the success or failure of these outcomes is the degree to which the system fulfilled the objectives that the president and Congress originally established in the Atomic Energy Act of 1946 and reconfirmed in the Atomic Energy Act of 1954. The broad policy statement and purposes of these acts were given previously. The policy statement is repeated here:

> It is hereby declared to be the policy of the people of the United States that, subject at all times to the paramount objective of assuring the common defense and security, the development and utilization of atomic energy shall, so far as practicable, be directed toward improving the public welfare, increasing the standard of living, strengthening free competition in private enterprise, and promoting world peace.[27]

Many AEC programs contributing to these objectives were not investigated in this research. These include:

- Weapons development programs.
- The "Atoms for Peace" program, which led to cooperative research with many nations.
- Atomic research in other fields, such as medicine and agriculture.
- Basic research and information exchange with other nations on physics, biology, controlled thermonuclear reactors.
- The Nuclear Test Ban Treaty.

The specific objective of the t.d.s. under study here, and one that became a national objective, was to develop a safe and economic nuclear power plant as an alternative source of energy for electric power generating stations. This objective is central to the evaluation of outcomes given below.

Outcomes Judged Favorable to System Performance:

- The primary objective was met. The product developed is economically and environmentally competitive with other sources, both nationally and internationally.
- Despite the fundamental constraint on the system—namely, the fission process—and the potential hazards associated with nuclear power, the nuclear industry and its product have had an outstanding safety record.
- The product provides a new energy source to supplement or replace rap-

idly dwindling fossil fuels, which in the long term may have a higher value in uses other than generation of electricity.

- With some exceptions, the deployment and use of the product is within the traditional framework of government and industry institutions, even though it was developed with massive government intervention.
- The resulting supply industry is at least as competitive as the industry traditionally serving the user utilities.
- Cost of development is commensurate with the size of the projected market for the product and for related services; it is also commensurate with the amount of potential savings in electric power costs. Potential profits, however, were not assessed.

Outcomes Judged Unfavorable to System Performance:
- Public education on nuclear risks appears to have been inadequate.
- Although public health and safety risks are acceptable to the utilities and to the AEC's regulatory division, they are not acceptable to some interest groups.
- There is evidence of inadequate AEC program planning and performance in the areas of nuclear waste management and reactor safety.
- Reactors with large power ratings are required in order to compete economically with fossil-fuel plants.
- Government monopoly and secrecy in connection with technology, materials, and equipment were and, in one important area, still remain a deterrent to private development of the nuclear industry.

As seen above, most criticisms of the system are associated with the issues of public health and safety. From the viewpoint of its critics, the system was shortsighted in not assigning high enough priority to reactor safety and waste management developments and/or to public education in these two areas. Some believe that the inherent nature of the fission process, the finite (although extremely small) probability of a catastrophic accident, and the possibility of diversion and illegal use of special nuclear materials create such a potentially large hazard to society that the product should not be used, regardless of how well the technological delivery system performs.

There have been and continue to be specific technical problems associated with the introduction of nuclear power plants—some associated with the reactor, and others with nonnuclear components of the very large facilities. Such problems may be expected in any new complex technology. Industry has pushed the technology rapidly, and a period of product demonstration and standardization is now needed. Criteria for reactor licensing have been modified, based on extensive reviews by the AEC with considerable influence from critics, the judiciary, and various interest groups. Changes in reactor design, construction, and operation should continue to occur as operating experience is gained. The utility industry is confident that current problems can be resolved satisfactorily, as is evidenced by their continued purchase of nuclear power plants. The government's Nuclear Regulatory Commission, while recognizing that problems exist, does not judge them to be severe enough to make reactor operation an unacceptable risk to the public.

The dual role of the AEC as the developer and promoter of nuclear power on the one hand and the regulator of its use on the other was questioned by some individuals and interest groups. These critics felt that the AEC's development and promotion function detracted from its objectivity in establishing licensing standards for reactor design, construction, and operation. The AEC attempted to minimize the possibility of conflict of interest in the two roles by establishing two separate organizations, each reporting to the five-member commission. In 1972 President Nixon proposed that the two functions be separate agencies; there would be one agency for regulation, and the development function would become part of an agency for energy R&D. This was accomplished in 1974.

There are no meaningful, quantifiable evaluations that can be put on the list of favorable and unfavorable outcomes in order to arrive at an overall performance evaluation. Nevertheless, the subjective evaluation of the author is that the technological delivery system was successful in meeting its primary objective. The fundamental bases for this conclusion are:

- The controversy surrounding the product stems primarily from the radioactive products resulting from the fission process—an inherent constraint on the system—and the risks which they pose to the public if mismanaged.
- The intended users of the product have judged the product to be economically and environmentally acceptable, thereby fulfilling the primary objective.

THE SYSTEM'S ADAPTABILITY TO OTHER TECHNOLOGICAL DEVELOPMENTS

Assuming that the evaluation of the system as successful is correct, one might ask what can be learned from it—what aspects of the technological delivery system can be applied advantageously to other technological delivery systems having similar objectives. For example, how could it be applied to government-industry development of other energy sources, such as fusion, solar energy, and geothermal energy?

The development studied had many characteristics not likely to be duplicated in other developments: for example, it emerged from the high-pressure development of an awesome military weapon; it was originally totally owned and controlled by the government, under extreme secrecy; and one aspect of fission—namely, the resulting radioactivity—is very hazardous. With these factors in mind, we may now consider what aspects of the system might be usefully transferred to another technological development system, and under what conditions. The propositions given here will be based primarily on observations made from the analysis of the nuclear system given above and from comments of persons interviewed. Since the objective of the set of process questions was to identify determinants of the system's outcomes and key aspects of the decision-making, policy-formulation, and implementation processes, the answers will serve as a useful tool in answering the question at hand. The significant features of the nuclear power t.d.s. were identified from the process questions as follows:

- The Joint Committee on Atomic Energy.
- The Atomic Energy Commission.
- Government-industry partnership in development of the technology.
- Government administrative control of the technology.

Before specific parts of the system are examined, general criteria for government intervention will be proposed. Major government financial support may be justified when:

- The financial risks and uncertainties in the development are too large for industry to undertake, but the potential benefits to society are sufficiently large to warrant the expenditure.
- The benefits will serve a large fraction of the society, not just the direct users of the technology.
- There is a base technology to be developed by and/or transferred from government.

In this context, it is possible to discuss potential application to other technological developments of the four key features listed above.

The Joint Committee on Atomic Energy

The initial and primary reason for establishing the JCAE and the AEC institutional forms was the secrecy placed on nuclear energy development and the control deemed necessary because of its great importance to national security. That reason no longer exists for nuclear power and would not be likely to exist for another energy source development.

There are both advantages and disadvantages to a joint committee in Congress. On the one hand, it centralizes policy making on a particular subject in a single congressional group, and this results in a coordinating mechanism for legislative development. On the other hand, it tends to become too much of a unified body and thereby eliminates one important aspect of Congress— namely, the bringing of two separate points of view to bear on a subject. In the case of the JCAE, there was an apparent increase in the power of Congress at the expense of the president, which may or may not have been an advantage. However, Congress as a whole did not necessarily benefit from this power increase. Because of the concentration of knowledge and authority that takes place with a joint committee, issues become somewhat isolated from the rest of Congress; therefore, the decision-making process can be considered to be less democratic. The JCAE also became somewhat inbred and dominated by a few of its members. A joint committee does provide a single entry point for input from high-intensity interest groups, such as the executive agency and industry, which helps to coalesce differing points of view in Congress.

The final answer to the question of the desirability of a joint committee involves many complex issues and organizational components not dealt with in this book. It is the opinion of the author that the JCAE was an effective body in assisting in the development of atomic energy, but that the need for the joint-committee approach stemmed mainly from the nature of the initial problem. One must ask: if a joint committee for energy is desirable, why not a joint committee for defense, etc.? From this type of question, one can see the serious implications that an across-the-board system of joint committees would have on the total organization of Congress.

The AEC

As is the case with the JCAE, the original reasons for a commission form of agency management no longer exist. Orlans has stated that "familiarity has bred a growing criticism of the commission form of organization, a mechanism once praised for promoting wise, balanced, and non-partisan policies is increasingly condemned for precisely the same reasons, only what was deemed wisdom and balance is termed caution and timidity, while nonpartisanship is regarded as an abdication of executive and presidential responsibilities." [28] The commission form and the method by which the members are appointed did insulate the AEC somewhat more from political pressures than would a single administrator appointed by the president and subject to the usual removal conditions. Some see the removal from the turmoil of domestic politics as unwise in the long run, in that it does not provide the checks and balance of power traditional in the United States form of government. The commission structure also has the inherent weakness of administration by committee. For nonregulatory agencies, a single administrator would probably be the best choice. The different points of view provided by the commission form of management can be obtained from a competent staff and from advisory and adversary groups established and supported by the agency for the purpose of bringing out counter-views on policy issues.

The commission form is appropriate, however, for government regulatory bodies. Regulatory bodies are responsible for formulating a type of "administrative law," and therefore legislate within the powers granted by Congress. They issue rules, procedures, and policies, normally considered appropriately immune from politics. Because of these types of responsibilities, a deliberative body in the form of a commission is desirable and should be maintained for nuclear regulatory responsibilities.

Government-Industry Partnership in Development of the Technology

The general technical development approach summarized in the six steps presented in the section entitled, "Innovation and Progressiveness in the Production and Delivery of Outputs," is an effective way to arrive at a near-optimum commercial design choice. If fiscal support is adequate, investigating several design concepts in the early stages of development will minimize the probability of failure of the final product.

Partnership between government and industry is also desirable for assuring that government R&D is applicable to problems ultimately requiring solutions

before commercial utilization of the product can be achieved. The cooperative approach for conducting programs between government and industry or, where antitrust laws permit, within industry combines, provides a mechanism for cost sharing and interchange of the technology. The contracting policies as practiced by the AEC represent another effective mechanism for assisting in technology transfer and training of industry manpower. The government's policies with respect to scientific and technical education and training were beneficial in building up a staff in nongovernment institutions which was competent in a technology initially dominated by the government.

The legacy of the AEC laboratories and associated research staff is an asset that should have value to developments with high technology content. As pointed out in the section entitled, "Innovation and Progressiveness in the Production and Delivery of Outputs," such laboratories are most effective for the research and prototype-development phases. The demonstration phase should be conducted by industry, both so that it may bring to bear its cost-cutting know-how, and because this is the first stage approaching commercial introduction.

Government Administrative Control of the Technology

Secrecy is a deterrent to technology development. A policy of broad dissemination of information not only is desirable from the technical development standpoint, but also should result in better public understanding of the technological delivery system outputs.

Government monopoly of some materials and services may be justifiable for reasons such as national security, or in cases where materials are in short supply and must be rationed. Outside of such concerns, the policies practiced by the government in nuclear matters had the aim of nurturing a capability within industry, so that the product and related markets could be turned over to industry as they approached the commercial stage and as the new industry was assessed to be able to sustain viability. This appeared to be an effective means of government assistance in the development of a major new industry.

Administrative constraints will, however, limit the technical alternatives that can be considered. If overall optimum systems are to be developed, the technical managers in the t.d.s. must have the opportunity to consider all available alternatives. For example, the current commercial reactors emerged from the evaluation of alternatives within the constraints placed by the fission process. If the t.d.s. is to be an energy research and development system, however, then all energy system alternatives must be open to it. This conclusion supports the recent formation of ERDA, which is responsible for all energy research and development by the federal government. Such an agency is in a position not only to evaluate alternatives, but also to coordinate developments when outputs are known to require multiple selections—e.g., coal gasification and liquefaction for the short term and fusion or solar energy for the long term.

Much of the AEC's and JCAE's strengths came from three important factors:

(1) they had sole domain in the Executive Branch and Congress over nuclear matters; (2) their responsibilities and authorities were clearly defined; and (3) the mechanism for their interaction was defined by law. Monopoly of a development in one government agency can be both a weakness and a strength, since it eliminates interagency competition.

There should be opportunities for input from interest groups (both proponents and opponents) and from the public, both to allow their participation in policy formulation and to obtain their feedback during implementation. The AEC contracting policies and cooperative programs with industry generally provided open channels for proponent inputs. Legislative and administrative hearings are also effective, and tend to enlarge the spectrum of interest groups. In addition, mechanisms should be developed to deliberately seek out inputs from adversary groups. In this way, their inputs can be factored in at an early stage of the development.

If the final objective was to turn the product over to industry, then the types of policies employed by government for disengagement were effective in making the transfer from government to industry without major disruptions in the system's operation (see section entitled, "Innovation and Progressiveness in the Production and Delivery of Outputs," for a summary discussion of this point).

CONCLUSION

In a highly technological society such as that of the United States, there are likely to be new opportunities in the future for government initiative and government-industry partnership in executing a large technology development program. For example, the policy requirements for controlled thermonuclear development would appear to parallel many of the research and development policy considerations implemented in the fission power program. However, Palfrey [29] once said the following about atomic energy development: "The problems here are original, and their solutions elusive, because of the singular characteristics of the atom and its course of development. Generalizations and assumptions, drawn from the outside and applied to the atomic statute, will become distortions unless tightly related to the facts of the enterprise, to the setting in which the law was enacted, and to the Government's objectives." The same caution is appropriate in considering the general applicability of the nuclear t.d.s. to other delivery systems. The approach to such an endeavor should be to examine the features assessed above to be important to the nuclear t.d.s. for specific applicability to the system of interest. The final evaluation of the adaptability of the technological delivery system presented here can be made only when the nature and objectives of the specific development are know.

Persons Interviewed

1. Abbadessa, John P. Controller, AEC, 1962 to 1974; with General Accounting Office, 1953–62.
2. Bauser, Edward. Executive director, JCAE, 1968 to 1974; formerly captain with the Navy's nuclear submarine project.
3. Behnke, Wallace. Executive vice-president, Commonwealth Edison Company, Chicago, Illinois.
4. Bethe, Hans. Professor and physicist, Cornell University; formerly consultant on nuclear matters to General Electric, General Atomic, and Power Reactor Demonstration Corporation.
5. Dickeman, Raymond L. President, Exxon Nuclear; formerly an executive with General Electric Company, Atomic Power Division and Hanford Atomic Products Operation.
6. Farmer, Sam J. Assistant laboratory director, Battelle-Northwest; vice-president and counsel to General Atomic Division, General Dynamics Corporation, 1956–68; counsel to Electric Boat Division, General Dynamics Corp. 1954–68; counsel to Electric Boat Division, General Dynamics Corp. 1954–56; attorney, AEC Hanford Operations Office, 1950–54.
7. Green, Harold P. Professor of law, the National Law Center, The George Washington University, Washington, D.C.; coauthor of *Government of the Atom* (New York: Atherton, 1963) and author of many journal articles on the atomic energy development.
8. Heisenberg, Werner. Professor and physicist, Max Planck Institute for Physics and Astrophysics, Munich; early participant in Germany's nuclear developments and consultant to the German government.
9. Hennessey, Joseph F. Attorney at law, Bechhoefer, Snapp, Sharlitt, Trippe, Hausman and Drucoff, Washington, D.C.; general counsel of the AEC, 1962–71; earlier, counsel to AEC's Oak Ridge operations office, AEC's Divisions of Production and Reactor Development.

10. Holifield, Chet. Member U.S. House of Representatives from California; member of the JCAE, 1946 to 1974; chairman of the JCAE, 1961–62, 1965–66, 1969–70.

11. Hollingsworth, Robert. General manager of the AEC, 1964 to 1974; former deputy general manager, assistant general manager, and assistant director, AEC Division of Production.

12. Hosmer, Craig. Member U.S. House of Representatives from California; member of the JCAE, 1958 to 1974.

13. Johnson, Wilfred E. Retired; AEC commissioner, 1966–72; former manager, General Electric Company, Hanford Atomic Products Operation.

14. Lee, Byron. Vice-president, Commonwealth Edison Company, Chicago, Illinois.

15. McCormack, Mike. Member U.S. House of Representatives from Washington; member of the JCAE, 1973 to present; formerly, scientist, Hanford Research Laboratory.

16. O'Neill, Robert D. Director, Office of Congressional Relations, AEC, 1967 to 1974; staff member, Office of Congressional Relations, AEC, 1958–67.

17. Orlans, Harold. Brookings Institution, Washington, D.C.; author of *Contracting for Atoms*. (Washington, D.C.: Brookings Institution, 1967).

18. Pittman, Franklin K. Director of AEC Division of Waste Management and Transportation, 1971 to present; former director, Office of Industrial Development; director, AEC Division of Reactor Development; executive of Atomics International and Kerr McGee's nuclear division.

19. Ramey, James. AEC commissioner, 1962–73; executive director, JCAE, 1956–62; AEC legal staff 1947–56; earlier, with TVA.

20. Sandler, Richard. Congress Project and nuclear energy aide to Ralph Nader, Washington, D.C.

Glossary

ATOMIC OR NUCLEAR ENERGY. The energy released by a nuclear reaction or by radioactive decay. (*See also* Fission; Fusion; Nuclear reactor; Radioactivity.)

ATOMIC NUMBER. The number of protons in the nucleus of an atom, and also its positive charge. Each chemical element has its characteristic atomic number, and the atomic numbers of the known elements form a complete series from 1 for hydrogen to 103 for the man-made element lawrencium.

ATOMIC WEAPON. An explosive weapon in which the energy is produced by nuclear fission or fusion.

ATOMIC WEIGHT. The mass of an element relative to other elements. The atomic weight of an element is approximately equal to the total number of protons and neutrons in its nucleus.

BOILING-WATER REACTOR (BWR). A nuclear reactor in which water, used as both coolant and moderator, is allowed to boil in the reactor core. The resulting steam can be used directly to drive a turbine.

BREEDER REACTOR. A nuclear reactor designed to convert more uranium-238 or thorium into useful nuclear fuel than the uranium-233, uranium-235, or plutonium it consumes. The new fissile materials are created by capture in the fertile materials of neutrons from the fission process. The four types of breeder reactors now being considered in the United States are: the liquid-metal fast breeder (LMFBR); the gas-cooled fast breeder (GCBR); the molten-salt breeder (MSBR); and the light-water breeder (LWBR).

BREEDING (OR CONVERSION). The process of converting a nonfissile material, such as U-238 or Th-232, into a fissile material—Pu-239 or U-233, respectively.

BREEDING RATIO. The ratio of the number of fissile atoms produced in a breeder reactor to the number of fissile atoms consumed in the reactor. The term "breeding ratio" is used when the ratio is greater than unity. (*See also* Conversion ratio.)

CONTAINMENT. The provision of a gastight shell or other enclosure around a nuclear reactor to confine fission products that otherwise might be released to the atmosphere in the event of an accident.

CONVERSION. *See* Breeding.

CONVERSION RATIO. The ratio of the number of fissile atoms produced in a reactor to the number of fissile atoms consumed. The term "conversion ratio" is used when the ratio is less than unity. (*See also* Breeding ratio.)

CONVERTER REACTOR. A nuclear reactor that produces some fissile material, but less than it consumes.

COOLANT. A substance circulated through a nuclear reactor to remove or transfer heat. Common coolants are water, air, carbon dioxide, liquid sodium, and helium.

CORE. The central portion of a nuclear reactor, which contains the fuel elements and the moderator if it exists.

DECAY, RADIOACTIVE. The spontaneous transformation of one nuclide either into a different nuclide or into a different energy state of the same nuclide.

DECAY HEAT. The heat produced by the decay of radioactive nuclides.

DEPLETED URANIUM. Uranium having less uranium-235 than the 0.71 percent found in natural uranium.

DEUTERIUM. An isotope of hydrogen whose nucleus contains one neutron and one proton, and is therefore about twice as heavy as the nucleus of normal hydrogen, which has only a single proton. It occurs in nature as 1 atom to 6,500 atoms of normal hydrogen and is not radioactive.

ENERGY. The capability of doing work.

ENRICHED URANIUM. Uranium in which the proportion of uranium-235 present has been artificially increased above that found in nature. Uranium for light-water reactors, e.g., is enriched to about 2 percent to 6 percent; uranium for weapons is enriched above 90 percent.

FAST REACTOR. A nuclear reactor in which the fission chain reaction is sustained primarily by fast neutrons, neutrons with velocities at or near their initial emission velocities from the fission process, rather than by thermal- or intermediate-velocity neutrons.

FERTILE ISOTOPES. Isotopes that can be converted to fissile isotopes through capture of a neutron.

FERTILE MATERIAL. A material not itself fissionable by thermal neutrons, which can be converted into a fissile material by irradiation in a nuclear reactor. The two basic fertile materials are uranium-238 and thorium-232. When these fertile materials capture neutrons, they become fissile plutonium-239 and uranium-233, respectively.

FISSILE ISOTOPES. Isotopes that are fissionable by absorption of a thermal (very low-energy) neutron. The three basic fissile isotopes are uranium-235, plutonium-239, and uranium-233, of which only U-235 occurs in nature.

FISSILE MATERIAL. While sometimes used as a synonym for fissionable material, this term has also acquired a more restricted meaning, namely, any material that will undergo fission with neutrons of all energies.

FISSION. The splitting of a heavy nucleus into two approximately equal parts (which are radioactive nuclei of lighter elements), accompanied by the release of a relatively large amount of energy and generally one or more neutrons. Fission can occur spontaneously, but usually is caused by nuclear absorption of neutrons or other particles.

FISSIONABLE MATERIAL. Any material that will undergo fission with fast neutrons only. The two important fissionable isotopes are uranium-238 and thorium-232.

FISSION PRODUCTS. The nuclei formed by the fission of heavy elements, plus nuclides formed by the fission fragments' radioactive decay.

FUEL CYCLE. The series of steps involved in supplying fuel for nuclear power reactors. It includes mining, refining, and enriching uranium; fabrication of fuel elements; their use in a nuclear reactor; chemical processing of elements to recover remaining material; reenrichment of the fuel; and refabrication into new fuel elements.

FUEL ELEMENT. A rod, tube, plate, or other shape or form into which nuclear fuel is fabricated for use in a reactor.

FUEL REPROCESSING. The processing of spent (irradiated) reactor fuel to recover the residual fertile and fissile materials and to separate out the radioactive waste.

FUSION. The formation of a heavier nucleus from two lighter ones, such as hydrogen isotopes, with the attendant release of energy.

GAS CENTRIFUGE PROCESS. A method of isotope enrichment in which heavier isotopes are partially separated from lighter ones by centrifugal force.

GASEOUS DIFFUSION PROCESS. A method of enrichment based on the fact that gas atoms or molecules with different masses will diffuse through a porous barrier or membrane at different rates.

ISOTOPE. One of two or more atoms with the same atomic number but with different atomic weights. Isotopes usually have very nearly the same chemical properties but somewhat different physical properties.

LICENSED MATERIAL. Source material, special nuclear material, or byproduct material received, possessed, used, or transferred under a general or special license issued by the Atomic Energy Commission.

MEGAWATT. One million watts, one thousand kilowatts; abbreviated: Mw. Thermal and electrical megawatts are abbreviated Mw_{th} and Mw_e, respectively.

MEGAWATT-DAY PER TON. A unit that expresses the burn-up of nuclear fuel in a reactor; specifically, the number of megawatt-days of heat output per metric ton of fuel in the reactor; abbreviated: Mwd per ton.

METRIC TON. 1,000 kilograms (2,205 pounds).

MILLS PER KILOWATT-HOUR. Cost in one-thousandth dollars per thousand watt-hours of electrical energy; abbreviated: mills per kwh.

MODERATOR. A material, such as water, heavy water, or graphite, used in a nuclear reactor to slow down high-velocity neutrons emitted by fissioning atoms to intermediate or thermal velocities, thus increasing the likelihood of capture to cause further fission.

NATURAL URANIUM. Uranium as found in nature, containing 0.7 percent uranium-235, 99.3 percent uranium-238, and a trace of uranium-234. It is also called normal uranium.

NORMAL URANIUM. *See* Natural uranium.

NUCLEAR POWER PLANT. Any device, machine, or assembly that converts nuclear energy into some form of useful power.

NUCLEAR REACTOR. A device in which a fission chain reaction can be initiated, maintained, and controlled. Its essential component is a core with fissile fuel. It usually has a moderator, reflector, shielding, coolant, and control mechanisms. It is the basic machine of nuclear power.

NUCLIDE. A general term applicable to all atomic forms of the elements. It is not a synonym for "isotope," which properly has a more limited definition. Whereas isotopes are the various forms of a single element, nuclides comprise all the isotopic forms of all the elements.

PLUTONIUM. A heavy, radioactive, man-made element whose atomic number is 94. Its most important isotope is fissile plutonium-239 (Pu-239), produced by neutron irradiation of uranium-238. It is used for reactor fuel and in weapons.

PRESSURIZED-WATER REACTOR (PWR). A power reactor in which heat is transferred from the core to a heat exchanger by water kept under high pressure to prevent it from boiling. Steam is generated in a secondary circuit.

PU-239. The plutonium isotope whose atomic weight is 239.

Q. One Q equals 10^{18} British thermal units of energy.

RADIATION. The emission and propagation of energy through matter or space by electromagnetic waves, or by particles. Nuclear radiation is that emitted from atomic nuclei in various nuclear reactions.

RADIOACTIVITY. The spontaneous decay or disintegration of an unstable atomic nucleus, usually accompanied by emission of ionizing radiation.

SEPARATIVE WORK UNIT. A measure of the effort expended in separating the uranium into two streams, one enriched and the other depleted.

SOURCE MATERIAL. As defined in the Atomic Energy Act of 1954, any material, except special nuclear material, which contains 0.05 percent or more of uranium, thorium, or any combination of the two.

SPECIAL NUCLEAR MATERIAL. As defined in the Atomic Energy Act of 1954, this term refers to plutonium, uranium-233, enriched uranium, or any material artificially enriched with any of these substances.

SPECTRAL SHIFT. A method of controlling the reactor by modifying the neutron energy spectrum through the process of varying the ratio of heavy water to light water in the moderator.

THORIUM. An element used as the fertile material in the HTGR's and in some breeders under development.

TOLL ENRICHMENT. A business arrangement whereby privately owned uranium is enriched in uranium-235 content in government facilities upon payment of a service charge.

TRITIUM. A radioactive isotope of hydrogen. It is man-made and is heavier than deuterium.

U-233, U-235, U-238. Uranium isotopes of atomic weights, 233, 235, and 238, respectively.

URANIUM. A radioactive element with atomic number 92 and, as found in natural ores, an average atomic weight of approximately 238. The two principal natural isotopes of uranium are uranium-235 (0.7 percent of natural uranium), which is fissile, and uranium-238 (99.3 percent of natural uranium), which is fertile.

URANIUM HEXAFLUORIDE. A volatile compound of uranium and fluorine. In gaseous form, this is the process material for the gaseous diffusion and gas centrifuge methods of enrichment.

WASTES, RADIOACTIVE. Equipment and materials, particularly products of fission and neutron capture, from nuclear operations, which are radioactive and for which there is no further use. Wastes are generally classified as high level (having radioactivity concentrations of hundreds to thousands of curies per gallon or cubic foot), low level (in the range of one microcurie per gallon or cubic foot), or intermediate.

APPENDIX C

Acronyms and Abbreviations

ACRS	Advisory Committee on Reactor Safeguards
AEC	Atomic Energy Commission
AFL	American Federation of Labor
AGR	Advanced graphite reactor
AIF	Atomic Industrial Forum
ANL	Argonne National Laboratory
APDA	Atomic Power Development Associates
APPR	Army Package Power Reactor
ATR	Advanced Test Reactor
B&W	Babcock and Wilcox Company
BORAX	Boiling Reactor Experiment
BWR	Boiling-water reactor
C-E	Combustion Engineering Company
CIO	Congress of Industrial Organizations
CIP	Cascade Improvement Program
CUP	Cascade Power Uprating Program
EBR	Experimental Breeder Reactor
EBWR	Experimental Boiling-Water Reactor
EEI	Edison Electric Institute
EGCR	Experimental Gas-Cooled Reactor
ERDA	Energy Research and Development Administration
ETR	Engineering Test Reactor
FPC	Federal Power Commission
GAC	General Advisory Committee
GAO	General Accounting Office
GCFR	Gas-cooled fast breeder reactor
GE	General Electric Company
GETR	General Electric Test Reactor

G-GA	Gulf-General Atomic
HRE	Homogeneous Reactor Experiment
HTGR	High-Temperature Gas-Cooled Graphite Reactor
HWOCR	Heavy-Water-Moderated, Organic-Cooled Reactor
JCAE	Joint Committee on Atomic Energy
KAPL	Knolls Atomic Power Laboratory
kw	Kilowatt
kwh	Kilowatt-hour
LASL	Los Alamos Scientific Laboratory
LMFBR	Liquid-metal fast breeder reactor
LOFT	Loss of Fluid Test Facility
LSBR	Large seed-blanket reactor
LWBR	Light-water breeder reactor
LWR	Light-water reactor; includes the BWR and PWR types
MED	Manhattan Engineer District
MSBR	Molten-salt breeder reactor
MSRE	Molten Salt Reactor Experiment
MTR	Materials Testing Reactor
Mw	Megawatt or one million watts
Mw_e	Electrical megawatt
MW_{th}	Thermal megawatt
NATO	North Atlantic Treaty Organization
NCA	National Coal Association
NCPC	National Coal Policy Conference, Inc.
NDRC	National Defense Research Committee
NFS	Nuclear Fuel Services, Inc.
NRC	Nuclear Regulatory Commission
N-Reactor	New Production Reactor (Hanford)
NRTS	National Reactor Testing Station
NSSS	Nuclear steam supply system
ORNL	Oak Ridge National Laboratory
OSRD	Office of Scientific Research and Development
PBF	Power Burst Facility
PDRP	Power Demonstration Reactor Program
PRDC	Power Reactor Development Company
psi	Pounds per square inch
PWR	Pressurized-water reactor
R&D	Research and development
REA	Rural Electrification Administration
SAR	Submarine Advanced Reactor
SGHWR	Steam-Generating Heavy-Water Reactor
SIR	Submarine Intermediate Reactor
SNM	Special nuclear materials
SPERT	Special Power Excursion Reactor Test

SRE	Sodium-graphite Reactor Experiment
STR	Submarine Thermal Reactor
SWU	Separative work unit
t.d.s.	Technological delivery system
TREAT	Transient Reactor Test
TVA	Tennessee Valley Authority
VESR	Vallecitos Experimental Superheat Reactor
WETR	Westinghouse Test Reactor
WPPSS	Washington Public Power Supply System

Notes

CHAPTER I

1. Public Law 79-585 (60 Stat. 755) (1946).
2. C. M. Nader, "American Natural Scientists in the Policy Press: Three Atomic Energy Issues," Ph.D. dissertation, Columbia University, 1964.
3. Harold P. Green, "Nuclear Technology and the Fabric of Government," *The George Washington Law Review* 33 (October 1964), p. 160.
4. John Gorham Palfrey, "Atomic Energy: A New Experiment in Government-Industry Relations," *Columbia Law Review* 56 (1956), p. 373.
5. Harold P. Green and Alan Rosenthal, *Government of the Atom* (New York: Atherton Press, 1963).
6. Harold Orlans, *Contracting for Atoms* (Washington, D.C.: The Brookings Institution, 1967).
7. Walter H. Zinn, Frank K. Pittman, and John F. Hogerton, *Nuclear Power, U.S.A.* (New York: McGraw-Hill, 1964).
8. Samuel Glasstone and Alexander Sesonske, *Nuclear Reactor Engineering* (Princeton: Van Nostrand Company, 1967).
9. Emmette S. Redford, *Democracy in the Administrative State* (New York: Frederick C. Mosher, 1969).

CHAPTER II

1. Richard G. Hewlett and Oscar E. Anderson, Jr., *The New World, 1939/1946,* (University Park: Pennsylvania State University Press, 1962), p. 12.
2. *Ibid.*, p. 15.
3. *Ibid.*
4. *Ibid.*, p. 16.
5. Copy of letter presented in Ralph E. Lapp, *The New Priesthood* (New York: Harper and Row, 1965), p. 48.
6. Hewlett and Anderson, *The New World,* p. 19.
7. *Ibid.*, p. 24.
8. *Ibid.*, p. 41.
9. *Ibid.*, p. 112.
10. *Ibid.*, p. 211.

11. *Ibid.*, p. 305.

12. *Ibid.*, p. 379.

13. *Ibid.*, p. 402.

14. *Ibid.*, p. 44.

15. *Ibid.*, p. 78.

16. Harold Orlans, *Contracting for Atoms* (Washington, D.C.: The Brookings Institution, 1967), p. 5.

17. Hewlett and Anderson, *The New World,* p. 322.

18. *Ibid.*, p. 323.

19. *Ibid.*, p. 324.

20. *Ibid.*, p. 325.

21. *Ibid.*, p. 345.

22. Hewlett and Anderson, *The New World,* p. 407.

23. *Ibid.*

24. Harry S. Truman, "Atomic Energy," *Vital Speeches* 12 (October 15, 1945), pp. 8–10.

25. Hewlett and Anderson, *The New World,* p. 412.

26. *Ibid.*, p. 429.

27. See *ibid.*, Chapter 13, for a detailed accounting of various views on the bill, and Nader, "American Natural Scientists in the Policy Process: Three Atomic Energy Issues and Their Foreign Policy Implications," Ph.D. dissertation, Columbia University, 1964.

28. Nader, "American Natural Scientists in the Policy Process," p. 78.

29. Hewlett and Anderson, *The New World,* p. 439.

30. *Ibid.*

31. *Ibid.*, p. 436.

32. Harry S. Truman, *Years of Trial and Hope,* Memoirs, Vol. 2 (New York: Doubleday, 1956). See also discussion by Nader, "American Natural Scientists in the Policy Process," pp. 114–15.

33. Public Law 79-585 (60 Stat. 755) (1946).

34. *Ibid.*, Section 3.

35. U.S., Congress, Senate, *The Atomic Energy Act of 1946,* 79th Cong., 2nd sess., April 19, 1946, Senate Rept. 1211, Section 3.

36. *Ibid.*, Section 4.

37. *Ibid.*, Section 5.

38. *Ibid.*

39. *Ibid.*, Section 10.

40. *Ibid.*, Section 11.

41. *Ibid.*, p. 12.

42. Public Law 79-585 (60 Stat. 755) (1946), Section 3a.

43. Public Law 820, 81st Cong. (64 Stat. 979) (1950).

44. Orlans, *Contracting for Atoms,* p. 147.

45. *Ibid.*, p. 152.

46. Public Law 585 (60 Stat. 755), Section 2.

47. United States, Atomic Energy Commission (hereafter cited as U.S., AEC), *Semiannual Report to the Congress by the USAEC, July–December 1946* (Washington, D.C.: GPO, January 31, 1947). (The semiannual reports were published from 1947 to 1959 and will be cited hereafter as follows: U.S., AEC, *Semiannual Report to Congress,* [e.g.] *July–December 1946.* Since 1959, the reports have been made annually and will be cited as follows: U.S., AEC, *Annual Report to Congress, 1962.* It should be noted that the publication date in both cases is one month following the biennium or year, as the case may be.)

48. Richard G. Hewlett and Francis Duncan, *The Atomic Shield, 1947/1952, A His-*

tory of the United States Atomic Energy Commission, Vol. 2 (University Park: Pennsylvania State University Press, 1969), p. 30.

49. *Ibid.,* p. 336.

50. *Ibid.,* p. 155.

51. *Ibid.,* p. 337.

52. Hewlett and Anderson, *The New World,* p. 338.

53. *Ibid.,* p. 339.

54. U.S., AEC, *Semiannual Report to Congress, January–June 1955,* p. 4.

55. U.S., AEC, *Semiannual Report to Congress, July–December 1957,* p. 305.

56. U.S., AEC, *Semiannual Report to Congress, July–December 1947.*

57. Public Law 93-438.

58. *Weekly Energy Report,* February 4, 1975.

59. *Ibid.,* p. 2.

60. U.S., AEC, *Annual Report to Congress, 1961,* p. 155.

61. U.S., AEC, *Civilian Nuclear Power—A Report to the President—1962* (Washington, D.C.: GPO, November 1962); and *The 1967 Supplement to the 1962 Report to the President* (Washington, D.C.: GPO, February 1967).

62. Orlans, *Contracting for Atoms,* p. 1.

63. James R. Newman, "The Atomic Energy Industry," *Yale Law Journal* 60, 8 (December 1951), pp. 1324–25.

64. Public Law 585 (60 Stat. 755) (1946), Section 15.

65. *Ibid.*

66. U.S., Congress, JCAE, *Current Membership of the Joint Committee on Atomic Energy, Congress of the United States,* 92nd Cong., 2nd sess., Joint Committee Print, p. 3.

67. *Ibid.*

68. Public Law 83-703 (68 Stat. 919) (1954), Section 202.

69. U.S., Congress, JCAE, *Current Membership,* p. 4.

70. Public Law 83-703 (68 Stat. 919) (1954), Section 261.

71. Public Law 85-79 (71 Stat. 274) (1957).

72. Public Law 88-72 (77 Stat. 84) (1963).

73. U.S., Congress, JCAE, *Current Membership,* p. 5.

74. Public Law 83-703 (68 Stat. 919) (1954), Section 58.

75. *Ibid.,* Section 161.

76. U.S., Congress, JCAE, *Current Membership,* p. 7.

77. Harold P. Green and Alan Rosenthal, *Government of the Atom* (New York: Atherton Press, 1963), p. 266.

78. Harold P. Green and Alan Rosenthal, *The Joint Committee on Atomic Energy: A Study in Fusion of Governmental Power* (Washington, D.C.: The George Washington University, 1961), p. 6.

79. *Nucleonics Week* 14, 20 (May 17, 1973), p. 1.

80. Orlans, *Contracting for Atoms,* p. 170.

81. Green and Rosenthal, *Government of the Atom,* p. 105.

82. U.S., AEC, *Semiannual Report to Congress, July–December 1946.*

83. Hewlett and Duncan, *The Atomic Shield,* p. 30.

84. *Ibid.*

85. *Ibid.,* p. 29.

86. *Ibid.,* p. 120.

87. *Ibid.,* p. 121.

88. *Ibid.,* p. 116.

89. *Ibid.,* p. 117.

90. *Ibid.,* p. 119.

91. *Ibid.*, p. 120.
92. *Ibid.*, p. 121.
93. U.S., AEC, *Semiannual Report to Congress, July–December 1948.*
94. *Ibid.*
95. Hewlett and Duncan, *The Atomic Shield,* p. 208.
96. *Ibid.*, p. 196.
97. *Ibid.*, p. 208.
98. *Ibid.*, p. 209.
99. *Ibid.*, p. 210.
100. *Ibid.*, p. 211.
101. *Ibid.*, p. 212.
102. *Ibid.*, p. 213.
103. *Ibid.*, p. 423.
104. See U.S., AEC, *Semiannual Report to Congress, 1950,* p. viii.
105. Hewlett and Duncan, *The Atomic Shield,* p. 494.
106. *Ibid.*
107. *Ibid.*, p. 511.
108. Gordon Dean, *Report on the Atom* (New York: Alfred A. Knopf, 1957), p. 121.
109. Hewlett and Duncan, *The Atomic Shield,* p. 425.
110. *Ibid.*, p. 427.
111. *Ibid.*, p. 531.
112. *Ibid.*, p. 669.

CHAPTER III

1. Walter H. Zinn, Frank K. Pittman, and John F. Hogerton, *Nuclear Power, U.S.A.* (New York: McGraw-Hill, 1964), p. 9.
2. Glenn T. Seaborg and William R. Corliss, *Man and Atom* (New York: E. Dutton and Company, Inc., 1971), p. 27.
3. U.S., AEC, *Semiannual Report to Congress, January–June 1952,* p. 17.
4. *Ibid.*
5. *Ibid.*, p. 14.
6. U.S., AEC, *Semiannual Report to Congress, July–December 1953,* p. 18.
7. U.S., AEC, *Semiannual Report to Congress, July–December 1954,* p. 22.
8. *Ibid.*
9. U.S., AEC, *Semiannual Report to Congress, July–December 1953,* p. 19.
10. U.S., AEC, *Semiannual Report to Congress, July–December 1954,* p. 23.
11. U.S., AEC, *Semiannual Report to Congress, January–June 1954,* p. 20.
12. *Ibid.*
13. U.S., AEC, *Semiannual Report to Congress, July–December 1954,* p. 22.
14. U.S., AEC, *Semiannual Report to Congress, January–June 1954,* p. 23.
15. U.S., AEC, *Semiannual Report to Congress, January–June 1953,* p. 21.
16. U.S., AEC, *Semiannual Report to Congress, July–December 1954,* p. 28.
17. *Ibid.*
18. *Ibid.*
19. *Ibid.*, p. 29.
20. U.S., AEC, *Semiannual Report to Congress, January–June 1954,* p. 28.
21. U.S., AEC, *Semiannual Report to Congress, July–December 1954,* p. 26.
22. U.S., AEC, *Semiannual Report to Congress, January–July 1954,* p. 121.
23. *Ibid.*, p. 125.
24. *Ibid.*, p. 135.
25. U.S., AEC, *Semiannual Report to Congress, July–December 1952,* p. 20.

26. *Ibid.*, p. 23.

27. U.S., AEC, *Semiannual Report to Congress, July–December 1953,* p. 20.

28. *Ibid.*

29. U.S., AEC, *Semiannual Report to Congress, January–June 1954,* p. 26.

30. *Ibid.*

31. U.S., AEC, *Semiannual Report to Congress, July–December 1954,* p. 25.

32. *Ibid.*, p. 27.

33. U.S., AEC, *Semiannual Report to Congress, January–June 1954,* p. 27.

34. U.S., Congress, JCAE, *Atomic Power Development and Private Enterprise,* Hearings, 83rd Cong., 1st sess., June 24, 25, 29; July 1, 6, 9, 13, 15, 16, 20, 22, 23, 27, and 31, 1953, p. 4. (Hereafter cited as *1953 Hearings.*)

35. U.S., Congress, JCAE, *Atomic Power and Private Enterprise,* Joint Committee Print, JCAE, December 1952, p. III.

36. *Ibid.*

37. U.S., Congress, JCAE, *1953 Hearings.*

38. *Ibid.*, p. 2.

39. *Ibid.*, p. 1.

40. *Ibid.*, p. 2.

41. *Ibid.*

42. *Ibid.*

43. *Ibid.*, p. 3.

44. U.S., AEC, *Semiannual Report to Congress, January–June 1953,* p. 19.

45. US., Congress, JCAE, *1953 Hearings,* p. 7.

46. *Ibid.*, p. 71.

47. *Ibid.*, p. 9.

48. *Ibid.*, p. 30.

49. *Ibid.*, p. 31.

50. *Ibid.*, p. 33.

51. *Ibid.*, p. 23.

52. *Ibid.*, p. 24.

53. *Ibid.*, p. 25.

54. *Ibid.*, pp. 420–34.

55. *Ibid.*, p. 436.

56. *Ibid.*

57. *Ibid.*, p. 301.

58. *Ibid.*, p. 284.

59. *Ibid.*, p. 280.

60. *Ibid ,* p. 285.

61. U.S., Congress, JCAE, *Atomic Power and Private Enterprise,* p. 325.

62. *Ibid.*, p. 31.

63. Zinn, Pittman, and Hogerton, *Nuclear Power, U.S.A.,* p. 9.

64. U.S., Congress, JCAE, *Atomic Power and Private Enterprise.*

65. U.S., Congress, House, *Legislative History of the Atomic Energy Act of 1954,* Report. 83rd Cong., 2nd sess., 1954, House Doc. 328, pp. 2134–35. (Hereafter cited as *Leg. Hist. 1954.*)

66. Harold P. Green and Alan Rosenthal, *The Joint Committee on Atomic Energy: A Study in Fusion of Governmental Power* (Washington, D.C.: The George Washington University, 1961), p. 149. (Hereafter cited as *The JCAE.*)

67. Thomas Morgan, *Atomic Energy and Congress* (Ann Arbor: The University of Michigan Press, 1956), p. 146.

68. U.S., Congress, JCAE, *1953 Hearings.*

69. U.S., Congress, House, *Leg. Hist. 1954,* pp. 1638–42.

70. *Ibid.,* p. 1641.

71. *Ibid.,* p. 1642.

72. *Ibid.,* p. 1644.

73. *Ibid.,* p. 1646.

74. *Ibid.*

75. Morgan, *Atomic Energy and Congress,* p. 150.

76. U.S., Congress, House, *Congressional Record,* 83rd Cong., 2nd sess., 1954, 100 (Daily Edition, July 23, 1954), p. 11021.

77. U.S., Congress, House, *Leg. Hist. 1954,* p. 1648.

78. Green and Rosenthal, *The JCAE,* p. 158.

79. U.S., Congress, House, *Leg. Hist. 1954,* p. 1658.

80. *Ibid.,* pp. 3860–61.

81. Green and Rosenthal, *The JCAE,* p. 160.

82. *Ibid.,* pp. 160–73.

83. U.S., Congress, House, *Leg. Hist. 1954,* p. 2132.

84. *Ibid.,* p. 2133.

85. *Ibid.,* p. 1952.

86. *Ibid.,* p. 1953.

87. *Ibid.,* p. 1954.

88. *Ibid.,* p. 1982.

89. *Ibid.,* p. 2237.

90. *Ibid.*

91. *Ibid.,* p. 3747.

92. *Ibid.,* p. 754.

93. *Ibid.,* p. 847.

94. *Ibid.,* p. 853.

95. *Ibid.,* p. 855.

96. *Ibid.*

97. *Ibid.,* p. 871.

98. *Ibid.*

99. *Ibid.,* p. 872.

100. *Ibid.*

101. *Ibid.,* p. 861.

102. *Ibid.,* p. 863.

103. *Ibid.,* p. 3566.

104. Green and Rosenthal, *The JCAE,* p. 196.

105. U.S., Congress, House, *Leg. Hist. 1954,* p. 2964.

106. *Ibid.,* p. 3916.

107. *Ibid.,* p. 2986.

108. *Ibid.,* p. 3924.

109. *Ibid.,* p. 3007.

110. Green and Rosenthal, *The JCAE,* pp. 196–206.

111. *Ibid.,* p. 197.

112. See U.S., Congress, House, *Leg. Hist. 1954,* for a report of the Dixon-Yates debates.

113. *Ibid.,* p. 999.

114. *Ibid.,* p. 2983.

115. Gordon Dean, *Report on the Atom* (New York: Alfred A. Knopf, 1957), p. 329.

116. U.S., Congress, 1954 Atomic Energy Act, Section 44.

117. Public Law 86-50 (73 Stat. 81) (1959); Public Law 88-394 (78 Stat. 376) (1964); Public Law 91-161 (83 Stat. 444) (1969).

CHAPTER IV

1. For further discussion of this point, see Harold P. Green, "The Strange Case of Nuclear Power," *Federal Bar Journal* 17 (April–June 1957), p. 100.

2. For a discussion of political subsystems, see Emmette S. Redford, *Democracy in the Administrative State* (New York: Oxford University Press, 1969), Chapter IV.

3. U.S., AEC, *Semiannual Report to Congress, July–December 1954,* p. vii.

4. For references and further discussion of this topic, see U.S., AEC reports to Congress from 1947 to date.

5. Richard G. Hewlett and Francis Duncan, *The Atomic Shield, 1947/1952: A History of the United States Atomic Energy Commission,* Vol. 2 (University Park: Pennsylvania State University Press, 1969), p. 194.

6. U.S., Congress, JCAE, *Five-Year Power Reactor Development Program Proposed by the Atomic Energy Commission,* JCAE Print, March 1954, p. 5.

7. *Ibid.,* p. 10.

8. U.S., AEC, *Annual Report to Congress, 1964,* p. 87.

9. U.S., AEC, *Annual Report to Congress, 1965,* p. 121.

10. Public Law 89-32 (79 Stat. 120) (1965).

11. U.S., AEC, *Annual Report to Congress, 1965,* p. 122.

12. U.S., AEC, *Annual Report to Congress, 1966,* p. 152.

13. U.S., AEC, *Annual Report to Congress, 1971,* p. 114.

14. U.S., AEC, *Semiannual Report to Congress, January–June, 1955,* p. 36.

15. U.S., AEC, *Semiannual Report to Congress, January–June, 1957,* p. 50.

16. *Ibid.*

17. *Ibid.*

18. *Ibid.,* p. 51.

19. U.S., AEC, *Annual Report to Congress, 1959,* p. 20.

20. U.S., AEC, *Annual Report to Congress, 1961,* p. 83.

21. U.S., AEC, *Annual Report to Congress, 1962,* p. 132.

22. *Ibid.,* p. 135.

23. U.S., AEC, *Annual Report to Congress, 1967,* p. 95.

24. *Ibid.*

25. U.S., AEC, *Semiannual Report to Congress, July–December 1958,* p. 28.

26. U.S., AEC, *Annual Report to Congress, 1960,* p. 45.

27. *Ibid.*

28. U.S., AEC, *Annual Report to Congress, 1962,* p. 130.

29. U.S., AEC, *Annual Report to Congress, 1966,* p. 161.

30. U.S., AEC, *Annual Report to Congress, 1965,* p. 118.

31. U.S., AEC, *Annual Report to Congress, 1964,* p. 97.

32. Samuel Glasstone and Alexander Sesonske, *Nuclear Reactor Engineering* (New York: Van Nostrand, 1963), p. 740.

33. U.S., AEC, *Annual Report to Congress, 1969,* p. 90.

34. U.S., AEC, *Semiannual Report to Congress, July–December 1957,* p. 119.

35. U.S., AEC, *Semiannual Report to Congress, January–June 1958,* p. 83.

36. U.S., AEC, *Annual Report to Congress, 1961,* p. 105.

37. U.S., AEC, *Semiannual Report to Congress, July–December 1958,* p. 33.

38. Green, "The Strange Case of Nuclear Power," p. 102.

39. *Ibid.*

40. *Atomic Energy Reporter, News and Analysis* 1, 23 (November 9, 1955), p. 179.

41. *Atomic Energy Reporter, News and Analysis* 1, 18 (October 5, 1955), p. 142.

42. U.S., AEC, Press Release No. 589, January 10, 1955.

43. U.S., Congress, JCAE, *Cooperative Power Reactor Demonstration Program, 1963,* Hearings, 88th Cong., 1st sess. July 9, August 7, and October 15, 1963, p. 226. (Hereafter cited as *1963 Hearings.*)

44. *Ibid.*

45. U.S., AEC, Press Release No. 695, September 21, 1955.

46. Green, "The Strange Case of Nuclear Power," p. 112.

47. U.S., Congress, JCAE, *1963 Hearings,* p. 228.

48. U.S., Congress, JCAE, *Authorizing Appropriations for the Atomic Energy Commission,* 85th Cong., 1st sess., August 2, 1957, H. Rept. 978, p. 15.

49. *Ibid.*

50. *Ibid.,* p. 17.

51. Public Law 85-79 (71 Stat. 274) (1957).

52. Public Law 85-162 (71 Stat. 403) (1957).

53. U.S., AEC, Press Release No. 953, January 7, 1957.

54. Green, "The Strange Case of Nuclear Power," p. 118.

55. U.S., AEC, Press Release No. 1 IN-360, August 23, 1962.

56. U.S., Congress, JCAE, *Accelerating the Civilian Reactor Program,* Hearings on S 2725, HR 10805, 84th Cong., 2nd sess., May 23, 24, 25, 28, and 29, 1956, p. 1. (Hereafter cited as *1956 Hearings.*)

57. U.S., AEC, *Semiannual Report to Congress, January–June 1956,* p. 35.

58. U.S., Congress, JCAE, *1956 Hearings,* p. 53.

59. *Ibid.,* p. 59.

60. *Ibid.,* p. 27.

61. *Ibid.,* p. 13.

62. *Ibid.,* p. 77.

63. *Ibid.,* p. 8.

64. *Ibid.,* p. 15.

65. *Ibid.,* p. 33.

66. *Ibid.,* p. 109.

67. *Ibid.,* p. 259.

68. *Ibid.,* p. 485.

69. *Ibid.,* p. 165.

70. *Ibid.,* p. 140.

71. *Ibid.,* p. 180.

72. *Ibid.,* p. 176.

73. *Ibid.,* p. 353.

74. Public Law 85-79 (71 Stat. 274) (1957).

75. U.S., Congress, House, *The Congressional Record,* 85th Cong., 1st sess., 1957, 103, Pt. 11, p. 14251.

76. *Ibid.,* p. 15038.

77. *Ibid.,* p. 15022.

78. *Ibid.*

79. *Ibid.,* p. 15310.

80. U.S., AEC, *Semiannual Report to Congress, July–December 1958,* p. 34.

81. U.S., Congress, JCAE, *Technical Aspects of the Report on the Gas-Cooled, Graphite Moderated Reactor,* Hearings, 85th Cong., 2nd sess., April 22, 1958. (Hereafter cited as *April 1958 Hearings.*)

82. *Ibid.,* p. 1.

83. *Ibid.,* p. 48.

84. *Ibid.,* p. 51.

85. *Ibid.,* p. 64.

86. *Ibid.,* p. 24.

87. *Ibid.,* p. 12.

88. U.S., Congress, Senate, *The Congressional Record*, 85th Cong., 2nd sess., 1958, 104, Pt. 11, p. 14641.

89. *Ibid.*, p. 13810.

90. *Ibid.*, p. 13805.

91. *Ibid.*, p. 13820.

92. U.S., Congress, House, *Conference Report*, 85th Cong., 2nd sess., July 21, 1958, House Rep. 2237.

93. U.S., Congress, Senate, *The Congressional Record*, 85th Cong., 2nd sess., 1958, 104, Pt. 11, p. 13802.

94. U.S., AEC, *Semiannual Report to Congress, July–December 1958*, p. 34.

95. *Ibid.*

96. U.S., AEC, *Annual Report to Congress, 1959*, p. 29.

97. See, for example, U.S., AEC, *Annual Report to Congress, 1961*, p. 99.

98. U.S., AEC, *Annual Report to Congress, 1964*, p. 101.

99. U.S., AEC, *Annual Report to Congress, 1965*, p. 125.

100. *Nucleonics Week* 14, 14 (April 5, 1973), p. 1.

101. Vera Edinger, *The Hanford Story*, monograph, March 1964, p. 7.

102. U.S., AEC, *Annual Report to Congress, 1959*, p. 64.

103. U.S., AEC, *Annual Report to Congress, 1963*, p. 46.

104. U.S., AEC, *Annual Report to Congress, 1964*, p. 62.

105. U.S., AEC, *Annual Report to Congress, 1965*, p. 76.

106. U.S., AEC, *Annual Report to Congress, 1967*, p. 38.

107. U.S., AEC, *Annual Report to Congress, 1964*, p. 17.

108. U.S., AEC, *Annual Report to Congress, 1971*, p. 126.

109. *Ibid.*

110. *Nuclear News* 16, 1 (January 1973), p. 30.

111. U.S., AEC, *Annual Report to Congress, 1973*, Vol. 1, *Operating and Developmental Functions*, p. 97.

112. *Nuclear News* 7, 3 (March 1964), p. 32.

113. U.S., Congress, JCAE, *Proposed Expanded Civilian Nuclear Power Program*, 85th Cong., 2nd sess., August 1958, p. V. (Hereafter cited as *Expanded Program*.)

114. *Ibid.*, p. 3.

115. *Ibid.*

116. *Ibid.*, p. 4.

117. *Ibid.*, p. 8.

118. *Ibid.*, p. 9.

119. *Ibid.*

120. U.S., AEC, *Semiannual Report to Congress, July–December 1958*, p. 16.

121. For a more complete review of the AEC's reactor program status as of the end of 1958, see U.S., AEC, *Semiannual Report to Congress, July–December 1958*, pp. 16–38, 250–80.

122. U.S., Congress, JCAE, *Expanded Program*, p. 9.

123. *Ibid.*

124. *Ibid.*, p. 11.

125. U.S., Congress, JCAE, *Comments of Reactor Designers and Industrial Representatives on the Proposed Expanded Civilian Nuclear Power Program*, Report, 85th Cong., 2nd sess., December 1958, p. 60.

126. *Ibid.*, p. 117.

127. U.S., Congress, JCAE, *Selected Materials on Atomic Energy Indemnity Legislation*, 89th Cong., 1st sess., June 1965, p. 8.

128. U.S., AEC, *Semiannual Report to Congress, January–June 1957*, p. 44.

129. U.S., Congress, JCAE, *Selected Materials on Atomic Energy Indemnity Legislation*, Committee Print, 89th Cong., 1st sess., June 1965, p. 180.

130. *Ibid.*

131. U.S., Congress, JCAE, *Government Indemnity,* Hearings, 84th Cong., 2nd sess., May 15–21 and June 14, 1956.

132. U.S., Congress, JCAE, *Selected Materials on Atomic Energy Indemnity Legislation,* p. 104.

133. U.S., Congress, JCAE, *Government Indemnity and Reactor Safety,* Hearings on S 715 (HR 1981), 85th Cong., 1st sess., March 27, 1957, p. 8. (Hereafter cited as *1957 Hearings.*)

134. *Ibid.,* p. 10.

135. *Ibid.,* p. 11.

136. *Ibid.*

137. *Ibid.,* p. 122.

138. *Ibid.,* p. 131.

139. *Ibid.,* p. 146.

140. *Ibid.*

141. *Ibid.,* p. 147.

142. *Ibid.,* pp. 259–71.

143. *Ibid.,* p. 7.

144. U.S., Congress, JCAE, *Selected Materials on Atomic Energy Indemnity Legislation,* p. 130.

145. *Ibid.*

146. U.S., Congress, House, *The Congressional Record,* 85th Cong., 1st sess., 1957, 103, Pt. 8, p. 10711.

147. *Ibid.,* p. 10719.

148. *Ibid.,* p. 10721.

149. *Ibid.,* p. 10725.

150. U.S., Congress, Senate, *The Congressional Record,* 103, Pt. 11, p. 15056.

151. *Ibid.,* p. 15059.

152. *Ibid.,* p. 15050.

153. Public Law 85-256 (71 Stat. 576) (1957), cited as the Price-Anderson Act, an amendment to the Atomic Energy Act of 1954.

154. U.S., Congress, House, *Congressional Record,* 103, Pt. 8, p. 10717.

155. Public Law 89-210 (79 Stat. 855) (1965).

156. *Nucleonics Week* 14, 24 (June 14, 1973), p. 2.

157. Atomic Industrial Forum, Inc., *INFO,* No. 78 (January 1975), p. 4.

158. U.S., Congress, JCAE, *Proposed Extension of AEC Indemnity Legislation,* Hearings, 89th Cong., 1st sess., June 22–24, 1965, p. 121.

159. *Ibid.,* p. 138.

160. *Ibid.,* pp. 143–45.

161. *Nucleonics Week* 14, 24 (June 14, 1973), p. 1.

162. U.S., AEC, *Annual Report to Congress, 1962,* p. 7.

163. U.S., AEC, *Civilian Nuclear Power—A Report to the President—1962* (Washington, D.C.: GPO, November 20, 1962), p. 13.

164. *Ibid.,* p. 30.

165. *Ibid.,* p. 33.

166. *Ibid.,* p. 42.

167. *Ibid.,* p. 11.

168. *Ibid.*

169. U.S., Congress, JCAE, *1963 Hearings,* p. 2.

170. *Ibid.*

171. *Nucleonics Week,* 14, 21 (May 24, 1973), p. 8.

172. U.S., Congress, JCAE, *1963 Hearings,* p. 2.

173. *Ibid.*, p. 38.

174. U.S., AEC, *Annual Report to Congress, 1963,* p. 90.

CHAPTER V

1. U.S., AEC, *Civilian Nuclear Power—A Report to the President—1962* (Washington, D.C.: GPO, November 20, 1962), p. 13.

2. *Ibid.*

3. U.S., AEC, *Annual Report to Congress, 1963,* p. 48.

4. U.S., AEC, *Annual Report to Congress, 1964,* p. 84.

5. *Ibid.*, p. 86.

6. U.S., AEC, *Annual Report to Congress, 1965,* p. 122.

7. *Nuclear News* 18, 6 (mid-April 1975), p. 16B.

8. U.S., AEC, *Annual Report to Congress, 1965,* p. 123.

9. *Ibid.*, p. 124.

10. U.S., AEC, *Civilian Nuclear Power—The 1967 Supplement to the 1962 Report to the President* (Washington, D.C.: GPO, February 1967), p. 5.

11. *Ibid.*, p. 7.

12. U.S., AEC, *The Nuclear Industry—1971* (Washington, D.C.: GPO, 1971), p. 8.

13. *Ibid.*, p. 136.

14. U.S., AEC, *Nuclear Power Growth 1974–2000* (Washington, D.C.: February 1974), p. 8.

15. *Ibid.*, p. 20.

16. U.S., AEC, *The Nuclear Industry—1971,* p. 2.

17. Arthur D. Little, Inc., *Competition in the Nuclear Power Supply Industry,* Report, prepared for the U.S. AEC and the U.S. Department of Justice, NYO-3853-1 (Washington, D.C.: GPO, December 1968).

18. *Nucleonics Week* 16, 5 (January 30, 1975).

19. Arthur D. Little, Inc., *Competition in the Nuclear Power Supply Industry,* p. 25.

20. U.S., AEC, *The Nuclear Industry—1971,* p. 46.

21. *Ibid.*, p. 23.

22. *Ibid.*, p. 46.

23. *Ibid.*, p. 136.

24. *Nuclear News* 18, 3 (February 1975), p. 30.

25. *Ibid.*, p. 133.

26. *Ibid.*, p. 136.

27. *Ibid.*, p. 134.

28. U.S., AEC, *The Nuclear Industry—1971,* p. 153.

29. *Nuclear News* 16, 4 (March 1973), p. 159.

30. *Ibid.* 18, 3 (February 1975), p. 29.

31. *Ibid.*

32. Thomas E. Kauper, "National Energy Policy and the Antitrust Laws," paper presented at the Western Conference of Public Service Commissions, Portland, Oregon, June 4, 1973.

33. Public Law 91-560 (84 Stat. 1472) (1970).

34. Kauper, "National Energy Policy and the Antitrust Laws," p. 15.

35. "Atomic Lemons," *Wall Street Journal,* May 3, 1973, p. 1.

36. Atomic Industrial Forum, Inc., *INFO,* No. 59 (May 1973), pp. 6–7.

37. *Ibid.*

38. "Letters to the Editor," *Wall Street Journal,* June 6, 1973.

39. *Weekly Energy Report,* February 17, 1975, p. 3.

40. "Problems Abound—But So Does Optimism," *Nuclear News* 16, 3 (February 1973), p. 20.

41. *Nuclear News* 16, 9 (June 1973), p. 48.

42. U.S., Congress, JCAE, *Amending the Atomic Energy Act of 1954 to Provide for Private Ownership of Special Nuclear Materials,* 88th Cong., 2nd sess., Legislative Report, S. Rept. 1325, H. Rept. 1702, August 5, 1964, p. 7.

43. U.S., AEC, *Annual Report to Congress, 1963,* p. 17.

44. U.S., Congress, JCAE, *Private Ownership of Special Nuclear Materials,* Hearings on S 1160 (HR 5035), 88th Cong., 1st sess., July 30, 31, and August 1, 1963, p. 14. (Hereafter cited as *Private Ownership Hearings—1963.*)

45. *Ibid.,* p. 142.

46. *Ibid.*

47. *Ibid.*

48. U.S., Congress, JCAE, *Private Ownership of Special Nuclear Materials,* Hearings on S 2635, 88th Cong., 2nd sess., June 9–11, 15, 25, 1964, p. 225. (Hereafter cited as *Private Ownership Hearings—1964.*)

49. *Ibid.,* p. 232.

50. *Ibid.,* p. 265.

51. *Ibid.,* p. 269.

52. U.S., Congress, JCAE, *Private Ownership Hearings—1963,* p. 167.

53. U.S., Congress, JCAE, *Private Ownership Hearings—1964,* p. 46.

54. *Ibid.,* p. 261.

55. *Ibid.*

56. *Ibid.,* p. 294.

57. *Nuclear News* 17, 15 (December 1974).

58. U.S., Congress, JCAE, *Private Ownership Hearings—1964,* p. 158.

59. U.S., Congress, JCAE, *Amending the Atomic Energy Act of 1954,* p. 16.

60. *Ibid.*

61. *Ibid.*

62. U.S., Congress, House, *The Congressional Record,* 88th Cong., 2nd sess., 1964, 110, Pt. 15, p. 20142.

63. *Ibid.,* p. 20143.

64. *Ibid.,* p. 20145.

65. *Ibid.*

66. U.S., AEC, *Annual Report to Congress, 1964,* pp. 12–15.

67. U.S., Congress, JCAE, *Private Ownership Hearings—1964,* p. 160.

68. Richard G. Hewlett and Francis Duncan, *The Atomic Shield, 1947/1952: A History of the United States Atomic Energy Commission,* Vol. 2 (University Park: Pennsylvania State University Press, 1969), p. 147.

69. *Ibid.,* p. 148.

70. *Ibid.,* pp. 148, 272–82.

71. *Ibid.,* p. 173.

72. *Ibid.*

73. David E. Lilienthal, statement for press conference in Denver, Colorado, December 17, 1948. Published in U.S., Congress, JCAE, *Atomic Power and Private Enterprise,* 1952.

74. Henry D. Smyth, prepared remarks for the Western Division of the American Mining Congress at Denver, Colorado, September 25, 1952. Published in U.S., Congress, JCAE, *Atomic Power and Private Enterprise,* p. 96.

75. *Ibid.*

76. Hewlett and Duncan, *The Atomic Shield,* p. 148.

77. U.S., AEC, *Semiannual Report to Congress, June–December 1948,* pp. 160–65.

78. U.S., AEC, *Semiannual Report to Congress, July–December 1957,* p. 143.

79. *Ibid.*, p. 144.

80. *Ibid.*, p. 145.

81. *Ibid.*, p. 143.

82. *Ibid.*, p. 148.

83. U.S., AEC, *Semiannual Report to Congress, January–June 1956*, p. 1.

84. U.S., AEC, *Annual Report to Congress, 1962*, p. 209.

85. *Ibid.*, p. 210.

86. *Ibid.*, p. 211.

87. U.S., AEC, *Annual Report to Congress, 1966*, p. 80.

88. U.S., AEC, *Annual Report to Congress, 1971*, p. 135.

89. U.S., AEC, *Annual Report to Congress, 1970*, p. 104.

90. U.S., AEC, *Annual Report to Congress, 1969*, p. 35.

91. U.S., AEC, *Annual Report to Congress, 1971*, p. 137.

92. Battelle-Pacific Northwest Laboratories, "Assessment of Uranium and Thorium Resources in the United States and the Effect of Policy Alternatives" (Richland, Washington: Battelle Laboratories, December 1974).

93. "Summary of EPRI Special Report No. 5, Uranium Resources to Meet Long Term Requirements," prepared by Milton F. Searl and staff, Electric Power Research Institute, November 1974.

94. U.S., AEC, *The Nuclear Industry—1971*, pp. 35–36.

95. *Ibid.*, p. 35.

96. Wilfred E. Johnson, "The Potential and Problems of Nuclear Power," remarks made at the National Energy Forum, Washington, D.C., September 24, 1971, AEC Public Release S-18-71.

97. Public Law 88-489 (78 Stat. 602) (1964).

98. U.S., AEC, *The Nuclear Industry—1969*, p. 54.

99. U.S., Congress, JCAE, *Future Ownership of the AEC's Gaseous Diffusion Plants*, Hearings, 91st Cong., 1st sess., July 8 and 9, August 5, 7, and 8, 1969, p. 188. (Hereafter cited as *Future Ownership of Diffusion Plants.*)

100. Hewlett and Duncan, *The Atomic Shield*, p. 147.

101. *Ibid.*, p. 669.

102. U.S., Congress, JCAE, *Future Ownership of Diffusion Plants*, pp. 15–19.

103. *Ibid.*

104. U.S., AEC, *The Nuclear Industry—1971*, p. 31.

105. U.S., AEC, *Annual Report to Congress, 1971*, p. 126.

106. U.S., AEC, *The Nuclear Industry—1971*, p. 31.

107. U.S., AEC, *The Nuclear Industry—1969*, p. 52, December 30, 1969.

108. U.S., AEC, *The Nuclear Industry—1971*, p. 30.

109. Johnson, "The Potential and Problems of Nuclear Power."

110. U.S., Congress, JCAE, *Future Ownership of Diffusion Plants*, p. 84.

111. *Ibid.*, p. 85.

112. *Ibid.*, p. 87.

113. *Ibid.*, p. 89.

114. U.S., Congress, JCAE, *Uranium Enrichment Pricing Criteria*, Hearings, 91st Cong., 2nd sess., June 16 and 17, 1970, p. 110.

115. *Ibid.*, p. 111.

116. *Ibid.*, p. 112.

117. *Ibid.*, p. 111.

118. *Ibid.*, p. 6.

119. U.S., AEC, *Annual Report to Congress, 1969*, p. 43.

120. U.S., AEC, *Annual Report to Congress, 1970*, p. 108.

121. U.S., Congress, JCAE, *Future Ownership of Diffusion Plants*, p. 375.

122. *Ibid.*, p. 254.

123. *Ibid.,* p. 255.
124. *Ibid.,* p. 132.
125. *Ibid.,* p. 312.
126. *Ibid.*
127. *Ibid.,* pp. 187, 195–222.
128. *Ibid.,* p. 341.
129. *Ibid.,* p. 225.
130. U.S., AEC, *Annual Report to Congress, 1971,* p. 121.
131. *Ibid.,* p. 124.
132. U.S., AEC, *Annual Report to Congress, 1972,* p. 32.
133. *Nuclear News* 16, 2 (February 1973), p. 42.
134. U.S., AEC, *1973 Financial Report,* p. 27.
135. U.S., AEC, *1974 Financial Report,* p. 28.
136. *Ibid.*
137. U.S., AEC, *1973 Financial Report,* p. 27.
138. U.S., AEC, *Annual Report to Congress, 1972,* p. 32.
139. *Nuclear News* 15, 5 (May 1972), p. 36.
140. *Ibid.* 18, 4 (March 1975), p. 18.
141. *Ibid.* 18, 8 (June 1975), p. 42.
142. *Ibid.,* p. 56.
143. *Ibid.* 18, 2 (February 1975), p. 31.
144. *Ibid.* 18, 5 (April 1975), p. 60.
145. *Ibid.* 17, 14 (November 1974), p. 68.
146. *Ibid.* 18, 7 (May 1975), p. 38.

CHAPTER VI

1. U.S., AEC, Press Release No. P-118, April 25, 1972.
2. Public Law 83-703 (68 Stat. 921) (1954).
3. U.S., Congress, JCAE, *Study of AEC Procedures and Organization in the Licensing of Reactor Facilities,* Committee Print, 85th Cong., 1st sess., April 1957.
4. Public Law 83-703 (68 Stat. 953) (1954).
5. U.S., 10 Code of Federal Regulations 50. (Hereafter cited as CFR.)
6. U.S., 10 CFR 100.
7. Clifford K. Beck, "Engineering Out the Distance Factor," *Atomic Energy Law Journal* 5, 4 (1963), p. 245.
8. Public Law 83-703 (68 Stat. 919) (1954), Section 185.
9. Public Law 86-373 (73 Stat. 688) (1959), Section 274h.
10. Public Law 83-703 (68 Stat. 938) (1954), Section 105c.
11. Public Law 85-256 (71 Stat. 579) (1957), Section 6b.
12. *Ibid.,* Section 7.
13. Public Law 87-615 (76 Stat. 409) (1962), Section 2.
14. *Ibid.,* Section 191.
15. Public Law 85-256 (71 Stat. 579) (1957), Section 5.
16. Public Law 87-615 (76 Stat. 409) (1962), Section 191a.
17. Sidney G. Kingsley, "The Licensing of Nuclear Power Reactors in the United States," *Atomic Energy Law Journal* 7, 4 (1965), p. 309.
18. *Nuclear News* 18, 3 (1975).
19. U.S., AEC, *Annual Report to Congress, 1973,* Vol. 2, Regulatory Activities.
20. U.S., AEC, *1972 Atomic Energy Programs, Regulatory Activities* (Washington, D.C.: GPO, January 31, 1973), p. III.
21. *Ibid.*
22. *Nucleonics Week* 13, 52 (December 28, 1972), p. 6.

23. Atomic Industrial Forum, Inc., *INFO*, No. 54 (December 1972), p. 2.

24. *Ibid.*

25. U.S., AEC, *1972 Atomic Energy Programs, Regulatory Activities,* p. IV.

26. Public Law 91-190 (83 Stat. 852) (1969).

27. U.S., Office of the President, Executive Order 11514, March 5, 1970, amending Executive Order 11472, May 29, 1969. (35 *Federal Register* 4247.)

28. U.S., 10 CFR 50 (Licensing and Production and Utilization Facilities), Section 50.34 and 50.34a, pp. 286–89.

29. Public Law 91-224 (84 Stat. 91) (1970).

30. U.S., AEC, *Annual Report to Congress, 1973,* Vol. 2, Regulatory Activities, p. 46.

31. U.S., Congress, JCAE, *Nuclear Reactor Safety Hearings,* 93rd Cong., Pt. I, January 23, September 25, 26, 27, and October 1, 1973, p. 341.

32. U.S., AEC, *Annual Report to Congress, 1973,* Vol. 2, Regulatory Activities, p. 31.

33. U.S., AEC, *Annual Report to Congress, 1973,* Vol. 2, Regulatory Activities.

34. Public Law 86-373 (73 Stat. 688) (1959).

35. *Minnesota* v. *Northern States Power Co.* 447 *Federal Reporter* 1143 (405 *U.S. Reports* 1035) (1972).

36. Public Law 55-425 (30 Stat. 1152) (1899), Section 13.

37. Public Law 92-500 (70 Stat. 498) (1972).

38. *Ibid.,* Section 402c (2).

39. *Ibid.,* Section 405c.

40. *Ibid.,* Section 405a.

41. *Ibid.,* Section 311b (2a).

42. Washington State, *Revised Code of Washington,* 80.50, Thermal Power Plant Site Locations.

43. Harold P. Green, "The Law of Reactor Safety," *Vanderbilt Law Review* 12 (1958), pp. 129–31.

44. U.S., Congress, JCAE, "A Study of AEC Procedures and Organization in the Licensing of Reactor Facilities," *JCAE Report* (1957), p. 8.

45. *Ibid.,* p. 104.

46. Green, "The Law of Reactor Safety," p. 130.

47. U.S., Congress, JCAE, "A Study of AEC Procedures and Organization in the Licensing of Reactor Facilities," p. 128.

48. *Ibid.,* p. 133.

49. *Ibid.,* p. 132.

50. *Ibid.,* p. 125.

51. *Ibid.,* p. 126.

52. *Ibid.,* p. 109.

53. *Ibid.,* p. 128.

54. Sheldon Novick, *The Careless Atom* (Boston: Houghton-Mifflin Company, 1969), pp. 147–48.

55. U.S., Congress, JCAE, "A Study of AEC Procedures and Organization in the Licensing of Reactor Facilities," p. 126.

56. Public Law 85-256 (71 Stat. 579) (1957).

57. William H. Berman and Lee M. Hydeman, *The Atomic Energy Commission and Regulating Nuclear Facilities* (Ann Arbor: University of Michigan Law School, 1961).

58. U.S., Congress, JCAE, *Government Indemnity and Reactor Safety,* Hearings on S 715 (HR 1981), 85th Cong., 1st sess., March 27, 1957, p. 11.

59. *Power Reactor Development Co.* v. *International Union of Electrical, Radio and Machine Workers, AFL-CIO et al.* (367 *U.S. Reports* 396) (1961).

60. *Nucleonics Week* 13, 19 (December 7, 1972), pp. 6–7.

61. *Minnesota* v. *Northern States Power Co.*

62. U.S., Congress, JCAE, *Environmental Effects of Producing Electric Power,* Hearings, 91st Cong., 2nd sess., January 27–30, and February 24–26, 1970, p. 1137.

63. *Ibid.,* p. 1138.

64. *Ibid.*

65. *Ibid.,* p. 1139.

66. *Ibid.*

67. For more information about the symposium the reader is referred to Harry Foreman (ed.), *Nuclear Power and the Public* (Minneapolis: University of Minnesota Press, 1970).

68. Public Law 85-256 (71 Stat. 579) (1957), p. 1111.

69. Richard S. Lewis, *The Nuclear Power Rebellion* (New York: Viking Press, 1972), pp. 128–29.

70. Lewis, *The Nuclear Power Rebellion.*

71. *Minnesota* v. *Northern States Power Co.*

72. U.S., Congress, Senate, *Amendment to the Atomic Energy Act of 1954, as Amended with Respect to Cooperation with the States,* 86th Cong., 1st sess., Rept. No. 870, September 1, 1959.

73. U.S., Congress, Senate Committee on Interior and Insular Affairs, *Calvert Cliffs Court Decision,* Hearings, 92nd Cong., 1st sess., Pt. 2, November 3, 1971, p. 622.

74. *Ibid.,* Pt. 2, pp. 622–66.

75. *Ibid.*

76. *Ibid.,* Pt. 2, p. 673.

77. *Ibid.,* Pt. 2, p. 716.

78. *Ibid.,* Pt. 1, p. 172.

79. *Ibid.,* Pt. 1, p. 173.

80. *Ibid.,* Pt. 1, p. 179.

81. *Ibid.,* Pt. 1, p. 236.

82. National Academy of Sciences and National Research Council, Advisory Committee on the Biological Effects of Ionizing Radiation, "The Effects on Populations of Exposure to Low Levels of Ionizing Radiation," *Resources and Man* (San Francisco: W. H. Freeman and Co., 1969).

83. U.S., Congress, JCAE, *Nuclear Reactor Safety,* Hearings, 93rd Cong., 1st sess., January 23, September 25–27, and October 1, 1973, p. 365.

84. Merrill Eisenbud, "Health Hazards from Radioactive Emissions," presented at the American Medical Association's Congress on Environmental Health, Chicago, Illinois, April 29–30, 1973.

85. U.S., AEC, *The Safety of Nuclear Power Reactors (Light Water Cooled) and Related Facilities,* Rept. No. WASH-1250, July 1973.

86. John P. Holdren, "Hazards of the Nuclear Fuel Cycle," *Bulletin of the Atomic Scientists,* October 1974, p. 18.

87. U.S., AEC, *Reactor Safety Study, An Assessment of Accident Risks in U.S. Commercial Nuclear Power Plants,* Rept. No. WASH 1400, August 1974.

88. F.A.S., *Public Interest Report* 3, 1 (January 1975), p. 4.

89. Paul F. Gast, "Divergent Public Attitudes toward Nuclear and Hydroelectric Plant Safety," presented at the 19th Annual Meeting of the American Nuclear Society, Chicago, Illinois, June 10–14, 1973.

90. Eisenbud, "Health Hazards from Radioactive Emissions."

91. U.S., AEC, *Semiannual Report to Congress, January–June 1954,* p. 22.

92. U.S., AEC, *Annual Report to Congress, 1961,* p. 115.

93. *Ibid.,* p. 116.

94. U.S., AEC, *Annual Report to Congress, 1971,* p. 116.

95. *Ibid.,* p. 117.

96. U.S., AEC, *Current Status and Future Technical and Economic Potential of Light Water Reactors*, Rept. No. WASH 1082 (Washington, D.C.: GPO, March 1968).

97. "Nuclear Safety (I): The Roots of Dissent," *Science* 177 (September 1, 1972), p. 771. "Nuclear Safety (II): The Years of Delay," *Science* 177 (September 8, 1972), p. 867. "Nuclear Safety (III): Critics Charge Conflicts of Interest," *Science* 177 (September 15, 1972), p. 970. "Nuclear Safety (IV): Barriers to Communication," *Science* 177 (September 22, 1972), p. 1080.

98. U.S., AEC, *Annual Report to Congress, 1973*, Vol. 1, Operating and Developmental Programs, Chapter 4.

99. U.S., Congress, JCAE, *Nuclear Reactor Safety*, Hearings, 93rd Cong., 2nd sess., January 22–24, and 28, 1974, p. 759.

100. *Ibid.*, p. 765.

101. *Nucleonics Week* 16, 5 (January 30, 1975), p. 2.

102. Mason Willrich and Theodore B. Taylor, *Nuclear Theft: Risks and Safeguards* (Cambridge, Massachusetts: Ballinger, 1974).

103. Ralph E. Lapp, *The Nuclear Energy Controversy* (Greenwich, Connecticut: Fact Systems, 1974), p. 76.

104. U.S., AEC, *Annual Report to Congress, 1971*, p. 75.

105. Alvin Weinberg, "Prophet of Nuclear Power," *The New Scientist* 53 (January 20, 1972), p. 142.

CHAPTER VII

1. Edward Wenk, Jr., "The Social Management of Technology," *Science for Society*, Proceedings of the National Conference on Goals, Policies and Programs of Federal, State and Local Science Agencies, edited by John E. Mock, held in Atlanta, Georgia, October 12–14, 1970 (Atlanta: National Science Foundation and Georgia Science and Technology Commission, 1971).

2. University of Washington, Social Management of Technology Project, unpublished results, National Science Foundation Grant GQ-2.

3. U.S., General Services Administration, *Government Organization Manual* (Washington, D.C.: GPO, July 1972).

4. *Nucleonics Week* 14, 20 (May 17, 1973), p. 1.

5. Byron S. Miller, "A Law Is Passed—The Atomic Energy Act of 1946," *University of Chicago Law Review* 15, 4 (Summer, 1948), p. 799.

6. *Ibid.*

7. *Ibid.*, p. 800.

8. Public Law 79-585 (60 Stat. 755) (1946), Section 1(a).

9. Don K. Price, *Government and Science* (New York: New York University Press, 1954), p. 68.

10. Don K. Price, *The Scientific Estate* (Cambridge, Mass.: Harvard University Press, 1965).

11. For a summary of the AEC programs for assisting in manpower training, see U.S., AEC, *Semiannual Report to Congress, July-December 1957*, pp. 179–88.

12. *Nucleonics Week* 14, 35 (August 30, 1973), p. 6.

13. For a summary of an analysis of a proposed nuclear plant, see D. L. Morrison's article, "Environmental Benefit-Cost Analysis for Nuclear Power Generation," in *Nuclear News* 15, 6 (June 1972), p. 50.

14. *Ibid.*, p. 57.

15. For a detailed discussion of the major role scientists played in developing legislation for the postwar control of the atom, see Claire M. Nader, "American Natural Scientists in

the Policy Process: Three Atomic Energy Issues and Their Foreign Policy Implications"
(Ph.D. dissertation, Columbia University, 1964).

16. Emmette S. Redford, *Democracy in the Administrative State* (New York: Oxford
University Press, 1969), p. 83.

17. *Ibid.,* p. 102.

18. Alvin Weinberg, "The Moral Imperatives of Nuclear Energy," *Nuclear News*
14, 12 (December 1971), p. 33.

19. *Ibid.,* p. 36.

20. *Ibid.,* p. 35.

21. *Nucleonics Week* 14, 30 (July 26, 1973), p. 4.

22. National Academy of Sciences and National Research Council, Committee on
Resources and Man, *Resources and Man* (San Francisco: W. H. Freeman and Company,
1969).

23. "Energy and Power," *Scientific American,* September 1969.

24. J. Barnard et al., "Development of the Commercial Breeders," *Nuclear News*
15, 12 (December 1972), p. 30.

25. Personal communications with D. E. Deonigi, Pacific Northwest Laboratory,
Battelle Memorial Institute, Richland, Washington.

26. *General Electric Investor* 4, 1 (Spring 1973).

27. Public Law 79-585 (60 Stat. 755), Section 1a.

28. Harold Orlans, *Contracting for Atoms* (Washington, D.C.: The Brookings Institution, 1967), p. 146.

29. John Gorham Palfrey, "Atomic Energy: A New Experiment in Government-Industry Relations," *Columbia Law Review* 56 (1956), p. 373.

Bibliography

Anthony, Robert N. *Planning and Control Systems: A Framework for Analysis.* Boston: Division of Research, Graduate School of Business Administration, Harvard University, 1965.

Atomic Energy Reporter, News and Analysis 1, 18 (October 5, 1955):142.

Atomic Energy Reporter, News and Analysis 1, 23 (November 9, 1955):179.

Atomic Industrial Forum, Inc. *Forum Member Views on Atomic Energy Development.* New York: The Forum, March 1962.

Atomic Industrial Forum, Inc. *INFO,* No. 54 (December 1972).

Atomic Industrial Forum, Inc. *INFO,* No. 59 (May 1973).

Atomic Industrial Forum, Inc. Ad Hoc Committee on Atomic Policy. *Report of the Committee.* New York: The Forum, March 1962.

Atomic Industrial Forum, Inc. Ad Hoc Committee on Practical Value. *Atomic Energy . . . A Realistic Appraisal.* A Forum Report. New York: The Forum, August 1955.

Atomic Industrial Forum, Inc. Ad Hoc Committee on Practical Value. *Power Reactors of "Practical Value."* New York: The Forum, September 1964.

"Atomic Lemons." *Wall Street Journal.* May 3, 1973, p. 1.

Barnard, J., L. F. Fidrych, A. S. Gibson, K. M. Horst, P. M. Murphy, and B. Wolfe. "Development of the Commercial Breeders." *Nuclear News* 15, 12 (December 1972):30.

Beck, Clifford K. "Engineering Out the Distance Factor." *Atomic Energy Law Journal* 5, 4 (1963):245.

Berman, William H., and Lee M. Hydeman. *The Atomic Energy Commission and Regulating Nuclear Facilities.* Ann Arbor: University of Michigan Law School, 1961.

Bloustein, Edward J., ed. *Nuclear Energy, Public Policy and the Law.* Dobbs Ferry, N.Y.: Oceana Publications, 1964.

Bulletin of the Atomic Scientists 12, 8 (October 1956):318.

Churchman, C. West. *The Systems Approach.* New York: Delacorte Press, 1968.

Commerce Clearing House. *Atomic Energy Law Reporter.* 1967.

Davidson, R. Kirby, and Walter H. Warrick. "Atomic Energy Legislation and Its Import." Manuscript. Lafayette, Inc.: Purdue University, January 1960.

Dean, Gordon. *Report on the Atom.* New York: Alfred A. Knopf, 1957.

Edinger, Vera. "The Hanford Story." Mimeographed. March 1964.

Eisenbud, Merrill. "Health Hazards from Radioactive Emissions." Presented at the

American Medical Association's Congress on Environmental Health, Chicago, Ill., April 29–30, 1973.

F.A.S. *Public Interest Report* 3, 1 (January 1975):4.

Foreman, Harry, ed. *Nuclear Power and the Public*. Minneapolis: University of Minnesota Press, 1970.

Gast, Paul F. "Divergent Public Attitudes toward Nuclear and Hydroelectric Plant Safety." Presented at the 19th Annual Meeting of the American Nuclear Society, Chicago, Ill., June 10–14, 1973.

A General Account of the Development of Methods of Using Atomic Energy for Military Purposes under the Auspices of the United States Government, 1940–45. Washington, D.C.: GPO, 1945.

General Electric Investor 4, 1 (Spring 1973).

Glasstone, Samuel, and Alexander Sesonske. *Nuclear Reactor Engineering*. New York: Van Nostrand, 1963.

Green, Harold P. "The Law of Reactor Safety." *Vanderbilt Law Review* 12 (1958):129–31.

Green, Harold P. "Nuclear Technology and the Fabric of Government." *The George Washington Law Review* 33 (October 1964):160.

Green, Harold P. "The Strange Case of Nuclear Power." *Federal Bar Journal* 17 (April–June 1957):100.

Green, Harold P., and Alan Rosenthal. *Government of the Atom*. New York: Atherton Press, 1963.

Green, Harold P., and Alan Rosenthal. *The Joint Committee on Atomic Energy: A Study in Fusion of Governmental Power*. Washington, D.C.: George Washington University, 1961.

Harms, Keith L. *Economic Considerations Bearing on Civilian Nuclear Power Development*. New York: Atomic Industrial Forum, March 1962.

Hewlett, Richard G., and Francis Duncan. *The Atomic Shield, 1947/1952: A History of the United States Atomic Energy Commission*, Vol. 2. University Park: Pennsylvania State University Press, 1969.

Hewlett, Richard G., and Oscar E. Anderson. *The New World, 1939/1946*. University Park: Pennsylvania State University Press, 1962.

Hodgetts, J. E. *Administering the Atom for Peace*. New York: Atherton Press, 1964.

Holdren, John P. "Hazards of the Nuclear Fuel Cycle." *Bulletin of the Atomic Scientists*. October 1974.

Hottel, H. C., and J. B. Howard. *New Energy Technology: Some Facts and Assessments*. Cambridge: M.I.T. Press, 1971.

International Institute for Environmental Affairs. *World Energy, the Environment and Political Action*. New York: The Institute, 1971.

Johnson, Wilfred E. "The Potential and Problems of Nuclear Power." Remarks made at the National Energy Forum, Washington, D.C., September 24, 1971. (AEC Public Release S-18-71.)

Johnson, Wilfred E. "Status of the Uranium Producing Industry." Remarks made at the American Mining Congress, Las Vegas, Nev., October 13, 1971. (AEC Public Release S-19-71.)

Kahn, Alfred J. *Theory and Practice of Social Planning*. New York: Russell Sage Foundation, 1969.

Kauper, Thomas E. "National Energy Policy and the Antitrust Laws." Paper presented at the Western Conference of Public Service Commissions, Portland, Ore., June 4, 1973.

Kepner, Charles H., and Benjamin B. Tregoe. *The Rational Manager*. New York: McGraw-Hill, 1965.

Kingsley, Sidney G. "The Licensing of Nuclear Power Reactors in the United States." *Atomic Energy Law Journal* 7, 4 (1965):309.

Kwee, S. L., and J. S. R. Mullender, eds. *Growing against Ourselves: The Energy-Environment Tangle.* Lexington, Mass.: Lexington Books, D. C. Heath and Co., 1972.

Lapp, Ralph E. *The New Priesthood.* New York: Harper and Row, 1965.

Lapp, Ralph E. *The Nuclear Energy Controversy.* Greenwich, Conn.: Fact Systems, 1974.

"Letters to the Editor." *Wall Street Journal.* June 6, 1973, p. 20.

Lewis, Richard S. *The Nuclear Power Rebellion.* New York: Viking Press, 1972.

Lilienthal, David E. Statement for press conference in Denver, Colo., December 17, 1948. Published in U.S. Congress. JCAE. *Atomic Power and Private Enterprise.* 82nd Cong., 2nd sess., 1952.

Little, Arthur D., Inc. *Competition in the Nuclear Supply Industry.* Report prepared for the U.S. AEC and the U.S. Department of Justice. NYO-3853-1. Washington, D.C.: GPO, December 1968.

McCune, Francis K. *The Race for Atomic Power.* Remarks made before the Southeastern Electric Exchange, Boca Raton, Fla., March 23, 1955. Schenectady: General Electric, 1955.

Meadows, Donella H., Dennis L. Meadows, Jørgen Randers, and William W. Behrens, III. *The Limits to Growth.* New York: Universe Books, 1972.

Metzger, H. Peter. *The Atomic Establishment.* New York: Simon and Schuster, 1972.

Miller, Byron S. "A Law Is Passed—The Atomic Energy Act of 1946." *University of Chicago Law Review* 15, 4 (Summer 1948):799.

Minnesota v. *Northern States Power Co.* 447 *Federal Reporter* 1143 (405 *U.S. Reports* 1035) (1972).

Morrison, D. L., R. H. Malés, K. M. Duke, V. L. Sharp, and R. L. Ritzman. "Environmental Benefit-Cost Analysis for Nuclear Power Generation." *Nuclear News* 15, 6 (June 1972).

Nader, Claire M. "American Natural Scientists in the Policy Process: Three Atomic Energy Issues and Their Foreign Policy Implications." Ph.D. dissertation, Columbia University, 1964.

National Academy of Sciences and National Research Council. Advisory Committee on the Biological Effects of Ionizing Radiation. "The Effects on Populations of Exposure to Low Levels of Ionizing Radiation." *Resources and Man.* San Francisco: W. H. Freeman and Co., 1969.

National Petroleum Council. Committee on U.S. Energy Outlook. Other Energy Resources Subcommittee. Nuclear Task Group. *U.S. Energy Outlook.* Washington, D.C.: The Council, 1972.

Newman, James R. "The Atomic Energy Industry." *Yale Law Journal* 60, 8 (December 1951):1263–1394.

Newman, James R., and Byron S. Miller. *The Control of Atomic Energy.* New York: McGraw-Hill, 1948.

Novick, Sheldon. *The Careless Atom.* Boston: Houghton-Mifflin Co., 1969.

Nuclear News 7, 3 (March 1964):32.

Nuclear News 15, 5 (May 1972):36.

Nuclear News 15, 6 (June 1972):50.

Nuclear News 15, 12 (December 1972):44.

Nuclear News 16, 1 (January 1973):30.

Nuclear News 16, 2 (February 1973):42.

Nuclear News 16, 3 (February 1973):16.

Nuclear News 16, 4 (March 1973):32, 47.

Nuclear News 18, 3 (mid-February 1975).

"Nuclear Safety (I): The Roots of Dissent." *Science* 177 (September 1, 1972):771.

"Nuclear Safety (II): The Years of Delay." *Science* 177 (September 8, 1972):867.

"Nuclear Safety (III): Critics Charge Conflicts of Interest." *Science* 177 (September 15, 1972):970.

"Nuclear Safety (IV): Barriers to Communication." *Science* 177 (September 22, 1972):1080.

Nucleonics Week 13, 19 (December 7, 1972):6–7.

Nucleonics Week 13, 52 (December 28, 1972):6.

Nucleonics Week 14, 14 (April 5, 1973):1.

Nucleonics Week 14, 20 (May 17, 1973):2.

Nucleonics Week 14, 21 (May 24, 1973):8.

Nucleonics Week 14, 24 (June 14, 1973):2.

Nucleonics Week 14, 30 (July 26, 1973), p. 4.

Nucleonics Week 14, 35 (August 30, 1973):6.

Nucleonics Week 16, 5 (January 30, 1975):2.

Orlans, Harold. *Contracting for Atoms.* Washington, D.C.: The Brookings Institution, 1967.

Palfrey, John Gorham. "Atomic Energy: A New Experiment in Government-Industry Relations." *Columbia Law Review* 56 (1956):373.

Poage, Scott T. *Quantitative Management Methods for Practicing Engineers.* New York: Barnes and Noble, 1970.

Power Reactor Development Co. v. *International Union of Electrical, Radio and Machine Workers, AFL-CIO et al.* (367 *U.S. Reports* 396) (1961).

Price, Don K. *Government and Science.* New York: New York University Press, 1954.

Price, Don K. *The Scientific Estate.* Cambridge, Mass.: Harvard University Press, 1965.

"Problems Abound—But So Does Optimism." *Nuclear News* 16, 3 (February 1973):20.

Public Law 55-425 (30 Stat. 1152) (1899).

Public Law 79-585 (60 Stat. 755) (1946).

Public Law 81-820 (64 Stat. 979) (1950).

Public Law 83-703 (68 Stat. 919) (1954).

Public Law 85-79 (71 Stat. 274) (1957).

Public Law 85-162 (71 Stat. 403) (1957).

Public Law 85-256 (71 Stat. 576) (1957).

Public Law 86-50 (73 Stat. 81) (1959).

Public Law 86-373 (73 Stat. 688) (1959).

Public Law 87-615 (76 Stat. 409) (1962).

Public Law 88-72 (77 Stat. 84) (1963).

Public Law 88-394 (78 Stat. 376) (1964).

Public Law 88-489 (78 Stat. 602) (1964).

Public Law 89-32 (79 Stat. 120) (1965).

Public Law 89-210 (79 Stat. 855) (1965).

Public Law 91-161 (83 Stat. 444) (1969)

Public Law 91-190 (83 Stat. 852) (1969).

Public Law 91-224 (84 Stat. 91) (1970).

Public Law 91-560 (84 Stat. 1472) (1970).

Public Law 92-500 (70 Stat. 498) (1972).

Rama, Simon. *Cure for Chaos.* New York: David McKay Co., 1969.

Redford, Emmette S. *Dèmocracy in the Administrtive State.* New York: Oxford University Press, 1969.

Rocks, Lawrence, and Richard P. Runyan. *The Energy Criss.* New York: Crown Publishers, 1972.

Schooler, Dean, Jr. *Science, Scientists, and Public Policy.* New York: Free Press, 1971.

Scientific American Editors. *Energy and Power: A Scientific American Book*. New York: Scientific American, 1971.

Seaborg, Glenn T., and William R. Corliss. *Man and Atom*. New York: E. Dutton and Co., 1971.

Seidman, Harold. *Politics, Position, and Power: The Dynamics of Federal Organization*. New York: Oxford University Press, 1970.

Shipman, George A. *Designing Program Action–Against Urban Poverty*. University: University of Alabama Press, 1971.

Smyth, Henry D. Prepared remarks for the Western Division of the American Mining Congress at Denver, Colo., September 25, 1952. Published in U.S. Congress. JCAE. *Atomic Power and Private Enterprise*. Report. 82nd Cong., 2nd sess., December 1952.

Snow, C. P. *Science and Government: The Godkin Lectures at Harvard University, 1960*. New York: Mentor Books, 1962.

Snow, C. P. *The Two Cultures: And a Second Look*. New York: Mentor Books, 1964.

Stason, E. Blythe, Samuel D. Estep, and William J. Pierce. *Atoms and the Law*. Ann Arbor: University of Michigan Law School, 1959.

Strauss, Lewis L. *Men and Decisions*. Garden City, N.Y.: Doubleday, 1962.

Study of Critical Environmental Problems. *Man's Impact on the Global Environment: Assessment and Recommendations for Action*. Cambridge, Mass.: M.I.T. Press, 1970.

Teich, Albert H., ed. *Technology and Man's Future*. New York: St. Martin's Press, 1972.

Thomas, Morgan. *Atomic Energy and Congress*. Ann Arbor: University of Michigan Press, 1956.

Toffler, Alvin. *Future Shock*. London: Bodley Head, 1970.

Truman, Harry S. "Atomic Energy." *Vital Speeches* 12 (October 15, 1945):8–10.

Truman, Harry S. *Years of Trial and Hope*. Memoirs, Vol. 2. New York: Doubleday, 1956.

Tybout, Richard A. *The Reactor Supply Industry*. Bureau of Business Research Monograph No. 97. Columbus: The Bureau, College of Commerce and Administration, Ohio State University, 1960.

United States. 10 Code of Federal Regulations 50.

U.S. 10 CFR 100.

U.S. Atomic Energy Commission. *Annual Report to the Congress by the USAEC*. Washington, D.C.: GPO, 1959–1974.

U.S. AEC. *Civilian Nuclear Power—A Report to the President—1962*. Washington, D.C.: GPO, November 20, 1962.

U.S. AEC. *Civilian Nuclear Power—The 1967 Supplement to the 1962 Report to the President*. Washington, D.C.: GPO, February 1967.

U.S. AEC. *Current Status and Future Technical and Economic Potential of Light Water Reactors*. Rept. No. WASH 1082. Washington, D.C.: GPO, March 1968.

U.S. AEC. *Financial Reports 1956–1972*. Washington, D.C.: GPO, 1957–73.

U.S. AEC. *1972 Atomic Energy Programs, Regulatory Activities*. Washington, D.C.: GPO, January 31, 1973.

U.S. AEC. *The Nuclear Industry—1969*. Washington, D.C.: GPO, 1969.

U.S. AEC. *The Nuclear Industry—1971*. Washington, D.C.: GPO, 1971.

U.S. AEC. *Plans for Development as of February 1960*. Civilian Power Reactor Program, Pt. IV. Washington, D.C.: GPO, 1960.

U.S. AEC. Press Release No. 1, August 23, 1962.

U.S. AEC. Press Release No. 589, January 10, 1955.

U.S. AEC. Press Release No. 695, September 21, 1955.

U.S. AEC. Press Release No. 953, January 7, 1957.

U.S. AEC. Press Release No. P-118, April 25, 1972.

U.S. AEC. *Reactor Safety Study: An Assessment of Accident Risks in U.S. Commercial Nuclear Power Plants*. Rept. No. WASH 1400, August 1974.

U.S. AEC. *The Safety of Nuclear Power Reactors (Light Water Cooled) and Related Facilities*. Rept. No. WASH 1250, July 1973.

U.S. AEC. *Semiannual Report to the Congress by the USAEC*. Washington, D.C.: GPO, 1947-1959.

U.S. Budget Bureau. *President's Budget to Congress*. 1974.

U.S. Congress. House. *Conference Report*. 85th Cong., 2nd sess., July 21, 1958. H. Rept. 2237.

U.S. Congress. House. *The Congressional Record*. 83rd Cong., 2nd sess., 1954. 100 (Daily edition July 23, 1954).

U.S. Congress. House. *The Congressional Record*. 85th Cong., 1st sess., 1957. 103, Pt. 8.

U.S. Congress. House. *The Congressional Record*. 85th Cong., 1st sess., 1957. 103, Pt. 11.

U.S. Congress. House. *The Congressional Record*. 88th Cong., 2nd sess., 1964. 110, Pt. 15.

U.S. Congress. House. *Legislative History of the Atomic Energy Act of 1954*. Report. 83rd Cong., 2nd sess., 1954. H. Doc. 328.

U.S. Congress. House. Committee on Science and Astronautics. *A Study of Technology Assessment*. Report of the Committee on Public Engineering, National Academy of Engineering. 90th Cong., 1st sess., 1969.

U.S. Congress. House. Committee on Science and Astronautics. *Technology: Processes of Assessment and Choice*. Report of the National Academy of Sciences. 90th Cong., 1st sess., 1969.

U.S. Congress. JCAE. *Accelerating the Civilian Reactor Program*. Hearings on S 2725, HR 10805. 84th Cong., 2nd sess., May 23-25, 28, and 29, 1956.

U.S. Congress. JCAE. *Amending the Atomic Energy Act of 1954 to Provide for Private Ownership of Special Nuclear Materials*. Report. 88th Cong., 2nd sess., August 5, 1964. S. Rept. 1325, H. Rept. 1702.

U.S. Congress. JCAE. *Atomic Power and Private Enterprise*. Report. 82nd Cong., 2nd sess., December 1952.

U.S. Congress. JCAE. *Atomic Power Development and Private Enterprise*. Hearings. 83rd Cong., 1st sess., June 24, 25, and 29; July 1, 6, 9, 13, 15, 16, 20, 22, 23, 27, and 31, 1953.

U.S. Congress. JCAE. *Authorizing Appropriation for the Atomic Energy Commission*. 85th Cong., 1st sess., August 2, 1957. H. Rept. 978.

U.S. Congress. JCAE. *Comments of Reactor Designers and Industrial Representatives on the Proposed Expanded Civilian Nuclear Power Program*. Committee Print. 85th Cong., 2nd sess., December 1958.

U.S. Congress. JCAE. *Cooperative Power Reactor Demonstration Program, 1963*. Hearings. 88th Cong., 1st sess., July 9, August 7, and October 15, 1963.

U.S. Congress. JCAE. *Current Membership of the Joint Committee on Atomic Energy, Congress of the United States*. Committee Print. 92nd Cong., 2nd sess., 1972.

U.S. Congress. JCAE. *Environmental Effects of Producing Electric Power*. Hearings. 91st Cong., 2nd sess., January 27-30 and February 24-26, 1970.

U.S. Congress. JCAE. *Five-Year Power Reactor Development Program Proposed by the Atomic Energy Commission*. Report of the Subcommittee on Research and Development. 83rd Cong., 2nd sess., March 1954.

U.S. Congress. JCAE. *Future Ownership of the AEC's Gaseous Diffusion Plants*. Hearings. 91st Cong., 1st sess., August 5, 7, and 8, 1969.

U.S. Congress. JCAE. *Government Indemnity.* Hearings. 84th Cong., 2nd sess., May 15–21, and June 14, 1956.

U.S. Congress. JCAE. *Governmental Indemnity and Reactor Safety.* Hearings on S 715 (HR 1981). 85th Cong., 1st sess., March 25–27, 1957.

U.S. Congress. JCAE. *Naval Reactor Program and Shippingport Project.* Hearings. 85th Cong., 1st sess., March 7 and April 12, 1957.

U.S. Congress. JCAE. *Nuclear Power and Related Energy Problems—1968 through 1970.* Report. 92nd Cong., 1st sess., December 1971.

U.S. Congress. JCAE. *Nuclear Reactor Safety.* Hearings. 93rd Cong., 1st sess., January 23, September 25–27, and October 1, 1973.

U.S. Congress. JCAE. *Peaceful Uses of Atomic Energy.* Report of the Panel on the Impact of the Peaceful Uses of Atomic Energy. 84th Cong., 2nd sess., 1956.

U.S. Congress. JCAE. *Private Ownership of Special Nuclear Materials.* Hearings on S 1160 (HR 5035). 88th Cong., 1st sess., July 30, 31, and August 1, 1963.

U.S. Congress. JCAE. *Private Ownership of Special Nuclear Materials.* Hearings on S 2635. 88th Cong., 2nd sess., June 9–11, 15, and 25, 1964.

U.S. Congress. JCAE. *Proposed Expanded Civilian Nuclear Program.* Committee Print. 85th Cong., 2nd sess., August 1958.

U.S. Congress. JCAE. *Proposed Extension of AEC Indemnity Legislation.* Hearings. 89th Cong., 1st sess., June 22–24, 1965.

U.S. Congress. JCAE. *Report on Raw Materials.* 82nd Cong., 2nd sess., 1952. H. Rept. 2449.

U.S. Congress. JCAE. *Selected Materials Concerning Future Ownership of the AEC's Gaseous Diffusion Plants.* Committee Print. 91st Cong., 1st sess., 1969.

U.S. Congress. JCAE. *Selected Materials on Atomic Energy Indemnity Legislation.* Committee Print. 89th Cong., 1st sess., June 1965.

U.S. Congress. JCAE. *Study of AEC Procedures and Organization in the Licensing of Reactor Facilities.* Committee Print. 85th Cong., 1st sess., April 1957.

U.S. Congress. JCAE. "A Study of AEC Procedures and Organization in the Licensing of Reactor Facilities." *JCAE Report* (1957):8.

U.S. Congress. JCAE. *Technical Aspects of the Report on the Gas-Cooled, Graphite-Moderated Reactor.* Hearings. 85th Cong., 2nd sess., April 22, 1958.

U.S. Congress. JCAE. *Uranium Enrichment Pricing Criteria.* Hearings. 91st Cong., 2nd sess., June 16 and 17, 1970.

U.S. Congress. JCAE. Subcommittee on Energy. *Proposed Changes in AEC Arrangements for Uranium Enriching Services.* Hearings. 93rd Cong., 1st sess., March 7, 8, 26, and April 18, 1973.

U.S. Congress. Senate. *Amendment to the Atomic Energy Act of 1954, as Amended with Respect to Cooperation with the States.* 86th Cong., 1st sess., Rept. 870, September 1, 1959.

U.S. Congress. Senate. *The Atomic Energy Act of 1946.* 79th Cong., 2nd sess., April 19, 1946. S. Rept. 1211.

U.S. Congress. Senate. *The Congressional Record.* 85th Cong., 2nd sess., 1958, 104, Pt. 11.

U.S. Congress. Senate. Committee on Interior and Insular Affairs. *Calvert Cliffs Court Decision.* Hearings. 92nd Cong., 1st sess., Pt. 2, November 3, 1971.

U.S. Congress. Senate. Committee on Interior and Insular Affairs. Hearings. 92nd Cong., 2nd sess., February 8, 1972.

U.S. General Services Administration. *Government Organization Mannual, 1972/73.* Washington, D.C.: GPO, July 1972.

U.S. Office of the President. Executive Order 11514, March 5, 1970. 35 *Federal Register* 4247.

U.S. Office of the President. *Marine Science Affairs—A Year of Broadened Partici-pation*. The Third Report of the President to the Congress on Marine Resources and Engineering Development. Washington, D.C.: GPO, January 1969.

University of Michigan Law School. Summer Institute on International and Comparative Law. *Atomic Energy Industrial and Legal Problems*. Ann Arbor: The Law School, 1952.

University of Washington. Social Management of Technology Project. Unpublished results. National Science Foundation Grant GQ-2.

Washington State. *Revised Code of Washington*. 80.50, Thermal Power Plant Site Loca-tions.

Weekly Energy Report (February 17, 1975):3.

Weinberg, Alvin. "The Moral Imperatives of Nuclear Energy." *Nuclear News* 14, 12 (December 1971):33.

Weinberg, Alvin. "Prophet of Nuclear Power." *The New Scientist* 53 (January 20, 1972):142.

Wenk, Edward, Jr. *The Politics of the Ocean*. Seattle: University of Washington Press, 1972.

Wenk, Edward, Jr. "The Social Management of Technology." *Science for Society*. Pro-ceedings of the National Conference on Goals, Policies and Programs of Federal, State and Local Science Agencies. Edited by John E. Mock. Atlanta: National Science Foundation and Georgia Science and Technology Commission, 1971.

Willrich, Mason, and Theodore B. Taylor. *Nuclear Theft: Risks and Safeguards*. Cam-bridge, Mass.: Ballinger, 1974.

Zinn, Walter H., Frank K. Pittman, and John F. Hogerton. *Nuclear Power, U.S.A.* New York: McGraw-Hill, 1964.

Index

Italicized page references indicate material in tables or figures.